Enacting Gender
on the English Renaissance Stage

Enacting Gender

on the

English Renaissance Stage

Edited by
Viviana Comensoli
& Anne Russell

University of Illinois Press
Urbana and Chicago

© 1999 by the Board of Trustees of the University of Illinois
Manufactured in the United States of America
1 2 3 4 5 C P 5 4 3 2 1

This book is printed on acid-free paper.

Library of Congress Cataloging-in-Publication Data
Enacting gender on the English Renaissance stage / edited by
Viviana Comensoli and Anne Russell.
   p.   cm.
Includes bibliographical references (p.) and index.
ISBN 0-252-02423-0 (cloth : acid-free paper)
ISBN 0-252-06730-4 (pbk. : acid-free paper)
1. English drama—Early modern and Elizabethan,
1500–1600—History and criticism. 2. Sex role in literature.
3. English drama—17th century—History and criticism.
4. Gender identity in literature. 5. Renaissance—England.
6. Women in literature. 7. Men in literature. I. Comensoli,
Viviana. II. Russell, Anne, 1952–
PR658.S42 E63 1999
822'.309353—ddc21
                                                98-8991
CIP

Contents

Acknowledgments   vii

Introduction   1
 Viviana Comensoli and Anne Russell

PART 1

1. Making Defect Perfection: Shakespeare and the One-Sex Model   23
 Janet Adelman
2. "To Laugh with Open Throate": Mad Lovers, Theatrical Cures, and Gendered Bodies in Jacobean Drama   53
 Alan Walworth
3. Transmigrations: Crossing Regional and Gender Boundaries in *Antony and Cleopatra*   73
 Mary Floyd-Wilson
4. Marlowe's Ganymede   97
 Joyce Green MacDonald
5. Subjectivity, Time, and Gender in *Titus Andronicus, Hamlet,* and *Othello*   114
 R. L. Kesler

PART 2

6. Theaters, Households, and a "Kind of History" in Elizabeth Cary's *The Tragedy of Mariam*   135
 Rosemary Kegl

7. Playing the "Scene Self": Jane Cavendish and Elizabeth Brackley's *The Concealed Fancies*   154
   Alison Findlay
8. The Introduction of Actresses in England: Delay or Defensiveness?   177
   Michael Shapiro
9. Staging the Female Playgoer: Gender in Shakespeare's Onstage Audiences   201
   Laurie E. Osborne
10. Gender, Rhetoric, and Performance in John Webster's *The White Devil*   218
    Christina Luckyj

Bibliography   233
Contributors   259
Index   263

Acknowledgments

It is a pleasure to acknowledge the help we have received in the preparation of this collection of essays.

We would first like to extend special thanks to the contributors. We are also grateful to the many scholars in Canada, the United States, and Britain who anonymously reviewed individual essays in the early stages of the project. Our friends and colleagues Sylvia Bowerbank, Jane Kalbfleisch, Ted McGee, Lynn Shakinovsky, Paul Tiessen, and Eleanor Ty generously contributed valuable comments and suggestions, as did the anonymous readers for the University of Illinois Press.

We would like to thank our editors at the Press—Ann Lowry, Emily Rogers, and Pat Hollahan—for their generous and expert assistance and their support. Our research assistants Kathryn Brough, Kymberlee Cottingham, Viona Falk, Merina Hew, Ann Mackay, Siobhan McMenemy, Robert Parker, and Evan Smith made helpful contributions by performing a wide range of tasks at different stages of the project. Our department's secretarial staff, Joanne Buehler-Buchan, Susan Mück, and Sandra Wallace in particular, helped immensely with the preparation of the manuscript.

The Office of Research at Wilfrid Laurier University generously provided funding assistance in the form of research and book preparation grants.

Our greatest debts are to Elaine Auerbach, who proofread the volume, and Martin Dowding, who prepared the index. In addition, they gave invaluable advice, assistance, and support at every stage of the project.

Enacting Gender
on the English Renaissance Stage

Introduction

Viviana Comensoli and Anne Russell

Since the mid-1980s, an important shift has occurred in the study of English Renaissance drama and theatrical practices. Moving away from the New Critical preoccupation with character and the aesthetic and moral value of dramatic texts and performance, feminist and other forms of poststructuralist scholarship have stressed the theater's complex and multivocal engagement with early modern cultures and ideologies. Cultural historians have pointed to the heterogeneity of the signifying practices of the theater in early modern England. Situated in the suburbs beyond the legal control of city officials, the theater, as Steven Mullaney observes, "could not be contained within the strict or proper bounds of the community"; the theater's marginality, notes Nick Potter, placed "the players in a position of considerable ambiguity, able only to act the enactment of harmonies to which they could never quite belong themselves, or to question such harmonies from a position of dependence."[1] An institution characterized by diversity and contrariety, the commercial theater (both "public" open-air theaters and "private" enclosed hall theaters such as the Blackfriars theater) was the site of convergence for different segments of the population, and for wide-ranging discursive and dramatic traditions. The early modern theater, suggests Ivo Kamps, occupied a "liminal" space; in catering "to a heterogeneous audience while also striving for respectability and patronage,"[2] it became a site where cultural meanings were both promoted and contested. Central to the multivocality that characterized the English Renaissance theater was its pervasive fascination with gender, a category of signification which, through the stage conventions of crossdressing and the deployment of boy actors to play women's parts, was represented as protean and ambiguous. Although as a public institution the stage was required to endorse conventional paradigms of gender, it also inverted those structures by positing alternatives in ways that renegotiated difference and sometimes contradicted traditional norms.

Applying diverse theoretical and critical approaches, the essays in *Enacting Gender on the English Renaissance Stage* contribute to the evolving interest in the intersections of gender ideologies, theatricality, and cultural production in early modern England. The essays are grounded in and inspired by the critical and theoretical debates of the past twenty years. During the 1970s and early 1980s feminist criticism uncovered the patriarchal structures of early modern culture, challenging us to rethink its social hierarchies and to be attuned to the role of gender in their development. Building on this early work, more recent scholarship has brought interdisciplinary perspectives to early modern conceptualizations of gender, scrutinizing terms such as "man" and "woman," for example, in relation to their function in dramatic representation, and reorienting our thinking about the theater as a historically contingent institution. With respect to Elizabethan and Jacobean theatrical practices, critical debate has revolved around two principal areas of inquiry: (1) the theater's staging of the profound instability of the categories of gender, race, and sexuality; and (2) the complex role of the boy actor and the dynamics of the transvestite theater. In exploring these issues, feminist approaches have incorporated various and sometimes conflicting critical practices. Similarly, the essays in the present collection do not offer a single, unified analysis of gender as it is conceptualized and represented in the English Renaissance theater. The contributors engage canonical and less well studied texts by female and male dramatists, offering new insights into how the coordinates of gender (including not only the body, racial status, and subjectivity but also authorship and spectatorship) are inscribed in dramatic texts and performance. These structures redefine and are influenced by historical models of the gendered body, performance practices, and ideology. In its multivalent exploration of gender, the collection reflects the wide range of approaches informing the current state of Renaissance criticism.

One area of inquiry that has become increasingly contested revolves around early modern constructs of the gendered body and agency. A valuable point of intersection between feminist and other poststructuralist discourses has been their mutual interest in theorizing these structures as cultural constructions subject to redefinition in response to sociopolitical, discursive, and historical pressures. Postmodern theories have directed our attention to the displacement of the unified, self-reflexive subject by multiple systems of signification, and to the heterogeneity of the premodern body politic, representing it, like its modern counterparts, as "an effect of the multiplicity of historical meanings and values that intersect in individuals."[3] In considerations of premodern conceptualizations of "woman," for example, revisionist scholarship has brought to the debate a specifically postmodern concern, namely what Judith Butler has characterized as the desire within contemporary feminism "to reconcile the apparent need to formulate a politics which assumes the category of 'women' with the demand, often politically articulated, to problematize the category, interrogate its incoherence, its internal dissonance, its constitutive exclusions."[4] And scholars working with queer theory have demonstrated, following Foucault, that "sex" in the early modern period does not constitute a monolithic unity but a multidimensional, speculative construct, which, as Butler elsewhere argues, "compounds the semantic sense of sex as identity, sensation, and practice."[5] The disavowal of essentialist categories has, however, created a paradox for those for whom terms such as "woman," "racial status," "homosexual," and "hermaphrodite" are inextricable from the history and politics of oppression, and therefore crucial to our understanding of the gender ideologies that underwrite pre- and postmodern cultural production.[6]

In postulating what Alice Jardine has aptly called the "new semiosis of woman" and its correlative, the new semiosis of agency, the postmodern project, in discovering that which "has been 'left out,' de-emphasized, hidden, or denied articulation within Western systems of knowledge,"[7] has also tended to elide the importance of sexual difference, race, and subjectivity as categories of analysis on the basis that they invoke an unfractured notion of identity. Observing the general uneasiness in postmodernist discourses with the appeal to difference, Luce Irigaray comments that such an appeal is likely to be considered "reactionary or naive," a "*return to . . . nature.*"[8] In contemporary critical discourses on the representation of gender in the early modern theater, the disquiet one sometimes encounters with concepts such as agency and presence has, in the words of Carol Thomas Neely, tended "to oppress women, repress sexuality, and subordinate gender issues."[9] Karen Newman, in her study of women in early modern England as subjects and as objects of dramatic representation, has similarly argued that insufficient attention to difference has resulted in disregard for the numerous historical instances of women's resistance, denial, and transgression which attest to "gender specific anxiety about changing social relations."[10] Nor has the emphasis on the denaturalization of sexuality, together with the denial of the materiality and "race" of the gendered body, necessarily erased the universality of the "white" heterosexual subject, which the feminist scrutiny of gender as a historical construct intended to supersede. As Parveen Adams argues, while essentialism "has been challenged by theories that emphasize the space of representation and systems of representation . . . the essentialism that is being attacked in this challenge often returns even if in a more sophisticated form."[11]

The present collection goes beyond previous studies by engaging competing Renaissance discourses on gender which have not received wide critical currency. The contributors focus on representations of the subject, performance practices (including commercial and household productions), and audience response, analyzing the ways in which these elements variously corroborate and contradict dominant discourses of gender, both pre- and postmodernist. The essays in part 1 consider the interconnections of gender, theatrical traditions, and dramatic form in relation to early modern homologies of sex, race, and subjectivity; those in part 2 focus on the material conditions of the early modern theater—writing, playgoing, production, actors' bodies, transvestism, household dramas. Taken together, the essays demonstrate how the gendered conditions of (masculine) presence, (female) absence, and the heterosexual subject are by no means stable in the theater of the late sixteenth and early seventeenth centuries.

Part 1 shows how early modern epistemologies of gender encompass not only constructions of femininity and masculinity but also multiple representations of the gendered body, contemporary anxieties surrounding physiology and racial status, and the relation between historically changing forms of subjectivity and transformations in dramatic form. Revisionist scholarship has drawn attention to early modern conceptualizations of gender as a performative construct rather than as the expression of a stable ontological core. However, a debate has recently emerged centering on the historiography of gender and sexual difference as it has been theorized by Michel Foucault, Stephen Greenblatt, and Thomas Laqueur, whose considerations of medical, legal, philosophical, and literary texts have been instrumental in consolidating social-constructionist theories of the gendered body.[12] Although Laqueur's *Making Sex* (1990) is intended primarily as a refutation of nineteenth-century theories of the two-sex model of sexuality, his analysis of sixteenth-century anatomical and other medical treatises that account for sexual difference has been especially influential on interpretations of early modern gender systems. Laqueur contends that in Western cultures the fundamental biological division of human sexuality into male and female did not occur until the eighteenth century; by the nineteenth century the physical differentiation between male and female, together with the accompanying cultural or gendered differentiation between "man and woman," had become seen as firmly rooted in nature.[13] This oppositional view of sexual difference was a radical departure from the one-sex model of human anatomy and sexuality which until the eighteenth century had provided the dominant explanation for sexual differences as mere variations in a single, essentially male nature. The Galenic one-sex model, which depended on the hierarchical representation of sexual difference whereby the human body is defined according to a teleology of perfection, proceeding from imperfect to perfect, female to male, was thus replaced by a conceptualization of the body as determined by biological dimorphism.

Laqueur's thesis, and the work it has influenced, has enhanced our understanding of how the one-sex model may have contributed to early modern transvestite acting conventions and representations of sexual difference. Sexuality, however, as Jeffrey Weeks points out, "is a deeply problematic concept, and there are no easy answers to the challenges it poses."[14] In "Making Defect Perfection: Shakespeare and the One-Sex Model," the opening essay of the collection, Janet Adelman draws on a wide range of medical and related texts written between 1548 and 1615 to offer a valuable corrective to the hegemony of the one-sex model. She illustrates that the model's appeal to twentieth-century representations of early modern stage practices has been attended by historical inaccuracies, omissions, and oversimplifications. Adelman's examination of English vernacular texts establishes that "elements of a two-sex model were at home in Renaissance medical discourse," an observation which also has important implications for the English transvestite theater.

The categorical erasure of the female body, argues Adelman, is neither historically accurate nor unequivocally performed on the English Renaissance stage. Her point of reference for the theater is the open-endedness of the discourse about sexual difference and the ways in which *Antony and Cleopatra* participates in that discourse's multifariousness. Whereas Shakespeare's transvestite comedies ultimately efface the woman, Cleopatra reinstates her (female) presence "over the body of the boy actor," self-reflexively referring to "the presence of the boy underneath" not in order to "repair a lack in herself" but "in order to distance herself from his defective representation of her decidedly female grandeur." Drawing the spectator's attention to the lack, not of Cleopatra but of the boy actor, Shakespeare rewrites "the tropes of lack" as "the tropes of an endlessly generative fullness that underscores the lack in others," allowing for the possibility of "a theater allied with female generativity." Destabilizing the one-sex model in *Antony and Cleopatra,* Shakespeare may be "experiment[ing] with making defect perfection," and therefore participating in a widespread cultural debate about gender and sexual difference. Adelman's analysis has important implications for the theatrical practices which Shakespeare's plays foster and on which they depend, particularly the coexistence on the English transvestite stage of competing models for both gender and theater.

A fundamental question which Adelman's revisionist argument forces us to ask is why the Galenic one-sex model of homology suddenly swept the academy after the first wave of feminist criticism of Shakespeare had subsided. The premises that have led to the late twentieth-century elevation of Galen to singular prominence in the Renaissance are symptomatic of a pervasive critical tendency to efface the categories of gender and woman in analyses of early modern power structures and to view the male body, Adelman suggests, as "the gold standard, that against which the female must be defined."

In "'To Laugh with Open Throat': Mad Lovers, Theatrical Cures, and Gendered Bodies in Jacobean Drama," Alan Walworth also consults a wide selection of early modern medical treatises developed from classical models to explore how another Renaissance homology—the medical treatment of melancholia by means of a theatrical illusion or ruse—is premised on the effacement of female agency. Like the Galenic one-sex model, this homology has important ramifications for our understanding of the relation between early modern gender ideologies and theatrical traditions, and how they intersect with contemporary theory and practice, in this case psychoanalysis. Walworth demonstrates that the categories "male" and "female" as conceptualized in the treatises correspond to figurations of the gendered body found in plays by Fletcher, Brome, Middleton, Shirley, and Ford. These dramatists appropriate material from the treatises for the staging of scenes in which ailments such as lovesickness and other forms of melancholia are treated by the melancholic characters' deceptive (that is, theatrical) compliance with their delusions. In both the medical and theatrical representations of melancholia, patients are cured by a method of substitution in which the physician or his delegate replaces the patient's object of desire. This illusory cure or ruse is a form of substitution closely resembling the psychoanalytic phenomenon which Freud has called the transference, whereby the patient's desire for the love object is displaced onto the physician. The displacement reifies the politics of gender on which the ruse is premised.

The theatrical cure for lovesickness inscribed in Renaissance medical treatises and stage plays, like psychoanalytic discourses of transferential therapy, is based on "implicitly gendered constructions" of the body. Conceived as a predominantly male illness, melancholia relies on "a gendered distinction which informs the psychoanalytic account of melancholia as well." Like their classical counterparts, these early modern texts focus chiefly on male patients who are overwhelmed with a sense of loss, an indeterminate fear accompanied by the patient's preoccupation with the integrity of his body. Expanding on the Bakhtinian model of the classical (male) and grotesque (female) body, Walworth locates the melancholic's fear in the presentation of "grotesque openness as simultaneously the secret truth and the defining fantasy of the female body." Further underwriting the fantasy of the lost object of desire is the paradox that melancholia "turns grief for the (female) beloved's absence into an obsessive fantasy requiring that absence."

In the process of theatrical substitution, the female object of desire thus becomes effaced by her fantasy substitute.

Adelman and Walworth show how the transvestite theater's engagement with medical and philosophical discourses defines sexual difference as a relative construction in which the premise of woman as "lack" and the binary of the classical male body and the grotesque female body are variously contested (Adelman) and promoted (Walworth). Mary Floyd-Wilson argues that traditional models of the gendered body are further qualified by systems of differentiation such as Renaissance climatic-humoral theories of the body. "Transmigrations: Crossing Regional and Gender Boundaries in *Antony and Cleopatra*" contributes to the emerging critical interest in the early seventeenth-century shift away from categories of difference based on variations in degree to a notion of difference grounded in immutable distinctions of kind. It was a fundamental shift that accelerated the convergence of ideologies of the body, "color," and gender.

Like Adelman, Floyd-Wilson takes as her starting point Shakespeare's *Antony and Cleopatra,* arguing that the play, like a number of other dramas written for the English Renaissance stage, complicates early modern epistemologies of difference. Uncovering numerous treatises on natural philosophy in which the Renaissance climatic-humoral discourse is found, Floyd-Wilson shows how that discourse contributes to our understanding of *Antony and Cleopatra,* which stages a contradictory, often ambivalent interaction between regional identity and gender distinctions. The contradictory treatment of the gendered body is consonant with the unstable, "pre-racial" epistemologies of the body articulated in Renaissance treatises on climatic-humoral theory. Like those treatises, *Antony and Cleopatra* only precariously affirms the trope in which effeminacy is characterized as excess of bodily heat and moisture, an excess counterbalanced by the well-regulated masculine body. The trope is further disrupted by the English nation's own marginalized status as a "white," northern region. In the early seventeenth century, race had not yet been entirely codified "in tandem with ideological erasures taking place in the discourse of natural philosophy." The binary white/black became entrenched during the latter part of the seventeenth century, when physiological and climatic explanations of sexual and national differences yielded to imperialist constructions of racial difference. As England broadened its colonialist interests in the Atlantic slave trade, explanations of color difference, particularly between black and white complexions, began to move away from an emphasis on diversity toward the equation of black complexions with strangeness. Whereas early seventeenth-century climate theory, influenced by ancient physiology, characterized blackness as a "mystery," later scientific discourses would deny the inscrutability of blackness, thereby displacing the traditional Renaissance reverence for southern cultures. Within this critical historical juncture, *Antony and Cleopatra* momentarily captures the fluidity of physiological paradigms of racial and gender distinctions—a fluidity that, ironically, would enable early modern England to redefine the effeminizing terms of climatic-humoral theory and to construct a national identity founded in part on the equation of the northern male complexion with natural virtue. Shakespeare's anticipation of this engendering of nationhood clarifies the cultural stake in the play's final depreciation of Cleopatra's blackness and her fluidity as mere role-playing, her diminishing grandeur powerfully dramatizing how the long-standing respect for the ancient wisdom of Egypt begins to be translated into a colonial prejudice based on color differentiation.

While the essays by Adelman, Walworth, and Floyd-Wilson illustrate the theater's extensive engagement with extraliterary discourses and social practices that construct the gendered body, Joyce Green MacDonald and R. L. Kesler focus on the drama's exploitation of genre in its representation of sexual difference and evolving forms of subjectivity. An area of critical inquiry that has been the subject of increasing debate in Renaissance studies concerns the legitimacy of textual criticism. Although formalist analysis has sometimes been deemed to uphold universal categories, Fredric Jameson, Mikhail Bakhtin, and others have pointed out that textual forms and generic conventions do not necessarily constitute ahistorical modes of representation. Renaissance genres, partly because they are not yet subject to the rigid systems of codification introduced during the Enlightenment, are flexible and inclusive, the multivocality of generic languages (Bakhtin's "polyglossia") operating within individual texts. "Literary forms and artistic conventions," writes Mary Beth Rose, "are themselves social and ideological constructs whose varying patterns, sudden appearances at distinct historical moments, and shifting dominance serve as significant registers of cultural transformation."[15] As the essays by MacDonald and Kesler attest, the theater of Marlowe and Shakespeare refashions inherited models in such a way that literary forms are reconstituted as a network of codes of mediation—between text, audience, culture, and history—intersecting with a genre's figuration of gendered subjectivity.

For MacDonald, in "Marlowe's Ganymede," to recover the historical context of a genre such as Renaissance tragedy and a text such as Marlowe's Prologue to *Dido Queene of Carthage* is to construe history as an "imperial as well as sexual, textual as well as political" entity. Marlowe's reworking of the Ganymede-Jupiter myth as he found it in Ovid's *Metamorphoses* and Virgil's *Aeneid* confounds the spectator's expectations by thwarting epic conventions through a deliberate disruption of conventional binaries of gender and sexual difference: "love versus duty, the personal versus the public and historical, passion versus intellect, men versus women." MacDonald's reading of the interconnections between historical, generic, and erotic structures in Marlowe's Prologue situates the essay within in the recent shift in multidisciplinary scholarship away from the heterocentric perspective—which Bonnie Zimmerman has defined as "*the* perceptual screen provided by our . . . cultural conditioning" which "assumes heterosexuality to be the only natural form of sexual and emotional expression"[16]—toward a recognition of the significance of homoeroticism on the English transvestite stage. An increasingly contested assumption has been the claim that because "homosexuality" was a term invented by nineteenth-century sexologists, it was a form of subjectivity unknown in the early modern period. MacDonald advances the revisionist argument in her assertion that although "homosexuality" may be a term found only in post-Renaissance discourses, this does not deny that sexual or romantic love between same-sex individuals had any social or literary bases. She does so by clarifying how Marlowe reconstitutes the Ganymede myth through a "playfully subversive homoeroticism" which undermines the classical epic's privileging of marital sex as a fundamental component of heroic action. Dislodging conventional tragic structures through the interplay of epic, comic, and erotic elements, Marlowe undertakes a radical although ultimately indeterminate scrutiny of gendered identity and of the social hierarchies through which gender is mediated. In portraying the tragic encounter between Aeneas and Queen Dido, Marlowe's classical sources stress "the incompatibility of history and pleasure" and exclude the feminine from heroic action. Marlowe, on the other hand, playfully employs the "flirtatious and effeminate" Ganymede to challenge "heterosexual and familial, as well as generational, hierarchies" including the hierarchies of genre.

In "Subjectivity, Time, and Gender in *Titus Andronicus, Hamlet,* and *Othello,*" R. L. Kesler examines how Shakespeare's appropriation of dramatic paradigms speaks to the commercial theater's growing emphasis on the relation between tragedy, causality, and subjectivity. Central to this new emphasis is the construction in the drama of the universal male subject, a development that ultimately depends on the effacement of the feminine. Laurie A. Finke has observed that in early seventeenth-century tragedies the erasure of femininity and its equation with powerlessness involve "strategies" that "are most often violent, and include rape . . . and murder," the effect of which is the "reduction" of the women characters "to mere objects whose femininity is exclusively defined by their sexuality."[17] In the early tragedy *Titus Andronicus* this effacement, suggests Kesler, is only tentatively and ambivalently staged. The hero Titus (re)defines himself in a specifically early modern context by overcoming the dissolving feudal claims of family (claims represented in the denouement by the corpse of Lavinia), and by only gradually assuming a subjectivity free of such constraints. In Titus's self-redefinition, the play encodes the rupture of a subjectivity initially defined against and dependent upon "feminized values." The displacement gives way to a (male) subjectivity that "is fully causal, objective, and detached," and that functions, in the "phallocentric terms of the new science, . . . beyond any symbolic need for women." In a later tragedy such as *Hamlet* the figure of the single, isolated, masculine hero occupies center stage. *Hamlet* crystallizes the development in Renaissance tragedy of the causal plot: "the emergence of an independent and 'objective,' if self-obsessed and masculinized, subjectivity" constituted by the play's definition of Ophelia's femininity as "a story structured in absence." While *Hamlet* participates in Renaissance tragedy's construction of a hypermasculine subjectivity, creating the illusion of an individuality coextensive with its fate, *Othello* assumes the inferiority of that subjectivity. The play constructs identity as random, moving tragedy closer to comedy. In reconstituting the causal tragic plot, *Othello* reveals that the demise of the feminine ideal is associated "not with the consolidation of a heroic male subjectivity but with its disintegration."

Part 1 of the collection is concerned with the multiple ways in which early modern epistemologies of sex, race, and subjectivity inform representations of the gendered body in the drama; part 2 is grounded in the more specific consideration of women as authors, subjects, and objects of theatrical representation. In recent years an increasingly fruitful dialogue has evolved between critics who see performativity as a speech act and those who study performance as a set of bodily practices.[18] This dialogue has been particularly influential in critical analyses of crossdressing as plot motif and material practice in Renaissance drama, in which gender *is* performance. The essays in this section address performativity from a number of critical and theoretical perspectives to explore the equivocal positions women occupied in the drama, and how performance practices and spectatorship underwrote the theater's preoccupation with gender.

Although women were generally missing from the commercial theater as writers and performers, they were present as spectators; for court and household productions, however, women both performed and wrote. Household performances (including masques, interludes, and entertainments) took place in controlled circumstances within individual households, rather than at court, with the participation of primarily nonprofessional performers. Numerous discussions of noncommercial drama have focused on entertainments at court and in stately houses, especially on interludes, entertainments presented to Queen Elizabeth, and the Stuart court masque.[19] When Queen Henrietta Maria and the women of her court began to take speaking parts in performances of pastorals and masques, they sparked a debate in theatrical and polemical texts about whether women should perform.[20] Ann Thompson comments on two prologues "written and performed by men [in which] women are represented as trying to get on to the stage quite literally, and to challenge men's monopoly of the right to act and of the right to judge plays as privileged spectators."[21] Sophie Tomlinson suggests that plays performed in the early 1630s which address female acting demonstrate "a tension between allegiance to the theatrical profession—and implicitly to Henrietta Maria—and acquiescence with the ideological norms regarding women"; in contrast, the court theater "insisted on the legitimacy of women's talents finding expression and being put on to view."[22] Critical attention in the last few years has also turned to how early modern women represented themselves, as dramatists and as performers, in masques and other plays produced in the household, the only forum in which women who were not courtiers could participate theatrically. Suzanne Westfall has also shown how household performances in the Tudor period had religious, political, and dynastic significance.[23]

The essays by Rosemary Kegl and Alison Findlay open up new areas of investigation by considering the special significance of the household as a locus in which women could write and perform drama. They consider women dramatists in relation to traditions of private household performances, in which the construction of household histories is an important function. As well, both essays address the political significance of genre, and of generic disruption, for women writers of dramatic scripts.

In "Theaters, Households, and a 'Kind of History' in Elizabeth Cary's *The Tragedy of Mariam*," Kegl argues that while many critics have connected Cary's life to the events portrayed in *Mariam*, Cary's understanding of dramatic theory and practice is also significant to our understanding of the play. Closet drama, given its thematic concerns with political reformation, had an affinity with the dynastic "histories" so often presented in household performances. In some households closet dramas were declaimed, while in others they were read aloud. As Kegl notes, Cary and other members of her family enjoyed attending masques and other dramatic performances. The formal structures of *Mariam*—particularly its strict adherence to unity of time—stand in an "uneasy relationship" with the commercial stage as well as with household performances. While Philip Sidney's critique of popular drama prescribes temporal unity instead of the extended, episodic chronology of romances and other dramatic forms, the Chorus in *Mariam* draws attention to the sheer number of events that have taken place in the six hours of the play's action—events so numerous that the play "tends to replicate rather than reform the excesses of popular productions." Given the extent to which plot and language in *Mariam* emphasize the overturning of order in family, household, and state, it is significant that the play should disrupt certain conventions of closet drama and challenge the imperatives of dynastic order celebrated in so many household productions.

Jane Cavendish and Elizabeth Brackley, in their critique of genre, family, and dynasty, draw on their direct familiarity with the conventions of comedy and the masque. In "Playing the 'Scene Self': Jane Cavendish and Elizabeth Brackley's *The Concealed Fancies*," Alison Findlay addresses the ways in which social roles assigned by gender and class were central to dramatic self-representation in the household of a Royalist family during the Civil War. The essay focuses on the complex ways in which *The Concealed Fancies* explores gendered identity in its dramatization of prescribed social and familial roles. The characters Luceny and Tattiney, like the authors, are sisters whose marriages have been arranged in a system of homosocial exchange. The play examines the fluidity and instability of rituals such as courtship, in which "the performance of deference" is required of the male courtly lover until marriage, and of the wife after marriage. Arguing that the enactment of gender "empowers not only the female protagonists but also the authors who stand behind them," Findlay illustrates how Cavendish and Brackley's characters appropriate the word "mistress" to create new female subject positions and to "manipulate patriarchal models of mimesis" through insincere performance of the wife's role, a cause of anxiety for writers of early modern conduct books. Drawing on the work of Luce Irigaray and Elin Diamond, Findlay points out that although at the end of *The Concealed Fancies* Luceny and Tattiney marry the appropriate suitors, their use of mimicry subverts conventional discursive and ideological expectations. As the characters mimic wifely conformity, the rehearsals—or performances—"fracture the gendered human subject," a strategy suggesting that these characters do not always see themselves in terms of lack. Like their female protagonists, Cavendish and Brackley refashion themselves through discourse, revealing the connections between "the scripted performance and other forms of self-presentation in the household and beyond."

Findlay's analysis of *The Concealed Fancies* raises the strong possibility that women performed speaking roles in household dramatic performances. The essays by Michael Shapiro, Laurie E. Osborne, and Christina Luckyj analyze the relations between (female) lack, substitution, and performativity on the commercial stage, illuminating the material and metadramatic implications of crossdressing and the male gaze.

In "The Introduction of Actresses in England: Delay or Defensiveness?" Shapiro reminds us that in the commercial transvestite theater women did not appear on the stage—that gender was, quite literally, enacted. The conventions of transvestite performance, in which women were represented through substitution and displacement, emphasized women's physical absence from the stage as well as from the production processes of the professional theater. Shapiro begins by asking why male performers continued to play women's roles on the English stage at a time when professional actresses were performing in European cities, taking the position that explanations based on cultural attitudes to gender and sexuality should be supplemented by an analysis of the material conditions in which English and European theatrical companies existed.

Reassessing an extensive body of early modern records pertaining to professional actors and acting companies in England and on the Continent, Shapiro considers the regulation of performers by civil authorities, the differences in the training and recruiting of performers in Europe and England, and changes in the organization of the commercial theater in England before and after the Restoration. He suggests that the exclusion of women from English professional acting companies in the early seventeenth century may have been rooted partly in economic and legal structures. Laws which held a parish responsible for supporting children born within its boundaries made women potential "liabilities" on the provincial tours which London theatrical companies needed for financial survival. In addition, women may have been excluded from London troupes because they formed a threat to theatrical organizations and structures. If actresses had been employed to play women's roles in which young male performers served a form of apprenticeship, women, especially in London, could have been seen as potential rivals by male actors. When the patent theaters opened at the advent of the Restoration, after eighteen years of structural and economic disruption in the commercial theater, the apprenticeship system was not reinstated; instead, patent theaters relied on "nurseries" in which both male and female performers were trained. Shapiro's consideration of the legal and economic conditions which would militate against the participation of women as performers in the early seventeenth-century commercial theater reminds us how persistently the conventions and practices of the transvestite theater survived in early modern England, and how powerfully these conventions structured the representation and discourses of gender and sexual difference.

Although women were objects of representation on the stage, they were present in the theaters as spectators of female personation. Debate continues about precisely how many women, and of which social classes, attended the commercial theaters, but it is generally agreed that women formed a significant part of the audiences of both commercial and household performances.[24] Women were also writers of and performers in "amateur" productions in the court, household, and other spaces such as girls' schools. Jean E. Howard has noted that occasional, household performances were largely exempted from anxieties about, and regulations imposed on, professional performances, and that Stephen Gosson, disapproving of women attending the theater, proposed to "send the gentlewoman citizen out of the theatre" to the home.[25] Ironically, the private and domestic spheres in which women were assumed to be controlled were the very spaces in which women of noble rank were not only spectators but also performers and sometimes writers of drama.

Although the household and court offered a relatively freer theatrical space for women, Laurie Osborne's "Staging the Female Playgoer: Gender in Shakespeare's Onstage Audiences" argues that the position of women in the audiences of court entertainments is represented as problematic on the commercial stage of the early seventeenth century. Osborne examines Shakespeare's metadramatic representation of women auditors of courtly entertainments in light of contemporary anxieties that women spectators might themselves become spectacles. Women spectators are more "vulnerable sexual spectacles" than are Shakespeare's women characters who employ theatrical behavior "outside overtly theatrical contexts." Moreover, Shakespeare's women spectators of courtly performances are less autonomous than those represented in contemporary metadramatic plays like *The Knight of the Burning Pestle,* which were written for the public or commercial theater. Osborne emphasizes the significance of class—of the patrons, performers, and spectators—in the construction and reception of the metadramatic representations of women as spectators, suggesting that *Love's Labor's Lost,* for example, "validates female spectatorship, but only in the noblewomen and only in informal theatrical situations." In that play, when men promote the action of the performance it is only after the female spectacle has replaced the female spectator as the focus of attention. Women spectators in *Love's Labor's Lost, Hamlet,* and *A Midsummer Night's Dream* variously resist and succumb to the gaze which puts them in danger of being perceived as sexual spectacles by the male characters and by the audience in the theater. Critics such as Lisa Jardine and Laura Levine have emphasized that crossdressed male performers are vulnerable to being constructed as sexual spectacles, whether they are playing women characters or women characters crossdressed as male.[26] Osborne's essay suggests that in Shakespeare's plays women in the onstage audience are multiply spectacularized. Played by boy actors, as spectators of plays-within-plays, the women characters are subject to the gaze of the male characters, as well as to the gaze of the audience in the theater itself, ultimately becoming both spectators and spectacles.

The collection's final essay, Christina Luckyj's "Gender, Rhetoric, and Performance in John Webster's *The White Devil,*" also addresses the interplay between gender and performance, but in terms of how the conventions of the transvestite theater operates rhetorically and discursively. While crossdressed male performers construct and represent "femininity," in many plays the female characters disguised as men parody "masculinity." The consequent uncertainties about the ways in which performance constitutes gender are especially significant in Webster's play. Vittoria Corombona does not follow the suggestion that she evade the law by assuming a masculine disguise as a page. Instead, she defends herself in the courtroom, rhetorically "constructing and playing out a female stereotype." The metatheatrical presentation, however, is ultimately unreadable because multiple interpretations can be placed upon the "signs" of femininity by other characters who are spectators of Vittoria's performance. Thus, Luckyj concludes that in *The White Devil* a character's distance from "self-representation [can] open a space" for female subjectivity.

A complex variable, gender as enacted in the English Renaissance theater requires continuous critical revaluation and reconsideration. In this context, the question posed by the historian Joan Scott—"Which symbolic representations are invoked, how, and in what contexts?"[27]—to which we would add the equally important question, "how and under what symbolic and material circumstances are gender and sexual difference performed?" are crucial points of departure for unraveling the multiple structures (epistemological, performative, psychological, ideological) that underwrite early modern enactments of gender.

Notes

1. Steven Mullaney, *The Place of the Stage: License, Play, and Power in the Drama of Shakespeare and His Contemporaries* (Chicago: University of Chicago Press, 1988), 9; Nick Potter, "*As You Like It:* The Outlaw Court," in Graham Holderness, Nick Potter, and John Turner, *Shakespeare, Out of Court: Dramatizations of Court Society* (New York: St. Martin's Press, 1990), 88.

2. Ivo Kamps, "Materialist Shakespeare: An Introduction," in *Materialist Shakespeare: A History,* ed. Ivo Kamps (London: Verso, 1995), 8. On the contradictory aspects of the English Renaissance theater, see also Jean E. Howard, *The Stage and Social Struggle in Early Modern England* (London: Routledge, 1994), 13; and John Drakakis, "'Fashion It Thus': *Julius Caesar* and the Politics of Theatrical Representation," in *Materialist Shakespeare,* ed. Kamps, 280–91.

3. Regenia Gagnier, "Feminist Postmodernism: The End of Feminism or the Ends of Theory?" in *Theoretical Perspectives on Sexual Difference,* ed. Deborah L. Rhode (New Haven: Yale University Press, 1990), 23.

4. Judith Butler, *Bodies That Matter: On the Discursive Limits of "Sex"* (New York: Routledge, 1993), 188.

5. Judith Butler, "Against Proper Objects," *Differences: More Gender Trouble: Feminism Meets Queer Theory* 6 (Summer/Fall 1994): 3.

6. Feminist and "'third world' critics," writes Ania Loomba, have been especially wary of certain postmodernist assumptions and methodologies: "it has been variously alleged that the agency of the marginalized subject is obscured when that subject is theorized as discontinuous, or as merely 'the site' for the intersection of various discourses," an allegation which points to the enormous difficulties involved in problematizing difference. Concepts such as "race, gender, class, caste and other social differentials cannot be easily accommodated without risking endless fragmentation of subjectivity" ("The Color of Patriarchy," in *Women, "Race," and Writing in the Early Modern Period*, ed. Margo Hendricks and Patricia Parker [London: Routledge, 1994], 18).

7. Alice Jardine, *Gynesis: Configurations of Woman and Modernity* (Ithaca: Cornell University Press, 1985), 36.

8. Luce Irigaray, "The Female Gender," in *Sexes and Genealogies*, trans. Gillian C. Gill (1987; reprint, New York: Columbia University Press, 1993), 107, 109. For an illuminating account of how some "differences" have been exploited in postmodern literary criticism, and the distortions that have resulted when differences have been misconstrued, see Audre Lorde, *Sister Outsider: Essays and Speeches* (New York: Crossing Press, 1984), 114.

9. Carol Thomas Neely, "Constructing the Subject: Feminist Practice and the New Renaissance Discourses," *English Literary Renaissance* 18 (Winter 1988): 7. See also Walter Cohen's critique of the tendency on the part of new historicists to consider "gender in relation to the body or to power more than in relation to women," a practice which in effect erases women as "historical actors or subjects": women "can be victims or objects, but it is not . . . their experience that matters" ("Political Criticism of Shakespeare," in *Shakespeare Reproduced: The Text in History and Ideology*, ed. Jean E. Howard and Marion F. O'Connor [New York: Methuen, 1987], 38). Similarly, Mary Beth Rose points out that "scholars concerned with the representation of sexuality and gender construction in Renaissance literature" are increasingly recognizing that critical "inquiries must involve a full scrutiny of the discourses distinctive to, and the options available in, Renaissance England" and their connection to "the otherness of the past" ("Where Are the Mothers in Shakespeare? Options for Gender Representation in the English Renaissance," *Shakespeare Quarterly* 42 [Fall 1991]: 291).

10. Karen Newman, *Fashioning Femininity and English Renaissance Drama* (Chicago: University of Chicago Press, 1991), xviii. Other attempts to correct the inattention to difference with respect to early modern representations of gender include Linda Woodbridge, *Women and the English Renaissance: Literature and the Nature of Womankind, 1540–1620* (Urbana: University of Illinois Press, 1986); Catherine Belsey, *The Subject of Tragedy: Identity and Difference in Renaissance Drama* (London: Methuen, 1985); Margaret J. M. Ezell, *The Patriarch's Wife: Literary Evidence and the History of the Family* (Chapel Hill: University of North Carolina Press, 1987); and Barbara Kiefer Lewalski, *Writing Women in Jacobean England* (Cambridge, Mass.: Harvard University Press, 1993).

11. Parveen Adams, "A Note on the Distinction between Sexual Division and Sexual Differences," in *The Woman in Question*, ed. Parveen Adams and Elizabeth Cowie (Lon-

don: Verso Press; Cambridge, Mass.: MIT Press, 1990), 102. A case in point is the concept of "Renaissance self-fashioning," which, as Marjorie Garber observes of Stephen Greenblatt's well-worn phrase, has sustained the practice of theorizing gender while sexual difference is eclipsed by a return to an older historicism in which "a man" is said to "'make'" or invent himself (Marjorie Garber, *Vested Interests: Cross-Dressing and Cultural Anxiety* [New York: Routledge, 1992], 93; cf. 75–77). For a comprehensive discussion of how sexual difference has been insufficiently theorized in historicist-based discourses, see also Charles Shepherdson, "The *Role* of Gender and the *Imperative* of Sex," in *Supposing the Subject,* ed. Joan Copjec (London: Verso, 1994), 158–84.

12. See esp. Michel Foucault, *The History of Sexuality,* trans. Robert Hurley, 3 vols. (1978; reprint, New York: Vintage, 1978–87); Stephen Greenblatt, "Fiction and Friction," in *Shakespearean Negotiations: The Circulation of Social Energy in Renaissance England* (Berkeley and Los Angeles: University of California Press, 1988), 66–93; Thomas Laqueur, "Orgasm, Generation, and the Politics of Reproductive Biology," *Representations* 14 (Spring 1986): 1–41; and Laqueur, *Making Sex: Body and Gender from the Greeks to Freud* (Cambridge, Mass.: Harvard University Press, 1990).

13. Laqueur, *Making Sex,* 6–8.

14. Jeffrey Weeks, *Sexuality* (London: Routledge, 1986), 17. Although Laqueur is careful to note that sixteenth-century appropriations of Galen, Hippocrates, and Aristotle include exceptions to the one-sex model, his argument has recently been challenged for ultimately treating its subject monolithically. Patricia Parker, for example, has suggested that "the argument that posits for the period a normative teleology drawn from a particular selection of medical materials, or tends to represent the medical archive as more straightforward or univocal than it is, needs to be tested against a broader and more complicating textual field" ("Gender Ideology, Gender Change: The Case of Marie Germain," *Critical Inquiry* 19 [Winter 1993]: 339). See also Julia Epstein, "Either/Or—Neither/Both: Sexual Ambiguity and the Ideology of Gender," *Genders* 7 (Spring 1990): 99–142.

15. Rose, "Where Are the Mothers in Shakespeare?" 291. See also Fredric Jameson, *The Political Unconscious: Narrative as a Socially Symbolic Act* (Ithaca: Cornell University Press, 1981), 140–41; Jameson, *Marxism and Form* (Princeton: Princeton University Press, 1971); and Mikhail Bakhtin, *Rabelais and His World,* trans. Hélène Iswolsky (1965; reprint, Bloomington: Indiana University Press, 1984).

16. Bonnie Zimmerman, "What Has Never Been: An Overview of Lesbian Feminist Criticism," in *Making a Difference: Feminist Literary Criticism,* ed. Gayle Greene and Coppélia Kahn (1985; reprint, London: Routledge, 1990), 179.

17. Laurie A. Finke, "Painting Women: Images of Femininity in Jacobean Tragedy," in *Performing Feminisms: Feminist Critical Theory and Theatre,* ed. Sue-Ellen Case (Baltimore: Johns Hopkins University Press, 1990), 225.

18. This concern is central to Sue-Ellen Case's collection of essays *Performing Feminisms: Feminist Critical Theory and Theatre.* Reprinted in the same volume, Judith Butler's essay "Performative Acts and Gender Constitution: An Essay in Phenomenology and Feminist Theory" (270–82) has been widely cited in studies of early modern theatrical repre-

sentations of gender. See also Andrew Parker and Eve Kosofsky Sedgwick, "Introduction: Performativity and Performance," in *Performativity and Performance,* ed. Andrew Parker and Eve Kosofsky Sedgwick (New York: Routledge, 1995), 1–18.

19. For an indication of the popularity and numbers of both court and household entertainments, see C. E. McGee and John C. Meagher, "Preliminary Checklist of Tudor and Stuart Entertainments: 1485–1558," *Research Opportunities in Renaissance Drama* 25 (1982): 31–114; McGee and Meagher, "Preliminary Checklist of Tudor and Stuart Entertainments: 1599–1603," *Research Opportunities in Renaissance Drama* 24 (1981): 51–155; McGee and Meagher, "Preliminary Checklist of Tudor and Stuart Entertainments: 1603–1613," *Research Opportunities in Renaissance Drama* 27 (1984): 47–126; McGee and Meagher, "Preliminary Checklist of Tudor and Stuart Entertainments: 1614–1625," *Research Opportunities in Renaissance Drama* 30 (1988): 17–128.

20. Women regularly danced in masques and entertainments in the household, and took nonspeaking roles as masquers at the Stuart court until 1626, when Queen Henrietta Maria "declaimed" a speech (Sophie Tomlinson, "She That Plays the King: Henrietta Maria and the Threat of the Actress in Caroline Culture," in *The Politics of Tragicomedy: Shakespeare and After,* ed. Gordon McMullan and Jonathan Hope [London: Routledge, 1992], 189; see also Suzanne Gossett, "'Man-maid Begone!': Women in Masques," *English Literary Renaissance* 18 [1988]: 97). Young girls also took part in such performances; see, for example, *Cupid's Banishment: A Masque Presented to her Majesty by the Young Gentlewomen of the Ladies Hall, Deptford, May 4, 1617,* ed. C. E. McGee, *Renaissance Drama,* n.s. 19 (1988): 227–64. (*Cupid's Banishment* is also included in S. P. Cerasano and Marion Wynne-Davies, *Renaissance Drama by Women: Texts and Documents* [London: Routledge, 1996]: 83–89.) Women's active participation in initiating masques is a subject of recent critical interest: see Barbara Lewalski, "Enacting Opposition: Queen Anne and the Subversions of Masquing," in *Writing Women in Jacobean England,* 15–43; Erika Veevers, *Images of Love and Religion: Queen Henrietta Maria and Court Entertainments* (Cambridge: Cambridge University Press, 1989); and Marion Wynne-Davies, "The Queen's Masque: Renaissance Women and the Seventeenth-Century Court Masque," in *Gloriana's Face: Women, Public and Private, in the English Renaissance,* ed. S. P. Cerasano and Marion Wynne-Davies (Detroit: Wayne State University Press, 1992), 79–104.

For an example of the polemical debate that attended the subject of women performers see William Prynne, *Histrio-Mastix: The Player's Scourge or Actor's Tragedy* (1629) (New York: Garland, 1974).

21. Ann Thompson, "Women/'Women' and the Stage," in *Women and Literature in Britain 1500–1700,* ed. Helen Wilcox (Cambridge: Cambridge University Press, 1996), 101.

22. Tomlinson, "She That Plays the King," 197.

23. See Suzanne Westfall, *Patrons and Performance: Early Tudor Household Revels* (Oxford: Clarendon Press, 1990).

24. Alfred Harbage's argument, in *Shakespeare's Audience* (1941; reprint, New York: Columbia University Press, 1958), that audiences in the "public" theaters comprised a cross section of society was first challenged by Ann Jennalie Cook, *The Privileged Playgoers of*

Shakespeare's England (Princeton: Princeton University Press, 1981). See also Jean E. Howard, "Women as Spectators, Spectacles and Paying Customers in the English Public Theater," in *Stage and Social Struggle in Early Modern England,* 73–92; Andrew Gurr, *Playgoing in Shakespeare's London* (Cambridge: Cambridge University Press, 1987); and Richard Levin, "Women in the Renaissance Theatre Audience," *Shakespeare Quarterly* 40 (Summer 1989): 165–74.

25. Howard, *Stage and Social Struggle in Early Modern England,* 74–75; see Stephen Gosson, *The Schoole of Abuse* (1579; reprint, New York: Da Capo Press, 1972), 78.

26. Lisa Jardine, "'As Boys and Women Are for the Most Part Cattle of This Colour': Female Roles and Elizabethan Eroticism," in *Still Harping on Daughters* (New York: Columbia University Press, 1989), 9–36; Laura Levine, *Men in Women's Clothing: Anti-Theatricality and Effeminization, 1579–1642* (Cambridge: Cambridge University Press, 1994).

27. Joan W. Scott, "Gender: A Useful Category of Historical Analysis," *American Historical Review* 91 (December 1986): 1067. On the need to contextualize the symbolic presentation of gender in the performing arts, see Laurence Senelick, "Introduction," in *Gender in Performance: The Presentation of Difference in the Performing Arts,* ed. Laurence Senelick (Hanover, N.H.: University Press of New England, 1992), ix–xx.

PART I

I

Making Defect Perfection: Shakespeare and the One-Sex Model

Janet Adelman

> I saw her once
> Hop forty paces through the public street;
> And having lost her breath, she spoke, and panted,
> That she did make defect perfection,
> And, breathless, pow'r breathe forth.
> —*Antony and Cleopatra,* 2.2.229–33

I take *Antony and Cleopatra* as my starting point because Shakespeare's language about Cleopatra here allows for—perhaps even encourages—the critical fantasy that he is redressing a gender injustice. *Defect* and *perfection* are not neutral terms, particularly in descriptions of women: they are conceptual tokens in a long-standing argument about woman's nature relative to man's, as Milton well knew when he had Adam call Eve "this fair defect of nature" after the Fall (*Paradise Lost,* 10.891–92). The sense that woman is a defective man—a kind of glitch in nature's master plan, which was to produce men—is at least as old as Aristotle; we can hear its attenuated echoes in all language that characterizes woman as privative, woman as lack.

This language is of course familiar in Shakespeare, particularly in the transvestite comedies, and it is always called on initially to secure gender difference. From Portia's "they shall think we are accomplished / With that we lack" (*Merchant of Venice,* 3.4.61–62)[1] to Viola's "A little thing would make me tell them how much I lack of a man" (*Twelfth Night,* 3.4.282–83), *lack* registers the presence of the woman under the masculine costume by calling attention to what is absent in her. (The definition of woman as that which lacks man's "little thing" is so habitual that Shakespeare can afford to make an anatomical joke about it in *As You Like It:* after Rosalind swoons at the sight of Orlando's blood, Oliver says, "Be of good cheer, youth. You a man! You lack a man's heart," and the chastened Rosalind, no doubt thinking of another lack, answers, "I do so, I confess it" [4.3.164–66].) As soon as a woman puts on men's clothes in the comedies, she is compelled to remind us of what she does not have, as though the audience were in danger of forgetting; Hamlet, worrying over the issue of his own gender confusions, reminds himself and us that what Ophelia has between her legs is "nothing" (*Hamlet*, 3.2.113–15).

But if the allusions to *lack* in Shakespeare's transvestite comedies serve initially to secure difference by registering the woman's presence under the masculine costume, they also serve to undermine that difference. The joke, of course, is that the "women" do not in fact lack anything: the transvestite comedies repair the "lack" in women at least in part by calling attention to the body of the boy actor who underwrites the representation of women on stage. When transvestite theater reaches what appears to be its full potential in transvestite comedy, that is, it tends to do away with the anxieties attendant on sexual difference by doing away with sexual difference: lack disappears because women disappear.[2]

It is frequently assumed that the evocation of the boy actor must always function thus; but the strategy of *Antony and Cleopatra* is, I want to argue, quite different.[3] When Cleopatra alludes to the boy actor playing her—"I shall see / Some squeaking Cleopatra boy my greatness / I' th' posture of a whore" (5.2.219–21)—she does so not in order to repair a lack in herself by alluding to the presence of the boy underneath but in order to distance herself from his defective representation of her decidedly female grandeur. It goes without saying, I think, that only a playwright supremely confident in his boy actor's capacity to play a woman convincingly could risk these lines: they work only if we simultaneously see the boy actor speaking them and see the "real" woman who does not want to be play-acted parodically by some squeaking boy actor. Cleopatra is so sure of the power of her femininity that she can dismiss the underlying actor's body as a poor imitation of her: in her own mind at least, she is the perfection of which he is the defect.

If the theater of the transvestite comedies is characterized by its playing out of a lack in which women eventually disappear, the theater of *Antony and Cleopatra* reinstates female presence precisely over the body of the boy actor, and precisely by calling attention to his—not her—lack. She does not have Antony's "inches" (1.3.40), she reminds us early on, and she can only play at putting on Antony's sword (2.5.23); but in her, the tropes of lack are rewritten as the tropes of an endlessly generative fullness that underscores the lack in others: a fullness that makes hungry where most it satisfies, that draws everything into itself and threatens to make a gap in nature (2.2.238–39, 217–19). Through this rewriting, Shakespeare makes it possible to imagine a theater allied with female generativity, with what Cleopatra calls "the memory of my womb" (3.13.163),[4] a theater as far away as possible from the male spectacle promoted by Caesar—and from his own earlier transvestite comedies.

Recently we have been told that transvestite theater is the logical culmination of the reigning anatomical model of sexual difference in the Renaissance,[5] a model that in effect does away with women's bodies altogether. I refer of course to the Galenic or "one-sex" model as it was delineated by Thomas Laqueur and brought powerfully into the domain of literary studies by Stephen Greenblatt.[6] In this model, male and female genitals are (by now famously) structurally homologous; the female wears hers inside, rather than outside, only because she lacks the superior heat necessary to thrust hers out. Under the aegis of this model, the female body is by definition defective insofar as it is present at all; indeed, insofar as the "one sex" is inevitably male, anatomically speaking the female body can scarcely be said to be present. But despite—or sometimes because of—this disappearing act, English Renaissance literary scholars interested in gender have rushed to embrace the Galenic model, discovering in it in effect a new orthodoxy, one of the things that we can now take for granted in the Renaissance.[7]

The appeal to any medical model is by no means an obvious or a necessary move; though one of Galen's recent adherents can claim self-assuredly that "our notions of our bodies are, after all, constructed primarily through their descriptions in the discourses of medicine and science,"[8] it's by no means clear in the twentieth century, let alone the sixteenth, that our notions of our bodies are more indebted to medicine and science than, say, to religious doctrine or to all the cultural and individual practices—and accompanying psychic fantasies—that teach us who we are in a bodily sense from birth onward. And the appeal to this particular medical model seems to me especially vexed, for two reasons. First, because the model may not in fact be entirely historically accurate, or not accurate in quite the hegemonic way that its proponents suppose.[9] And second, because elevation of the one-sex model to hegemonic status—as the single prototype that determined the way that early modern people thought about anatomical sexual difference—sometimes turns out to be only the most recent way of reinforcing lack, made respectable by its apparent claim to historical accuracy. But Shakespeare himself seems far from certain that there is only one sex; seen from within the context of contemporary medical discourses about gender difference, Shakespeare's willingness to experiment with making defect perfection in *Antony and Cleopatra* may signal his participation in a complex conversation about anatomical sexual difference—a conversation that we are not likely to hear if we know in advance that there is only one way to think anatomically about sexual difference in the Renaissance. We might frame our thinking about his participation in this conversation by asking: if it makes sense to see Shakespeare's foregrounding of the boy actor in the theater of his transvestite comedies as the logical end of the one-sex model, of what model(s) might those aspects of Cleopatra's theater most allied with a generative womb-space be the logical end? For what model(s) might Cleopatra speak when she recuperates the female body specifically from the inadequacies of the squeaking boy actor?

In the interests of beginning to make this conversation audible, I want to test out the hegemony of the Galenic model in a very limited arena: medical or medically inflected texts published in England in the English language from roughly mid-sixteenth century to the time of Shakespeare's death. What exactly is the status of the one-sex model in these texts? Is it in fact the only show in town? We need to begin, I think, by asking what exactly we mean by the one-sex model, what counts as evidence for it. There's no question that the medical discourses assumed certain similarities between male and female bodies: the as-yet-functionally-unacknowledged ovaries are normally called stones or testicles and are non-Aristotelianly assumed to produce their own version of seed, one weaker and less effective than male seed. There's also little question that the male body remains the gold standard, that against which the female must be defined. But neither of these assumptions by itself has much power to surprise or allure; neither constitutes what contemporary critics seem to mean by allusions to the one-sex model. The aspect of the one-sex model that seems particularly sexy in contemporary discourse is the invertibility of male and female sexual organs, the structural homology that apparently did away with anatomical sexual difference and could turn a woman into a man merely by raising her temperature. This is what excites our imagination. But how hegemonic was *this* aspect of the one-sex theory in vernacular medical works in sixteenth-century England? How prominent is it, for example, in the developing vernacular medical discourse and in popular works about the body?

A nod toward the Galenic model does indeed turn up in the work of Thomas Vicary, "Serjeant of the Surgeons to Henry VIII, Queen Mary, Edward VI, and Queen Elizabeth; Master of the Barber-Surgeons' Company; and Chief Surgeon to St. Bartholomew's Hospital, London, 1548–62" (all of which makes him sound well placed to have a hegemonic opinion). But unlike his twentieth-century counterparts, Vicary is distinctly unexcited by (almost uninterested in) the homology, which he in any case presents more as a loose analogy than as a principle of invertibility that does away with anatomical sex difference. He makes the transition from unisex to female anatomy by noting that "the Testikles be without; but in women it abydeth within, for their Testicles stande within, as it shal be declared hereafter."[10] He then continues: "Next foloweth the Matrix in women: The Matrix in woman is an official member, compounde and Nerueous, and in complexion colde and dry. And it is the felde of mans generation; and it is an instrument susceptiue, that is to say, a thing receying or taking . . . : the likenes of it is as it were a yarde reuersed or turned inwarde, hauing testikles likewise, as aforesaid: also the Matrix hath two concauities or selles" (77). Vicary here echoes an earlier English vernacular medical text: in *The Cyrurgie of Guy de Chauliac,* an anonymous Middle English translation in manuscript of Guy de Chauliac's 1363 *Inventarium seu collectorium in parte cyrurgicali medicine,* women have their stones within and the matrix has the same hollowness and hole as the yard and is as large as the yard "turned again or put within."[11] But neither of these works embraces the full-blown doctrine of homology: like the *Cyrurgie,* Vicary does not mention the role of heat in extruding or retaining the genitals within and never implies the convertibility of female to male. Moreover, Vicary's phraseology—"the liknes of it is as it were"—suggests a self-conscious analogy, twice distanced from fact, rather than a literal description of a structural identity. Even as an analogy, that is, the homology between matrix and yard appears here in a weak form—weaker than other terms of comparison that Vicary invokes shortly after this one: "the necke [of the matrix] . . . in her concauitie hath many inuolutions and pleates, ioyned together in the maner of Rose leaues before they be fully spread or ripe, and so they be shut togeather as a Purse mouth" (77). "A whole world view makes the vagina look like a penis to Renaissance observers," Laqueur says (*Making Sex,* 82); but for Vicary, the vagina can look as much like a rose or a purse as like a penis. And while he clearly knows the Galenic model, he does not seem to deduce from it any "transcendental claim that there exists but one sex" (Laqueur, *Making Sex,* 69), any principle of covert maleness in the female: his matrix is as much like a classically female rose as like a yard.

And as far as I have been able to discover, this rather weak form of the one-sex model is its sole appearance in a sixteenth-century English vernacular medical text.[12] It does not appear, for example, in the work of a later anatomist, John Banister, "Master in Chururgerie, and Practioner in Phisicke," whose compilation *The Historie of Man* (London, 1578) advertises itself as "sucked from the sappe of the most approved Anathomistes, in this present age, compiled in most compendious forme, and now published in English, for the utilitie of all godly Chirurgians, within this Realme." Either his most approved anathomistes did not rely heavily on the one-sex model or he did not choose to suck that particular bit of sap from them: though he is perfectly willing to compare women to men in other respects—they do not have the same protuberances in their throats that men have, they are more fatty than men, they have special veins which dispense milk to their paps, and so forth—he declines to compare female genital parts to male, indeed declines to write about female genital parts at all. He describes the male genitalia at length in book 6, on "the instrumentes servyng to the propagation of mankynd," but refuses to lift "up the vayle of Natures secretes, in womens shapes" (fol. 89v)[13] even long enough to dismiss the female genitalia by saying that they are inverted versions of the male, as he might modestly have done. In language that everywhere suggests his anxiety about sexual difference even while he declines to write about it, he announces in his introductory "Epistle to the Chirurgians" that he has "endevoured to set wyde open the closet doore of natures secretes, whereinto every Godly Artist may safely enter, to see clearly all the partes, and notable deuises of nature in the body of man. From the female, and that (as I suppose) for sundry good considerations, I have wholly abstained my penne: least, shunning Charibdis, I should fall into Scylla headlong" (Biv). The pen of the Godly artist can safely penetrate the space of nature's closet only insofar as that space is imagined as inside the body of a man; in a woman's body, the closet would be transformed into an engulfing whirlpool. And apparently there is no penis hidden behind this woman's secret fold of flesh;[14] in a metaphoric transformation that neatly reverses the premise of the Galenic model, Banister's penetrations locate not the covert penis in women but the feminized space of Nature's closet in men.

Despite this reversal, Banister does in fact go on in his Proeme to cite one of the familiar tropes of the one-sex model, the transformation of women into men; but here, too, the model is most conspicuous by its absence.

> It is straunge to us that women have beardes, albeit not so every where: for in Caria it is a thyng familiar: whereas some of them beyng a while frutefull, but after widowes, and for that suppressed of naturall course, put on virilitie, being then bearded, hearie, and chaunged in voyce. Shall it be counted a fable that toucheth the transformation of one kinde into an other, as the Male into the Female and so contrariwise? Surely Plinie saith. No: since him selfe to have sene a woman chaunged into man, in the day of mariage, he playnly avoucheth. (Biiv)

Here, if anywhere, we would expect an allusion to the one-sex model that might explain such transformations; but we would be disappointed. For despite its association with the one-sex model in Paré, Montaigne, Crooke, and elsewhere, the transformation of woman to man here seems to represent less the slipperiness of gender categories in the one-sex model than the slipperiness of species, the "transformation of one kinde into an other": far from being one flesh, woman and man seem here, temporarily at least, to belong to distinct species. And in fact Banister's use of the trope of transformation emphatically dissociates that trope from the discourse of Galenic homologies: it occurs not in the section describing the genitals but in the section cataloguing the amazing diversity of animals and people in remote times and places; whatever its use elsewhere, here it serves as part of Banister's effort to save the authority of the ancients by arguing that what seems impossibly strange in their accounts—and therefore evidence of their errors—may be merely the strangeness of what is temporally or geographically removed from us. The transformations of gender that are local and contemporary in Montaigne or Paré are significant here specifically as the sign of the far away and long ago; they testify to the strangeness of the remote, not to a currently ruling notion of sexual homology.

Banister, in short, does not have recourse to the structural homologies of the one-sex model even when we might expect him to allude to them for convenience or convention's sake; although of course we have no way of knowing how strenuous an act of suppression this might have entailed on his part, he writes as though this aspect of the theory simply doesn't exist for him or for his audience. In fact, on the one occasion on which he allows himself to describe both male and female genitals, he assumes not their likeness but their difference; if we are one flesh, he suggests, we are one flesh not in our genitals but in our brains, which turn out to house the replicas of our two distinct sexual parts:

> Behynd this vaulted part in the extreme part of the brayne towardes *Cerebellum,* and in the upper part of the thyrd ventricle, Nature hath feyned certaine eminent partes, whiche in their upper partes, represent the likenes or Image of Testicles, and so called therfore of Anathomistes *Testes:* neare unto the which, two other particles yet somewhat greater are to be discerned, called according to their figure clunes, the haunches or buttockes. Betwene which lyeth that hole, whiche is already noted to from the thyrd, to the fourth ventricle, and seemeth like unto the fundament. Furthermore in the forepart of these Testicles (as we call them) stretchyng to the thyrd ventricle, an other part of the brayne appeareth, which not unaptly, but very elegantly expresseth the shape or privye part of a woman. With this body is sene a litle hard Glandule, in colour contrary to the substaunce of the brayne, that is to say, somewhat yellow, covered with the thinne Membran.
>
> This Glandule is called *Pinalis,* or *Conarium,* fitly representyng the shape of the yard. So that in the brayne wanteth nether the figure of the Testicles, buttockes, fundament, womans shape, nor yard. (fol. 101v)

Whatever his worries about falling into Scylla by writing about the female genitals, Banister is not at all shy about sex on—or in—the brain: he writes as though we carry around in our heads not only the idea of two distinct sexes but their physical embodiment as well. Apparently ignorant of—or unimpressed by—the correspondence of matrix to yard, Banister is clearly delighted by the elegance, fitness, and aptness with which our brains—whatever sex we are—contain all sexual possibilities. If we are one sex, this astonishing anatomical fantasy seems to suggest, we are one in that the very flesh of our brains elegantly expresses our bifold sexual difference.

Banister's bizarre anatomy matters, I think, not because it reflects widespread opinion (my guess is that few followed Banister in his delight at a brain that was missing nothing, that elegantly expressed both male and female parts) but because it suggests that Galen's one-sex model had not driven out other ways of thinking medically about sexual difference in sixteenth-century England. If humoral theory might, for example, explain the failure of a woman to extrude a set of genitals in every way homologous with man's and so might be understood as the basis for the Galenic model, it might equally well be understood as the basis for a theory of sexual difference.[15] In the hodgepodge of questions published under the name of *The Problemes of Aristotle* ("with other Philosophers and Phisicians, wherein are contained divers questions, with their answers, touching the estate of mans bodie" [London, 1597]) sexual difference is everywhere assumed and is explained through humoral theory, which accounts, for example, for why women grow more hair than men, why man's seed is white and woman's red, why women's pulses are slower and their voices shriller than men's, why women aren't ambidextrous, why men don't have paps as large as women's. Despite frequent reference to Galen and a near-obsessive interest in comparison of the sexes, the homologies of his one-sex model are entirely absent from this humoral account of the estate of man's body:[16] in this popular compendium,[17] female difference and the dangers attaching to that difference are far more visible than any potentially reassuring sense that the woman is merely a weak and defective man.

Problemes is of course securely grounded in the sense of woman's defectiveness, teleologically and biologically: the female is "a monster in nature" (E8r), sick even when she is well ("A slow and weake pulse doth betoken the coldnes of the hart and an evil complexion. And therefore a woman which is in health hath a slower and weaker pulse then a man" [D4r]). But the satisfactions of proclaiming women inferior turn out to be short-lived, for this monster problematically tends to contaminate its biological and teleological superior at the point of origin. In its construction of difference, *Problemes* returns again and again to the "corrupt undigested blood" of menstruation (E3r), and it rehearses all the old tropes about the pernicious effects of this "infectious matter" (E4r). Familiarly, the eyes of a menstruating woman stain glass (B2r), and her menstrual blood kills trees and makes dogs run mad (E4r–E4v); even her hair—which grows more abundantly than man's hair, because she is moister—is dangerous at certain times of the month: "Albertus doth saie, that if the haire of a woman in the time of hir flowers be put into dung, a venemous serpent is engendred of it" (A4r). Even the graying of red hair turns out to be attributable to menstrual blood: red hair turns white sooner than other hair, we are told, "bicause that rednes is an infirmitie of the hayre, for it is engendred of a weake and infirme matter, that is to say, of a matter corrupted with the flowers of a woman" (A6r). But red hair is by no means alone in its contaminating origin: if nature expels menstrual blood "euery moneth, as being an enimie vnto life" (E4r–E4v), man himself turns out to be substantially made from this enemy. The author refutes the idea that "the seede of the father and the mother doth go into the substance of the childe in the wombe" by assigning the superior position of pure efficient cause ("according to Aristotle, and other Philosophers") to the male seed (E3v), but this of course leaves the woman's seed in the position of pure material cause. And that female seed is a distillation of her menstrual blood, red rather than white "bicause the flowers are corrupt vndigested blood, and therefore it hath the colour of blood" (E3r). By this logic, *Problemes* concludes, "onely the flowers of the woman are the materiall cause of the yoong one" (E4r).[18]

Insofar as sexual difference collapses in *Problemes*, it collapses not along the teleological axis of the Galenic model, in which a defective woman may become a perfected man, but along a genetic axis, in which the male is always potentially susceptible to his female origin because he is made of her infectious matter. So susceptible that some males don't make it past that pernicious origin as male at all:

> Question. *How are Hermaphrodites begotten?*
> Answer. . . . bicause nature doth alwaies tend vnto that which is best, therefore she doth alwaies intend to beget the male, and not the female, bicause that the female is onely for the males sake, and a monster in nature. Therefore the male is somtime begotten in all principall parts, and yet through the euill disposition of the wombe, and object, and inequalitie of the seede, when nature cannot perfect and ende the male, she doth bring foorth the female, or Hermaphrodite. (E8r)

Whatever the ontological superiority of the male, its female origins—not only the womb but the over-powerful female seed and a nature imagined as feminized—can convert it to their own substance: what begins as teleologically male ends as substantially female. In its struggle to affirm gender difference by affirming an essential maleness against an accidentally caused femaleness (or the hermaphroditism that seems roughly equivalent), this passage ends by recording the collapse of difference, but not in a Galenic direction: not through finding a defective penis in woman but through finding an accidental womb in what should have been a man.

The Problemes of Aristotle is far from systematic or intellectually coherent in its representations of sexual difference. For the most part, it assumes physiological sexual difference, but a difference in which maleness is always liable to be contaminated by femaleness; when such contamination reaches its maximum point, sexual difference itself disappears into the hermaphrodite, or the female who is teleologically male. Insofar as it approaches a one-sex model, it does so from a direction opposite to that of the Galenists; and it nowhere suggests the genital homology that is the hallmark of the contemporary Galenist. But *Problemes*—like the other works I've been examining—is primarily concerned with "the estate of mans bodie" and only secondarily with the issue of anatomical sexual difference. What of works devoted specifically to women's bodies? Thomas Raynold's *The Byrth of Mankynde, otherwyse named the Womans Booke* was the only gynecological work available in English before 1612.[19] Raynold's work was immensely popular—if we judge by editions in English, more popular than any of the other works I have discussed; after the first edition in 1545, it was reprinted in 1552, 1560, 1565, 1585, 1588, 1598, 1604, 1613, 1626, and 1634.[20] And despite its foregrounding of anatomy[21] and its frequent comparison of elements of the male and female body—veins, bladder, seed, and so forth—*The Byrth of Mankynde* never invokes the Galenic model.

As with the other works that I've cited, this absence is most striking when the occurrence of the tropes surrounding the one-sex model makes us anticipate its appearance. In introducing the figures illustrating female anatomy, for example, Raynold tells us that the first figure is that of a man's body. We might expect an argument for sexual homology to occur here; indeed, Laqueur's one reference to *The Byrth of Mankynde*—the caption to illustrations of the male body combined and used in it (*Making Sex*, 111)—could be read to suggest that the male body could serve indifferently for the female because they were homological, hence indistinguishable. But in fact Raynold is very careful to distinguish anatomically between male and female bodies precisely on the grounds of anatomical sexual difference. His commentary identifies G and H on his first figure as the right and left seed vessels, and then goes on to add "but this G and H hath no place in the women."[22] At the end of his description of the second figure, as though suddenly embarrassed by his use of a male figure, he says, "Here ye shalbe advertysed that although these ii. fyrst fygures be made principally for the man, yet may they serve as well to express the woman." Here, if anywhere, we might expect the argument from homology, but he goes on to make exactly the opposite case: "for the man and woman differ in nothyng but in the priuie parts" (sig. Hhhr). And by the 1560 edition, the troublesome body of a man has been replaced by the body of a woman (fol. 43v)—as though even the 1545 explanation would no longer suffice for a population interested in sexual dimorphism and the difference between bodies.[23]

When Raynold writes about the congruence between male and female sexual parts, he characteristically does so not in the service of an argument about homology but in the service of an argument about function. The comparable size of penis and womb passage would, in Galenic terms, be taken as evidence for the one-sex model: if the neck of the womb is the penis inside out, then the two should be roughly the same length. But Raynold reads this similarity not as evidence of homology but as evidence of Nature's wise management of differentiated generative function: "To make especyall mencion of the length of this womb passage were but folly, for the diuersitees therof. Notwithstanding in women it is estemed of the length of x, xi, xii, or xiii fingers bredth, sum more sum lesse: And this we may say that nature hath so prouided that it is of sufficient length to receaue the priuy part of man in the tyme of generation dyrectynge the same towardes the womb porte" (fol. 10r). Anatomy here demonstrates nothing about homology or about female inferiority, ontological or biological; instead, it demonstrates the fitness with which the differentiated genital parts are created.

This is in fact Raynold's emphasis throughout the *Byrth,* an emphasis that undercuts the teleological logic of homology and is in fact specifically designed to combat the misogyny that usually accompanies that logic. Here, for example, is Raynold on the subject of women's seed: it is "not so stronge, ferme and myghty in operation as the seed of man . . . howbeit as conuenient and propre for the pourpose for the whiche it was ordeynid, as the seede of man for his pourpose" (fol. 15r). The simultaneous similarity and difference of the seed—men and women share the same substance, but the man's is stronger—that might elsewhere be read as evidence both for female inferiority and for homology here serve Raynold's argument about the perfection of differentiated function, an argument that he makes with a self-conscious glance over his shoulder at his misogynous predecessors:

> This foresaid seede, as we saide before, is nothyng so firme, perfect, absolut, and myghty in woman as in man: and yet can you not cal this any imperfection or lacke in woman: for the woman in her kynd, and for thoffice and pourpose wherfor she was made is euen as absolute and perfect as man in his kynd: nether is woman to be callyd (as sum do) unperfecter then man (for bycause the man is moore myghtyer and strong: the woman wekar, more feble) for by this reason the horse, the lyon, the olyphant, camel, and many other beestes shold be callid more perfect than man: to the which man is not able to compare in naturall myght and strength. (fol. 24r)

Women are not imperfect men, he argues; they are perfect in their own kind.[24] The argument from kind in fact suggests that, far from being an inferior version of man, woman may be an entirely separate species: "imperfection is when that any perticular creature doth lacke any properte, instrument, or qualite, which communely, by nature is in all other or the moore part of that kynde: comparyng it to other of the same kinde, and not of an other kynde" (fol. 24v).

It's worth noting that Raynold rescues women from infamy only at the cost of excoriating men in whom he finds "woman lyke" qualities, as though he can value what is womanly only by separating it rigorously from what is manly. His instance of imperfection within kind is the effeminate man: "But truely comparing one man to another, such as be geldyd and want the genitories be moch febler, weeke and effeminat then other: in voyce woman lycke, in gesture and condition nise, in softnesse of skyn, and plumpnesse of the body fatter and rounder: in strength and force impotent nothing manly ne bold: the which imbecyllite in them may well be named imperfection" (fol. 24r–24v). Admiring women is clearly not without its attendant anxieties. Nonetheless, in the context of works on reproductive difference, Raynold's is refreshing in the boldness with which it refutes the notion of female imperfection.

Even menstrual blood, that ancient token of women's defect, becomes for him evidence of nature's wisdom:

> The cause and reason why Nature created this perpetuall course of termes in women is this: for so much as almyghty god had to institute that women shoulde be the vessels, wherin the seede of mankinde wold be conceaued, efformed or fashioned, augmented, nourished and brought to perfection: This could not be doone unlesse there were a commodious and conuenient place, to this office assigned and destinat wherefore nature created the womb or matrix to be the sayd receptacle, and house of office wherin she mought at her leaser wurke her divine feates about the seede once conceaued. Agayne it is not ynough the sede to be placed, unlesse also it have foode and nourishment, to thencrease and augmentation of the same: Wherefore prudent lady nature ful wysely hath prouided that there shulde always be prest and ready, a continual course and resort of blud in the vaynes of the matrice as a very naturall source, spryng, fountayne, or wel evermore redy to arrouse, water, and nourishe the feature so sone as it shal be conceaued. . . . Which food although it is ordayned for this necessarye purpose, yet when the purpose fayleth . . . it shold be to the place but a burden, and unprofitable lode, there to remayne or linger. (fol. 34v–35v)

Spring, fountain, or well: Raynold's images of natural fecundity and purity are an antidote to all the old associations of menstrual blood with poison and infection. Even the commonplace that menstruation is the purgation of excesses and impurities in the blood occasions his scorn:

> But here ye shall note that they be greatly disceaued and abused, which call the termes, the womans purgation, or the clensyng of there blud: as who shuld say, that it were

the refuce, drosse, and vilar part of the outher blud remaynyng in the body, naturally euery monyth sequestrat, and separated from the purer for the vylite and euel qualite therin comprehendyd: for undoutedly the blud is euen as pure and holsum as all the rest of the blud in eny parte of the boody els.

Is it to be thought that nature wold feade the tender and dilicate infant in the mothers womb, with the refuse of the blud, or not rather with the purist of it. (fol. 44r–44v; sig. I.vir–I.viv)

The peroration to his discussion of menstruation triumphantly dismisses his predecessors (predecessors whose line of argument is still current at the end of the century, for example, in *The Problemes of Aristotle*): "Yet much more are to be detestid and abhorred the shamefull lyes and slaunders that Plynie, Albertus Magnus De Secretes Mulierum, and dyvers othermo, have wrytten, of the venomous and daungerous infectyue nature of the womans flowers or termes: The which al be but dreames and playne dotage: to reherse there fon wurdes here were but losse of ynke and paper: wherfore let them passe with their auctours" (fol. 45r; sig. I.viir).

When Raynold looks at the uterus, he does not see a defective or inverted penis; he sees an organ perfect in its own kind, wisely prepared by a beneficent lady nature whose feminized virtues are reflected in the specifically female place she provides for the generation of mankind. Defending his decision to publish his work in English against those who claim that men who read about woman's private parts might "conceaue a certayn lothsomnes and abhorringe towardes a woman," he declares, "I know nothing in woman so pryve, ne so secret that thei shold nede to care who knew of it: neyther is there any part in woman moore to be abhorred, then in man"; rather charmingly, he adds that by his opponents' logic, physicians and surgeons should abhor their wives, "And I myselfe lyke wise, which writyth this booke, shold meruey lously aboue many other abhore or lothe wemen: but to be short, there is no such thyng, neyther any cause therto why" (Prologue, sigs. C.vir–C.viv).[25] Even when he seems to accept man's ontological superiority as efficient cause of generation, he relocates that claim in a context that gives priority to women: "And all though that man, be as princypall moovar and cause of the generation, yet (no displeasur to men) the woman dothe confer and contribute much more, what to the encresement of the chyld in her wombe, and what to the nourysshment therof after the byrth, then doth the man. And doutlesse if a man wold demaund to whome the chylde oweth moost his generation: ye may murthely make answere that, to the mother: whether ye regarde the paynes in bearyng, other elles the conference of most matter in begetting" (fol. 1v).[26] Full of affectionate regard for lady nature's wisdom in making women, attentive to the lived experience of childbearing and child-nurturing as opposed to the ontology that always locates woman as secondary, Raynold sees in the uterus not a defective penis but a replica of the human heart: the bottom of the matrix "is not parfactly round bowlwyse," he tells us, "but rather lyke the forme of a mans harte" (fol. 11v).

Byrth remained the only gynecological handbook in English until well into the seventeenth century; its first competitor, the 1612 translation of Guillemeau's *Child-birth, or the Happy Deliverie,* displayed no interest in anatomy or in the one-sex model.[27] But something had obviously changed at the beginning of the seventeenth century:[28] whereas the texts in English in the sixteenth century seem for the most part ignorant of or uninterested in the one-sex model, Helkiah Crooke in *Microcosmographia. A Description of the Body of Man* (1615) specifically mentions it—apparently in order to argue against it. This puts him in the curious position of being simultaneously the model's best—indeed, virtually its first—full expositor in English, and its severest critic.[29]

Like Raynold, Crooke is especially concerned to refute the idea that a woman is by definition an imperfect or defective man ("For the female sexe as well as the male is a perfection of mankinde. . . . The truth is, that as the soule of a woman is the same divine nature with a mans, so is her body a necessary being, a first and not a second intention of Nature, her proper and absolute worke not her error or prevarication" [258]); like Raynold, he understands the womb not as a defect but as a "most noble and almost divine Nurse" (262).[30] But unlike Raynold's, Crooke's refutation turns explicitly on his relation to the one-sex model.

At first, in book 4 ("Of the Naturall Parts belonging to Generation, as well in Men as in Women"), Crooke seems to be a proponent of the one-sex model: Nature made, he tells us, "another sexe of mankinde, not altogether of so hot a temper or constitution, because she should have a superfluity of bloode for the nourishment of the infant; as also that the partes of generation for want of heate to thrust them foorth remaining within, might make a fit place wherein to conceive, breede, and perfect the same" (199). But Crooke transforms the emphasis of the model even as he enunciates it, seeing in it the signs not of imperfection but of perfection. The coldness that keeps woman's (apparently homologous) genitals inside her is no longer evidence of her weakness or of the failure of nature's plan (to produce men); it is now a necessity, providing both the superfluity of blood necessary for food and the interior "fit place" for generation.[31] Each time Crooke returns to the Galenic model in book 4, he amplifies this theme: men and women have the same sexual parts, he tells us, but women's "for want of heate [are] reteined within. . . . Although heerin Nature hath excellently acquitted her selfe, that the abatement of naturall heate, which in man is the onely naturall and necessary cause of their dissolution, should so admirably become in women the original of generation, whereby we should attaine a kinde of eternity even of our bodies" (216). Even when he flirts with the idea of women as imperfect men, he ultimately insists on their perfection: "A woman is so much lesse perfect then a man by how much her heate is lesse and weaker then his; yet as I saide is this imperfection turned unto perfection, because without the woman, mankinde could not have been perfected by the perfecter sexe," he says (216–17), leaving both the perfecting agent and the "perfecter sexe" startlingly ambiguous.

Moreover, Crooke's embrace of the one-sex model—even in the new improved version in which imperfection becomes perfection—is far from secure. Abundant heat thrusts men's testicles "foorth of the body," he tells us, "whereas in women they remain within, because their dull and sluggish heate is not sufficient to thrust them out. The trueth of this appeareth by manifold stories of such women, whose more active and operative heate hath thrust out their Testicles, and of women made them men: as we shall relate hereafter more at large in our Controversies" (204). But the truth turns out not to be so readily discerned. Crooke is above all interested in the controversies to which he refers his reader here;[32] and by the time he arrives at the controversy to which he has referred us (the eighth controversy of book 4, "How the parts of generation in men and women doe differ"), he strenuously refutes both these manifold stories and the Galenic logic on which they are based:

> But what shall we say to those so many stories of women changed into men? . . . If such a thing shal happen, it may well be answered that such parties were Hermophradites, that is, had the parts of both sexes, which because of the weaknesse of their heat in their nonage lay hid, but brake out afterward as their heate grew unto strength. Or we may safely say, that there are some women so hot by nature that their *clitoris* hangeth foorth in the fashion of a man's member, which because it may be distended and againe grow loose and flaccid, may deceive ignorant people. Againe Midwives may oft be deceived because of the faultie conformation of those parts, for sometimes the member and testicles are so small, and sinke so deepe into the body that they cannot easily be discerned. (250)

In his view, someone with a man's parts inside is a defective man or a hermaphrodite, not a woman. And while heat here—as in the Galenic model—is the operative force that brings the genitals out, a "woman" does not become a "man" simply because her genitals have been extruded; in fact, the apparent resemblance of clitoris to penis in this case is fit only "to deceive ignorant people."[33] As the stories become suspect, so does the truth to which they had apparently testified: Crooke repeats Galen's version of the one-sex model once again in this controversy only to dispute it on the basis of both the number and the structure of the sexual parts, triumphantly concluding, "Me thinks it is very absurd to say, that the neck of the wombe inverted is like the member of a man. . . . Howsoever therefore the necke of the wombe shall be inverted, yet will it never make the virile member" (250).

Once he takes this position, Crooke never wavers from it. In book 5 ("Wherein the Historie of the Infant is acurately described") he refutes the model again at length, taking up the attack explicitly under the banner of female perfection in the first of the controversies, "Of the Difference of the Sexes":

> The Peripatetiks thinke that Nature ever intendeth the generation of a Male, and that the Female is procreated by accident out of a weaker seede which is not able to attaine the perfection of the male. Wherefore *Aristotle* thinketh that the Woman or female is nothing else but an error or aberration of Nature . . . ; yea he preceedeth further and saith, that the female is a bye worke or prevarication, yea the first monster in Nature. [The marginal note to this paragraph reads: "*Aristot.* Error."]
>
> *Galen* . . . , following *Aristotle* something too neere, writeth, that the formative power which is in the seede of man being but one, doth alwayes entend the generation of one, that is, the Male; but if she erre from hir scope and cannot generate a male, then bringeth she foorth the female which is the first and most simple imperfection of a male, which therefore he calleth a creature lame, occasionall and accessary, as if she were not of the mayne, but made by the bye. [Margin: "*Galens* Error."]
>
> Now heerin he putteth the difference betwixt her and the Male, that in males the parts of generation are without the body, in Females they lye within because of the weaknesse of the heate, which is not able to thrust them foorth. And therefore he saith, that the necke of the wombe is nothing else but the virile member turned inward, and the bottome of the wombe nothing but the *scrotum* or cod inverted.
>
> But this opinion of *Galen* and *Aristotle* we cannot approve. For we thinke that Nature as well intendeth the generation of a female as of a male: and therefore it is unworthily said that she is an Error or Monster in Nature. For the perfection of all naturall things is to be esteemed and measured by the end: now it was necessary that woman should be so formed or else Nature must have missed of her scope, because shee intended a perfect generation, which without a woman cannot be accomplished. [Margin: "Disprooved."]
>
> These things which *Galen* urgeth concerning the similitude, or parts of generation differing onely in scite and position, many men do esteeme very absurd. Sure we are that they favour little of the truth of Anatomy, as we have already prooved in the Booke going before: wherein we have shewed how little likenesse there is betwixt the necke of the womb and the yard, the bottome of it and the cod. Neither is the structure, figure, or magnitude of the testicles one and the same, nor the distribution and insertion of the spermatick vessels alike,[34] wherefore we must not thinke that the female is an imperfect male differing only in the position of the genitals. [Margin: "no similtude betwixt their Genitals."] (271)

Ultimately, for Crooke, the Galenic model of homology is incompatible with the idea of woman's perfection; his final "wherefore we must not thinke" rests his case for woman as perfect in herself—not as the "imperfection of the male"—on his refutation of the homological model.

Crooke's insistence that he is in good company—"many men do esteeme [Galen's position] very absurd"—suggests that he was not alone in his views, and his advertised position as King James's physician seems to give those views a certain amount of authority; the second edition of *Microcosmographia* (1618) announces itself as "published by the kings Maiesties especiall Direction and Warrant, according to the first integrity, as it was Originally written by the Author."[35] If it is the case that the one-sex model had become current enough in England by 1615 to require refutation by a very well-placed medical authority, it also seems to be the case that the model enters vernacular English medical discourse largely via this distinctly hegemonic refutation of it.

The transvestite theater of Shakespeare's comedies may perhaps be the logical culmination of the one-sex model, but it seems not to be the chronological culmination of it: at least in vernacular medical writing in England in the sixteenth century, there is little evidence of the model's hold on the imagination.[36] In fact, if we can imagine a heyday of the model in early modern England, a moment at which the model became important enough to require an extensive commentary (and refutation) in English, Crooke's work suggests that such a moment would coincide not with the period of Shakespeare's transvestite comedies but with the period of the tragedies, in which the inward space of male subjectivity—the space Greenblatt associates with the later development of the novel[37]—is problematically formed out of the matrix of the female.[38] This misalliance might teach us caution both in the assumption that there is one reigning model of sexual difference at any given time and in the application of historical to literary texts, particularly if the historical texts are used to disable certain kinds of discourse on the grounds of their ahistoricity.

Given the relative lack of evidence for the presence of the Galenic model in sixteenth-century England, why has the idea been taken up as a new orthodoxy among critics of early modern English literature? Contemporary users of the one-sex model tend to find it liberating insofar as it appears to break down the stability of gender categories. But at least in Shakespearean tragedy, there is nothing liberating about the breakdown of gender categories: men like Hamlet or Lear famously dread the woman's part in themselves, and women who possess the rod are a source of horror. Moreover, the model apparently does away with the anatomical basis for gender—and hence for gender fixity—only at the cost of doing away with women's bodies: there is only one sex, and that sex is male. Laqueur himself notes the defensive functions which the Galenic model might have served for its original proponents and their early modern kin: "An almost defensive quality suggests that the politics of gender off the page might well have engendered the textual insistence that there really were no women after all" (*Making Sex,* 98); he speculates that the model "was framed in antiquity to valorize the extraordinary cultural assertion of patriarchy, of the father, in the face of the more sensorily evident claim of the mother" (*Making Sex,* 20). Is it fair to suggest that engagement with the model may occasionally serve a comparable function for some of its contemporary proponents as well? Certain aspects of the recent history of criticism suggestively ally themselves with the shift Laqueur notes. Despite Crooke's association of the one-sex model with misogyny, that model certainly can be put to feminist uses; but it can also be used—particularly in conjunction with an insistence on the maleness of the boy actor—to argue, for example, that Shakespeare is not representing women at all. But if Shakespeare is not representing women, then certain traditional feminist concerns become irrelevant; and under the guise of engagement with a historical model that does away with sexual difference, perhaps we can imagine not only an all-male theater but also a time and place where women—and the threat their difference represents to men—simply disappear.

If recourse to the Galenic model can serve to minimize this threat, it can also serve to acknowledge it—but only (I shall argue) by consigning it to the dustbin of history. "The implication of this developmental account," Greenblatt says, "is that men grow out of or pass through women" (*Shakespearean Negotiations,* 81). Though Greenblatt himself never imagines Galenic man regressively pulled back to this point of origin, others have taken his implication in that direction, explaining the "conviction that men can turn into—or be turned into—women; or perhaps more exactly, can be turned *back* into women" and the fear of that "disastrous slide back into the female" as a consequence of the Galenic model.[39] But even if we knew that this model was a force in the imaginations of Shakespeare and his contemporaries, could it support this reading of it? The model does suggest that all of us wear our genitals inside until they are sorted into male and female, for most of us *in utero*. But—because of its emphasis on teleology rather than origin—it reads that similarity in terms of the female's failed maleness, not in terms of the male's originary femaleness: in Galen's famous mole's-eye simile, "the female genitalia 'do not open' and remain an imperfect version of what they would be were they thrust out" (Laqueur, *Making Sex,* 28). Moreover, though Nature often produces a woman where she intended a man through a kind of teleological goof-up *in utero,* and a woman *ex utero* may occasionally climb the teleological ladder and become a man if she attains to his superior heat and thrusts her genitals outward, Nature never reverses herself and produces a woman out of an already finished man. As Crooke reports, "the ancients have thought that a woman might become a man, but not on the contrary side a man become a woman" (*Microcosmographia,* 249).[40] But the unidirectionality of the model does not prevent critics—even critics who are fully aware of its theoretical and medical impossibility—from deriving fantasies of reversion to femaleness from the model; Orgel, for example, writes as though not only the fantasies of reversion but social customs as pervasive as breeching are based in it: "In the medical literature we all start as women, and the culture confirmed this by dressing all children in skirts."[41]

Given that one has to swim against the tide of the unidirectionality of the model itself, why locate the fear of reversion to femaleness within that model? I can answer that question only from within the confines of my own methodological assumptions—assumptions that will certainly not be granted by everyone;[42] but seen from within those confines, the move to locate the regressive pull of the female in the one-sex model looks strikingly consistent with the defensive purposes Laqueur outlines, in its consequences if not its intentions. Greenblatt's language—that "men grow out of or pass through women"—suggests a far more homely origin for fears of reversion to femaleness than the Galenic model: it suggests the presence of the maternal body largely occluded by Galenist theory and by its contemporary proponents.[43] As many feminist critics—often not cited by the contemporary Galenists—have argued, the regressive pull of the female is a psychological derivative of both the biological facts of human reproduction and the social customs that left the young boy initially almost entirely in the domain of his mother or her female substitutes and defined him as quasi-female until maleness was conferred on him by separation from women.[44] But it is easier and certainly more reassuring to ascribe the pull back toward femininity to a questionable interpretation of a detail in an outmoded medical model that we can locate safely in the "out there" of history (though it may not in fact have been historically present) than to causes that remain disturbingly familiar to us. Under the aegis of the Galenic model, we can write as though that pull were only a historical curiosity: it can't happen here.

Where then does this leave us in our thinking about Shakespeare and the Galenic model? First of all, I think we need to be more cautious in appealing to the unique explanatory force of this model for Shakespeare or for his theater. I think we need to recognize that—whether or not Shakespeare was ever aware of the medical debates[45]—his work may be in dialogue with several different medical models of sexual difference. If we may sometimes catch glimpses of the Galenic one-sex model in his plays, we may also catch glimpses of, for example, the quite different model for the collapse of sexual differentiation implicit in *The Problems of Aristotle*. More broadly speaking, it seems to me possible to see in Shakespeare the beginnings of a shift from definition by *telos* to definition by *origin*, a shift of the kind implicit in Raynold when he writes that the child owes more to the mother than the father: think of Richard defining himself in relation to his mother's womb (*3 Henry VI*, 3.2.153–64), Lear anxiously feeling the presence of the "mother" rising within him (2.4.54), Leontes regretting that he could not remove all his wife's blood from his son as effectively as he can remove the child physically from her (2.1.56–58). And as for Cleopatra? If the logical end of the Galenic model is the transvestite theater of the comedies, perhaps Cleopatra's claim for a female theatrical space—and one written over the conventions of the transvestite theater—is the logical (if not chronological) end of Crooke's vigorous reinstatement of the female body over against the claims of the one-sex model. Perhaps Shakespeare—like Raynold before him and Crooke after him—is engaged in *Antony and Cleopatra* in his own version of making defect perfection.

Notes

1. All quotations from Shakespeare are from *William Shakespeare: The Complete Works*, ed. Alfred Harbage (Baltimore: Penguin, 1969).

2. This disappearance is, of course, not absolute; but insofar as we "see" the male surface and are encouraged to look "beneath" it to the male body of the actor, the bodily femaleness of a Rosalind or a Viola disappears into a purely imaginary space—a disappearance aided by the absence of mature sexual women from these plays.

3. For the counterargument, specifically the claim that reference to the boy actor disrupts the illusion of femininity in *Antony and Cleopatra*, see, for example, Madelon Sprengnether, "The Boy Actor and Femininity in *Antony and Cleopatra*," in *Shakespeare's Personality*, ed. Norman N. Holland et al. (Berkeley and Los Angeles: University of California Press, 1989), 191, 202. Peter Stallybrass similarly assumes that Cleopatra's reference to the boy actor unfixes her femininity: in a provocative reading of moments at which boy actors were called upon to bare their breasts as fetishized objects prosthetically establishing gender, he notes that Cleopatra's baring of her breast occurs in close proximity to this defeminizing reference ("Transvestism and the 'Body Beneath': Speculating on the Boy Actor," in *Erotic Politics: Desire on the Renaissance Stage*, ed. Susan Zimmerman [New York: Routledge, 1992], 71).

4. I am here repeating an argument that I have made at greater length and in different terms in *Suffocating Mothers: Fantasies of Maternal Origin in Shakespeare, "Hamlet" to "The Tempest"* (New York: Routledge, 1992), 192; see 343–44, n. 64 for others who gender Cleo-

patra's theater female and stress Shakespeare's alliance with her in it. For many critics, that alliance is based not in Cleopatra's generativity but in the inherent femaleness or effeminizing power of the theatrical; see Jyotsna Singh's account of the association between the female and the theatrical in the antitheatrical and antifeminist texts and Shakespeare's reworking of this association in *Antony and Cleopatra* ("Renaissance Antitheatricality, Antifeminism, and Shakespeare's *Antony and Cleopatra*," *Renaissance Drama*, n.s. 20 [1989]: 99–121), and Laura Levine's extensive account of the idea of the self—especially the masculine self—that underlies this association in the antitheatrical tracts and in *Antony and Cleopatra* (*Men in Women's Clothing: Anti-Theatricality and Effeminization, 1579–1642* [Cambridge: Cambridge University Press, 1994], 1–25, 44–72).

5. In Stephen Greenblatt's powerful formulation, "a conception of gender that is teleologically male and insists upon a verifiable sign that confirms nature's final cause finds its supreme literary expression in a transvestite theater" ("Fiction and Friction," chap. 3 of *Shakespearean Negotiations: The Circulation of Social Energy in Renaissance England* [Berkeley and Los Angeles: University of California Press, 1988], 88); portions of this chapter—including this very influential sentence—were published in an essay of the same title in 1986, in *Reconstructing Individualism,* ed. Thomas C. Heller et al. (Stanford: Stanford University Press, 1986).

6. See Greenblatt, *Shakespearean Negotiations,* 78–93. Laqueur's initial enunciation of the one-sex model (in "Orgasm, Generation, and the Politics of Reproductive Biology," *Representations* 14 [Spring 1986]: 1–41) was greatly expanded in his *Making Sex: Body and Gender from the Greeks to Freud* (Cambridge, Mass.: Harvard University Press, 1990). Though I think that Laqueur overstates the uniform hegemony of the one-sex model and hence overlooks not only geographic differences but also the extent to which elements of a two-sex model were at home in Renaissance medical discourse, his assessment of the stakes of a stridently two-sex model that poses woman as inalterably other seems to me very compelling.

7. A random sampling of those who have assumed the hegemony of the one-sex model reads like a Who's Who of prominent and up-and-coming Renaissance literary critics. That the model often is tangential to the argument at hand but is cited anyway suggests its status: it is something that people in the know need to show that they know. See Peter Stallybrass, "Reading the Body: *The Revenger's Tragedy* and the Jacobean Theater of Consumption," *Renaissance Drama* 18 (1987): 145; Margreta de Grazia, "The Motive for Interiority: Shakespeare's *Sonnets* and *Hamlet*," *Style: Texts and Pretexts in the English Renaissance* 23 (Fall 1989): 440; Stephen Orgel, "Nobody's Perfect," *South Atlantic Quarterly* 88 (Winter 1989): 13; Alan Sinfield, *Faultlines: Cultural Materialism and the Politics of Dissident Reading* (Berkeley and Los Angeles: University of California Press, 1992), 134; Elizabeth D. Harvey, *Ventriloquized Voices: Feminist Theory and English Renaissance Texts* (London: Routledge, 1992), 4, 33, 87–88; Jonathan Crewe, "In the Field of Dreams: Transvestism in *Twelfth Night* and *The Crying Game*," *Representations* 50 (Spring 1995): 120. In more recent work, both Orgel and Stallybrass have softened their Galenist stances, noting that the Galenic model exists in tension with other medical models (Stephen Orgel,

Impersonations: The Performance of Gender in Shakespeare's England [Cambridge: Cambridge University Press, 1996], 19–24; Ann Rosalind Jones and Peter Stallybrass, "Fetishizing Gender: Constructing the Hermaphrodite in Renaissance Europe," in *Body Guards,* ed. Julia Epstein and Kristina Straub [London: Routledge, 1991], 81, 106, n. 2); in addition, Jones and Stallybrass warn specifically against privileging biological discourse (88). But even in muted form, the Galenic model remains integral to these works. Others have disavowed the claim to Galenic hegemony more strenuously, both insofar as it underestimates other nonmedical discourses that produce gender difference or structure the body as fundamentally female (see, for example, Jean E. Howard, "Crossdressing, the Theatre, and Gender Struggle in Early Modern England," *Shakespeare Quarterly* 39 [Winter 1988]: 422–23, and Levine, *Men in Women's Clothing,* 109, 169, n. 3) and insofar as it represents medical discourse as far more monolithic than it in fact is (see, for example, Heather Dubrow on the multivocality of the gynecological tracts ["Navel Battles: Interpreting Renaissance Gynecological Manuals," *American Notes and Queries* 5, n.s. (1992): 67–71, and "Friction and Faction: New Directions for New Historicism," *Monatshefte* 84 (Summer 1992): 213–14]; see also Gail Kern Paster on humoral gender difference [*The Body Embarrassed: Drama and the Disciplines of Shame in Early Modern England* (Ithaca: Cornell University Press, 1993), 17, 79, 82–83] and especially on the pervasiveness of physiological gender difference articulated through a theory of heat ["The Unbearable Coldness of Women: Women's Imperfection in the Humoral Economy," forthcoming in *English Literary Renaissance* 28 [Dec. 1998].) The fullest critiques are those of Katharine Park and Robert A. Nye, who argue—occasionally intemperately—against the privileging of biology over metaphysics and against the false homogeneity of the model, insisting especially on the tensions between Aristotle and Galen ("Destiny Is Anatomy," *New Republic,* 18 Feb. 1991: 53–57), and Patricia Parker, who demonstrates the extent to which the Galenic model of unidirectional change from (imperfect) female to (perfect) male was undercut in sixteenth-century France by other discourses that insisted on male impotence and the reverse change ("Gender Ideology, Gender Change: The Case of Marie Germain," *Critical Inquiry* 19 [Winter 1993]: 337–64). As far as I know, no one has examined the extent to which the model—whether or not it was overvalued or complicated by other discourses, medical and otherwise—was in fact present in English vernacular medical writing.

8. Harvey, *Ventriloquized Voices,* 4.

9. While both Laqueur and Greenblatt pose the hegemony of the Galenic model, neither forecloses other possibilities with the insistence that has often become the rule in their followers. Particularly in the longer version of his argument, Laqueur is careful to delineate the strains within the model; in fact, part of his point is to show the ways in which even those resistant to the model nonetheless think in its terms. Greenblatt too insists, at least initially, on the "friction" between opposing medical models (*Shakespearean Negotiations,* 78–79), though the latter end of his chapter tends to forget this insistence.

10. Thomas Vicary, *The Anatomie of the Bodie of Man,* ed. Frederick J. Furnivall and Percy Furnivall, Early English Text Society, e.s., 53 (London: Oxford University Press, 1888;

reprint, Millwood, N.Y.: Kraus, 1975), 76–77; this is a reprint of the edition of 1548 as reissued by the surgeons of St. Bartholomews in 1577. According to the Furnivalls ("Foretalk," vi), no copies of the 1548 edition and only one copy of the 1577 edition survive, which may indicate that the work was not widely disseminated.

11. My citation modernized from the Early English Text Society edition of the *Cyrurgie*, ed. Margaret S. Ogden [Oxford: Oxford University Press, 1971], 67.

12. The model does occur in Juan Huarte's *Examen de ingenios, The Examination of mens Wits, in which, by discouering the varietie of natures, is shewed for what profession each one is apt, and how far he shall profit therein*, Englished by R. Carew (printed by A. Islip for R. Watkins, 1594; STC 13890), a work that might be considered quasi-medical insofar as it uses humoral theory in its attempt to assign vocations to men according to the properties of their minds, originally for the benefit of the king of Spain (Aiii). Huarte invokes Galen in order to explain exactly how much coldness and moisture a woman should have in order to maximize the chances of producing wise children, "to which end," he says, "it behooueth first to know a particular point of Philosophy, which although in regard to the practices of the art, it be verie manifest and true, yet the vulgar make little reake therof. And from the notice of this, dependeth all that, which as touching this first point is to be deliuered: and that is, that man (though it seem otherwise in the composition which we see) is different from a woman in nought els (saith Galen) than only in hauing his genitall members without his body" (268–69). But this occurrence of the model suggests that it was far from determinative for Renaissance observers; Huarte clearly prides himself on knowing something that only the few know, something specifically different from what the vulgar see. (I owe this reference to Heather Dubrow, who has generously supplied me with bibliographic and other aid throughout this project.)

13. Signatures are continuous throughout Banister's volume; folio numbers begin after the prefatory material ends, with the beginning of book 1. I give signatures for the prefatory material, folio numbers for the later material, following the conventions of recto and verso for both signature and folio to avoid confusion.

14. I am here reworking Greenblatt's famous—and beautifully crafted—sentence describing Duval's discovery of Marin le Marcis's penis: "empowered by the court of law, the physician reaches in behind the woman's secret fold of flesh and feels with his finger's end a swelling penis" (*Shakespearean Negotiations*, 77)—a sentence that might single-handedly account for the sexiness of the one-sex model.

15. Paster's *Body Embarrassed* explicates a variety of ways in which the theory of humoral difference enforces gender difference; see esp. 79–83 for a critique of Laqueur's reading of humoral homology.

16. By the time *The Problemes of Aristotle* was incorporated into *Aristotle's Masterpiece* in the eighteenth century, the homological model had found a home in it. See Vern L. Bullough, *Sex, Society, and History* (New York: Science History Publications, 1976), 99–100, for the Galenic model in this popular sex manual; see also Laqueur's similar citation of it (*Making Sex*, 4). But in its 1595 and 1597 incarnations, homology of sex organs is strikingly missing.

17. According to Bullough, "at least twenty-six different printed versions of *Problems* are recorded before 1500" (*Sex, Society, and History*, 94). London editions in English in 1595, 1597, and 1603 testify to its continued popularity; I quote from the edition of 1597.

18. *Problemes* does locally assuage the sense of inevitable contamination attaching to menstruation as material cause by dividing menstrual blood into two kinds: "Question. *Whether are the flowers which are expelled, & the flowers which the child is ingendred of, all one? Answer.* No, bicause the one are uncleane, and unfit for that purpose: but the other very pure and cleane, and therefore that blood is fit for generation" (E5v). But given the repeated characterization of menstrual blood as venomous, and the insistence that woman's seed is red because it is made from corrupt menstrual blood, this one-time-only division does not carry much weight.

19. See Audrey Eccles, *Obstetrics and Gynaecology in Tudor and Stuart England* (Kent, Ohio: Kent State University Press, 1982), 11–12, for the publication history of *The Byrth of Mankynde*. Richard Jonas had translated the Latin translation (*De partu hominis*) of Roesslin's German work in 1540; Raynold's 1545 work, which draws on Jonas's translation but augments it significantly, is the basis for all later editions of *The Byrth of Mankynde*. The spelling of Raynold's name is contested; it is Raynald in Eccles and Raynalde in Joan Larsen Klein's brief but useful introduction to her excellent selection of excerpts from *Byrth* (*Daughters, Wives, and Widows: Writings by Men about Women and Marriage in England, 1500–1640* [Urbana: University of Illinois Press, 1992], 177–79). I have followed the spelling on the title page of the 1545 edition for both author and title. Klein concludes from Raynolds's use of "stones" for ovaries that "he is following in part the old theory that the reproductive organs in women inversely mirror those of men" (179). Given that "stones" was the only terminology available and that Raynold declines to invoke the old homologies where we might most expect them, I disagree; here as elsewhere, "stones" seems to me a linguistic carryover that does not presuppose the whole of the one-sex model.

20. These are the listings in A. W. Pollard and G. R. Redgrave, *A Short Title Catalogue of Books Printed in England, Scotland, and Ireland, 1475–1640* (London: Bibliographical Society, 1956); STC queries the 1585 date. Raynold is very self-conscious about the status of his work as potentially popular; see the prologue for his elaborate defense of its publication in English, despite the misuses to which it might be prone.

21. Raynold insists that his long section on anatomy—roughly one-third of the total length—is the necessary preface to an understanding of woman's reproductive functioning and its ailments and cures. This section—book 1—is his most striking addition to Jonas's 1540 edition.

22. *Byrth*, Hh.viiir, or fol. 46r. I have used folio numbers (given in arabic numerals in the original) whenever possible in referring to *Byrth*, since signature markings are often missing. Both signatures and folio numbers sometimes get scrambled in the 1545 edition; in addition, folio numbers start only at the conclusion of the prologue and often repeat (as they do here: this is in the second batch of pages in the 40s). Where the folio numbers are missing or confusing, I have used signatures. I have followed the conventions of recto and verso for both signatures and folio numbers to avoid unnecessary confusion.

23. The status of the anatomical figures accompanying the various editions of *Byrth* is confusing. Editions of the 1545 *Byrth* available to me, for example, do not contain the combined masculine figures to which Laqueur refers (*Making Sex,* 111). Moreover, although Raynold (1545) describes male parts and apologizes for the maleness of his first and second figures, and although the 1560 edition prides itself on correcting the sex of the 1545 figures, the 1545 text available on microfiche contains only two figures, labeled 1 and 2, and both distinctly female (the first is marked "Prima figurarum muliebrium" and is taken from Vesalius [see Laqueur, *Making Sex,* 111]; the second, with its long strand of hair and flayed breast, is even more decidedly female). But since Raynold's descriptions of his (female) third and fourth figures seem to apply to the figures labeled 1 and 2, and since he alludes to far more figures than appear in his 1545 text, there may have been a mismatch from the start, at least in some editions. (In 1545, he describes eleven figures in all; with the omission of the first two, his descriptions correspond roughly to the nine that appear in the 1560 edition and in later editions.) This already-confusing situation is made still more confusing by the omission of all the anatomical figures in the 1545, 1552, and 1560 editions on microfilm, despite detailed descriptions of them in the text (were they excised? if so, when and by whom?) Assuming that the 1545 figures sometimes were—or were intended to be—like those of the 1560 and later editions, what do they tell us about the hegemony of the one-sex model? Most were derived from Vesalius and appear in other anatomical texts (see, for example, Eccles, *Obstetrics,* plate 2, for *Byrth*'s figures 3 and 9; see Laqueur, *Making Sex,* 81, 82, 84, for *Byrth*'s figures 4 and 9). *Byrth*'s figure 9, taken from Vesalius's *Fabrica,* is in fact one of Laqueur's prime visual examples of homology: "Here [the female genitalia] are not specifically arrayed, as in the *Tabulae* or the *Epitome,* to demonstrate that these structures are isomorphic with those of the male; they are just *seen as* such" (*Making Sex,* 82). This remarkably penis-like structure certainly seems to make a strong case for the one-sex model and presumably does so in the works Laqueur cites; but its status in *Byrth* and its descendants is far from clear. Oddly, the 1560 edition omits any description of it; and the 1545 description (like, for example, the 1598 description) focuses not on the extended (and hence apparently penis-like) neck of the womb but on the internal structure of the womb itself, opened up for our better viewing. In the absence of any reference to homology either in the text proper or in the description of this figure, we may question the extent to which it would have been "seen" as a penis, by Raynold or his audience; read from within Raynold's text, it might equally well have been seen as an illustration of his claim that the bottom of the matrix resembles a man's heart (see 36). The anatomical figures clearly were passed around and attached to texts with quite different understandings of anatomical sex difference; without specific textual pointers, it seems to me dangerous to assume that we know what people in the Renaissance saw when they looked at them.

24. Raynold is of course far from the first to attempt to qualify the sense that female anatomy is by definition imperfect; for discussion of this debate in the Renaissance, see Ian Maclean, *The Renaissance Notion of Woman* (Cambridge: Cambridge University Press, 1980), 29–33. But Raynold may be among the first to make this argument on the basis of

differentiation of function. According to Maclean, "after 1600, the vast majority of doctors reject these axioms [of isomorphism] in favour of the argument from specific sexual function," assigning each sex "an appropriately differentiated physiology"; he attributes the "earliest suggestion of such an approach" to Julius Caesar Scaliger's possibly ironic 1557 attack on Cardano (33–34). Strictly speaking, an understanding of differentiated function depended on anatomical discoveries—especially of the female ovum—that were still in the future; but Raynold's insistence on the different purposes of male and female seed, like his discussion of the fit between yard and womb port, seem to me to contain at least a suggestion of such an approach. If I read Raynold correctly here, he is significantly in advance of his continental colleagues.

25. But see Paster for a reading of the ways in which Raynold's language here may in fact reinforce the shame he is apparently trying to mitigate (*Body Embarrassed*, 186–87).

26. Greenblatt distinguishes between *then* and *now* in part by distinguishing between teleological and genetic accounts of identity: if the (teleological) one-sex model finds its expression in the transvestite theater, "by contrast, a conception of gender that is symbolically female insists upon a genetic rather than a teleological account of identity, interests itself in the inward material matrix of individuality, and finds its supreme literary expression in the novel" (*Shakespearean Negotiations*, 88). Like *The Problems of Aristotle*'s account of hermaphrodites, Raynold's insistence on the importance of origins, especially of the literal matrix of material and maternal origins, suggests that Greenblatt's distinction—however compelling in itself—does not map conveniently onto the historical divide between transvestite theater and novel.

27. The model is also absent from the brief anatomical section on the uterus in Edward Jorden's *A Briefe Discourse of a Disease called the Suffocation of the Mother* (London, 1603), STC reel 757, C3r. Its absence is more surprising in Guillemeau, given that he was writing in France during the apparent heyday of the one-sex model and was Paré's student (see Eccles, *Obstetrics*, 12). The omission may signal Guillemeau's relative lack of interest in anatomy in this work rather than his lack of interest in the one-sex model: unlike Raynold, who insists on an anatomical foundation, Guillemeau fills his work with practical advice and anecdotes about occasions on which surgeons have saved the day. He does refer to one famous (and comic) form of homology, however: "Some do obserue, that the Nauell must be tyed longer, or shorter, according to the difference of the sexes, allowing more measure to the males: because this length doth make their tongue, and priuie membres the longer: whereby they may both speake the plainer, and be more seruiceable to Ladies. And that by tying it short, and almost close to the belly in females, their tongue is lesse free, and their naturall part more straite: And to speake the truth, the Gossips commonly say merrily to the Midwife; if it be a boy, *Make him good measure;* but if it be a wench, *Tye it short*" (Jacques Guillemeau, *Child-birth, or The Happy Deliverie of Women* [London: Printed by A. Hatfield, 1612], 99). See Heather Dubrow on the non-Galenic implications of a similar passage from Culpepper ("Navel Battles," 68–69).

28. Presumably the trial surrounding the sensational transformation of Marie le Marcis to Marin le Marcis in 1601, as reported by Duval in his *Des Hermaphrodites* in 1603

(see Laqueur, *Making Sex,* 136–37, and Greenblatt, *Shakespearean Negotiations,* 73–75), reawakened interest in the Galenic model in England. But if the trial reanimated the apparently moribund model, it's worth asking what pressures, ideological or otherwise, gave that reanimation its force, since the story of the transformation itself need not have carried a Galenist moral (see, for example, Banister's reading of such transformations, 28–29). Though Paré gave a Galenist reading of the earlier transformation of Marie Garnier to Germain (see Laqueur, *Making Sex,* 126–27, and Greenblatt, *Shakespearean Negotiations,* 81), in the *Essais*—the source through which Marie's transformation was most likely to have become known in England—Montaigne reads it not through the lens of the Galenic model but as an instance of the power of imagination; in his extraordinary account, the incorporation of "this masculine member in girls" testifies not to genital homology but to the intensity of their desire for the penis, a desire that imagination rewards by providing them with one ("Of the Power of the Imagination," in *The Complete Essays of Montaigne,* trans. Donald M. Frame [Stanford: Stanford University Press, 1965], 69; see also Laqueur, *Making Sex,* 128–29). In Parker's important account of Montaigne's use of the story, whatever Galenist force it possesses is mitigated by the insistent fears of impotence and hence effeminization that surround it ("Gender Ideology," 343–50, 357–64).

29. In my view, Crooke has been misrepresented in this matter: despite his strenuous refutation of the Galenic model, he tends to turn up in critical discourse as a proponent of it. See, for example, de Grazia, who cites him in support of the Galenic model ("Motive," 440), and Eccles, who quotes him out of context to demonstrate that woman's imperfection was thought to be "a scientific fact" and overlooks his refutation of the homological model, instead citing Bartholin's, fifty years later, as evidence that the idea was on its way out by the late seventeenth century (*Obstetrics,* 26). Even Laqueur, who cites Crooke's arguments against the model at some length, tends to emphasize the perversity of his anatomical reasoning rather than the fact that he disavows the model (*Making Sex,* 90). Recently, Orgel has argued that Crooke does not in fact disavow the Galenic model: "He has, in effect, one theory when his attention is focused on men, another when it is focused on women; the latter, though it contradicts and, indeed, to post-Enlightenment eyes ought to preclude the former, does not, in Crooke's account, negate or even supercede it" (*Impersonations,* 22); "the scientific truth or falsehood of either theory is not at issue—the two claims are parts of two different arguments, and they are not in competition" (24). But this account seems to me not quite accurate. Crooke introduces homology first as part of his discussion of the need for generative parts (*Microcosmographia,* 199), not in his discussion of men specifically; he maintains it in his discussion both of men's generative parts (204) and of "the proportion of these parts both in Men and Women" (216). His first explicit refutation of homology comes not in his discussion of woman's generative parts but in question 8 of the Controversies to book 4 ("How the parts of generation in men and women doe differ"); it is repeated in question 1 ("Of the Difference of the Sexes," 270–72) of book 5, on the "Historie of the Infant." In other words, *Microcosmographia* sorts its theories only very inexactly according to focus on men or women. Nor is it content merely to make the two claims only as equally valid parts of

two different arguments. After Crooke explicitly refutes the homological model, he never again embraces it. The terms in which he introduces the refutation of homology in book 5 suggest that he sees the theories very much in competition ("Notwithstanding all this, against this opinion there are two mighty arguments" [249]), and the triumphant series of marginal notations with which he concludes his discussion—"*Aristot.* Error," "*Galens* Error," "Disprooved," and "No similitude betwixt their Genitals"—suggest not only that he sees the arguments in competition but also that he expects the latter argument to negate and supercede the former. (Both truth-claims and combativeness are in fact commonplace in Crooke. See, for example, his dismissal of the idea that testicles don't make seed, in questions 2 and 3 of the Controversies to book 4: "We will therefore bid adue vnto Aristotle his faigned conceite"; "But the truth is that onely ignorance of Anatomy brought in this old wiues tale" [245]). While we should respect the untidiness of Renaissance argument that Orgel notes, I don't think that we need to see refutation by consecutive argumentation as a post-Enlightenment fallacy here.

30. The womb is in fact unusually active—and male seed unusually inactive—in Crooke: the womb is the place "wherein [the] dull and sleepy faculties [of the male seed] may be raised and rowsed up" (258); "and that which was before but potentiall, it bringeth into act" (262).

31. This revised understanding of woman's humoral deficiency seems to have been conventional in the early seventeenth century; it occurs again in William Whately's *A Bride-Bush or A Wedding Sermon* (London, 1617): "The woman is made to be fruitfull; and therefore also more moist and cold of constitution. Hence it is that their naturall heate serves not to turne all their sustenance into their owne nourishment; but a quantity redounding is set apart in a conuenient place to chearish and nourish the conception" (44).

32. Most of the books of the *Microcosmographia* are structured by an expository section followed by a (usually longer) set of controversies. Book 5 is an extreme instance: the expository section runs from 257 to 270; the "Dilucidation or Exposition of the Controversies concerning the Historie of the Infant"—thirty-three in all—runs from 270 to 345. (The extent to which Crooke's "Controversies" are in fact his is in doubt; he tells his readers inconspicuously in his "Preface to the Chyrurgeons" that he has taken the Controversies largely from Laurentius, with some "additions, subtractions, and alterations," and that book 5 is "almost wholy out of *Laurentius* sauing for some passages." Since Crooke nonetheless presents the controversies as his own, often citing Laurentius as though he were not translating from him, I have followed critical custom in referring to their author as Crooke.) By omitting Crooke's reference forward to the Controversies in the passage about stories of female to male transformation, Orgel minimizes Crooke's investment in sorting out "trueth"; Crooke returns to these stories in the passage cited below not as someone who "sees no need to reconcile the conflicting scientific arguments" (*Impersonations,* 22) but specifically to set the record straight ("what shall we say to those so many stories?" [250]).

33. Laqueur points out that, after the "discovery" of the clitoris, this organ was routinely (if confusingly) assimilated to the one-sex model as another equivalent to the penis (*Making Sex,* 64–65, 92–93).

34. Since like terminology is often taken to indicate homology of genital structure, it may be worth noting that Crooke uses the same terms—"testicles" and "spermatick vessels"—to describe male and female parts specifically in the process of discrediting the one-sex model. One might read this—as Laqueur does—as the failure even of its adversaries to free themselves from the model; or one might read it as an indication of a time lag between the development of a new model and the development of a new terminology.

35. Most people accept Crooke at his—or his title page's—word; but Carol Neely has called my attention to Jonathan Andrews's argument that he was only one of a number of physicians attached to the royal household rather than James's personal physician, as *Microcosmographia* advertised ("Bedlam Revisited: A History of Bethlem Hospital 1634–1770" [Ph.D. diss., Queen Mary and Westfield College, London University, 1991], 246). Though I was unable to follow up on all of her suggestions, I have profited throughout from Carol Neely's wonderfully detailed and responsive reading of this essay.

36. Orgel elegantly underscores the mismatch between the theorists of homology and the transvestite theater ("the medical theorists are for the most part French and Italian, and France and Italy did not develop transvestite theaters" ["Nobody's Perfect," 18]). But he nonetheless writes in this essay as though Galenic homologies unproblematically defined thinking about sexual difference in England, ignoring his own incipient critique (13); even in this essay's later incarnation in *Impersonations* he maintains that "outside the professional scientific community homology remained the predominant theory" (24).

37. See Greenblatt, *Shakespearean Negotiations,* 88, and n. 26, above.

38. See *Suffocating Mothers,* especially the discussions of *Hamlet, King Lear, Macbeth,* and *Coriolanus.*

39. These instances are taken from Orgel ("Nobody's Perfect," 14, and *Impersonations,* 25) and Sinfield (*Faultlines,* 134). Among those who assume the "female" origin of men within the Galenic system, see also, for example, Carol Thomas Neely, "Constructing Female Sexuality in the Renaissance: Stratford, London, Windsor, Vienna," in *Feminism and Psychoanalysis,* ed. Richard Feldstein and Judith Roof (Ithaca: Cornell University Press, 1990), 212–13; Susan Zimmerman, "Disruptive Desire: Artifice and Indeterminacy in Jacobean Comedy," introduction to *Erotic Politics: Desire on the Renaissance Stage* (New York: Routledge, 1992), 40; and Valerie Traub, *Desire and Anxiety: Circulations of Sexuality in Shakespearean Drama* (London: Routledge, 1992), 51. But a system defined by the teleological rather than the genetic does not readily point toward female origin; Parker (rightly, in my view) reads the fear of effeminization as a critique—rather than a confirmation—of the Galenic model insofar as it reverses the unidirectionality of the model (see "Gender Ideology," esp. 360–62).

40. See Laqueur, *Making Sex,* 141–42, and Parker, "Gender Ideology," 338–39. Huarte seems to depart from his fellow-Galenists insofar as he entertains the possibility that the transformation can work in both directions: "if when nature hath finished to forme a man in all perfection, she would conuert him into a woman, there needeth nought els to be done, saue only to turne his instruments of generation inwards. And if she haue shaped a woman, and would make a man of her, by taking forth her belly and her cods, it would

quickly be performed. This hath chanced many times in nature, aswell whiles the creature hath been in the mothers womb, as after the same was borne, wherof the histories are full" (*Examination of mens Wits*, 269). But although he writes that these transformations can take place both before and after birth, Huarte is particularly interested in *in utero* transformations, apparently because they explain cross-gender characteristics: "To whom this transformation hath befallen in the mothers womb, is afterwards plainly discouered, by certain motions which they retaine, vnfitting for the masculin sex, being altogither womanish, & their voice shrill and sweet. And such persons are enclined to perform womens actions, and fall ordinarily into vncouth offences. Contrariwise, nature hath sundrie times made a male with his genetories outward, and cold growing on, they haue turned inward, and it became female. This is knowen after she is borne, for she retaineth a mannish fashion, aswel in her words, as in all her motions and workings" (269–70). Moreover, whatever the theoretical possibilities of post-uterine transformation from male to female, the only male-to-female transformation Huarte describes is *in utero* (269), the only post-uterine transformation female-to-male (270). In practice, that is, Huarte follows traditional wisdom, combining a version of the Aristotelian position (that a man may become a woman *in utero*) with the Galenic position (that only a woman can become a man after birth).

41. Orgel, "Nobody's Perfect," 14; see also *Impersonations*, 25, for a slight variant on this sentence ("In this version of the medical literature we all start as women").

42. The assumption, for example, that our critical methodologies serve our psychological needs at the same time as they serve as signs of our attentiveness to ruling critical trends and to changes in the status of our knowledge.

43. Among those who use the theory, Traub is exceptional in her insistence on consideration of this body; see, for example, *Desire and Anxiety*, 51–52.

44. For early formulations of this thesis, see especially Madelon (Sprengnether) Gohlke, "'I Wooed Thee with My Sword': Shakespeare's Tragic Paradigms," in *Representing Shakespeare: New Psychoanalytic Essays*, ed. Murray M. Schwartz and Coppélia Kahn (Baltimore: Johns Hopkins University Press, 1980), 170–87, and Coppélia Kahn, *Man's Estate: Masculine Identity in Shakespeare* (Berkeley and Los Angeles: University of California Press, 1981); and see my *Suffocating Mothers* for a full account both of this psychic tension and of the numerous other feminist critics from whose work I have drawn.

45. Given what we know of his reading habits, I would speculate that Shakespeare was far more likely to have encountered medical descriptions of generation through Plutarch's "Of the Naturall Love or Kindnes of Parents to their Children" (in *The Philosophie, Commonlie called The Morals*, trans. Philemon Holland, "Doctor in Physicke" [London, 1603]) than through any of the specifically medical works; and, at least in this essay, Plutarch writes within the "wise nature" school akin to Raynold and Crooke.

2

"To Laugh with Open Throate":
Mad Lovers, Theatrical Cures, and
Gendered Bodies in Jacobean Drama

Alan Walworth

"Love is merely a madness," says Rosalind in *As You Like It,* adding that such a condition "deserves as well a dark house and a whip as madmen do" (3.2.400–402).[1] Rather than confining the lovesick Orlando, however, the disguised Rosalind offers instead to cure him of his affliction by a distinctly theatrical method. She will play the part of his beloved, and the two of them will enact a series of scenes in which she will "now like him, now loathe him; then entertain him, then forswear him; now weep for him, then spit at him." Through such role playing therapy, Orlando will ultimately overcome his "mad humor of love" (3.2.415–18).

The conceit of love as a madness curable only by theatrical means assumes a more literal form in a number of later Jacobean and Caroline dramas, in which the lovestruck patients are treated not by an invitation into conscious role playing but by a deceptive compliance with their mad delusions. Such a scenario draws upon that traditional treatment for melancholia, introduced in classical medical texts and perpetuated in Renaissance treatises, which Michel Foucault terms the cure by "theatrical representation" or "ruse."[2] The appropriation of this tradition by English Renaissance dramatists has been discussed at length in Lawrence Babb's meticulous study of Elizabethan melancholia.[3] More recently, Winfried Schleiner has considered the deployment of this "cure by the imagination" in Shakespeare,[4] while Donald Beecher has traced the drama's utilization of a related "theatrical device" tradition in which lovesick patients are cured by coitus with a substitute for the object of desire.[5] These parallel ruse and substitution traditions converge in Shakespeare and Fletcher's *The Two Noble Kinsmen* (1613), in which a doctor cures the low-born Jailer's Daughter, mad from unrequited love for the noble Palamon, by delegating one of her earlier wooers to impersonate the absent beloved and ultimately take the girl to bed. The success of this treatment vindicates the doctor's original prognosis: "it is a falsehood she is in, which is with falsehoods to be combated" (4.3.93–94), a formulation echoed in Foucault's claim that, in the theatrical ruse, "illusion can cure the illusory."[6]

In the following essay I attempt a dialogue with these historical studies from a psychoanalytic perspective, expanding on Schleiner's suggestion that in the theatricalized ruse "the modern psychotherapist has a Renaissance analogue."[7] More specifically, I examine the relation between this Renaissance cure, which features a physician or physician's delegate standing in for a love object and employs what Beecher calls a "principle of substitution" and a "transfer of affections," and that other therapeutic phenomenon whose effect, as Freud describes it, is to "replace some earlier person by the person of the physician," the psychoanalytic transference.[8] While the coercive, manipulative, and often publicly theatricalized treatment of delusions in the Renaissance ruse clearly differs sharply in its premises and procedures from the normatively voluntary, collaborative, and private interpretation of neurotic symptoms in the "talking cure," the two practices both exploit a transferential dynamic which, as Freud himself pointed out, is not limited to the analytic situation.[9] The very differences within the Renaissance medical discourses offer a parallel to the diverging theories of transference: while the traditional lovesickness cure of coitus with a substitute anticipates the Freudian dynamic of the analyst taking the place of a love object, the cure by compliance with the patient's melancholic delusions situates the physician in the transferential role of the Lacanian "subject supposed to know," able to enter into and dispel the delusion by appearing to have a more authoritative understanding of its internal logic than the patient. Both the compliance and substitution traditions accord with Lacan's definition of transference as "a conquest of the truth *via* the paths of deception";[10] thus Foucault's description of the theatrical ruse as "the point at which illusion, turned back upon itself, will open to the dazzlement of truth" parallels Slavoj Žižek's dictum that "the transference is an essential illusion by means of which the final Truth . . . is produced."[11]

I want to pursue this homology in order to suggest that both Renaissance and psychoanalytic discourses of transferential cure are predicated on implicitly gendered constructions of the body's openness and enclosure. I will begin by exploring the Renaissance tradition of theatrical cures for deluded melancholics through the parallel theoretical approaches of Lacanian psychoanalysis and the Bakhtinian model of "classical" and "grotesque" bodies.[12] Though these melancholics are generally not specified as suffering from lovesickness, their case histories nevertheless demonstrate all the more palpably the gendered dynamics of bodily loss and fantasmatic incorporation which, I will go on to argue, inform at a displaced level the representation of mad lovers and their cures in Jacobean drama. Ultimately, I want to suggest that both medical and literary discourses of the period employ transferential dynamics of desire and deception, figured in tropes of loss, incorporation, and control, to mediate cultural anxieties surrounding the female body as a potential site of grotesque and transgressive openness.

Unknown Losses, Open Wounds

Stories of mad delusions and the equally inventive means of humoring and curing them first appear in classical medical texts, from the first-century works of Galen and Aretaeus through the sixth-century writings of Aetius of Amida and Alexander of Tralles. In the late sixteenth century, these stories were repeated and embellished in continental sources, including Levinus Lemnius's *Touchstone of Complexions* (first published in Latin in 1561), Tomasso Garzoni's *Hospitall of Incurable Fooles* (published in Italian in 1586), and Andre Du Laurens's *Preservation of the Sight* and Simon Goulart's *Admirable and Memorable Histories* (published in French in 1597 and 1600, respectively). These writers lent their own authority to the classical tradition; Lemnius was "an eminent physician of Zeeland who gave up medicine to enter the ministry," while Du Laurens was "the principal physician of Henry IV and chancellor of the faculty of Montpellier."[13] The popularity of these continental works not only prompted translations (Lemnius's text, for example, went through four English editions between 1565 and 1633), but also led to the proliferation and adaptation of theatrical ruse stories in a number of equally popular seventeenth-century English works: William Vaughan's *Approved Directions for Health* went through seven editions between 1600 and 1633; Thomas Walkington's *Opticke Glasse of Humors* appeared in four editions between 1607 and 1639; Robert Burton's exhaustive *Anatomy of Melancholy* saw five editions between 1621 and 1638.[14]

The widely diverse stories in these texts focus primarily on male patients, many of whom, as Robert Burton points out in *The Anatomy of Melancholy*, are "afraid of some losse, danger, that they shall surely lose lives, goods, and al they have, but why they know not."[15] For many of the patients this indeterminate fear, which anticipates Freud's description of melancholia as an "unknown loss," becomes localized in a preoccupation with bodily integrity. Some are haunted by the prospect of mutilation: one young man, after having been attacked by a boar, remains unshakeable in his deluded conviction that the animal has eaten his leg, while another man, after having merely viewed a crocodile, becomes convinced that he has lost both an arm and a leg.[16] Other patients fear that they will lose their heads, or that they have already lost them, or that they have become "nothing but head."[17] Such fantasies of dismembered body parts provide a literal counterpart to Freud's cryptic metaphor of melancholia as an "open wound," even as they resemble the uncanny images of "dismembered limbs, a severed head, a hand cut off at the wrist" which Freud interprets in terms of castration anxiety.[18] Lacan further associates such images of "castration, mutilation, dismemberment, dislocation, evisceration, devouring, bursting open of the body" with the earliest self-experience of the "fragmented body" or "body in bits and pieces,"[19] imagery which is even more pronounced in those patients of the treatises who believe they have been transformed into breakable pitchers, pots, or urinals, or that their entire bodies, feet, or in one case buttocks are made of fragile glass.[20] Related fantasies involve a fear of bodily dissolution, as in the accounts of men who believe they have become a burning candle wick or a melting stick of butter,[21] a reversion to a primal state in which, according to Lacan, the ego's tenuous unity "fades away, dissipates, becomes disorganized, dissolves."[22] Other efforts to maintain bodily integrity involve the closing of orifices, including refusals of ingestion such as men who faint when offered a glass of water or who refuse to eat because they imagine themselves to be either godlike or dead.[23] A corresponding set of delusions focuses on evacuation, as in the cases of men who urinate whenever they hear music, or painful retention, as in men who refuse to urinate or who believe that they have frogs or toads crawling in their stomachs.[24]

In Freud's account of melancholia, the ego identifies with the lost object in a fantasy of oral incorporation, associated with the melancholic's typical refusal of actual nourishment. Lacan designates this object of melancholic "unknown loss" and fantasmatic incorporation as the *objet petit a,* associating it with a primal separation and hence with those objects which fall from or enter through such orifices as the mouth, breasts, phallus, vagina, and anus.[25] Lacan's emphasis on such threshold sites suggests a psychic corollary with Bakhtin's historical model of the open, unfinished "grotesque" body and its similarly exaggerated investment in "the parts through which the world enters the body or emerges from it."[26] If the melancholic patients of the treatises demonstrate fears of the Bakhtinian grotesque body and attempt to maintain instead an enclosed, seamless "classical" body in which "inner processes of absorbing and ejecting were not revealed," the psychoanalytic association of such bodily retentions and exclusions with irrevocable loss and fantasmatic incorporation deflates the pretensions of such an impossible ideal.[27]

Freud characterizes the melancholic incorporation of loss as a failure of the normal "transference" of libidinal energy from the ego to a new external object.[28] In contrast, the theatrical cures of the treatises work through a deceptive externalization of the lost and/or incorporated object itself, as in the case of the physician who "replaces" a patient's supposedly lost head by securing upon it a lead weight painfully heavy enough to dispel the delusion. And while Lacan refers to the "presence of the *objet a,* rediscovered always and everywhere, in the movement of the transference,"[29] such a transferential "movement" of the incorporated object becomes literalized in the cure for the delusion of frogs or toads in the stomach: the physician gives the patient a purgative, causes him to defecate and, through a theatrical sleight of hand, triumphantly displays the feces containing the living creatures which have supposedly been expelled. In the transferential deception, the opening of the body's orifices allows for the externalization of the expelled *objet a* in the form of a theatrical device. Externalization through expulsion becomes an even greater theatrical spectacle in the story of the "sillie melancholike man" who refuses to urinate for fear of drowning the town, and is cured only by his friends setting several abandoned houses ablaze, ringing the alarm bells, and convincing him "that he should pisse quickelie and quench the fire."[30] These anxieties surrounding the orifices of the grotesque body, through which, according to Bakhtin, "dung and urine . . . appear in hyperbolic quantities and cosmic dimensions,"[31] correspond with the Lacanian model of "mastery and control," which seeks to retain the incorporated *objet a* in spite of the physical imperatives that "the stomach is empty and needs to be filled, or the bladder is full and needs to be emptied."[32] The release of orifices at the culmination of the theatrical cure provides a literal parallel to what Lacan calls the transferential "opening" and "closing" of the unconscious, which is "like the bladder" in its rhythms.[33]

As Judith Butler points out, the attempt to maintain rigid control of the body's orifices and establish secure boundaries between interior and exterior necessarily undoes itself: "For inner and outer worlds to remain utterly distinct, the entire surface of the body would have to achieve an impossible impermeability. This sealing of its surfaces would constitute the seamless boundary of the subject; but this enclosure would invariably be exploded by precisely that excremental filth that it fears."[34] For Lacan, the subject derives its very identity from this impossible incorporation and retention of the lost object, to the point of "stuffing" itself with its own waste products. What Catherine Clément calls Lacan's "superb joke," namely that "desire feeds on waste," is grossly literalized in the treatise account of a man who "for his nourishment did eate his owne excrements."[35] But ultimately the incorporation of bodily waste is only a failed attempt to fill the hollow void of the fantasized lost object, "an object that has attained an existence that is all the more absolute because it no longer corresponds to anything in reality."[36] Thus Lacan includes "the nothing" among his "unthinkable list" of fantasy objects and posits the "fading" of the subject who becomes indistinguishable from the nothing on which it stuffs itself.[37] Ultimately, "it is as points of lack, as nothings, that the objects in fantasy serve to constitute the subject's identity,"[38] a terminal point seemingly reached in the brief but strangely poignant treatise account of "a melancholike man, which affirmed himselfe the most wretched and miserable in all the world, because he was nothing."[39]

The treatises present these melancholic dynamics of loss and incorporation, figured in terms of bodily openness and enclosure, as a predominantly male affliction, a gendered distinction which informs the psychoanalytic account of melancholia as well. In her analysis of Freud's paradigm, Juliana Schiesari points out that "the very notion of an 'open wound' already seems to evoke the question of castration and thus implicitly that of sexual difference."[40] More specifically, she notes the ways in which constructions of melancholia over the centuries have conferred upon its male sufferers "the cultural prestige of inspired artistry and genius," while in contrast "women's losses" have been "delegitimated or made to seem insignificant by men's melancholic display of loss."[41] While Freud avoids the issue of sexual difference in his discussion of melancholia, his implicitly gendered argument has contributed to what Hélène Cixous describes as a prevailing theoretical asymmetry in which male mourning "incorporates the lost object" while women's supposed inability to mourn loss is figured in "a body that overflows, disgorges, vomiting as opposed to masculine incorporation."[42] And while Bakhtin's discussion of the Renaissance grotesque body similarly ignores gender, more recent critics such as Peter Stallybrass have argued that the Renaissance patriarchal construction of women as tenuously held property involves the fear of a specifically female "openness" at such sites as "the mouth, chastity, the threshold of the house."[43] Stallybrass goes on to suggest that the masculine need to contain this transgressive female body leads to "the unstable conceptualization of woman as simultaneously enclosed and open," a view supported by Katharine Eisaman Maus's claim that the conflicting discourses of Renaissance male poetic subjectivity present the woman's body as at once "closed in upon itself" and yet a "paradigm of penetrability."[44] Such anxiety surrounding the female body may have been related to similar ambivalences regarding the very distinction between male and female, as suggested by Thomas Laqueur's association of Bakhtin's grotesque body with the one-sex model of "an open body in which sexual attributes were matters of degree rather than kind."[45] These conflicting and unstable significations of the female's potential grotesque openness and the male's potential feminization may inform the parallel between the treatise stories of frogs, toads, or serpents expelled from the stomach—one of the few delusions reported as frequently for women as for men—and the accounts in Renaissance obstetrics texts of women who give monstrous birth to "frogs, toads, serpents, lizards."[46] In the story of one melancholic woman, the eroticized detail that she had "swallowed" an imaginary serpent and thus voluntarily opened herself to her own dilemma further suggests the disturbing permeability of the female body.[47]

William Vaughan's *Approved Directions for Health* (1612), which presents tales from the parallel tradition of cures for lovesickness, contains a theatrical ruse story that reveals an even more anxious preoccupation with the grotesque female body, in spite or perhaps because of the fact that it atypically features a woman in the authoritative role of healer. Vaughan recounts the case of the beautiful teacher Hippatia, who becomes an object of unrequited love for one of her young male scholars. In order to dissuade the student from his desires, she invites him to her chamber, raises her petticoat, reveals "a filthy, bloudy, and mattry smock" which she has procured for the occasion, and warns the young man not to love "such filthy trompery over-cast and disguised with a glozing beautie."[48] Once again falsehood is cured with falsehood, as the theatrical ruse of an illusory physical corruption dispels the student's transferential, equally illusory idealization of his teacher. Hippatia's clever device, a doubly deceptive conjunction of veiling and revealing, epitomizes cultural ambivalences by presenting grotesque openness as simultaneously the secret truth and the defining fantasy of the female body.

Simon Goulart's *Admirable and Memorable Histories* (1607) similarly articulates anxieties about the open female body, presenting a transferential cure which may well have influenced the theatrical ruse scenarios of the Jacobean drama even as it anticipates the gendered ambivalences of psychoanalytic theory. Goulart recounts the unconventional cure of "a *Romaine* woman growne melancolike for that she had bene married against her will to one whom shee loved not, and smothering her furie with a sad silence."[49] As Stallybrass points out, Renaissance constructions of the female body involve metonymic displacements in which "silence, the closed mouth, is made a sign of chastity"; conversely, as Karen Newman observes, "an open mouth and immodest speech are tantamount to open genitals and immodest acts."[50] But since here the silence of the wife's closed mouth marks a resistance to and presumable sexual aloofness from the husband she "loved not," it becomes an object of medical intervention, comparable to the psychoanalytic practice for which, as Sarah Kofman observes, "there is no worse crime than silence, for it covers women's sex with its 'thick veil,' renders it inaccessible, indomitable, implacable: terrifying."[51] And just as Freud was first led to see the importance of "the question whether a woman is 'open' or 'shut'" through his analysis of Dora and his discoveries about the transference,[52] the physician Dr. Brasavole similarly effects the opening of the female patient through a transferential substitution. Assuming the husband's role, the doctor "salutes her lovingly as if shee had beene his wife," then "approcheth to kisse her" in a gesture anticipating Freud's own assumption that Dora "would like to have a kiss from me."[53] But as Freud mishandled the supposed transference in Dora's case, so the silent wife responds not with a kiss but with a rebuke, as "shee pulls of his Cappe, and all that Brasavole carried on his head, fitting for his age and the fashion of that time and casts it to the ground."

Despite this apparent miscalculation, Goulart's insistence that the cure was successful suggests that it effected a kind of negative transference. Like Freud's implicitly transferential description of traditional wedding-night substitutions, in which a stand-in for the groom deflects upon himself the deflowered young bride's vengeful desire to castrate or decapitate her new husband, Goulart's anecdote presents a role-playing substitute willing to replace the husband and suffer the furious wife's castrating de-"Cappe"-itation of his headpiece.[54] Having directed her smothered fury at the doctor, whom she now takes to be no more than a drunken old man, the young woman begins "to laugh with open throate" and is cured of her melancholy. This progression from the "sad silence" of a stubbornly closed mouth to the unrestrained laughter of the "open throate" centers, like Freud's Irma dream, on a reluctant female patient who has not yet "opened her mouth properly."[55] The silent wife of the treatise must open her mouth in submission to male authority, a dynamic similar to Kofman's claim that "the psychoanalytic solution restores speech to woman only the better to rob her of it, the better to subordinate it to that of the master."[56] But the doctor's apparent success has been won at a cost, exposing him to attack, ridicule, and what Cixous describes as the subversive potential of a female "laughter that breaks out, overflows."[57]

Thus the transferential cure in both Renaissance and psychoanalytic contexts points to a historically persistent anxiety centering on the open female body, from Bakhtin's description of the grotesque mouth as a "wide-open bodily abyss," to Lacan's equation of Irma's throat with "the abyss of the feminine organ."[58] Such preoccupations with bodily openness and enclosure are further explored, albeit in displaced form, in the theatrical cures of Jacobean drama.

"A Strange Conceite"

The inherently theatrical stories of the treatises were being dramatized on the continental stage by the early 1570s. Thomas Milles recalls a comedy, presented before Charles IX of France, which enacted the popular tale of the "dead" man who wouldn't eat and was cured when his caretakers wrapped themselves in winding sheets, announced that they too were dead, and invited him to join them in a meal.[59] In transferring the theatrical cure from the melancholic patients of the treatises to the mad lovers of the stage, Jacobean dramatists freely employed this device on both male and female lovers, perhaps reflecting the growing tendency of medical literature to conceptualize lovesickness no longer as the exclusive prerogative of aristocratic males but as a disease suffered with equal frequency and intensity by women.[60] At the same time, playwrights shifted the explicit focus from the body and its processes to desire and its deceptions. Nevertheless, this shift from drive to desire, from libido to love, perpetuates in displaced form the preoccupations with bodily openness and enclosure explored in the treatises, while further emphasizing the gender asymmetries found there.

In a typical scenario of the drama, the love-maddened woman is subjected to the coital substitution ruse which the medical tradition had previously reserved for male patients.[61] Perhaps under the vestigial stigma of intruding upon a preserve formerly reserved for aristocratic males, the lovesick woman typically suffers from an unrequited love for a man above her own social station. Because the object of her obsession is indifferent and absent, a more socially acceptable substitute steps in and attempts to deflect the woman's unrequited passion upon himself, a dynamic which, like the psychoanalytic transference, "displaces love upon a stranger who is only a stand-in."[62] This ruse, which works successfully upon the Jailer's Daughter in *The Two Noble Kinsmen,* is also attempted in Richard Brome's *The Northern Lasse* (1629), though in this case the mad Constance sees through the ruse of the doltish suitor passing himself off as her beloved Sir Phillip. The subplot, which features a comic twist on this type of cure, nevertheless maintains its essential outlines: Constance Holdup the whore disguises herself as the mad Constance, pretends to succumb to another suitor who also passes himself off as Sir Phillip, and withholds her true identity until he has "wedded her, bedded her, and put her in her right wits againe" (4.4.121–22).[63] Once the counter-ruse is revealed, the substitute Constance demands and obtains a hundred pounds in return for relinquishing any marriage claims upon her seducer. In each of these cases, the cure hinges on the assumption that the woman's desire can easily be deflected from her original object to a substitute.

The typical deception cure for mad male lovers, on the other hand, reverses this traditional scenario. The male is at no disadvantage in social station and finds his passion reciprocated by the female beloved, but nonetheless remains trapped in a maze of delusions. Hence in this version of the theatrical cure the female beloved is not replaced by a substitute love object, but becomes in effect a stand-in for herself. She partakes in the mad lover's recovery, employing a disguise ruse which enables her to follow and comfort him in his deluded travails before finally revealing herself at the culmination of the cure. In Thomas Middleton's *The Nice Valour; or The Passionate Mad-Man* (1616), a deluded noble, known only as the Passionate Lord, is cured by a former lover who pursues him disguised as a Cupid. In James Shirley's *Love Tricks* (1625), Infortunio, maddened by Selina's initial rejection of his suit, roams the forest until he is cured by his now-reciprocating beloved disguised as a shepherd. In John Ford's *The Lover's Melancholy* (1628), the despondent Prince Palador is finally consoled when the boy page who has been keeping watch over him at last reveals herself as his lost love Eroclea. And in John Fletcher's *The Noble Gentleman* (1626), the mad Shattillion is so absorbed in the delusion of his beloved's captivity that he is unable to recognize her even as she trails him undisguised. Finally, she participates in an elaborate theatrical ruse involving a comic single combat, proclaiming (in a line reminiscent of the doctor's in *The Two Noble Kinsmen*) that "a strange conceite hath wrought this malady, / Conceites again must bring him to himself" (5.1.316–17).[64]

In the typical cures for mad male lovers, then, the beloved becomes the physician, while for mad female lovers the physician, or physician's delegate, becomes the beloved. The reciprocity of these two motifs had already been exploited in Shakespeare's *As You Like It,* where Rosalind offers to cure Orlando's love "madness" by becoming at once both the beloved disguised as a healer and a healer impersonating the beloved. Both these sleight-of-hand modes of cure depend on a complex theatrical interplay of presence and absence: while the male lovers can only accept the beloved's presence through a disguise ruse which feigns her absence, the female lovers can only accept the beloved's absence through a bedtrick ruse which simulates his presence. This dialectic of presence and absence in the early modern ruse parallels the inherent tensions within the psychoanalytic concept of transference. As Cynthia Chase maintains, Freud's essay "The Dynamics of the Transference" wavers uncertainly over the question of whether transference makes emotional conflicts fully present or only deals with them *"in absentia."* Such an opposition, paralleling Saussure's distinction between metonymy as a combination of terms *in presentia* and metaphor as a selection of terms *in absentia,* leads Chase not only to point out that transference is etymologically related to both linguistic tropes but also to argue that in Freud's essay "the sense of the metonymical status of transference conflicts sharply with the sense of its metaphorical status."[65] Lacan further underscores this fundamental dialectic, maintaining that "connexion and substitution"—metonymy and metaphor, respectively—are "the formulas we give to the signifier in its *transference*-function."[66] This tension between the metaphoric and metonymic poles of transference underlies the "strange conceite" of the Jacobean drama's theatrical cures. More specifically, in these plays the opposition between bodily openness and enclosure found in the treatises coexists with, and is partially displaced onto, an opposition between metonymic presence and metaphoric absence. Though such figurative linguistic tropes may seem remote from bodily processes, from a psychoanalytic perspective the two dimensions are inextricably implicated; as Juliet Flower MacCannell observes, "For Lacan we never know the body except as a figure."[67]

This figuring of the body in the contrasting cures for male and female lovers corroborates MacCannell's further claim that "the two modes, metaphor and metonymy, are indeed silently, invisibly, but unarguably *gendered*."[68] The association of metonymy with the contiguous, umbilical connection to the maternal body and thus with presence and feminine openness informs Kristeva's linking of the trope with Bakhtin's open, grotesque body (and its carnival mode of language).[69] The association of metaphor with separation from the maternal body and with masculine enclosure leads Jean Laplanche to speak of the ego itself as a "psychical metaphor" based upon the introjected image of "a *body* apprehended as a totality, defined only by the existence of an envelope separating an 'inside' from an 'outside.'" The notion that this metaphoric process of individuation establishes the boundaries of the closed body surface is in accord with MacCannell's claim that "the tendency in metaphor is towards closure, encircling, drawing boundaries. . . . It will always centre and exclude."[70] The seeming paradox noted by Schiesari, namely that in the psychoanalytic theory of melancholia "Freud's 'open wound' becomes a metaphor of closure," appears less contradictory if melancholic incorporation is itself predicated on the closure of metaphor.[71]

Jacobean dramatists exploit the dynamic of metaphoric closure and metonymic openness found in the treatises, selectively appropriating this tradition in a way which heightens its gendered distinctions. The male lovers of the stage resemble the melancholics of the treatises in their symptoms of metaphoric bodily enclosure and incorporation of the lost fantasy image. In contrast, the female lovers of the drama come closest to the earlier medical tradition not in their pathology but in their cure by a deceptive humoring of delusions, sleight-of-hand substitutions, and the metonymic "opening up" of the body. This heightening of gendered contrasts offers an intriguing counterpoint to the celebrated gender indeterminacy of the transvestite Renaissance theatre.

For the female lovers, constructed as physically and psychically open to metonymic displacements along a potentially endless continuum, any male present can serve as a substitute object of desire.[72] In *The Two Noble Kinsmen* the doctor who prescribes the theatrical ruse instructs the substitute to impersonate Palamon through a process of metonymic association, to sing and wear flowers and perfumes, "for Palamon can sing, and Palamon is sweet, and ev'ry good thing" (4.3.86–87). The impostor's attempt to assume a metaphoric resemblance to the actual Palamon can be achieved only through his metonymic assumption of the trappings and behavior associated with the absent beloved. But the girl's father challenges the doctor's recommendation that the ruse go so far as a sexual consummation, a dialogue which stages the competing paternal and medical claims to authority over the female body.[73] The Jailer's Daughter is persuaded that the substitute is indeed her beloved Palamon, and she herself is the first to suggest that the two of them go to bed together (5.2.86). At the doctor's prompting, the substitute accepts the offer and leads the girl away. But the sexual culmination of the cure must necessarily take place offstage, and we do not see the daughter again, receiving instead only the father's assurance that "she's well restor'd, / And to be married shortly" (5.4.27–28). Consequently, there remains a missing link in the metonymic chain of associations which supposedly leads the girl back to the recognition of her original wooer and acceptance of her prescribed social and marital roles. Seemingly, the transferential cure which manipulates the transgressive openness of the female body can be represented as successful only insofar as it causes that body to disappear altogether.

A similar associational logic informs Brome's *The Northern Lasse,* when the impostor to be foisted upon the mad Constance is advised to insert himself into the girl's metonymic chain of thought: "take her into the Orchard; twas there she fell in love they say" (3.2.123–24). But in Brome's play women do not simply acquiesce to deceptive ploys. Since the medical tradition frequently advocated curing the lovesick patient's unrequited desire by filling the place of the absent beloved with a prostitute—a figure whose occupation is inherently predicated on a transferential standing in for another—it is fitting that the prostitute Constance Holdup should prove the most adept manipulator of the theatrical ruse. By assuming the role of her lovesick namesake, substituting not for the object of desire but for the desiring subject, she utilizes her sexually open body to turn the tables on the man who attempts a substitution ruse on her. And while this Constance skillfully carries metonymic displacements to new levels of complexity, the other Constance resists such slippages altogether. The seeming incomprehensibility of her metonymic verbal free associations—as Ellie Ragland-Sullivan points out, "any metonymy is always an apparent nonsense"[74]—prompts the caretakers to attempt a substitution ruse in the form of a doltish suitor who is himself named Non-sence. Constance, however, true to her name and her absent beloved, quickly sees through the ruse and rebukes the impostor. Her reversal of the cure—as one witty bystander observes, "She has done a cure on him. Hee spoke sense now" (3.2.279)—halts metonymic displacement in favor of a metaphoric fixing of signification, corroborating Lacan's dictum that "metaphor occurs at the precise point at which sense emerges from non-sense."[75]

The metaphoric rejection of displacement and adherence to the fantasy image, presented as an exceptional resistance in female lovers, is the typical pathology for males, who refuse not only any proffered substitute but also the actual beloved herself. By incorporating the fantasy of the lost object of desire, melancholia paradoxically turns grief for the (female) beloved's absence into an obsessive fantasy requiring that absence. In a process of metaphoric substitution, the actual beloved becomes in effect a rejected signifier, excluded from the chain of associations and subsumed beneath her fantasy image.

Having metaphorically excluded the beloved, the male lovers of the plays, like the melancholic male patients of the treatises, adhere to various forms of enclosure. The deluded Shattillion of *The Noble Gentleman,* certain that everyone around him is trying to draw him into "open Treason" (1.3.29), proclaims that the woman following him so determinedly is actually a spy sent by the king "to dive into me" (1.3.51), and that she wishes "to make me open and betray my self" (1.3.83). To protect himself against such a breach, he determines at last to close himself off completely from the outside world: "I'l nere stirr from my house, and keep my doores / Lockt day and night" (4.3.162–63), anticipating Lacan's metaphor in which transference "closes the door, or the window, or the shutters."[76] Shattillion demonstrates what Lacan calls the typically masculine mode of desire, "that what he relates to is the *objet a,* and that the whole of his realization in the sexual relation comes down to fantasy."[77] But in order for the male lover to adhere to the safely immutable fantasy image, the actual beloved must be denied and denigrated. Convinced that the woman who follows him and claims to be his lost beloved is a spy, Shattillion threateningly cries out, "I will descend my chamber, / And cut thy throat, I sweare I'le cut thy throat" (4.3.115–16). As Lacan observes, "I love you, but, because inexplicably I love in you something more than you—the *object petit a*—I mutilate you."[78]

The adherence to the fantasy object becomes more clearly manifest when the male lover uncharacteristically lets down his defenses. Through a theatrical ruse akin to Hamlet's mousetrap, the doctor in *The Lover's Melancholy* successfully diagnoses Prince Palador's disease by watching his reactions during a "Masque of Melancholy," in which the performing courtiers present themselves as various forms of melancholy closely based on Burton's *Anatomy.* While the device succeeds in determining the prince's malady as love melancholy, it merely causes him to withdraw further into an isolated enclosure. The only one who knows the identity of the beloved is the honest counselor Rhetias, to whom the prince had earlier lowered his guard, urging him to "be open" and in turn commanding him to "open my bosom" (2.1.147, 217).[79] Rhetias unlooses the prince's buttons and finds hidden within a portrait of Eroclea, the incorporated *objet a* of his desire. Palador insists that this internalized image is his true beloved and the standard by which any pretender must be measured; when his beloved Eroclea later reveals her identity, he rebukes her as a "cunning impostor" and proclaims that "if thou beest / Eroclea, in my bosom I can find thee" (4.3.129–30). Palador's stubbornness typifies the obsessive identification with the lost love object whereby, as Lacan maintains, "what one cannot keep outside, one always keeps an image of inside."[80] Such adherence to the fantasy image and corresponding reluctance to recognize and acknowledge the actual beloved also appears in Shirley's *Love Tricks:* Infortunio, even after being cured of his madness, nonetheless requires nearly an entire act before he will accept that his healer is actually his beloved Selina. The male lover suspects that he is being tricked with the substitution ruse typically worked on the drama's female patients, a suspicion which links the metaphoric and metonymic operations of the theatrical cure.

The male lover's preoccupation with bodily openness, and the risks of feminization which it entails, appears most powerfully in General Memnon of Fletcher's *The Mad Lover* (1616). Falling in love with a princess, the general resembles the female patients noted above by suffering from unrequited love for someone above his social station. His men chide him for not observing the masculine code of enclosure: "How have you borne your selfe, how nakedly / Laid your soul open" (1.1.168–69).[81] Taking literally his beloved's mocking command that he send her his heart, Memnon decides that to win her he "must be incisde first, cut and open'd" (2.1.17). In his efforts to attain an actual woman rather than fixating on a safe fantasy image, Memnon determines to perform a literalized version of the theatrical ruse upon himself, to expel the incorporated object and become a gory limit case of the grotesque open body. He goes so far as to order a surgeon to perform the operation, warning with comic illogic that should the heart be even slightly scratched or defaced in the process he will cut the man's throat. While Lacan points to the pound of flesh in *The Merchant of Venice* as a paradigmatic instance of the *objet a,* here Memnon in his theatricalized sleight-of-hand with his own internal object becomes an overdetermined combination of Shylock, Antonio, and Portia all in one, simultaneously assuming the roles of implacable butcher, sacrificial victim, and hair-splitting arbiter. Attempting to utilize Memnon's self-destructive openness as a cure, his companions present him with a prostitute disguised as the princess, employing the substitution ruse commonly applied to male patients in the medical tradition but more often associated with the open female body in the drama. Memnon, however, sees through the ploy and is dissuaded from his intent only by a final ruse in which his brother, a rival for the princess's affection, feigns suicide. Only when Memnon sees his own gesture of suicidal externalization itself externalized in another does he relinquish his impossible desire.

Through these various scenarios, the theatrical ruse of Jacobean drama both delineates and problematizes oppositional constructions of male and female desire. While the female lovers of these plays long for what Kristeva terms the "metonymic object of desire," the male lovers fixate on the "metaphorical object of love," associated with "fantasy" and "the poeticalness of the discourse of love."[82] Such metaphoric "love," exemplified in Petrarchan idealization, actually requires a failure of attainment. In more specifically psychoanalytic terms, the desire of the mad female lover hinges on what Jean Laplanche terms a "metonymization of the object," in which the woman is constructed as emotionally and bodily open to potentially endless displacements of the object of desire, while the mad male lover demonstrates a "metaphorization of the aim," characterized by "fantasmatic incorporation and introjection," in which the love object remains unchanged but satisfaction is shifted from actual attainment to the isolated, enclosed realm of fantasy.[83] The transferential dynamic of the theatrical cure, however, underscores the ambivalence of these constructions. MacCannell maintains that "the work of the transference is to revalue the *objet petit a* no longer as abject, fallen, a sign of separation and splitting, but as a new kind of connexivity," suggesting a progression from an enclosed separation (metaphor) to an open connection (metonymy).[84] Similarly, the transferential ruse of Jacobean drama overcomes masculine enclosure and what Frank Whigham calls metaphor's "solipsistic circle," even as it utilizes a supposed feminine openness through the "linear linkage" of metonymy.[85] But the melancholic self-absorption of the male lovers suggests that the final recognition and acceptance of the beloved represents no more than yet another transference in the search for the irrevocably lost and hence endlessly displaced object of desire. The female lovers, on the other hand, must negotiate a treacherous path between a compliance which subjects them to a regulating and exploiting authority and a resistance which only further ensconces them within a cultural ideal of feminine silence and chastity.

Notes

1. All quotations from Shakespeare are from *The Riverside Shakespeare,* 2d ed., ed. G. Blakemore Evans (Boston: Houghton Mifflin, 1997).

2. Michel Foucault, *Madness and Civilization: A History of Insanity in the Age of Reason,* trans. Richard Howard (New York: Vintage, 1988), 187–91.

3. Lawrence Babb, *The Elizabethan Malady: A Study of Melancholia in English Literature from 1580 to 1642* (East Lansing: Michigan State University Press, 1951).

4. Winfried Schleiner, *Melancholy, Genius, and Utopia in the Renaissance* (Wiesbaden: Otto Harrassowitz, 1991), 274–309. An earlier and more readily available version of Schleiner's discussion is found in "Prospero as a Renaissance Therapist," *Literature and Medicine* 6 (1987): 54–60.

5. Donald A. Beecher, "Antiochus and Stratonice: The Heritage of a Medico-Literary

Motif in the Theatre of the English Renaissance," *Seventeenth Century* 5, no. 2 (1990): 118–20. For additional historical background on the coital cure, see Jacques Ferrand, *A Treatise on Lovesickness,* ed. Donald A. Beecher and Massimo Ciavolella (Syracuse, N.Y.: Syracuse University Press, 1990), 563–64, n. 10.

6. Foucault, *Madness and Civilization,* 187.

7. Schleiner, *Melancholy, Genius, and Utopia in the Renaissance,* 287.

8. Beecher, "Antiochus," 128, 122; Sigmund Freud, "Fragment of an Analysis of a Case of Hysteria," in *The Standard Edition of the Complete Psychological Works of Sigmund Freud,* trans. and ed. James Strachey, 24 vols. (London: Hogarth Press, 1953–73), 7:116.

9. Freud points out that "psycho-analytic treatment does not *create* transferences, it merely brings them to light" ("Fragment of an Analysis," *Standard Edition,* 7:117); and Lacan similarly maintains that "there may be, properly speaking, transference effects that may be structured exactly like the gamut of transference phenomena in analysis" (*The Four Fundamental Concepts of Psycho-Analysis,* trans. Alan Sheridan, ed. Jacques-Alain Miller [New York: Norton, 1981], 125).

10. Jacques Lacan, "Introduction to the Names-of-the-Father Seminar," trans. Jeffrey Mehlman, *October* 40 (1987): 95.

11. Foucault, *Madness and Civilization,* 189; Slavoj Žižek, *The Sublime Object of Ideology* (London: Verso, 1989), 59.

12. In this approach I am indebted to the work of Valerie Traub and Gail Kern Paster, who in their criticism of Renaissance drama have persuasively argued for a parallel between Lacanian psychoanalytic theory and Bakhtin's historical model of "classical" and "grotesque" bodies (Valerie Traub, *Desire and Anxiety: Circulations of Sexuality in Shakespearean Drama* [London: Routledge, 1992], 50–52; and Gail Kern Paster, *The Body Embarrassed: Drama and the Disciplines of Shame in Early Modern England* [Ithaca: Cornell University Press, 1993], 17–19). See also Peter Stallybrass and Allon White on the theoretical validity of attempts "to synthesize the Bakhtinian opposition between the classical and grotesque body with the Lacanian terms of the symbolic and the Imaginary" (*The Politics and Poetics of Transgression* [London: Methuen, 1986], 175).

13. Babb, *Elizabethan Malady,* 191–92.

14. The specific Renaissance treatises and editions cited below include Levinus Lemnius, *The Touchstone of Complexions,* trans. Thomas Newton (London, 1581); Reginald Scot, *The Discoverie of Witchcraft* (London, 1584); Andre Du Laurens, *A Discourse of the Preservation of the Sight: of Melancholike Diseases; of Rheumes, and of Old Age,* trans. Richard Surphlet (Oxford, 1599); Tomasso Garzoni, *The Hospitall of Incurable Fooles,* trans. E. Blount (London, 1600); Edward Jorden, *A Briefe Discourse of a Disease Called the Suffocation of the Mother* (London, 1603); Simon Goulart, *Admirable and Memorable Histories Containing the Wonders of Our Time,* trans. Ed. Grimeston (London, 1607); Thomas Walkington, *The Opticke Glasse of Humors. Wherein the Foure Complections are Succinctly Painted Forth* (London, 1607); William Vaughan, *Approved Directions for Health* (London, 1612); Thomas Milles, *The Treasurie of Aunciant and Moderne Times* (London, 1613); and Robert Burton, *The Anat-*

omy of Melancholy (Oxford, 1621). For additional continental sources see Schleiner, *Melancholy, Genius, and Utopia in the Renaissance*, 277–80 and 287–88.

15. Burton, *Anatomy*, 234.

16. Milles, *Treasurie*, 478–79; Du Laurens, *Discourse*, 102.

17. The fear of losing one's head is mentioned in Burton, *Anatomy*, 233. The story of the man without a head appears in Du Laurens, *Discourse*, 101; Milles, *Treasurie*, 477; Burton, *Anatomy*, 371; Goulart, *Histories*, 372; and Walkington, *Glasse*, 69v–70r. The man who was nothing but head appears in Garzoni, *Hospitall*, 17.

18. Sigmund Freud, "Mourning and Melancholia," *Standard Edition*, 14:253; "The 'Uncanny,'" *Standard Edition*, 17:244.

19. Jacques Lacan, "Aggressivity in Psychoanalysis," in *Écrits: A Selection*, trans. Alan Sheridan (New York: Norton, 1977), 11.

20. Du Laurens, *Discourse*, 101–3; Scot, *Discoverie*, 53; Goulart, *Histories*, 370, 372, 375; Walkington, *Glasse*, 69v, 71v–72r; Lemnius, *Complexions*, 151r–151v.

21. Garzoni, *Hospitall*, 18; Walkington, *Glasse*, 70r, 70v; Du Laurens, *Discourse*, 103.

22. Jacques Lacan, *The Seminar of Jacques Lacan: Book II: The Ego in Freud's Theory and in the Technique of Psychoanalysis 1954–1955*, trans. Sylvana Tomaselli, ed. Jacques Alain-Miller (New York: Norton, 1988), 178.

23. The men who would not drink appear in Goulart, *Histories*, 394–98. The frequently told story of the "dead" man appears in Lemnius, *Complexions*, 151v–152r; Walkington, *Glasse*, 71r; Du Laurens, *Discourse*, 102; Milles, *Treasurie*, 477–78; Burton, *Anatomy*, 371; Goulart, *Histories*, 371, 372, 373–74. The man who believed he was a god appears in Walkington, *Glasse*, 71r.

24. Men who urinate at the sound of music appear in Walkington, *Glasse*, 70. The man who refuses to urinate appears in Du Laurens, *Discourse*, 103; Walkington, *Glasse*, 72r–72v; Burton, *Anatomy*, 371. Men with live creatures in their stomachs appear in Lemnius, *Complexions*, 151r; Goulart, *Histories*, 375.

25. Lacan discusses the melancholic incorporation of the *objet petit a* in "Desire and the Interpretation of Desire in *Hamlet*," trans. James Hulbert, in *Literature and Psychoanalysis: The Question of Reading: Otherwise*, ed. Shoshana Felman, *Yale French Studies* 55/56 (1977): 11–52. His most succinct account of the *objet a* in relation to the body's orifices appears in "The Subversion of the Subject and the Dialectic of Desire in the Freudian Unconscious," *Écrits*, 314–15.

26. Mikhail Bakhtin, *Rabelais and His World*, trans. Hélène Iswolsky (Bloomington: Indiana University Press, 1984), 26.

27. Ibid., 29. For the centrality of the body's orifices in both psychoanalytic and social terms within the context of Jacobean drama, see Peter Stallybrass, "Reading the Body: *The Revenger's Tragedy* and the Jacobean Theater of Consumption," *Renaissance Drama* 18 (1987): 137.

28. Sigmund Freud, "Mourning and Melancholia," *Collected Papers*, trans. Joan Riviere, 5 vols. (New York: Basic Books, 1959), 4:159. This translation substitutes "transference"

for the "displacement" of the *Standard Edition*. For the etymological and conceptual links between the two terms in Freudian theory, see Cynthia Chase, "'Transference' as Trope and Persuasion," in *Discourse in Psychoanalysis and Literature,* ed. Shlomith Rimmon-Kenan (London: Methuen, 1987), 217.

29. Lacan, *Four Fundamental Concepts of Psycho-Analysis,* 143–45, 200, 269.

30. Du Laurens, *Discourse,* 103. See also Walkington, *Glasse,* 72r–72v; Burton, *Anatomy,* 371.

31. Bakhtin, *Rabelais and His World,* 336.

32. Maire Jaanus, "The *Démontage* of the Drive," in *Reading Seminar XI: Lacan's Four Fundamental Concepts of Psychoanalysis,* ed. Richard Feldstein, Bruce Fink, and Maire Jaanus (Albany: State University of New York Press, 1995), 129, 121.

33. Lacan, *Four Fundamental Concepts of Psycho-Analysis,* 143, 187.

34. Judith Butler, *Gender Trouble: Feminism and the Subversion of Identity* (New York: Routledge, 1990), 134.

35. Catherine Clément, *The Lives and Legends of Jacques Lacan,* trans. Arthur Goldhammer (New York: Columbia University Press, 1983), 99; Goulart, *Histories,* 379.

36. Lacan, "Desire and the Interpretation of Desire," 37.

37. Lacan, "Subversion of the Subject," 315.

38. Jonathan Scott Lee, *Jacques Lacan* (Amherst: University of Massachusetts Press, 1991), 145.

39. Du Laurens, *Discourse,* 102.

40. Juliana Schiesari, *The Gendering of Melancholia: Feminism, Psychoanalysis, and the Symbolics of Loss in Renaissance Literature* (Ithaca: Cornell University Press, 1992), 41.

41. Ibid., 12, 10.

42. Hélène Cixous, "Castration or Decapitation," trans. Annette Kuhn, *Signs* 7, no. 1 (1981): 54.

43. Peter Stallybrass, "Patriarchal Territories: The Body Enclosed," in *Rewriting the Renaissance: The Discourses of Sexual Difference in Early Modern Europe,* ed. Margaret W. Ferguson et al. (Chicago: University of Chicago Press, 1986), 126.

44. Stallybrass, "Patriarchal Territories," 135; Katharine Eisaman Maus, "A Womb of His Own: Male Renaissance Poets in the Female Body," in *Sexuality and Gender in Early Modern Europe: Institutions, Texts, Images,* ed. James Grantham Turner (Cambridge: Cambridge University Press, 1993), 274.

45. Thomas Laqueur, *Making Sex: Body and Gender from the Greeks to Freud* (Cambridge, Mass.: Harvard University Press, 1990), 122–25.

46. For female sufferers of this delusion, see Du Laurens, *Discourse,* 101; Jorden, *Discourse,* 24v; and Burton, *Anatomy,* 371. The obstetrics passage from Paré is quoted in Maus, "Womb of His Own," 277.

47. Du Laurens, *Discourse,* 101.

48. Vaughan, *Directions,* 93–94.

49. Goulart, *Histories,* 381–82.

50. Stallybrass, "Patriarchal Territories," 127; Karen Newman, *Fashioning Femininity and*

English Renaissance Drama (Chicago: University of Chicago Press, 1991), 11. For a further consideration of the "metonymic chain" whereby "a woman who leaves her house is a woman who talks is a woman who drinks is a woman who leaks," see Paster, *Body Embarrassed,* 46. On "the centrality of the mouth and the tongue in the topography of the staged body," see Stallybrass, "Reading the Body," 122.

51. Sarah Kofman, *The Enigma of Woman: Woman in Freud's Writings,* trans. Catherine Porter (Ithaca: Cornell University Press, 1985), 48.

52. Freud, "Fragment of an Analysis," *Standard Edition,* 7:67.

53. Ibid., 74.

54. Sigmund Freud, "The Taboo of Virginity," *Standard Edition,* 11:191–208. Freud's claim that a husband is never more than a "substitute" for the bride's father situates marriage as an already inherently transferential situation only further exploited by the wedding-night substitution.

55. Sigmund Freud, *The Interpretation of Dreams, Standard Edition,* 4:111.

56. Kofman, *Enigma of Woman,* 48.

57. Cixous, "Castration or Decapitation," 55.

58. Bakhtin, *Rabelais and His World,* 317; Lacan, *Seminar: Book II,* 164.

59. Milles, *Treasurie,* 478.

60. For a historical account of the medical tradition's increasing attention to female lovesickness from the medieval period to the Renaissance, see Mary Frances Wack, *Lovesickness in the Middle Ages: The "Viaticum" and Its Commentaries* (Philadelphia: University of Pennsylvania Press, 1990), 109–25.

61. Carol Thomas Neely, "The Cultural Re-gendering of Madness in Early Modern England: The History of Case Histories and the Jailor's Daughter's Cure" (paper presented at the seminar on Shakespeare and the Arts of Healing, annual meeting of the Shakespeare Association of America, Atlanta, Apr. 1993).

62. Julia Kristeva, *Tales of Love,* trans. Leon S. Roudiez (New York: Columbia University Press, 1987), 13.

63. All quotations from *The Northern Lasse* are from Richard Brome, *A Critical Edition of Brome's "The Northern Lasse,"* ed. Harvey Freid (New York: Garland, 1980).

64. All quotations from John Fletcher, *The Noble Gentleman* are from vol. 3 of *The Dramatic Works in the Beaumont and Fletcher Canon,* ed. Fredson Bowers (Cambridge: Cambridge University Press, 1966–89).

65. Chase, "'Transference' as Trope and Persuasion," 218.

66. Jacques Lacan, "Agency of the Letter," *Écrits,* 170.

67. Juliet Flower MacCannell, *Figuring Lacan: Criticism and the Cultural Unconscious* (London: Croom Helm, 1986), 94.

68. Ibid., 100. On the gendering of metaphor and metonymy, see also Jane Gallop, *Reading Lacan* (Ithaca: Cornell University Press, 1985).

69. Julia Kristeva, *Desire in Language: A Semiotic Approach to Literature and Art,* trans. Thomas Gora, Alice Jardine, and Leon S. Roudiez, ed. Leon S. Roudiez (New York: Columbia University Press, 1980), 78.

70. Jean Laplanche, *Life and Death in Psychoanalysis,* trans. Jeffrey Mehlman (Baltimore: Johns Hopkins University Press, 1976), 135; MacCannell, *Figuring Lacan,* 97.

71. Schiesari, *Gendering of Melancholia,* 41. In an essay on alimentary imagery in Jacobean drama, Frank Whigham suggests that the theater's evocation of bodily processes similarly exploits an opposition between the "metonym" of "excessive and improper openness" and the "metaphor" of "inappropriate closing off" ("Reading Social Conflict in the Alimentary Tract: More on the Body in Renaissance Drama," *ELH* 55 [Summer 1988]: 336).

72. Valerie Traub similarly argues that "Shakespearean drama and psychoanalytic theory share in a cultural estimation of the female reproductive body as a Bakhtinian 'grotesque body'" (*Desire and Anxiety,* 51).

73. See Schleiner, *Melancholy, Genius, and Utopia in the Renaissance,* 301–3.

74. Ellie Ragland-Sullivan, *Jacques Lacan and the Philosophy of Psychoanalysis* (Urbana: University of Illinois Press, 1986), 250.

75. Lacan, "Agency of the Letter," 158.

76. Lacan, *Four Fundamental Concepts of Psycho-Analysis,* 131.

77. Jacques Lacan, *Feminine Sexuality: Jacques Lacan and the École Freudienne,* trans. Jacqueline Rose, ed. Juliet Mitchell and Jacqueline Rose (New York: Norton, 1982), 157.

78. Lacan, *Four Fundamental Concepts of Psycho-Analysis,* 268.

79. All quotations from John Ford are from John Ford, *The Lover's Melancholy,* ed. R. F. Hill (Manchester: Manchester University Press, 1985).

80. Lacan, *Four Fundamental Concepts of Psycho-Analysis,* 243.

81. All quotations from John Fletcher's *The Mad Lover* are from vol. 5 of *The Dramatic Works in the Beaumont and Fletcher Canon.*

82. Kristeva, *Tales of Love,* 30.

83. Laplanche, *Life and Death in Psychoanalysis,* 137.

84. MacCannell, *Figuring Lacan,* 168.

85. Whigham, "Reading Social Conflict," 336.

3

Transmigrations: Crossing Regional and Gender Boundaries in *Antony and Cleopatra*

Mary Floyd-Wilson

Much of the critical commentary on Shakespeare's *Antony and Cleopatra* sees a parallel between the perceived "masculinity" and "femininity" of its title characters and the dialectical opposition of Rome and Egypt.[1] While an earlier generation of criticism has suggested that Cleopatra and Antony embody universal gender roles, adumbrating a world-stage polarity of a feminine East versus a masculine West, feminist and postcolonial critics have argued that the play presents the instability of gender binaries and the West's construction of itself and the "Orient."[2] Regardless of the theoretical perspective, it is widely accepted that there are direct correspondences between geography and gender in *Antony and Cleopatra;* Cleopatra, in particular, is perceived to be "one with her feminized kingdom as though it were her body."[3] In a subtle reading of Antony's dissolution and Cleopatra's regenerative powers, Janet Adelman cites the play's "affiliation of 'masculine' Rome with the solid and bounded, 'feminine' Egypt with the fluid"; according to "the Roman point of view, the melting of the boundaries of the self is necessarily its effeminization, its pull back toward that matrix."[4] Gail Kern Paster has expanded our understanding of early modern gender distinctions by locating the "boundaries of the self" within the historicized specificities of humoral discourse and the hierarchy of Mikhail Bakhtin's bodily canons. For the most part, woman is conceived to be "naturally grotesque—which is to say, open, permeable, effluent, leaky. Man is naturally whole, closed, opaque, self-contained"; moreover, within this paradigm the "male body ... can assume the shameful attributes of the incontinent female body."[5] In obvious ways, Paster's work provides further support for reading Cleopatra as quintessentially female and "as abundant, leaky, and changeable as the Nile."[6]

However, early seventeenth-century natural philosophy also suggests that varying degrees of a body's internal liquidity and temperature determine what modern readers would classify as "racial" characteristics.[7] Renaissance climate theory avers that a region's atmospheric temperature, moisture level, soil, and topography help fix an inhabitant's humoral complexion, coloration, and temperament.[8] Consider, for example, *Titus Andronicus,* which associates Aaron the Moor's complexion and "fleece of woolly hair" with his native climate and "cloudy melancholy" (2.3.34, 33).[9] Popular accounts of climate theory establish that parallel physiological processes take place in northern, southern, and temperate regions;[10] the heat of the sun not only darkens the skin of the Egyptians but also dries the body's humors; conversely, cold northern air seals up the body's moisture, producing white skin and "gross," thick humors. Further complicating these distinctions in early modern texts is an inherited contradiction within classical climatic discourse itself. The Aristotelian tradition holds that external temperature has a counteractive effect on the body. Hot climates draw out internal heat, producing cold complexions, while the inverse takes place in the north. The Hippocratic theory maintains a correspondent relation between external temperatures and the body; cold climates, for example, produce cold complexions.[11] What remains stable throughout the discourse is the distribution of moisture: hot regions dry the body's humors, while cold climes preserve internal moisture. Since it is derived from Mediterranean sources, classical humoral discourse presupposes a temperate climate, and climate theory explicitly locates temperance in the middle regions. Yet even within temperate regions, certain "differences of style of life, climate and diet" produce puzzling questions about the body, such as whether the "hottest female is colder than the coldest male."[12] Once translated to less temperate regions, conflicts in the discourse are exacerbated. Just as distinctions in rank intersect with and confound the body's boundaries (the lower orders proving "leakier" than chaste ladies, for example), extreme climates further disrupt gender categories.

In fact, climate theory draws on and complicates the schematic opposition between the spirit and the flesh implicit in the antithesis of the classical male body and the grotesque female body.[13] Since extreme cold and heat produce disparate effects, it is widely held in early modern climatic discourse that the "body and the mind are swayed in opposite directions," so that "southerners excel in intellect, [and northerners] in body."[14] Northerners "have a greater abundance of blood and humor [and] with more difficulty separate themselves from these earthly dregs," while the southerners' relatively dry complexion gives them an unearthly "power of contemplation, . . . meditation," and wisdom.[15] Moreover, the gendered connotations of these differences are commingled. The powerful spirit of the south proves masculine in its strength, yet feminine in its subtlety, while the northern flesh is feminine in its excess, yet masculine in its strength. In general terms, only the middle regions readily produce temperate *men,* balanced in mind and body, while the extreme northern and southern climates generate intemperance, which translates easily to effeminacy.

Not only does most early modern climate theory assume a tripartite structure, it also identifies England as a septentrional nation.[16] And not surprisingly, there is some anxiety regarding climate theory in the discourse itself, stemming in part from an inability to reconcile regional determinations of a body's solidity and fluidity with accepted gender distinctions. On a local level, Englishmen are distinguished from Englishwomen as the dryer and more self-contained sex, with the supposition that "men have marble, [and] women waxen minds,"[17] but on the world stage the English find themselves characterized as soft-fleshed, inconstant, and permeable as the result of a northern climate which produces excessively moist complexions. As northern and southern regions, marginalized from the temperate zone, England and Egypt actually share a certain peripheral status. While *Antony and Cleopatra*'s construction of Egyptian and Roman identities and values depends explicitly on an East/West binary, it has been taken for granted that Jacobean England would "see Cleopatra [and Egypt] through *Western* eyes."[18] Certainly early modern Britain's perspective on Cleopatra entails a complex identification with western, masculine Rome.[19] And Jacobean nationalism is informed by Britain's invocation of mythological Roman origins, which subsumed the paradigm of a westward movement of empire.[20] Implicitly underscoring the East/West binary, Leonard Tennenhouse has argued that Cleopatra "embodies everything that is not English according to . . . British nationalism,"[21] but I would contend that England's opposition to Egypt could disrupt as well as secure its western, masculine perspective. In fact, as a northern nation, England's latitudinal relationship to southern Egypt and temperate Rome upsets the purportedly archetypal binaries of East/West, Female/Male.

It is not coincidental that *Antony and Cleopatra* focuses consistently on regional differences *and* the instability of gender roles. Antony's melting effeminacy is attributable not only to his lovesick "dotage" but also to the influence of the Egyptian climate on his relatively "northern" body. Contrasted sharply with Antony's leaky vulnerability and unguarded passions is the opaque surface of Cleopatra's body. Although both characters possess passionate temperaments, we can easily discern Antony's vacillating allegiances; yet we are never certain of the sincerity or depth of Cleopatra's affections. In significant ways, Cleopatra's climatically determined "racial" status challenges the northern construction of gender differences;[22] as a woman, her complexion should be soft and impressionable, but as an Egyptian she proves elusive and resistant to interpretation. The paradox of Cleopatra's ambiguous allure is not only that she represents the threatening excesses of Egyptian effeminacy, particularly exemplified by her seeming deceptions, but that those same qualities, if appropriated, would help remedy northern deficiencies.

Both Antony and Cleopatra derive their greatness (and their ruin) from their particular excesses; while the "vilest things / Become themselves" in Cleopatra (2.2.239–40), Antony's "faults, in him, seem as the spots of heaven" (1.4.12). However, their excesses move in opposing directions; to a certain extent Cleopatra's strengths are represented as transcending the body, while Antony's best qualities remain rooted in his corporeality. Explicitly identified as "hereditary / Rather than purchased," Antony's natural complexion inclines him toward a kind of fleshly bounty or surfeit, a virtue or vice, depending on one's perspective (1.4.13–14).[23] Arguably, Antony is more "northern" than Roman in his constitution; in fact, Jean Bodin cites Marc Antony's reputed fleshiness as analogous to the northerner's "heavy" body, and certainly his demise in Shakespeare's play recalls the commonplace notion that northern bodies are predisposed to melt in southern climates.[24] Paradoxically, Antony's greatest weakness also marks him as exceptional; in Cleopatra's vision, his internal bounty raises him above the elements in which he lives. By rejecting Roman restraint in favor of Antony's liberal excesses, the play seems to rewrite "heroic masculinity" in northern terms.[25]

Rather than equating Cleopatra's body with the Nile, we need to consider how the invocation of climate theory establishes a more complex relationship between the queen's complexion and Egypt. In climatic-humoral terms, Cleopatra's blackness and elusiveness are the natural effects of her environment: "Think on me, / That am with Phoebus' amorous pinches black" (1.5.27–28). And in various ways, these qualities make her motives inaccessible both to Shakespeare's Romans and Jacobean England. Yet the play's sly metadrama and anachronistic references to gypsies may have reminded Shakespeare's audience that Egypt is a world that is irrevocably lost. And while the mysteries of Egypt remain impenetrable, Cleopatra's characteristic subtlety, whether "infinite variety" or "cunning," becomes a quality that can "transmigrate" over time and place. Cleopatra's mystery can never be unraveled, yet the play suggests that it can be appropriated and represented through artifice and performance.[26] While northern virtues prove inherent and inimitable, the southerner's natural gifts metamorphose into qualities that can be acquired and enacted.

In ascribing particular characteristics to the peoples of various climates, Renaissance authors drew on a long history of classical geography which contrasted wise Egyptians with barbaric Scythians in the descriptions of remote borders beyond the ideal temperate zone.²⁷ Furthermore, as Karl Dannenfeldt suggests, the "revival of Platonism and Neoplatonism in the Renaissance enhanced the role of Egypt as the original land of theologians and philosophers."²⁸ Egypt's warm climate plays a crucial, yet rarely acknowledged, role in its history as a land associated with the origins of wisdom. The Hermetic texts, which Marsilio Ficino translated and which helped form the basis of his Neoplatonist philosophy, explain that "Egyptians are particularly favored.... In *Stobaeus* XXIV, II, Horus asks his mother Isis, 'By what cause, Mother, do men who live outside our most holy place lack our quickness of apprehension?'" Indeed, *Stobaeus* establishes that as a result of planetary aspects and a favorable climate, Egyptians are "exceptionally intelligent and wise."²⁹

While modern scholars readily concede that Renaissance authors traced the origins of sagacity to Egypt, few have explored the corresponding links they made between black bile, black skin, and wisdom.³⁰ Yet the interrelatedness of climate theory and humoralism makes these links quite apparent. Bodin not only assigns the origins of "blackness" to the concoction of humors by environmental heat but also notes that "the southern people, through continued zeal for contemplation, befitting black bile, have been promoters and leaders of the highest learning."³¹ Juan Huarte, in *The Examination of Men's Wits* (1594), sees direct correspondences between the Egyptian climate, coloration, and wit: the "Aegyptians . . . haue not forlorne that their delicacie of wit and promptnesse, nor yet that rosted colour which their auncestors brought with them from Aegypt."³² In the early modern period, their characteristically dry complexion links the southerners' blackness to wisdom. According to Huarte, "in this region [Egypt], the sunne yeeldeth a feruent heat: and therfore the inhabitants haue their brain dried, and choler adust, . . . the much heat of the countrey rosteth the substance of these members and wrieth them, as it draweth togither a peece of leather set by the fire; and for the same cause, their haire curleth, and themselves also are wily."³³ Hence, the Egyptian climate not only darkens the skin but also produces a natural wisdom or cunning. Given the ambiguous status of Cleopatra's coloration in the classical sources, it seems likely that the conspicuous blackness of Shakespeare's queen is intended to invoke both the myth of Egypt and the climatic-humoral discourse that underscores that myth.

Traditionally set in opposition to the ancient Egyptians are the northern Scythians, whose hearty bodies, inactive minds, and pale skin are attributed to their cold environment. In "Air, Waters, and Places," the earliest Greek tract to establish a connection between region and humoral physiology, Hippocrates sees a direct correspondence between the Scythians' fleshy bodies and sluggish temperaments, and their climatic conditions. This northern race has "ruddy complexions on account of the cold, for the sun does not burn fiercely there. But the cold causes their fair skins to be burnt and reddened."[34] In addition, "The body cannot become hardened where there are such small variations in climate; the mind, too, becomes sluggish . . . their bodies are heavy and fleshy, . . . they are watery and relaxed. The cavities of their bodies are extremely moist, . . . under such climatic conditions, the bowels cannot be dry."[35] Significantly, the softness of their flesh blurs physical distinctions between Scythian men and women: "All the men are fat and hairless and likewise all the women, and the two sexes resemble one another."[36] Hippocrates concludes that as a result of their excessively moist complexion, these northerners are the "most effeminate race of all mankind."[37] As "Scythian" becomes shorthand for "northern" in the early modern period, the English find themselves commonly bracketed with the Scythians in continental texts.[38]

As modern scholars have noted, Renaissance physiology readily links soft complexions, mental sluggishness, and effeminacy. Huarte, for example, draws on Aristotle, Hippocrates, and others to argue that while the supposedly tender flesh of women denotes excess moisture, those men whose predominant humors are phlegm and blood also possess tender flesh and prove "simple & dullards."[39] Huarte applies this same rubric of humoral differences geographically, associating closed, dry bodies with southern regions while characterizing northerners as fleshy, moist, and slow: "the Flemmish, Dutch, English, and French, . . . their wits are like those of drunkards: . . . & this is occasioned by the much moisture, wherwith their brain is replenished, and the other parts of the bodie: the which is knowen by the whitenesse of the face . . . and aboue this they are generally great, and of tall stature, through the much moisture, which breedeth encrease of flesh."[40]

For a positive portrait of northern attributes, early modern writers turn to Tacitus, who describes the Saxons as morally superior to the degenerate Romans.[41] Citing the influence of a cold climate, Tacitus observes the ancient Germans' penchant for drinking and carousing: "[n]o nation indulges more freely in feasting and entertaining than the German."[42] The Germans' excesses, however, serve to fortify their virtues—they are generous and bounteous to others, counting it "a sin to turn any man away from [their] door."[43] Moreover, their liberal-hearted natures make Germans incapable of cunning or political craft, for they are barely "sophisticated enough to refrain from blurting out their inmost thoughts . . . every man's soul is laid completely bare"; their hearts are "open to sincere feelings or . . . quick to warm to noble sentiments."[44] In the late sixteenth century, Fynes Moryson insists that "the Nature of the English is very singular aboue other Nations in liberality and bounty . . . if it be not rather prodegality or folly."[45] It is during the early seventeenth century that English writers begin to push the "question of a common ancestry" with the Germans, striving to see themselves in Tacitus's laudatory commentary.[46]

Despite the positive slant which Tacitus provides, the early modern English continue to struggle with the perceived disadvantages of their northern complexion. A treatise published in England in 1591 urges northerners to purge the "grosse humour ingendred in them, by reason of the grossnes, and coldnes of the aier wherin they live."[47] And as late as 1649 John Milton expresses anxiety concerning the "natural political deficiencies" that the English climate produces, and urges his countrymen to temper their northern excesses by "import[ing] civil virtues from the 'best ages' and those situated in more favorable climates."[48] Thomas Wright's *The Passions of the Mind in General* (1604) directly addresses the presumed correspondence between regional complexion and political acumen.[49] Of particular interest to Wright is how a "certain natural complexion and constitution of the body, . . . inclineth and bendeth them of hotter Countries more unto craftiness and warinesse than them of colder Climates" (84). Conceding that "these Northerne Climates are accounted" to produce "simple and unwise" citizens, he notes that Englishmen in particular tend to "reveal and disclose themselves very familiarly and easily" (82, 84). To remedy this weakness, Wright encourages his English readers to learn how to discover other men's passions, as well as how to govern their own. For Wright, skin color in particular signifies and promotes a person's simplicity or subtlety: "The very blushing also of [English] people showeth a better ground whereupon Virtue may build than certain brazen faces, who never change themselves, although they commit, yea, and be deprehended in enormous crimes" (82). Despite this defense of his countrymen's northern complexion, Wright concludes that the English are exceedingly open and vulnerable to foreign interpretation. Urging his nation to "be directed" in presenting a "prudent carriage," he suggests that they adopt a temperate measure of southern wariness (85). As Wright anxiously reveals, Englishmen in the early seventeenth century fear that their natural complexion may predispose them to a passive and effeminate role on the world stage, especially in the play of politics.[50]

Throughout the seventeenth and well into the eighteenth century, climate theory remains a popular and viable explanation for differences in coloration and national disposition. However, as England's involvement in the Atlantic slave trade escalates, natural philosophy begins to shift its focus away from diversity in complexions toward what is increasingly seen as the peculiarity of blackness. One example of this trend in the mid-seventeenth century is a posited link between the origins of blackness and artifice. In *Pseudodoxia Epidemica,* Sir Thomas Browne describes certain "Artificial Negroes, or Gypsies [who] acquire their complexion by anointing their bodies with Bacon and fat substances, and so exposing them to the Sun"; moreover, he suggests that this counterfeit practice might plausibly be the source of all seemingly "natural" black complexions.[51] In *Anthropometamorphosis* (1650) John Bulwer contends that man may have become "black by an advenient and artificial way of denigration, which at first was a meer affectation arising from some conceit they might have of the beauty of blacknesse, and an Apish desire which might move them to change the complexion of their bodies into a new and more fashionable hue. . . . And so from this artifice the *Moores* might possibly become Negroes, receiving atramentitious impression by the power and efficacy of imagination . . . which were continued by Climes, whose constitution advantaged the artificial into a natural impression."[52]

It is significant that both Browne and Bulwer continue to invoke the efficacy of "climes" to maintain color, yet insist on the artificial origins of that color.[53] This deviation in natural philosophy strives to collapse the tripartite framework, which embraces a spectrum of complexions, into a binary of normative white and aberrant black, effectively erasing the association between blackness and natural wisdom.

Well before these natural philosophers traced the origins of blackness to "Apish desire[s]," however, seventeenth-century Englishmen saw the natural vulnerabilities of their complexion inversely reflected in the southerner's darker countenance. In its consideration of geography and complexion, *Antony and Cleopatra* not only typifies the traditional associations of early modern climatic-humoral discourse but also anticipates England's impulse to link southern origins with artifice. Although Cleopatra's complexion is attributed to Egypt's clime, her mystery is recast as theatricality. The play sustains Cleopatra's "infinite variety" by obscuring her "true" motives with endless playing;[54] however, the play's allusion to a non-Egyptian boy actor as the agent of Cleopatra's playing reworks the north's relationship to the south. In this metadramatic moment, the southerner's cunning becomes effeminate artifice, while the northern male is stabilized, slyly revealing his own subtlety.

Antony and Cleopatra's opening scene establishes that from a Roman perspective it is Antony who resembles the Nile, "[o]'erflow[ing] the measure" (1.1.2), a comparison which points up the effect of the Egyptian environment on his body. Traditionally, critics have argued that Cleopatra's presence, Egypt's luxury, and love-sick dotage effeminize the Roman, but it is also true that Antony's relatively northern constitution is especially vulnerable to the southern climate and its excesses. After losing battles and loyal followers, Antony's loss of control is further represented as watery dissolution. Eventually his thoughts grow "indistinct / As water is in water," and the boundaries of his identity seem to melt until he "cannot hold this visible shape" (4.14.10–11, 14).[55]

We soon discover that while Caesar condemns Antony's indulgent ways in Egypt, he readily praises Antony's previous success as a soldier who endured severe environmental conditions. Although Egypt weakens Antony, a more northern climate seems to enhance his natural strengths. In his nostalgic recollection of Antony's mettle, Caesar describes Antony as a soldier, fighting famine

> (Though daintily brought up) with patience more
> Than savages could suffer. Thou didst drink
> The stale of horses and the gilded puddle
> Which beasts would cough at. Thy palate then did deign
> The roughest berry on the rudest hedge.
> Yea, like the stag when snow the pasture sheets,
> The barks of trees thou browsed. On the Alps
> It is reported thou didst eat strange flesh,
> Which some did die to look on. And all this
> . . . .
> Was borne so like a soldier that thy cheek
> So much as lanked not.
>
> (1.4.60–71)

It is no accident that Octavius's memory locates Antony-as-ideal-soldier in a northern environment—a cold region, barren of natural resources apart from the "roughest berry," the "barks of trees," and the presence of strange flesh. According to commonplace Renaissance notions of military science, northern climates produce the fiercest soldiers: they are men who bear cold patiently and wage war easily in the winter.[56] In his commentary on the military prowess of northern nations, Bodin notes that "when hunger comes upon the Scythians, they cut the veins of horses under the ears, suck the blood, and feast on the flesh, as tradition reports about the army of Tamerlane."[57] While Octavius concedes that Antony's Roman background is contrastively "dainty," Antony proves himself to be as hearty and robust as the "savages" apparently acclimated to such conditions. Octavius praises the command Antony wields over his body in the face of such a harsh environment, yet Antony behaves as if he were a native, his bodily strength and military powers seemingly enhanced by the brutal circumstances.[58] Arguably, Antony's fleshiness helps him to survive this harsh environment so well that his "cheek . . . / lanked not." However, when a northerner moves southward, his military strength is challenged: "bring a Scithian from his natiue habitation to the South," writes Bodin, "and you shall find him presently to droop, and fall away with sweat and faintnesse," for "the armies that come out of the North, grow weake and languish, the more they goe towards the South . . . [the more they become] molten with sweat, and languished with heat."[59] Moreover, hot climates will exacerbate the northerner's natural inclination to feasting and drinking.[60]

The abstemious Caesar censures Antony's present voluptuousness, characterizing him as the "abstract of all faults" (1.4.9). Despite Caesar's sweeping criticism, it is clear that Antony's faults are not the sum of all vices, but particularly carnal ones; he possesses an appetite for mirth, drinking, and sport (1.4.4–7, 16–21). As Lepidus notes, Antony's temperament predisposes him to these weaknesses, his faults being "what he cannot change," rather "[t]han what he chooses" (1.4.14–15). While Caesar scoffs at Antony's "composure," which "must be rare indeed / Whom these things cannot blemish," it is the same "rare" composure that earned Caesar's respect in the Alps (22–23). Although the Romans mock Antony's intemperance in Egypt, there is some recognition that a heart that "burst[s] / The buckles on his breast" in the "scuffles of great fights" necessarily "reneges all temper" (1.1.6–8). Antony's excesses mark him as conspicuously un-Roman, yet they also "seem as the spots of heaven" (1.4.12).

Peter Erickson contends that Cleopatra's final dream "endows [Antony] with the quality of 'bounty,'" and that the "image of . . . unending profusion replaces Octavius's preferred version of his [Antony's] heroic deprivation."[61] While it is true that Cleopatra and Caesar recollect Antony differently, Antony's natural characteristics remain constant in both visions; it is his body's interaction with the environment that varies. While Antony's internal plenitude easily counters Caesar's landscape of deprivation, it inevitably surfeits in Cleopatra's fertile Egypt. To attribute Antony's liberality solely to Cleopatra's imagination underestimates the import of Enobarbus's acknowledgment of his master's bounty. As a Roman, Enobarbus feels compelled to leave a master who proves "so leaky" (3.13.63). But when Antony answers this desertion with the return of Enobarbus's treasure, together with his own "bounty overplus" (4.6.22–23), Enobarbus's heart begins to break in the face of such splendid generosity:

> O Antony,
> Thou mine of bounty, how wouldst thou have paid
> My better service, when my turpitude
> Thou dost so crown with gold!
>
> (4.6.31–34)

Although Enobarbus recognizes that by overflowing the measure Antony displays a lack of policy, he concedes that this excess shows a nobility that outstrips more temperate actions.

Rather than simply endowing Antony with bounty, Cleopatra's vision celebrates the possibility of a world defined by Antony's generous rule:

> For his bounty,
> There was no winter in't, an *Anthony* it was
> That grew the more by reaping: his delights
> Were dolphin-like, they showed his back above
> The element they lived in.
>
> (5.2.86–90)[62]

In contrast to Caesar's place-specific recollection, Cleopatra's fancy first locates Antony everywhere and then in water, insisting that his best attributes rise above the "element they lived in." While Caesar imagines that Antony fills a "vacancy with his voluptuousness" (1.4.26), Cleopatra suggests that Antony's bounty flows from his natural constitution and that his defining quality is infinite renewal. Cleopatra's vision of Antony prizes the same attributes that northerners claim as virtues.

While the south's exceptional climate and fertile luxury exaggerate Antony's innate qualities, Cleopatra's complexion is engendered by Egypt. And in contrast to the play's representation of Antony's melting boundaries, the Egyptians' associations with melting and overflow are much more equivocal. Cleopatra most often invokes melting imagery as a curse or threat of destruction, as if willing the Nile to rise at her command. In declaring her devotion to Antony, she swears that if she proves disloyal, her own body will overturn the drying effects of Egypt's climate. Her hypothetical scenario of disaster is predicated on her possessing a cold heart:

> If I be [cold-hearted],
> From my cold heart let heaven engender hail,
> And poison it in the source, and the first stone
> Drop in my neck: as it determines, so
> Dissolve my life!
>
> (3.13.158–62)

As the storm "discandies," all of Cleopatra's progeny and all Egyptians will lie dead and graveless from the melting ice. The discandying that Cleopatra envisions appears to mirror Antony's own dissolving state, with the exception that her melting is an imagined punishment for betrayal, couched in an invocation that preserves her authority. Antony, in contrast, when his followers desert him, associates "discandying" with the ultimate surrender of one's self to another, lamenting that

> The hearts
> That spanieled me at heels, to whom I gave
> Their wishes, do discandy, melt their sweets
> On blossoming Caesar.
>
> (4.12.20–23)

Cleopatra's repeated ties to the serpent of the Nile further define her relationship to the environment. As with the crocodile's impenetrability, Cleopatra's temperament, complexion, and, arguably, her "cunning" are created by the "operation of [the] sun" (2.7.27). In the early modern period, the crocodile is noted for its dry, impervious skin; if Egypt is submerged in water, the opaque boundaries of the scaled serpent's body would certainly remain intact.[63] In response to Lepidus's questioning, Antony describes the crocodile as a creature that is bred by its environment; however, in a mysterious metamorphosis, it seems to transcend that which produces it: "It is shaped, sir, like itself, and it is as broad as it hath breadth; it is just so high as it is, and moves with its own organs. It lives by that which nourisheth it, and the elements once out of it, it transmigrates" (2.7.41–44).[64] The most specific detail Antony offers about the crocodile is that "the tears of it are wet" (2.7.48). Certainly, Antony plays on the proverbial sense that a crocodile's tears signify craft; however, it is not until the late sixteenth and early seventeenth centuries that this idea gains proverbial status.[65] Antony's equivocal statement conveys a less definitive response, suggesting that Roman knowledge proves impotent in the face of natural Egyptian mysteries.

Antony's jesting tone with Lepidus recalls Enobarbus's teasing of him on the interpretation of Cleopatra's tears. As with the crocodile's ambiguous yet patently "wet" teardrops, the mystery of Cleopatra's passions captures a transition in early modern distinctions between the natural and the artificial. While Antony contends that Cleopatra is "cunning past man's thought" (1.2.142), Enobarbus counters him with a playful inversion of the correspondences between microcosm and macrocosm: "her passions are made of nothing but the finest part of pure love. We cannot call her winds and waters sighs and tears: they are greater storms and tempests than almanacs can report. This cannot be cunning in her; if it be, she makes a shower of rain as well as Jove" (1.2.143–48). On one hand, Enobarbus suggests that Antony should simply appreciate the "performance" of Cleopatra's passions. But despite Enobarbus's apparent cynicism, the slipperiness of his statement indicates that we cannot ultimately know whether Cleopatra's affections are dissimulation. Intriguingly enough, contemporary mutations of the word "cunning" duplicate the period's changing perception of southerners. In its original sense, "cunning" denotes a *natural* ability or capacity for learning and wisdom, as in a predisposition determined by one's natural complexion; according to the OED it is not until 1583 that the word comes to mean craft, deceit, or a disposition to artifice. Although Antony observes that "every passion fully strives / To make itself, in [Cleopatra], fair and admired" (1.1.50–51), we remain unsure as to whether Cleopatra filters her emotions through an awareness of audience, or whether her "passions" possess an agency that defies Roman notions of true and false expression.

Although Enobarbus conveys some ambivalence in his response to Cleopatra's sighs and tears, he customarily views weeping as policy or effeminacy. When Agrippa remarks that Antony purportedly wept at Julius Caesar's and Brutus's slayings, Enobarbus intervenes with his version of events: "That year indeed he was troubled with a rheum. / What willingly he did confound, he wailed. / Believe't, till I weep too" (3.2.57–59).[66] Enobarbus does not simply cast doubt on the rumor that Antony wept; he undercuts any possible emotional tenor that those alleged tears may convey. For Enobarbus, weeping is a loss of manhood ("Transform us not into women" [4.2.36]), and artifice itself ("I am onion-eyed" [35]). In conspicuous contrast to Enobarbus's Roman thoughts, Antony sees a regenerative bounty in weeping: "Grace grow where those drops fall" (4.2.38). Antony's sentiments anticipate a Christian view of transformation, and, advantageously for the north, they imply that those who are prone to melt with heartfelt tears are especially open to grace. From a Roman perspective, Antony's bounty and overflow of tears mark him as effeminate, yet a revisionist, northern view would recast these qualities as masculine virtues.

As the boundaries of Antony's body melt, the play suggests that Cleopatra's complexion has changed over time. In her "salad days" she was both "green in judgment, [and] cold in blood" (1.5.73–74), but as she has aged, she seems to have grown dryer and hotter.[67] As a description of the young Cleopatra's humoral complexion, this verdant imagery connotes a typically effeminate impressionability. While she was colder and moister, Cleopatra, it seems, played a more passive role in her liaisons: with Caesar, she was "a morsel for a monarch," while Pompey could "make his eyes grow in [her] brow; / . . . anchor[ing] his aspect" there (1.5.31–33).[68] If we believe her claim that she has changed, then it would appear that Cleopatra has grown less impressionable, in humoral terms, and, according to northern constructions, less "feminine."

Jonathan Harris observes that "[f]or all of Cleopatra's undeniable corporeality, her body has an odd habit of disappearing altogether at precisely those moments when it seems most overwhelmingly present."[69] The incorporeal aspect of Cleopatra's allure is connected to her "racial alterity"[70] and to the complex interaction between her body and the elements. When Cleopatra describes her body plainly in climatological terms—"Think on me, / That am with Phoebus's amorous pinches black / And wrinkled deep in time" (1.5.27–29)—she alludes to the drying effect of the sun's heat on the body's humors.[71] Commenting on the paradox of Cleopatra's age, Adelman notes that she is associated "with an antiquity outside the range of time altogether, certainly outside the range of Caesar's time."[72] Cleopatra's ageless antiquity has its basis in contemporary climatic discourse, which classifies southerners as descendants of the oldest civilizations and correlates their natural qualities with those of the elderly.[73] Within the framework of climatic discourse, northerners resemble fleshy youths, and middle climates produce temperate men at their fittest, while southerners are analogous with the old—their bodies are weak and dry, but their minds possess sublime wisdom. At the same time, dry complexions prove less vulnerable to decay or physical change. In *The Masque of Blackness*, Ben Jonson contends that neither "cares, [nor] age can change" the Ethiopians' complexion—"Death her self . . . / Can never alter their most faithful hue."[74] In a similar vein, Enobarbus captures the timeless quality of Cleopatra's appearance: "Age cannot wither her" (2.2.236). Cleopatra's complexion represents the antiquity of Egypt and its impenetrable mysteries.

Not only is Cleopatra's "corporeality" quite ambiguous; she also seems to resist the customary correlations made between the female and flesh.[75] Her curious appeal is often presented in vaporous terms; she does not "cloy" or surfeit the appetite like "other women" (2.2.237, 238). Indeed, the material connotation of "cloying" suggests a weighing-down of the flesh typically associated with the grotesque body; contemporary usage of the term indicates that a soul may be cloyed by the "heavy bondage of the flesh" (OED). Instead Cleopatra seems to lack a real substance, "mak[ing] hungry / Where most she satisfies" (2.2.238–39). Agrippa's exclamation of "Rare Egyptian!" (219) in response to Enobarbus's famed report of the queen whose "own person, / . . . beggared all description" (2.2.198–99) catches her exceptional status, while also implying that she may be as subtle as the air that "[h]ad gone to gaze" on her (218). ("Rare" can imply the subtlety of one's temperament or constitution, as in Caesar's ironic use of the word in reference to Antony's indulgent ways.)

In the play's closing scenes Cleopatra repeatedly rejects any ties to gross corporeality. To be commanded by "poor passion" is equivalent in her mind to being "the maid that milks / And does the meanest chares" (4.15.77–78); in its associations with a loss of control, maternity, fluidity, and the lower orders, this image of the milkmaid represents the grotesque body that Cleopatra renounces.[76] Traditionally critics have stressed Cleopatra's identification with the milkmaid, a reading corroborated by the standard emendation to this line: it is established practice for editors of the play to substitute "No more but e'en a woman, and commanded / By such poor passion as the maid that milks" for the Folio's "No more but in a woman."[77] The change may appear inconsequential, yet if considered precisely, the Folio implies Cleopatra's critical detachment from the blubbering milkmaid. In the moment following Antony's death, Cleopatra acknowledges her grief only by critiquing it. She condemns "poor passion" and in the next breath seeks resolution. When expressing her dread of being staged in Rome, she seems most repulsed by the coarse physicality of the Roman people:

> mechanic slaves
> With greasy aprons, rules, and hammers shall
> Uplift us to the view. In their thick breaths,
> Rank of gross diet, shall we be enclouded,
> And forced to drink their vapor.
>
> (5.2.209–13)

As she prepares for her suicide, she separates herself further from "earthly dregs" while relegating the Romans to the mundane. The circularity of physical life and the materiality of the feminine are equated in Cleopatra's picture of Caesar, who, like the lowest beggar, is nursed by "dung" (5.2.7–8). Whether one interprets the text as "dug" or "dung," either sense preserves Cleopatra's renunciation of physicality, while likening Caesar to the body held captive by fleshly needs. Embracing death, she claims to "have nothing / Of woman in [her]"; she is "marble-constant" (5.2.238–40). As with the crocodile, Cleopatra's regional identity predisposes her to this transformation: she becomes "fire, and air," giving her "other elements . . . / to baser life" (5.2.288–89).

Although often interpreted as evidence of her leaky body, Cleopatra's death is an ironic reversal of maternal imagery; she does place herself in the role of the nurse, and the asp becomes the "baby at [her] breast" (5.2.308), but rather than nourishing this baby, she is feeding herself "[w]ith most delicious poison" (1.5.27). Cleopatra's death is the direct antithesis of Antony's messy demise.[78] Antony literally grows heavier while he is dying, and at the moment of his death Cleopatra laments, the "crown o' th' earth doth melt" (4.15.63). In contrast, Cleopatra's corpse shows neither "external swelling" nor blood; as Caesar observes, "she looks like sleep, / As she would catch another Antony / In her strong toil of grace" (5.2.344–46). Even in death her body maintains its opacity.

Neither the Romans nor the play's audience ascertain the truth of Cleopatra's loyalties. Although we have certain evidence of her manipulations and endless playing, we never gain absolute proof of betrayal. When politic Caesar attempts to read the queen, it is Cleopatra who triumphs, leaving "great Caesar [an] ass / Unpolicied" (5.2.306–7). When Caesar and Cleopatra finally confront one another, their scene is notable for its insistent focus on the *prospect* of unfolding

Cleopatra's motives, without ever making them clear. Caesar discovers that Cleopatra has reserved portions of her property, and praising her for the "wisdom in [her] deede" (5.2.150), he entreats her not to blush. Whether she is blushing or she soon will blush, her thoughts remain concealed. She explains away her withheld property as "some lady trifles" intended to induce the "mediation" of Livia and Octavia once she lives among the Romans (5.2.165–70); however, as Adelman notes, this explication may be a "cunningly staged device to convince Octavius that she has no desire to die."[79] Railing against her betrayer, Seleucus, Cleopatra suggests that her passions are nearly transparent, and that soon she may "show the cinders of [her] spirits / Through th' ashes of [her] chance" (5.2.173–74). In the early eighteenth-century editions of the play "chance" was glossed as "cheeks," augmenting the physiological reference in these lines and indicating that Cleopatra threatens to display heated spirits through her burnt cheeks; yet, even without this emendation, the lines suggest that what is produced as a result of external heat is accidental, and naturally obscures whatever burns within.[80]

Antony and Cleopatra repeatedly teases its audience with the possibility that Cleopatra's "true" mind and affections will be revealed, while it fosters the Egyptian paradox that her unreadability is natural. Roman accusations of betrayal and cunning presume that a familiar fixed self lurks beneath Cleopatra's playing. Since Egypt's climate produces her ineffable subtlety, drawing out her baser elements, Cleopatra's mysterious essence defies Roman definitions of truth and artifice. However, while the play sustains Cleopatra's ancient mystery, it also forecasts the disintegration of Egyptian culture and the loss of southern greatness.

Egypt's ruin is neatly captured by the Romans' anachronistic references to Cleopatra as "gypsy." The gypsy figure, as represented in a wide range of early modern texts, conflates England's rapidly shifting responses to blackness and natural Egyptian wisdom and anticipates the issues raised in the writings of Browne and Bulwer.[81] In 1547, Andrew Borde described Egyptians as displaced nomads, identified by their "swarte" skin and an inherent falseness, for unlike other nations they "go disgisyd in theyr apparel. . . . [and] Ther be few or none of the Egipcions that doth dwel in Egipt."[82] Later texts not only associate gypsy figures with craftiness and lost origins, but also emphasize the artifice of their complexion. In *Lanthorne and Candle-Light* (1609), Thomas Dekker finds it particularly disturbing that one might perceive the gypsy's complexion to be "natural": "A man that sees them would sweare they had all the yellow Iawndis, or that they were Tawny Moores bastardes, for no Red-oaker man caries a face of a more filthy complexion; yet are they not borne so, neither has the Sunne burnt them so, but they are painted so."[83] Throughout the sixteenth and seventeenth centuries, English law makes frequent mention of these troubling vagabonds; more significantly, it insists that "gypsies" are not southerners darkened by a foreign climate but Englishmen or "counterfeit" Egyptians wearing "black-face."

When these vagabonds are portrayed in later works such as Jonson's masque *Gypsies Metamorphosed* (1621) and the plays *The Spanish Gipsy* (Middleton and Rowley, 1623), *More Dissemblers Besides Women* (Middleton, 1623), and *The Lost Lady* (William Berkeley, 1637), their presence seems to necessitate an unmasking scene.[84] Quite simply, the gypsy's unmasking reworks the cultural associations of ancient Egyptian blackness derived from climatic-humoral theory. Rather than portraying blackness as powerfully unreadable, the dramatization of the gypsy-washed-white neatly equates blackness with artifice and establishes the revealed whiteness as the true and "natural" complexion. Unmasking the false gypsy both denies the mysterious agency attributed to blackness in climatic-humoral discourse and precipitates the erasure of a Renaissance reverence for southern civilizations.

Shakespeare's play anticipates these unmasking scenes most specifically in Cleopatra's metadramatic reference to the "quick comedians" who will stage her "Alexandrian revels":

> Antony
> Shall be brought drunken forth, and I shall see
> Some squeaking Cleopatra boy my greatness
> I' th' posture of a whore.
>
> (5.2.218–21)

At first glance, Cleopatra's allusion to the boy actor simply validates the "reality" of a male English body beneath the costuming of the Egyptian queen. At the same time, the play's privileging of climatological associations has established Cleopatra's seemingly performative qualities as natural and resistant to imitation. Cleopatra insists that in representation, her greatness will be "boyed" or reduced to the mere "posture" of a woman defined by carnality; in other words, the spirit of Cleopatra's greatness, which encompasses her unreadability and "infinite variety," will necessarily be lost in the translation of Egyptian culture.

Yet the reductive representation of Cleopatra's powers proves to be a cultural victory for the north, encapsulating the triumph of youthful barbarism over an ancient civilization.[85] Since ancient Egypt is gone, representations of Cleopatra inevitably reinvent her power as performativity. Paralleling the movement in English natural philosophy, the scene's metadrama dissociates Cleopatra's southern characteristics from her natural body, diminishing the status of her Egyptian "greatness"; at the same time, by equating Egyptian "greatness" with artifice, the English gain access to its mysterious agency by mere imitation. While *Antony and*

Cleopatra suggests that Cleopatra's agency originates with her southern complexion and challenges northern constructions of the gendered body, the play's metadramatic reference to the boy player stages Cleopatra's power as *northern* artifice—as a performance which succeeds in armoring and reifying the white male body.

As with her emblematic creature, the crocodile, the ancient Egyptian queen is naturally opaque and unreadable. However, by linking her mystery to the conscious and definitive artifice of gypsies and players, Shakespeare's *Antony and Cleopatra* suggests that Cleopatra's indecipherable quality can transmigrate over time and place, to be appropriated by the impolitic northerner. While ancient Egypt threatens the fixity of western distinctions (masculine/feminine; truth/artifice) the wandering, painted gypsies of the early modern period effeminize blackness as ornament and stabilize the northern male complexion as naturally virtuous. From a seventeenth-century English perspective, Egypt has degenerated, Rome has fallen, and Cleopatra's vision of Antony's natural bounty looks toward the northern horizon.

Notes

I would like to thank Reid Barbour, Lanis Wilson, and several anonymous reviewers for their helpful advice on revising this essay.

1. See *A New Variorum Edition of Shakespeare: Antony and Cleopatra,* ed. Marvin Spevack (New York: Modern Language Association, 1990), esp. 646–47, 652–53, and 63–84. For an essay that challenges binary views of the play see Jonathan Gil Harris, "'Narcissus in Thy Face': Roman Desire and the Difference It Fakes in *Antony and Cleopatra,*" *Shakespeare Quarterly* 45 (Winter 1994): 408–25.

2. See John Drakakis's introduction to *New Casebooks: Antony and Cleopatra* (New York: St. Martin's Press, 1994), 4–5. For a postcolonial perspective, see Ania Loomba, *Gender, Race, Renaissance Drama* (Manchester: Manchester University Press, 1989), 78–79 and 124–30.

3. Janet Adelman, *Suffocating Mothers: Fantasies of Maternal Origin in Shakespeare's Plays, "Hamlet" to "The Tempest"* (London: Routledge, 1992), 191.

4. Ibid., 187.

5. Gail Kern Paster, *The Body Embarrassed: Drama and the Disciplines of Shame in Early Modern England* (Ithaca: Cornell University Press, 1993), 92.

6. Harris, "'Narcissus in Thy Face,'" 409.

7. It is beyond the scope of this essay to trace the role of early modern natural philosophy in the eventual construction of "race." As an explanation of blackness, climate theory comes under scrutiny in the seventeenth century; however, it remains the dominant explanation of color difference and continues, in various forms, well into the eighteenth century. For a history of environmental theory, see Clarence J. Glacken, *Traces on the Rhodian*

Shore (Berkeley and Los Angeles: University of California Press, 1967). For a recent consideration of the role natural philosophy plays in English characterizations of American Indians in the sixteenth and seventeenth centuries, see Joyce Chaplin, "Natural Philosophy and an Early Racial Idiom in North America: Comparing English and Indian Bodies," *William and Mary Quarterly* 54 (1997): 229–52. As England's involvement in the Atlantic slave trade grows, English authors increasingly cite the Hametic curse to estrange and "explain" blackness, but in the early seventeenth century the curse of Ham is "denied more often than affirmed" (see Winthrop D. Jordan, *White over Black: American Attitudes toward the Negro, 1550–1812* [Chapel Hill: University of North Carolina Press, 1968], 19). We should recognize that the escalating prominence of the legend of Ham during the seventeenth century works in tandem with ideological erasures taking place in the discourse of natural philosophy. Changing socioeconomic factors shift the focus in early European "science" from theories of human diversity, drawn from ancient physiology, to the "mystery" of blackness—and religious discourse responds with a scriptural explanation of that mystery.

8. "Complexion" can refer to "psychological and social as well as physiological characteristics" (see Nancy G. Siraisi, *Medieval and Early Renaissance Medicine* [Chicago: University of Chicago Press, 1990], 103).

9. All quotations from Shakespeare are from *The Pelican Shakespeare,* ed. Alfred Harbage (New York: Viking Press, 1977). The nurse in *Titus* invokes climate theory when she contrasts Aaron's black child with "the fair-faced breeders of our clime" (4.2.68).

10. Early modern references to climate theory appear in a variety of sources, cited throughout this essay, including historiography (Jean Bodin, William Harrison), medical texts (Thomas Walkington), and treatises on education (Juan Huarte) and psychology (Thomas Wright). Within this discourse, latitudinal divisions prove arbitrary, shifting with the author's regional perspective, but for the most part regions classified themselves and others according to a tripartite scheme of northern, middle, and southern regions well into the late seventeenth century.

11. On the counteractive process, see Pseudo-Aristotle's *Problemata,* problem 14, "The Effect of Locality on Temperament," *The Works of Aristotle,* trans. E. S. Forster (Oxford: Clarendon Press, 1927). See also my discussion of Hippocrates below. Early modern writers appeal to both traditions; for example, *Batman uppon Bartholome* (London, 1582) draws on the theory of counteration (19.391), whereas William Harrison's conclusions are derived from Hippocrates ("Description of Britain," in *Holinshed's Chronicles of England, Scotland, and Ireland,* 6 vols. [London, 1807–8], 1:193).

12. Ian Maclean, *The Renaissance Notion of Woman* (Cambridge: Cambridge University Press, 1980), 34.

13. For an illuminating consideration of gender in relation to the spirit and the flesh, see Phyllis Rackin, "Historical Difference/Sexual Difference," in *Privileging Gender in Early Modern England,* ed. Jean R. Brink, Sixteenth Century Essays and Studies 23 (Kirksville, Mo.: Sixteenth Century Journal Publishers, 1993): 48–51.

14. Jean Bodin, *Method for the Easy Comprehension of History* (1583), trans. Beatrice Reynolds (New York: Columbia University Press, 1945), 98.

15. Ibid., 113–14. For similar statements see Pierre Charron, *Of Wisdome*, trans. Samson Lennard (London, n.d. [before 1612]; reprint, Amsterdam: Scholars Facsimiles, 1971), 168.

16. See, for example, William Harrison, "Description of Britain" (193), and Thomas Walkington, *The Optick Glasse of Humors*, (1631; reprint, New York: Scholars Facsimiles, 1981), 31.

17. Shakespeare, *The Rape of Lucrece*, l. 1240.

18. Jack D'Amico, *The Moor in English Renaissance Drama* (Tampa: University of South Florida Press, 1991), 153 (emphasis added). The tripartite division of the world eventually loses ground, helping to consolidate England's more secure position in the Occident-Orient binary.

19. In her discussion of Cleopatra's racial identity, Joyce Green MacDonald writes: "To speak meaningfully about Cleopatra's race is to include in one's use of the term an account of the ideological work race did (and does), work which was often enabled by and proceeded in tandem with the writing of other kinds of difference from a subject who is conceived of in this case as not only white, but also Roman (or English), not only male but also a heterosexual dominant male" ("Sex, Race, and Empire in Shakespeare's *Antony and Cleopatra*," *Literature and History* 5, no. 1 [1996]: 60–77). As MacDonald indicates, the issue of Cleopatra's race may give rise to the conflation of Roman and English identities. Of course Shakespeare's depiction of Rome and its people is far from univocal and is, at times, disparaging. On Shakespeare's Rome, see Charles Martindale and Michelle Martindale, *Shakespeare and the Uses of Antiquity: An Introductory Essay* (London: Routledge, 1990); Vivian Thomas, *Shakespeare's Roman Worlds* (London: Routledge, 1989); Robert S. Miola, *Shakespeare's Rome* (Cambridge: Cambridge University Press, 1983); Paul A. Cantor, *Shakespeare's Rome: Republic and Empire* (Ithaca: Cornell University Press, 1976); and M. W. MacCallum, *Shakespeare's Roman Plays and Their Background* (London: Macmillan, 1910).

20. On British nationalism and the *translatio imperii*, see Patricia Parker, "Romance and Empire: Anachronistic *Cymbeline*," in *Unfolded Tales: Essays on Renaissance Romance*, ed. George M. Logan and Gordon Teskey (Ithaca: Cornell University Press, 1989), 189–207. In "Jacobean *Antony and Cleopatra*," H. Neville Davies discusses the play in relation to James I's association with Augustus (reprinted in *New Casebooks: Antony and Cleopatra*, 126–65).

21. Leonard Tennenhouse, *Power on Display: The Politics of Shakespeare's Genres* (New York: Methuen, 1986), 144.

22. For recent discussions of Cleopatra's racial status, see MacDonald, "Sex, Race, and Empire," 60–62; Kim F. Hall, *Things of Darkness: Economies of Race and Gender in Early Modern England* (Ithaca: Cornell University Press, 1995), 153–60; and Mary Nyquist, "'Profuse, Proud Cleopatra': 'Barbarism' and Female Rule in Early Modern English Republicanism," *Women's Studies: An Interdisciplinary Journal* 24, nos. 1–2 (1994): 85–130. Nyquist points out that despite the ambiguity concerning Cleopatra's color outside of the play, Shakespeare's Cleopatra is clearly black (100).

23. My understanding of Antony's "bounty" owes a general debt to discussions in Adel-

man, *Suffocating Mothers,* and Peter Erickson, *Patriarchal Structures in Shakespeare's Drama* (Berkeley and Los Angeles: University of California Press, 1985), 123–47.

24. Bodin, *Method*, 99. Bodin also notes that Antony's fleshiness marks him as trustworthy, in contrast to lean Cassius, who resembles a southerner. In *Julius Caesar,* Caesar also notes the differences between them, swearing he would trust Cassius more if he were fatter (1.2.198).

25. On the play's construction of "heroic masculinity" see Adelman, *Suffocating Mothers,* 190.

26. John Gillies considers this issue from a different perspective, asserting that in staging her death, "Cleopatra counters one form of theatre with another, and preserves her mystery from translation" (*Shakespeare and the Geography of Difference* [Cambridge: Cambridge University Press, 1994], 122).

27. On this tradition see Frank M. Snowden, Jr., *Before Color Prejudice: The Ancient View of Blacks* (Cambridge, Mass.: Harvard University Press, 1983), 50–51.

28. Karl Dannenfeldt, "Egypt and Egyptian Antiquities in the Renaissance," *Studies in the Renaissance* 6 (1959): 10.

29. Quoted in Wayne Shumaker, *The Occult Sciences in the Renaissance: A Study in Intellectual Patterns* (Berkeley and Los Angeles: University of California Press, 1972), 229. Although it is not the focus of this essay, Cleopatra's association with Isis further complicates her relationship to the myth of Egypt and its climate.

30. Martin Bernal notes that there "appears to have been a relation between blackness and Egyptian wisdom. Many medieval and Renaissance paintings portray one of the *magi*—presumably an Egyptian—as a Black" (*Black Athena: The Afroasiatic Roots of Classical Civilization,* vol. 1: *The Fabrication of Ancient Greece, 1785–1985* [New Brunswick, N.J.: Rutgers University Press, 1987], 242). For a general discussion of black bile and genial melancholy in the early modern period, see Lawrence Babb, *The Elizabethan Malady: A Study of Melancholia in English Literature from 1580 to 1642* (East Lansing: Michigan State College Press, 1951).

31. Bodin, *Method,* 111.

32. Juan Huarte, *The Examination of Men's Wits,* trans. Richard Carew (Gainesville, Fla.: Scholars Facsimiles and Reprints, 1959), 199.

33. Ibid., 188. "Choler adust" is a form of melancholy (see Babb, *Elizabethan Malady,* 33–34).

34. *Hippocratic Writings,* trans. J. Chadwick and W. N. Mann, ed. G. E. R. Lloyd (London: Penguin, 1978), 165.

35. Ibid., 164.

36. Ibid.

37. Ibid., 166.

38. See Bodin, *Method;* see also Jacques Ferrand, *A Treatise on Lovesickness* (1623), ed. Donald A. Beecher and Massimo Ciavolella (Syracuse, N.Y.: Syracuse University Press, 1990), 246, who refers to the English, "the Scythians, the Muscovites, and the Poles" as similar types.

39. Huarte, *Examination of Men's Wits*, 80.

40. Ibid., 116.

41. See Hugh A. MacDougall, *Racial Myth in English History: Trojans, Teutons, and Anglo-Saxons* (Hanover, N.H.: University Press of New England, 1982), 43.

42. *The Agricola and the Germania,* trans. H. Mattingly and S. A. Handford (Middlesex: Penguin, 1970), 104, 119.

43. Ibid., 119.

44. Ibid., 120. It is a commonplace in climatic discourse to identify northerners as heavy drinkers and great feasters, and the southerners' dry complexion as easily sated by a few delicacies. See Charron, *Of Wisdome*, 164; and Bodin, *Method*, 128.

45. Quoted in Fynes Moryson, *Shakespeare's Europe: Unpublished Chapters of Fynes Moryson's Itinerary,* ed. Charles Hughes (London: Sherratt and Hughes, 1903), 478.

46. MacDougall, *Racial Myth in English History,* 44, 46–47.

47. Quoted in Z. S. Fink, "Milton and the Theory of Climatic Influence," *Modern Language Quarterly* 2 (1941): 69.

48. Ibid., 76.

49. Thomas Wright, *The Passions of the Mind in General,* ed. William Webster Newbold (New York: Garland, 1986); all subsequent references are to this edition.

50. Although Wright insists that the "readability" of his countrymen's complexion actually affirms their virtue, he later identifies this quality as effeminate, attributing the "tenderness of [a woman's] complexion" to her "lack of heat, and . . . native shamefastness," and citing her readability, slow wit, and inconstancy as typically feminine qualities (ibid., 119, 110).

51. *The Works of Sir Thomas Browne,* ed. Geoffrey Keynes, vol. 2 (Chicago: University of Chicago Press, 1964): 467–68.

52. John Bulwer, *Anthropometamorphosis: Man Transform'd; Or, The Artificial Changeling* (London, 1650), 254–55.

53. For another perspective on the issue of race and cosmetics, see Hall, *Things of Darkness,* 86–92.

54. I am not suggesting that Cleopatra has "true" motives to discover, but that her mystery depends on the promise and denial of revelation.

55. For a recent discussion of Antony's dissolution see Cynthia Marshall, "Man of Steel Done Got the Blues: Melancholic Subversion of Presence in *Antony and Cleopatra,*" *Shakespeare Quarterly* 44 (Winter 1993): 385–408.

56. See Jean Bodin, *The Six Bookes of a Commonweale* (1606), trans. Richard Knolles, ed. Kenneth Douglas McRae (Cambridge, Mass.: Harvard University Press, 1962), 563. See also Bodin, *Method*, 97; and Charron, *Of Wisdome*, 165. My understanding of the relationship between military science and environmental theory in the early modern period is derived in part from Ian MacInnes, "Decocting Cold Blood: Climate Theory and Military Science in *Henry V*" (paper presented at the annual meeting of the Shakespeare Association of America, Chicago, Mar. 1995).

57. Bodin, *Method*, 128. See Gillies's discussion of this passage as an exemplification of Stoicism (*Shakespeare and the Geography of Difference,* 118).

58. See Adelman's reading of this landscape as constructing a defensive masculinity defined by "male scarcity" and a "denial of . . . the female" (*Suffocating Mothers*, 176).

59. Bodin, *Six Bookes of a Commonweale*, 551, 549.

60. Henry Peacham, in *The Complete Gentleman* (1622), for example, notes that "there is not any nation in the world more subject unto surfeits than our English" when they have traveled to "hotter climates" (ed. Virgil B. Heltzel [Ithaca: Cornell University Press, 1962], 161–62).

61. Erickson, *Patriarchal Structures in Shakespeare's Drama*, 141–42.

62. I have adopted the Folio reading of "Anthony it was" rather than "autumn 'twas," which is an eighteenth-century emendation; the Folio text supports the impression that Antony's bounty is constant (not seasonal) and inherent. See Spevack on the editorial history of this line (*New Variorum Edition*, 315–16).

63. For a survey of Renaissance notions about the crocodile, see Robert Ralston Cawley, *The Voyagers and Elizabethan Drama* (London: Oxford University Press, 1938), 52–63; in particular, Cawley notes that writers marveled at the creature's "impervious" skin and apparent invulnerability (56–57).

64. See Gillies's discussion of this description as "essentially untranslatable into the Roman code and hence unknowable" (*Shakespeare and the Geography of Difference*, 121); Cleopatra, not unlike the crocodile, is "unsearchable in her difference. She is ancient, black, sun-burned, reptilian" (122).

65. Cawley finds that "[c]ontrary to common belief, the Ancients knew nothing" of the notion of a weeping crocodile (*Voyagers and Elizabethan Drama*, 53); however, sixteenth-century texts abound with references to it. Although Cawley claims that the medieval treatise of Bartholomaeus Anglicus contains the earliest reference to a weeping crocodile, he refers us to the sixteenth-century English translation *Batman uppon Bartholome;* Batman's translation has incorporated Leo Africanus's *A Geographical Historie of Africa*, a text that was not available until the sixteenth century. The OED cites Mandeville as the earliest mention of the crocodile's deceitful tears; however, Mandeville merely notes that crocodiles "slay and eat men weeping" (*Mandeville's Travels* [London: Hakluyt Society, 1953], 1:202).

66. I have incorporated the Folio text's "weep" instead of "wept."

67. Aging is expected to affect an individual's humoral complexion; however, English humoral discourse indicates that it causes one to grow *colder* and dryer (see Ruth Leila Anderson, *Elizabethan Psychology and Shakespeare's Plays* [New York: Russell and Russell, 1966], 55).

68. Cleopatra's younger impressionability accommodates Pompey, much in the way that Isabella in *Measure for Measure* implicates women: "For we are soft as our complexions are, / And credulous to false prints" (2.4.129–30). For the argument that Cleopatra reflects what the Romans project see Harris, "'Narcissus in Thy Face.'"

69. Ibid., 417.

70. Ibid., 424.

71. Of course this imagery also establishes a sexual relationship between the queen and Phoebus; Jonson uses similar language in *The Masque of Blackness,* wherein the sun "draws

/ Signs of his fervent'st love" in the Ethiopian dames' "firm hues" (*Ben Jonson: The Complete Masques*, ed. Stephen Orgel [New Haven: Yale University Press, 1969], 52).

72. Janet Adelman, *The Common Liar: An Essay on Antony and Cleopatra* (New Haven: Yale University Press, 1973), 138.

73. See Charron, *Of Wisdome*, 167.

74. Jonson, *Masque of Blackness*, 52.

75. In "*Antony and Cleopatra*: A Shakespearean Adjustment," John Danby argues that "Caesar impersonates the World, [and Cleopatra] of course, incarnates the Flesh" (in *New Casebooks: Antony and Cleopatra*, 49).

76. See Paster for a provocative reading of Cleopatra's "antinursing" (*Body Embarrassed*, 239–44).

77. Danby cites this line as evidence of Cleopatra's association with the flesh and the "female principle" ("*Antony and Cleopatra*," 49). For a summary discussion of the line's editorial history, see Spevack, *New Variorum Edition*, 305–6.

78. Citing Paster's commentary on blood as a "trope of gender," Marshall notes that "[w]ounded, bleeding, and lacking agency, Antony takes on a typically feminine position" in death ("Man of Steel Done Got the Blues," 403).

79. This is posed as a question in Adelman, *Common Liar*, 15; see also Adelman's discussion of the various interpretations of this scene (191–92, n. 8, and 202, n. 17).

80. On the emendation, see Spevack, *New Variorum Edition*, 360.

81. In act 1, scene 1 Philo claims that Antony's heart "is become the bellows and the fan / To cool a gypsy's lust" (9–10); Antony refers to Cleopatra as a gypsy in act 4, scene 12: "Like a right gypsy hath at fast and loose / Beguiled me to the very heart of loss" (28–29). For background on the English gypsy, see Dale B. J. Randall, *Jonson's Gypsies Unmasked: Background and Theme of "The Gypsies Metamorphos'd"* (Durham, N.C.: Duke University Press, 1975).

82. Andrew Borde, *The Fyrst Boke of the Introduction of Knowledge* (1548; reprint, London: Early English Text Society, 1870), 217.

83. *The Non-Dramatic Works of Thomas Dekker*, ed. Alexander B. Grosart (1884–86; reprint, New York: Russell and Russell, 1963), 1:259.

84. In *The Lost Lady* the character is actually a lady disguised as an "Egyptian" rather than a gypsy; John Webster's *The Devil's Law-Case* (1617–21) and Richard Brome's *The English Moor* (1637) also stage unmasking scenes, but the characters are identified as Moors rather than gypsies.

85. Cleopatra's reference to a "boy" impersonating her greatness recalls the play's earlier references to Octavius as the "young Roman boy" (4.12.48) as well as the "greatness he has got" from Cleopatra (5.2.30).

4

Marlowe's Ganymede

Joyce Green MacDonald

Until recently, critics have found it difficult to discuss the Jupiter-Ganymede prologue to Christopher Marlowe's *Dido Queene of Carthage*. Commentary in twentieth-century editions of the play tends to limit itself to the play proper, skipping lightly over its introductory scene. In an otherwise detailed introduction, for example, H. J. Oliver asserts that "the homosexuality" of the induction need not bear "too much emphasis"; a textual note holds that "it is debatable" whether the prologue adds much to the play.[1] Although C. F. Tucker Brooke notes that "*Dido* is the only play in which Marlowe has made sexual love the real centre of the action," he implicitly bars the prologue from consideration of this notion by adding that "it contains (at least among his plays) his most elaborate portraits of women."[2] Writing in 1909, Edward Thomas failed to address the sexual context of the play directly, but noted that despite its "intractable" source material, Marlowe did nonetheless succeed in making the most of "the many opportunities of expressing luxury and barbaric simplicity of love and hate."[3] Havelock Ellis similarly alluded to the play's "mellifluous sweetness," but did not find it worthy of inclusion in his volume.[4] Even such fleeting impressions of the quality of the play's language allow it more credit than does the unelaborated 1887 pronouncement of George Saintsbury that "The 'Tragedy of Dido' . . . is the worst thing he [Marlowe] ever did."[5] F. S. Boas, whose tracing of a consistently Machiavellian pattern of behavior among Marlowe's heroes allowed the first application of an ordering framework for discussion of the plays, notes with regret that the "elaborate scene of dalliance" between Jupiter and Ganymede which opens the play, especially coming from a playwright "who treats love between man and woman with so delicate a touch, may have given a handle to those who . . . charged him with abnormal vice."[6]

Such glances at *Dido*'s critical history, or lack of it, suggest that there is something about the play, and possibly particularly about its Jupiter-Ganymede prologue, which set it outside of the normal range of Marlovian discussion. A more contemporary historicism than Boas's, interested in Machiavelli but also in wider social contexts of discontinuity which may unsettle the grounds for discussion of character and motivation which Boas defined, has placed Marlowe—but not necessarily *Dido*—within a matrix of Renaissance colonialism and mercantilism.[7] Following Foucault, another group of critics has begun to read *Dido* within the history and politics of same-sex attraction; this project is as politically committed to uncovering the uses of homoeroticism under late capitalism as it is to discussing how the figures of Jupiter and Ganymede—or, for that matter, of the African queen of the play's title—may have transmitted sexual meanings in antiquity or the Renaissance.[8] Historically conscious critical traditions, however, have not always acknowledged that the brief and overtly erotic encounter between the king of heaven and his young lover which opens *Dido* initiates the play's concern with the power of sexual love, that it exemplifies the sweet richness of the play's most accomplished poetry, or even that it departs from a view of sexuality that has established patriarchally governed heterosexuality as the norm and everything else as, to a greater or lesser degree, "abnormal." "Sodomy ruins difference," Jonathan Goldberg has remarked, indicating some of the potential carried by admission of the fact that something erotic is happening between Jupiter and his cupbearer, eroding the categorical distinctions on which so much interpretation of *Dido* and its source materials in Virgil depends.[9]

In this essay, I am also interested in recovering some of the historical context for Marlowe, but I conceive the history as being imperial as well as sexual, textual as well as political. Amplifying material found in books 1, 2, and 4 of the *Aeneid*, *Dido Queene of Carthage* fertilizes the imperial concerns which Marlowe displays in his translation of the first book of Lucan's *Pharsalia* (concerns evident in the *Aeneid* itself) with the erotic polish of a *Hero and Leander*, or the sexual dissidence of his Ovid translations.[10] In its will to eroticize history, *Dido*'s Jupiter-Ganymede prologue engages in the characteristically Marlovian act of confounding audience expectation and categories of genre and emotional experience. Indeed, Marlowe understands his Virgilian history largely in terms of the Ganymede materials' mythic treatments of sexuality and gender.[11] The Jupiter-Ganymede prologue at least invites readers to consider the possibility of a divorce between sexuality and gender and gender difference, and, by implication, a dissolution of the organizational binaries—love versus duty, the personal versus the public and historical, passion versus intellect, men versus women—around which readers of Dido's role in the *Aeneid* have built their analyses.[12] The prologue accomplishes these rather large claims by its presentation of a love affair between the king of the gods and his cupbearer which undercuts one of the chief of those organizational binaries governing sexuality—the maintenance of careful distinctions between social superior (adult males) and social inferior (in this case, boys). As he seduces the king of heaven, the Ganymede of Marlowe's prologue also aggressively invites his readers to slant their knowledge of the interpretive traditions surrounding what the play's title promises will be its proper Virgilian subject.

Marlowe's reading of the Trojan boy disrupts both the inscription of properly sanctioned heterosexual marriage in epic and epic's resolutely unerotic homosocial dignity. As important as the way in which Marlowe deploys his Ganymede to reflect on Dido's hopeless passion is the way in which he uses the boy and his mythographic presence to interrogate the comradely bond between men that is also part of the cost of empire, excavating the sexual tensions which form its underside.[13] By reading and rewriting Ganymede, *Dido Queene of Carthage* brings a linked range of textual histories and heterosexual authorities into its view.[14]

My observation that Marlowe's Ganymede is radically un-Virgilian might at first merely seem to restate the obvious, but this first obvious point seems to me to deserve further exploration, if for no other reason than that *Dido* criticism has been so largely dismissive of or silent on the impact of the prologue. It is true that Marlowe retains most of the events and characters Virgil includes in the Dido-Aeneas episode; on several occasions, he even puts Virgil's Latin directly into his own dramatic characters' mouths. But he also writes these characters and quotations and events into a new narrative structure, one initiated in the Jupiter-Ganymede prologue, whose assumptions and tone radically alter their Virgilian meanings. In Marlowe, Dido's sister Anna falls jealously in love with Iarbas, who loves only Dido; Iarbas's love for Dido and his resentment of Aeneas is much more fully developed than in Virgil; and the play ends with the triple deaths of Anna, Dido, and Iarbas. What epic treats as solemn moral tableau here verges on farce.

Before looking at how Marlowe's play challenges the gender certainties of epic, I want to emphasize how the prologue to *Dido* also invites prior contemplation of the functions and nature of sexuality. As a widow, queen, and founder of a city, Dido is torn between her sense of duty to her dead husband and to Carthage and her love for Aeneas. In Virgil, Dido's sister Anne urges her to yield to her love for the stranger: "Will you not seeke for children sweete? nor *Venus* comfort crave?"[15] In Marlowe's prologue, although Dido does eventually surrender to her passion, she initially feels that she is not the owner of her body or her sexuality. Her husband, Sichaeus, she exclaims, "toke from me my love, / He keepes it, in his grave it lieth, from thence it shall not move" (4.30–31).[16]

Scholars of antiquity have drawn our attention to the ways in which the concept of sexuality was used to make gender socially visible, giving both gender privilege and gender oppression material form.[17] The myth of Ganymede seems to have functioned in ancient Greece as a Foucaultian transfer point between sexuality and its social uses, as does the dilemma of Virgil's Dido in the *Aeneid.* In myth, Ganymede was the son of Tros, the ancient lord from whom the Trojan people took their name. The boy was taken to Olympus by Zeus, who had assumed the form of a mighty eagle, to serve as cupbearer to the gods. The myth of Ganymede has been analyzed as narrating a specific and socially functional homoeroticism, one initiating young boys into an ancient Greek social order which did not segregate sexuality from the prevailing homosocial male bonds. Indeed, to become the sexual object of an older man through ritual abduction was to enter the world of status and social distinction: "For those who are handsome and have illustrious ancestors," writes Strabo, "not to have lovers is disgraceful, since their rejection would be attributed to their bad character."[18] A costly goblet or cup was among the ritual gifts presented to the *eromenos,* the younger partner in the initiatory bond, by the *erastes,* the elder and more socially established partner, at the end of his period of seclusion.

In early modern England, the term "ganymede" had become the commonest slang term for a young man who was the minion of an older male.[19] Yet, apparently, such sexual congress was not publicly condemned unless it occurred in such a way as to violate categories of social status and experience which were regarded as important to the maintenance of social order. If the sexual relationship allowed a servant to control a master, for example, it would place an inferior in improper authority over a superior, and would be condemned. Such improper domination crossed lines governing relations between different classes and—most significantly for the *Dido* prologue—generations. In the Renaissance, the word "sodomy," a term which in current usage refers virtually exclusively to anal intercourse between men, could encompass not only this particular kind of sexual contact but also heterosexual activity other than vaginal intercourse, sexual contact between women, and bestiality, as well as such sins as gluttony, drunkenness, and even usury.[20] The sin of which the figure of Ganymede was the most visible emblem was multiple, various, sometimes linked to, but never entirely determined by, one's choice of erotic objects. Perhaps fittingly, Ganymede himself appeared in multiple guises in Renaissance culture, from popular slang to the most powerful visual representations of the neoplatonic rapture also associated with the myth.[21]

The literary sources of the Jupiter-Ganymede myth generally available to Renaissance readers reinforce this sense of oscillation and multiplicity. The *Metamorphoses,* for example, includes the story in Orpheus's catalogue of transformations wrought by love:

> The King of Goddes did burne erewhyle in loue of *Ganymed*
> The *Phrygian,* and the thing was found which Iupiter that sted
> Had rather bee than that he was. Yit could he not beteeme
> The shape of any other Bird than Aegle for too seeme
> And so he soring in the ayre with borrowed wings trust vp
> The *Trojane* boay who still in heauen euen yit dooth beare his cup,
> And brings him *Nectar* though against Dame *Junos* will it bee.[22]

Almost immediately after declaring that "every thing / Is subject vntoo royall Ioue," Golding's Ovid nonetheless announces a "neede" of "a meelder style too tell of prettie boyes / That were the derlings of the Gods" (10.153–54, 157–58); therefore, being "subject vntoo royall Ioue" would seem to be an experience differing both in kind and in degree from being a "derling" of the gods. Royal Jove is himself the victim of his own desires, finding it almost necessary, instead of merely appropriate, to become something other than what he is in order to love Ganymede ("the thing . . . which Iupiter . . . / Had rather bee than that he was"). Jove assumes the shape of an eagle, the emblem of imperial and divine might, and so regains some of the dignity he may have surrendered in lust by becoming the means through which the "*Trojane* boay" is transported to heaven. Indeed, both Jove and Ganymede are transported, Jove's flight simultaneously declaring his subjection to sexual passion and the paradoxical capacity of sexual passion to endow bodies with the power to transcend the flesh.

The other *locus classicus* for the Ganymede myth is found in book 5 of the *Aeneid,* which memorializes the boy's experience in a description of the prizes Aeneas distributes after the games he and his men celebrate on the first anniversary of the death of his father, Anchises.[23] That Ganymede should figure in this supremely *pius* homage to the father of the father of Rome illustrates the degree to which epic purpose rereads the myth, omitting its account of the power of Ganymede's beauty to arouse Jove's lust in favor of a new emphasis on a nonsexual masculine unity and hierarchy:

> A mantell riche to him that wan the chiefe was given of gold,
> Whom purple borders broade environned with divers fold,
> And wrought therin there standes a princely child of precious face,
> That in the woods with Dart in hand both Hart & Hinde doth chace,
> All lively, breathing like, whom, falling downe from *Jove* on hie:
> An Egle féerce uptooke, and in his pawes conveied to skie.
> His keepers wailing stand, and handes abroad to heaven they hold
> In vaine, and barking noyse of dogs against the clouds do skold.
>
> (5.281–88)

The *ekphrasis* gives us a Ganymede and a rapture which differ significantly from the Ovidian version, just as tense sexual comedy differs from epic. Virgil's Ganymede is a "princely child" whose "lively" beauty as he engages in the hunt has been especially well captured by the artist of the cloak on which his likeness appears. Unlike the Ovidian Ganymede, who stands in some indeterminate relation to Jove—as both pretty boy and prey—Virgil's Ganymede is a person of some status, employing gamekeepers who are helpless and horrified before his abduction. In paying the filial debt that will shape the civilization they will found together, Aeneas's troops author a disciplined version of Ganymede's abduction whose very omissions speak to the process of making meaningful distinctions between their experience and that which overtakes the Trojan boy: distinctions between duty and pleasure, between older and younger, between the homosocial and the homoerotic.

This ekphrastic description both dignifies Ganymede and distances us from his rape. Indeed, readers of the passage cannot be absolutely certain that any abduction (*raptus,* in Ovid's Latin) has actually occurred; Jove sends an eagle to take the boy for some unspecified purpose, rather than transforming himself into an eagle to take the boy because he desires him sexually. Although the central image is that of the eagle seizing the boy, the description also includes information on Ganymede's character and presence and on the states of mind of his gamekeepers and his disturbed hounds. That central image of abduction—the basis for that ambiguous rapture in Ovid's account—is virtually bracketed by these personal and emotional details, dramatizing the event while somehow minimizing it, cleansing it of the syntactical confusion (and, as was frequent in Renaissance poetic practice, of the sodomitical irregularities of which syntactical confusion could be the manifestation).[24]

Virgil's elegant memorialization also underlies a third classical treatment of Ganymede's story, namely that found in book 1 of Statius's *Thebaid* (c. A.D. 90 or 91). Following Virgil, Statius presents his Ganymede in an *ekphrasis,* as the object of a hero's contemplation. Once again, readers are doubly removed from the anguish which the image freezes in time. As Polynices, one of the Seven against Thebes, is being feasted by the king of Argos, he views a golden ceremonial goblet on which "was embossed work of images. . . . Here the Phrygian hunter is borne aloft on tawny wings, Gargara's range sinks downwards as he rises and Troy grows dim beneath him; sadly stand his comrades, in vain the hounds weary their throats with barking and pursue his shadow or bay at the clouds."[25] In accomplishing the censorship of the Ovidian Jove's lust for the Phrygian boy, thus avoiding prolonged contemplation of his search for the appropriate embodiment of Jove's awkward desire, Virgil and Statius produce a Ganymede who is subject to a divine power from which sexuality has been rarefied, a tragic victim whose status as "prettie" boy leaves Jove unmoved. The ekphrastic descriptions operate to spectacularize Ganymede's subjection, underscoring his helplessness and his companions' anguish as the heroes contemplating him pause in the accomplishment of their epic duties.

Set within a literary tradition which acknowledges Ganymede's sexual power only indirectly and ambiguously before disciplining it—if, indeed, it can acknowledge it at all—the prologue to Marlowe's *Dido* becomes all the more startling. Marlowe's Ganymede is both sexual subject and sexual object, pretty boy and sexual manipulator, penetrated and at least potentially penetrator, in ways which challenge the excision of physical love between men from the business of history.[26] Marlowe invites his audience to witness, and be amused by, transgression.

The fact that the Jupiter-Ganymede episode in *Dido* was intended to be performed by "the Children of her *Majesties Chapell*" further emphasizes the place of homoeroticism in Marlowe's vision of a newly sexualized and gendered historical order.[27] Of course, as far as we can tell, the play was never actually performed at all, but the designation of the play for a boys' performance—by young actors who were commonly known as "ganymedes"—opens another avenue for the exploration of its marking by dissident sexualities.[28]

The process of finding a theatrical framework within which to discuss Marlowe's Ganymede is instructively frustrating: much discussion of the boy actor in the English Renaissance theater assumes that the choice he forces audiences to make is a choice between varieties of heterosexual response, grounded in the patriarchal conditions which have made him theatrically necessary. That is, the specificity of the gender of the performers and of the erotic encounters they enact tends to be absorbed within a system of sexual signification which is insufficiently flexible to account for it fully. Hence, much feminist criticism of the phenomenon of the boy actor reads him for the greater degree of social and sexual possibility he may posit for women in the culture for which he performed, seeing the literally same-sex romantic complications he enacted on the transvestite stage of Renaissance England as being essentially about women rather than men (or boys).[29] Even critics who may insist upon the construction of gender as a social category sometimes hastily efface the significance of the material practices of institutions of gender difference. Informed by Thomas Laqueur's discussion of the lability of physiological ideas of gender in the early modern period, for example, Stephen Greenblatt argues that the period's all-male English acting troupes were both culturally unremarkable—despite the fact that England was the only European country which found them necessary—and surprisingly open to performances of gender subversion, while Kathleen McLuskie doubts that the sex of Renaissance performers was relevant to the issues of male cultural dominance within whose terms theatrical representation took place.[30] However, the problem one encounters in trying to apply theories about boy actors, crossdressed or not, to *Dido Queene of Carthage* and its Jupiter-Ganymede prologue is that instead of a boy "pretending" to be a woman who will inevitably become more or less available to a male lover, the prologue presents a boy actor playing a boy who is the sexual object of an older man (also played by a boy).

Lisa Jardine's claim that because the ideal spectator of the Renaissance public theater was male, and crossdressed boy heroines were virtually designed to arouse the spectator's homoerotic pleasure, is one powerful exception to critics' assumptions of the uncontested dominance of a heterosexual and patriarchal logic in the period's use of boy actors.[31] But as Laura Levine has convincingly argued, fear of the possibility of homoerotic response is only one aspect of the period's antitheatrical discourse, a discourse which is also shot through with fear of the ungendering, the virtual dissolution of notions of masculine selfhood.[32] Heterosexually generated gender identity is the keystone of the orderly self put at risk by the activity of unbridled play-watching: after the experience of seeing a play "every one bringes another homeward of their way verye friendly, and in their secret conclaves (covertly) they play the Sodomits, or worse," warned Philip Stubbes in his *Anatomie of Abuses* (1583).[33] The boys' performance of heterosexual desire mediated the very real dangers which a male-dominant culture saw in it while allowing spectators—women as well as men—to revel in the sodomitical fears projected onto theatrical pleasure by the most extreme of the antitheatrical tracts. Watching *Dido*'s prologue, in which boys play a pair of homosexual lovers who overturn expected hierarchies of generational and sexual authority (the older man is here clearly enthralled by the young Ganymede), is a more direct kind of reveling in those same fears, with the added frisson of a main action which performs precisely that danger of effeminization and sodomy which such writers as Stubbes feared the most in the power of stage plays.[34] If boys pretending to be women are "monsters, of both kindes, half women, half men,"[35] if taking the woman's role may in fact lead to becoming a woman, then the supposedly stable and essential category of gender identity is in fact disturbingly subject to fluctuation in the act of dressing or undressing the male body. The boy actor may in fact more truly be said to open up unsettling vistas where categories of sexual, gender, and generational difference are confounded, destabilized, inverted—rendered, in fact, sodomitical.

Moments when males take up the woman's part through means of adornment are scattered throughout the play.[36] Marlowe's prologue shows Jupiter in the act of offering Ganymede the "gems, / My *Juno* ware upon her marriage day" (42–43). As evidence of Jupiter's love, Ganymede would rather have "a jewell for mine eare, / And a fine brouch to put in my hat" (46–47). Three times during the play Dido handles objects of dress or adornment fetishized by her association of them with her love for Aeneas: the jewelry that her late husband Sichaeus gave her during their courtship (3.4.61–62), which she now offers to Aeneas; her own "emperiall Crowne" and scepter (4.4.34–35), which she offers him in order to persuade him to stay with her; and, after he has deserted her, the sword by which he first swore to love her, and "the garment which I cloath'd him in, / When first he came on shoare" (5.1.298–99). Jupiter seizes the tokens of his marriage to the queen of heaven in a "theft" so that Ganymede can "tricke" (45) himself with them and so transform their significance; in the terms of antitheatricalism, Ganymede will here effeminize himself, a process in which Jupiter, in his willing subservience to the boy and in defiance of the symbolic significance of his own marriage, will happily collude, and even initiate. By clothing and attempting to adorn Aeneas, Dido attempts to perform role-playing's transformative magic on him. Aeneas not only sturdily resists her proffered gifts, but holds out for "A Burgonet of steele" (4.4.42), an object which will proclaim his possession of a prior martial identity, and his intention of keeping it.[37]

If Marlowe's Jupiter is the king of the gods, he is also the besotted lover of a particularly attractive and manipulative boy. If history constructs sexuality—a conclusion with which the play's epic matter would apparently force us to concur—here is a play whose prologue leads us to contemplate the degree to which sexual desire may order, or disrupt, historical events. If a frequently coercive heterosexuality underwrites epic, here is a play whose prologue invites us to imagine an alternative sexual ground of culture, one which is collaborative and unconflicted. The prologue of Marlowe's *Dido* trades in a kind of sexual outlawry which coolly contradicts the prescriptions of a normative heterosexuality.

Two things mark the Ganymede myth as Marlowe approaches the classical tradition and sets a prologue to the tragic epic matter which follows. First, Marlowe's Jove much more nearly resembles Ovid's than does Virgil's, an odd departure in a play which is otherwise strictly Virgilian. In Marlowe, Jove is madly infatuated with one of Ovid's "prettie boyes," and seems perfectly comfortable with the homoerotic and unmarital implications of his love: "Come gentle *Ganimed* and play with me, / I love thee well, say *Juno* what she will" (1.1.1–2). Far from being a narrative which shies away from endangering Jove's authority through too close proximity to his passion, Marlowe's *Dido* insists that Jupiter is ready to lay both his power and his love at his Ganymede's feet:

> What ist sweet wagge I should deny thy youth?
> Whose face reflects such pleasure to mine eyes,
> As I exhal'd with thy fire-darting beames,
> Have oft driven backe the horses of the night,
> When as they would have hal'd thee from my sight:
> Sit on my knee, and call for thy content,
> Controule proud Fate, and cut the thred of time,
> Why are not all the Gods at thy commaund,
> And heaven and earth the bounds of thy delight?
>
> (1.1.23–31)

Marlowe's more truly radical departure from his classical texts, however, lies in his characterization of the Trojan boy himself. Ganymede is Ovid's pretty boy with a vengeance, wickedly aware of his own attractiveness and of Jupiter's enslavement by his charms, self-sufficiently sexual in a way which seems more (early) modern than classical. Scene 1 of *Dido* opens to discover "Jupiter dandling Ganimed upon his knee," and there is no doubt that Marlowe's Ganymede is an active and self-conscious seducer. While the ekphrastic descriptions in Virgil and Statius are silent on Jove's motivation for sending the eagle down to earth to snatch Ganymede up to Olympus, Marlowe's "Ganimed" is perfectly certain:

> Sweet *Jupiter,* if ere I pleasde thine eye,
> Or seemed faire walde in with Egles wings,
> Grace my immortall beautie with this boone,
> And I will spend my time in thy bright armes.
>
> (1.1.19–22)

The eagle into which Jove either transforms himself or which he sends on his mysterious errand, a trope which figures so prominently in neoplatonic interpretations of the myth, here becomes nothing more than a particularly striking and ingenious foil for Ganymede's "immortall beautie"; what merely "pleasde" Jove's eye when he first beheld the boy seemed perhaps especially "faire walde in with Egles wings."

That Marlowe's Jupiter is so openly besotted and his Ganymede so seductive brings the shadowy places in the Jupiter-Ganymede tradition into sharp detail. Not only is Jupiter's lust for Ganymede less ambiguously acknowledged than it is in Ovid, but Ganymede himself is endowed with a sexualized subjectivity present in none of the other sources we have considered. His pouting over Juno's mistreatment elicits a richly amplified vow of devotion from Jupiter, who concludes by offering him the "gems, / My *Juno* ware upon her marriage day" (42–43).

The amplification demonstrates Marlowe in the act of poetically imitating his

Virgilian material in a particularly pointed way. Marlowe's subject is the tragic love affair between the hero Aeneas and Dido, queen of Carthage, an episode which seems clearly to point to the incompatibility of history and pleasure and to exclude women from the progress and import of epic. Yet, as the *Aeneid* suggests, sexual desire and sexual jealousy played their roles in the origins of the Trojan war. Juno's "endles wrath" (*Aeneid,* 1.8) was driven not only by her anger at losing the title of the fairest to Venus but also by the fact that the Trojans were of the same blood as "*Ganimede* whom *Jove* to heaven had raught" (1.30). Marlowe seizes on this almost parenthetical implication of sexual jealousy in matters of epic import as an important source of the noncanonical energy of the Jupiter-Ganymede prologue. In Marlowe, and only in Marlowe, Ganymede accompanies Jupiter as the king of Heaven sets about the "geare" (1.1.121) of assuring Aeneas's brief repose in Carthage before he must resume his "wandring fate" (1.1.83). The presence of "that female wanton boy" (1.1.51) thus literally shadows Aeneas's choice of duty and history over love; if the founder of Rome must separate the two, Marlowe's Jove experiences no such compulsion. The play's use of Ganymede insists upon foregrounding his hierarchically transgressive sexual power—a power exercised, paradoxically, by his being flirtatious and effeminate—over Jove and the consequent fertilization of epic by the comic and the erotic. Indeed, Jove's offering of Juno's wedding jewels to Ganymede outrages the heterosexual and patriarchal order which underscores Aeneas's epic quest toward lordship and dynastic marriage. Juno's jealousy, after all, was further complicated by the fact that in order for Jupiter to seize Ganymede and install him as his cupbearer, Jupiter had first to displace Hebe, his and Juno's daughter, from that role.[38] The rape of Ganymede thus sodomitically overwrites the patriarchal emblem of a daughter's service to an all-supreme father. Marlowe uses his Ganymede as a weapon against heterosexual and familial, as well as generational, hierarchies.

Marlowe invites us to imagine Aeneas's refusal of Dido's love in light of this unseen accompaniment by an outrageously role-reversed passion. His playfully subversive homoeroticism works to question disciplined marital sexuality as a major constituent of Aeneas's political and cultural experience, just as critics have observed that Virgil's treatment of Dido opens the text to similar questions.[39] In doing so, Marlowe, I believe, works from material already contained within the Jupiter-Ganymede myth. If readers (Marlowe among them) know that Aeneas must and will forsake Dido and the fully requited passion she offers him, Marlowe complicates our progress toward that historically and culturally necessary result.

Prefacing his version of the emblematic encounter between Trojan hero and Carthaginian queen with a portrayal of Ganymede which forcibly recalls the Trojan boy's multiple places in classical myth and contemporary Renaissance culture,

Marlowe reveals himself to be engaged in a radical questioning of gender identity and its social hierarchy. His questions elicit no particular answers; but he poses them in guises so provocative that pushing them to the margin may be a gesture necessary for the preservation of the figures of unhappy Dido and unerotic Ganymede, on which the edifice of Aeneas's masculine heroism has been built.

Notes

1. H. J. Oliver, introduction to Christopher Marlowe, *Dido Queen of Carthage* and *The Massacre at Paris*, ed. H. J. Oliver, The Revels Plays (Cambridge, Mass.: Harvard University Press, 1968), xli, 4, nn. 1–2.

2. C. F. Tucker Brooke, *The Life of Marlowe and "The Tragedy of Dido Queene of Carthage,"* vol. 1 of *The Works and Life of Christopher Marlowe*, gen. ed. R. H. Case (London: Methuen, 1930–33), 123.

3. Edward Thomas, introduction to *The Plays of Christopher Marlowe* (London: Dent, 1909), xiii.

4. Havelock Ellis, "Christopher Marlowe," in *Christopher Marlowe* (London: Unwin; New York: Scribner's, 1903), xliii.

5. Cited in Millar MacLure, ed., *Marlowe: The Critical Heritage 1588–1896* (London: Routledge, 1979), 163.

6. F. S. Boas, *Christopher Marlowe: A Biographical and Critical Study* (Oxford: Clarendon Press, 1940), 53.

7. See especially Stephen Greenblatt, *Renaissance Self-Fashioning: From More to Shakespeare* (Chicago: University of Chicago Press, 1980), 193–221; Thomas Cartelli, *Marlowe, Shakespeare, and the Economy of Theatrical Experience* (Philadelphia: University of Pennsylvania Press, 1991); and Emily Bartels, *Spectacles of Strangeness: Imperialism, Alienation, and Marlowe* (Philadephia: University of Pennsylvania Press, 1993). Bartels is more interested than Greenblatt or Cartelli in identifying racial consciousness as one of the elements of colonialism which shapes Marlowe's work.

8. The Foucault text which is most important here is vol. 1 of *The History of Sexuality*, trans. Robert Hurley (New York: Random House, 1980). Examples of works in Renaissance studies which take Foucault's remark that sexuality functions as "an especially dense transfer point for relations of power" (103) as axiomatic include Alan Bray, *Homosexuality in Renaissance England* (1982; reprint, New York: Columbia University Press, 1995), and "Homosexuality and the Signs of Male Friendship in Elizabethan England," *History Workshop Journal* 19 (1990): 1–19; Bruce R. Smith, *Homosexual Desire in Shakespeare's England: A Cultural Poetics* (Chicago: University of Chicago Press, 1991), esp. 189–223; Gregory W. Bredbeck, *Sodomy and Interpretation: Marlowe to Milton* (Ithaca: Cornell University Press, 1991), esp. 3–23; Simon Shepherd, *Marlowe and the Politics of Elizabethan Theatre* (New York: St. Martin's Press, 1986), 197–207; and Jonathan Goldberg, *Sodometries: Renaissance Texts, Modern Sexualities* (Stanford: Stanford University Press, 1992).

9. Goldberg, *Sodometries*, 129. For a discussion of *Dido* see 126–36.

10. On the relationships between Marlowe's play and its primary sources, see Oliver, introduction to *Dido Queen of Carthage,* xxxiii–xxxix; Boas, *Christopher Marlowe,* 53–66; and Roma Gill, introduction to *The Complete Works of Christopher Marlowe,* ed. Roma Gill (Oxford: Clarendon Press, 1987), 1:xiiii–xiv. All of these critics emphasize the freedom and flexibility of Marlowe's imitation of classical models, although neither Oliver nor Gill discusses the Jupiter-Ganymede prologue as an illustration of that freedom. In a paper presented at the 1993 meeting of the Modern Language Association, Ian Frederick Moulton argued that the sexual content which Marlowe emphasizes in *All Ovids Elegies* affected its publication history.

11. Compare my assertion here with Bartels's isolation of the episode from the main action of the play: "Ganymede . . . is practically dumped from Jupiter's lap as the colonialist contest begins"; and her reading of the presentation of an explicitly sexual connection between men as an aspect of the play's presentation of other, heterosexual bonds: "(Jupiter's) 'play' with Ganymede, however much predicated upon desire, becomes a way of exhorting his power over Juno and putting her in her place" (*Spectacles of Strangeness,* 168, 37). The prologue's example of a non-normative sexuality continues to bear, as itself, on the rest of the play.

12. Although Dido is not the main subject in this paper, I have been strongly influenced by three works which emphasize the multiple strands of the Dido tradition and how they function in Virgil's epic and its literary afterlife to produce her as a multiple figure: Christopher Baswell, *Virgil in Medieval England: Figuring the "Aeneid" from the Twelfth Century to Chaucer* (Cambridge: Cambridge University Press, 1995); Ralph Hexter, "Sidonian Dido," in *Innovations of Antiquity,* ed. Ralph Hexter and Daniel Selden (New York: Routledge, 1992), 332–84; and John Watkins, *The Specter of Dido: Spenser and Virgilian Epic* (New Haven: Yale University Press, 1995), 30–61. That instability, and its manifestations in gender, are restated, re-presented for me in the Ganymede tradition.

13. On epic's treatment of masculinity, I follow David Quint's immensely useful *Epic and Empire: Politics and Generic Form from Virgil to Milton* (Princeton: Princeton University Press, 1993), 45: "Narrative itself . . . becomes ideologically charged, the formal cause or consequence of that Western male rationality and historical identity that epic ascribes to the imperial victors. . . . It tells of a power able to end the indeterminacy of war and to emerge victorious, showing that the struggle had all along been leading up to its victory and thus imposing upon it a narrative teleology—the teleology that epic identifies with the very idea of narrative."

14. On the establishment of links between constructions of gender and constructions of textual meanings that were part of the humanist project, see Stephanie H. Jed, *Chaste Thinking: The Rape of Lucretia and the Birth of Humanism* (Bloomington: Indiana University Press, 1989).

15. All quotations from Virgil's *Aeneid* are from *The Aeneid of Thomas Phaer and Thomas Twyne* (1584), ed. Steven Lally (New York: Garland, 1987); here, 4.36.

16. All quotations from *The Tragedie of Dido Queene of Carthage* are from vol. 1 of *Complete Works of Christopher Marlowe,* ed. Gill.

17. See, besides Foucault's *History of Sexuality,* David Halperin, *One Hundred Years of*

Homosexuality and Other Essays on Greek Love (New York: Routledge, 1990); John J. Winkler, *Constraints of Desire: The Anthropology of Sex and Gender in Ancient Greece* (New York: Routledge, 1990); and David Konstan and Martha Nussbaum, eds., *Sexuality in Greek and Roman Society* (special issue of *Differences* 2, no. 1 [1990]). Studies concentrating on sexuality and gender in ancient Rome include Amy Richlin, *The Garden of Priapus: Sexuality and Aggression in Roman Humor,* rev. ed. (New York: Oxford University Press, 1992), and Suzanne Dixon, *The Roman Mother* (Norman: University of Oklahoma Press, 1988).

18. Bernard Sergent quotes Strabo's *Geography* (*Homosexuality in Greek Myth,* trans. Arthur Goldhammer [Boston: Beacon Press, 1984], 8). Sergent's thesis is that the ancient world practiced initiatory relationships between older men and young boys on a widespread basis, that the period of social initiation into warriorhood and service was "complemented by a sexual one" (13) and that what survives in the many myths of male-male attraction is the practice of defining masculinity and male sexuality in homoerotic rather than heteroerotic terms. See his discussion of the Ganymede myth (205–13). Kenneth J. Dover notes that the homosexual relationships which were publicly approved were "strongly asymmetrical," with the authority and prestige accruing to the older male ("Greek Homosexuality and Initiation," reprinted in vol. 1 of *Homosexuality in the Ancient World,* Studies in Homosexuality [New York: Garland, 1992], 127–46, quotation on 130).

19. My use of the term "minion" derives from Smith, *Homosexual Desire in Shakespeare's England,* 73–76. On Renaissance uses of the term "ganymede," see also Bray, *Homosexuality in Renaissance England,* 16, 53, 60, 65, and 66.

20. In addition to Bray, "Homosexuality and the Signs of Male Friendship," and Smith, *Homosexual Desire in Shakespeare's England,* see Cynthia Herrup, "Law and Morality in Seventeenth Century England," *Past and Present* 106 (Feb. 1985): 102–23, and Bredbeck, *Sodomy and Interpretation.*

21. On the neoplatonic influence on visual representations of the Ganymede legend, see Erwin Panofsky, *Studies in Iconology: Humanistic Themes in the Art of the Renaissance* (New York: Harper and Row, 1962), 212–18; James Saslow, *Ganymede in the Renaissance* (New Haven: Yale University Press, 1986), 17–62; and Leonard Barkan, *Transuming Passion: Ganymede and the Erotics of Humanism* (Stanford: Stanford University Press, 1991), 80–101.

22. All quotations from Ovid's *Metamorphosis* are from *The XV. Bookes Entytuled Metamorphosis,* trans. Arthur Golding (London, 1567; reprint, Amsterdam: Walter J. Johnson and Theatrum Orbis Terrarum, 1977); quotation on 125.

23. For a cogent discussion of the importance of fatherhood and patrilinear identification to the *Aeneid,* see Quint, *Epic and Empire,* 59–62.

24. On the links between sodomy and grammatical irregularity, see Ernst Curtius, *European Literature and the Latin Middle Ages* (New York: Bollingen, 1953), 414–16. Barkan, in *Transuming Passion,* emphasizes the degree to which the humanist recovery of classical texts was itself thought to be liable to a highly gendered and sexualized philological perversity, and therefore the degree to which the Jupiter-Ganymede story was read

as exemplifying the interpretive "problem of deceptive relations between signifier and signified" (51–53, quotation on 52).

25. Statius, *Thebaid,* in vol. 1 of *Statius,* trans. J. H. Mozley (London: Heinemann; New York: Putnam's, 1928), 381.

26. In "B/O—Barthes's Text/O'Hara's Trick," Gregory W. Bredbeck defines how a system of signification based on (male) homosexuality instead of on a phallically centered heterosexuality might restate "heterosexual binaries as questions that frustrate the desire for atemporal truth: Am I passive or active *tonight?* Am I defined by penis or anus *in this instance?*" (*Publications of the Modern Languages Association of America* 108 [1993]: 268–82, quotation on 274). I believe that this multiplicity of identities and subject positions—at least for men, because Bredbeck's argument rests on a sexual subject who possesses both anus *and* penis—is precisely what Marlowe's treatment of the Ganymede myth invokes.

27. Gill, *Complete Works of Christopher Marlowe,* 1:114.

28. Michael Shapiro, in *Children of the Revels: The Boy Companies of Shakespeare's Time and Their Plays,* discusses the wide range of these troupes' probable acting styles ([New York: Columbia University Press, 1977], 103–38). He suggests that the frequent bawdry of the boys' plays was aimed at "underlining the incongruity between the erotic behavior of the characters and the sexual immaturity of the actors" (106). However, he does not speculate on why boys should have been thought appropriate performers of erotic scenes between ostensibly adult characters.

29. See, for example, Phyllis Rackin, "Shakespeare's Boy Cleopatra, the Decorum of Nature, and the Golden World of Poetry," *Publications of the Modern Language Association of America* 87 (1972): 201–12, and "Androgyny, Mimesis, and the Marriage of the Boy Heroine on the English Renaissance Stage," *Publications of the Modern Language Association of America* 102 (1987): 29–41; and Juliet Dusinberre, *Shakespeare and the Nature of Women* (New York: Macmillan, 1975), 231–71. Rackin and Dusinberre both suggest that the boy actor points the way toward a new ideal of gender which in its approaches to a doubly sexed ideal either transcends the social meanings of gendered identity (Rackin) or points a way toward how women can step out of their ordained social roles (Dusinberre). However, Valerie Traub insists that boys playing women performed the sexualization not of boys' bodies but of women's, and thus can be seen as opening a space for reading female homoeroticism in early modern culture ("The (In)significance of 'Lesbian' Desire in Early Modern England," in *Erotic Politics: Desire on the Renaissance Stage,* ed. Susan Zimmerman [New York: Routledge, 1992], 150–69). Traub's analysis suggests how the figure of the boy actor can be seen as dislodging the centrality of a compulsory heterosexuality as the only matrix for understanding the effects of Renaissance theatrical practice.

30. See Thomas Laqueur, *Making Sex: Body and Gender from the Greeks to Freud* (Cambridge, Mass.: Harvard University Press, 1990), and Stephen Greenblatt, "Fiction and Friction," chap. 3 of *Shakespearean Negotiations: The Circulation of Social Energy in Renaissance England* (Berkeley and Los Angeles: University of California Press, 1988), 66–93. Arguing that the pervasive "fascination with all that seems to unsettle sexual differentiation . . . never decisively overturns in the Renaissance discourse of sexuality the

proper generative order that depends upon a distinction between the sexes" (82), Greenblatt concludes that the heroines of Shakespeare's plays who "realize their identities through cross-dressing" are in effect "the representation of Shakespearean men, the projected mirror images of masculine self-differentiation" (92). Kathleen McLuskie, on the other hand, contends that in early modern play texts in which the portrayal "of fictional characters is produced by emblem and symbol," and in which theatrical practices follow "a set of formal encounters," the difficulties of sustaining "a stable representation of women" are "not great" in that the "signification of 'woman' is entirely contained within the text" and is independent of "the sexuality of the actor in question"; in Shakespeare's romantic comedies, the heroines' crossdressing is employed "partly as a means of asserting their true femininity" ("The Act, the Role, and the Actor: Boy Actresses on the Elizabethan Stage," *New Theatre Quarterly* 3 [1987], 122, 123).

31. Lisa Jardine, *Still Harping on Daughters: Women and Drama in the Age of Shakespeare* (Sussex: Harvester Press, 1983), esp. 17–31. In "Twins and Travesties: Gender, Dependency and Sexual Availability in *Twelfth Night*," Jardine develops the additional point that the gender of the boy actors complicates an easy assumption that we can "read" them as cognates for women on stage by pointing out that even though boy actors are emphatically *not* women, they may well solicit the same kinds of "erotic attention" (28) as women because of the similarly subordinate and dependent positions of minors and women in the early modern household (in *Erotic Politics,* ed. Susan Zimmerman, 27–38). Stephen Orgel also points out the social "interchangeability" of boys and women in the period (in "Nobody's Perfect: Or Why Did the English Stage Take Boys for Women?" *South Atlantic Quarterly* 88 [1989]: 13).

32. Laura Levine, "Men in Women's Clothing: Anti-Theatricality and Effemization from 1579 to 1642," *Criticism* 28 (1986): 121–43; reprinted in *Men in Women's Clothing: Anti-Theatricality and Effemization, 1579–1642* (Cambridge: Cambridge University Press, 1994), 10–25.

33. Phillip Stubbes, *The Anatomie of Abuses* (London, 1583; reprint, Amsterdam: Theatrum Orbis Terrarum; New York: Da Capo Press, 1972), sig. L8v. As Orgel further suggests, the thing "worse" than playing the sodomite "is presumably the sodomized" ("Nobody's Perfect," 17): that is, to accept the subordinate, passive, "feminine" role in heterosexually ordained erotic or social relations.

34. I know that the term "homosexual" did not come into the language until the nineteenth century, a point emphasized by such critics as Bray and Halperin, and that it may thus be unhistorical to label people and their affectional orientations in the Renaissance as "homosexual." I would add, however, that although the term "homosexual" may not have come into use until created by later sexologists, this does not necessarily mean that the existence of sexual and romantic love between men was "largely unrecognized and unformed" (Bray, *Homosexuality in Renaissance England,* 79), that it had no social—or, especially for my purposes here—literary being because people didn't have the label "homosexual" to attach to it. See Joseph Cady, "'Masculine Love': Renaissance Writing and the 'New' Invention of Homosexuality," *Journal of Homosexuality* 23, nos. 1 and 2 (1992): 9–40.

35. Stubbes, *Anatomie of Abuses,* sig. F5v.

36. On how self-adornment, particularly face-painting, was held to be a particularly egregious example of women's duplicity in Renaissance culture, see Frances Dolan, "Taking the Pencil out of God's Hand: Art, Nature, and the Face-Painting Debate in Early Modern England," *Publications of Modern Language Association* 108 (1993): 224–39. I am not implying an equivalence between women and boys, but rather, following Jardine in "Twins and Travesties," I recognize that reactions against the deceitfulness of disguising one's true gender identity mark both the face-painting debate's and the antitheatrical tracts' charges of sodomy. If anything, the antitheatrical tracts experience an even deeper fear of losing one's gendered self, and the capacity to discern the marks of gender in others, than do the arguments against face-painting.

37. Simon Shepherd, in *Marlowe and the Politics of Elizabethan Theatre,* does not mention Jupiter's gifts, but does discuss Dido's (193–95), seeing them as articles which articulate gender "through private and public meanings; personal feeling expressed through objects is not separable from control and competition" (195). I would agree that Dido is not so much trying to "control" Aeneas as she is trying to remake him, to redefine him in the image of the husband and lord who is the only love object sanctioned by her own formation within a patriarchal and heterosexual construction of sexual identity. That the redressing inevitably recalls the gifts exchanged between Jupiter and Ganymede suggests the extent to which male-female relations in the play are in fact shaped by the male-male bond shown in the prologue. See also Gregory Woods, "Body, Costume, and Desire in Christopher Marlowe," *Journal of Homosexuality* 23, nos. 1 and 2 (1992): 69–84, esp. 70–72.

38. Reviewing neoplatonic interpretations of the Ganymede myth, George Sandys, in *Ovid's Metamorphoses English'd* (Oxford, 1632), notes that "physically Hebe is said to be removed from [the office of cupbearer], for stumbling and indecently shewing her nakedness." In contrast, Ganymede was "rather assumed into heaven for the beauty of his mind, than that of his body" (359).

39. See, for example, Marilyn Skinner, *Reading Dido: Gender, Textuality and the Medieval Aeneid* (Minneapolis: University of Minnesota Press, 1994).

5

Subjectivity, Time, and Gender in *Titus Andronicus, Hamlet,* and *Othello*

R. L. Kesler

> O, why should nature build so foul a den
> Unless the gods delight in tragedies?
> —*Titus Andronicus,* 4.1.59–60

Spoken by Marcus at a moment intense in its evocation of the tragic,[1] and visually marked by the reentry of *Titus Andronicus*'s handless and tongueless heroine Lavinia to the stage, this sardonic utterance is at once theological and metapoetic, pointing not only to the represented circumstances of a world in which suffering seems inevitable but also to the representational circumstance of a theater in which the production of images of suffering, often inscribed in gender, had an important commercial role. On the metapoetic level, the theological question posed is easily resolved: suffering occurs because the "gods" who delight in tragedy, the actual patrons of the theater, demand it, authorizing and consuming the images of suffering that the theater provides, even while the system of "nature" that organizes and supports their desire remains obscure. The amenability of this moment in *Titus* to interpretation on these two levels, however, suggests a self-consciousness and cynicism about the circumstances of production in the commercial theater, and the possibilities of another frame of reference, constructed in the disjunction between different presumptions of knowledge. Like the more general flirtations of this play with stylistic excess and parody, the gap between the literal and metadramatic levels of interpretation points to the possibility that at least some audiences can know more about the play than its characters appear to, that they can be conscious not only of the terms of its represented world but also of the conventions governing its representation. In this difference lies the possibility of movement and the awareness of change.

Titus Andronicus, like other plays of its time, appeared in a commercial market increasingly saturated by a growing number of plays and conventions, in various respects similar, yet each striving to distinguish itself against its competitors and the growing literary record of the past. In such a representational market, irony serves a special function, distancing itself from the conventions within which it operates, defining them as past to the present it creates, and separating those who understand it from those it left behind. In such an environment, insight soon becomes conventionalized as knowledge, knowledge soon becomes cliché, and irony about cliché becomes insight. Audiences are constantly presented with the new and reeducated in their understanding of the old. In this chain of differences, predicated in the economies of production, time is redefined, not as recurrence but as progression and change; and knowledge is based not upon precedent but on anticipation, prediction, and investment.

The rough equivalence of dramatic units substituted the regularity of "method" for the larger integrating narratives that drama and other Renaissance forms fragmented into the separate concerns of individual plays. Yet even within the group of representations clustered around a set of common themes and operating under the general rubric of "tragedy," change was inevitable, and within them, even such superficially stable categories as "man" and "woman," together with the relationships of cruelty and domination that seem routinely to order them, underwent profound functional shifts.[2]

In the most obvious respects, tragedy is about the relocation of representation to the limited and closed perspective of the individual play ("beginning," "middle," and "end"). Within the individual play, it is also about change ("the change of fortune from good to bad") and the pattern through which it can be understood (using the causal plot as a way of mapping events and time). These are, in fact, two aspects of a single situation in which both character and subjectivity were redefined.[3] As the rules and conventions governing this redefinition emerged, the subjectivities allowable also became visible, some in more privileged positions than others. Given the generality of patriarchal conditions, it is hardly surprising to see differentiation by gender operating to define levels of privilege within this system. But the images of violence and cruelty deployed toward women had a deeper and more aggressive function. The plays grouped around the rubric of "tragedy" developed in a dialectic of neologism and acclimatization in which new levels of understanding consistently displaced and disprivileged their predecessors, defining them as obsolete. In consistently structuring the emerging and most privileged categories of knowledge around the figures of the male heroes, the plays masculinized privileged knowledge, defining it against the feminization of those older formulations now scheduled for obsolescence. In this gendering of knowledge, privilege, and time, images of violence and cruelty toward women performed the central function of placing those older modes of understanding beyond recovery. This process, historical and momentary, is easily forgotten in light of the image it helped to produce, namely the new bourgeois subjectivity with its claims to universality and the "natural." But it produced as well an iconography of cruelty through which masculine/feminine relationships were inscribed in violence, long after this moment of historical realization had passed.

The extraordinary cultural prominence of Shakespeare throughout the ensuing four hundred years of bourgeois consolidation is the backdrop, then, for the consideration here of violence and the relative positioning of the "masculine" and "feminine" in three plays, *Titus Andronicus, Hamlet,* and *Othello,* each in some ways representative of different periods of Shakespeare's career. Each points to a distinct function for the differential separating "man" from "woman," and each is linked to the others as a stage in this process. As a group, these texts demonstrate not only the complexity and fluidity with which categories in the drama were rearranged to suit local purposes but also the subtleties through which social and political categories operated to preserve power and advantage through times of rapid scientific, technological, and social change.

In thinking through the early stages of this process, it is important to note that this kind of gendering of violence and change was hardly limited to the theater. Evelyn Fox Keller has argued that the feminizing of Nature in Baconian science was part of its domestication in a larger rhetoric of male mastery, idealizing Nature and the feminine, while ensuring their domination.[4] Carolyn Merchant has argued that images of sexual violence were also deployed to sanction more permissive attitudes toward the exploitation of natural resources for commercial gain:

> The change in controlling imagery was directly related to changes in human attitudes and behavior toward the earth. Whereas the nurturing earth image can be viewed as a cultural constraint restricting the types of socially and morally sanctioned human actions allowable with respect to the earth, the new images of mastery and domination functioned as cultural sanctions for the denudation of nature.... Sanctioning mining sanctioned the rape or commercial exploration of the earth—a clear illustration of how constraints can change to sanctions through the demise of frameworks and their associated values as the needs, wants, and purposes of society change.[5]

Whether or not feminized images of Nature existed before this usage, as Merchant has argued, the identification of such previously inclusive categories with the feminine at the point of their dismantling, and the corresponding emergence of an independent and autonomous male subjectivity in contradistinction to them, were familiar Renaissance patterns in which the tragedies considered here participated.

The image with which this essay began, that of the suffering Lavinia in *Titus Andronicus,* is representative of an early stage of Shakespeare's career as well as the initial phase of the most competitive period of Renaissance dramatic production. Perhaps not surprisingly, it is in this phase of the development of the commercial drama, even after its gradual separation from its earlier embedding in church festival and complex civic functions, that such larger conceptual and narrative categories as Nature posed the most serious threat to the privileged definition of an independent masculinized subjectivity.[6] In the later parts of the play, Lavinia wanders bloody, handless, and tongueless, an icon of what this kind of violence can accomplish. She is able to identify her attackers only after she has made the transition from speech to writing, holding a staff in her mouth as a phallic surrogate for her absent tongue, confirming not only the irretrievability of her loss but also her entry into a world of écriture and history, absence and deferral.

As powerful as this image is, however, the earlier scenes surrounding her rape (2.3–4) are perhaps even more critical to the play's explanatory thematics. In these scenes, Lavinia accuses the Goth queen Tamora of infidelity with Tamora's black servant, Aaron. Moments later, at Aaron's instigation, Lavinia's betrothed, Bassianus, is killed by Tamora's sons and thrown into a pit, and Lavinia is dragged off to be raped. In the subsequent scene, Lavinia's brothers are lured into the pit, and, with gold previously sequestered near its mouth, implicated in the murder. The accusation of lust, the womblike pit, and the rape of Lavinia form a triptych of female sexuality, both transgressive and abject, while the association of the pit and sequestered gold with the wounding of the earth, the extraction of resources, and the investment of capital for later gain form an overlying layer of commercialism and exploitation, reminiscent of Merchant's account and joined to the first by the common theme of violence. In this complex nexus of associations, images of female sexuality are placed in an intense and complicated relation with an emergent ethic of causality and commerce, while older ideals of feudal honor and nobility are simultaneously feminized and denigrated in their victimization.

The association of the feminine with the victimization of feudalism and family is initially offset by the image of the sexually potent and uncontrollable Tamora. These contradictory images of female sexuality are, however, ultimately resolved by the larger terms of the causal plot, which clearly emerges by the end as the play's dominant thematic. The importance of the causal plot in *Titus Andronicus* is perhaps more obvious in comparison with the role it plays in Kyd's earlier *Spanish Tragedy*, which also centers around issues of identity and temporality, and similarly emphasizes the immobility of characters constrained by feudal and familial relations in a causally structured environment. In *The Spanish Tragedy*, some are represented as dying pointlessly, others as successfully redefining themselves in planned and "plotted" action. Perhaps most significantly, the choral commentary that frames the action of the play, articulating these positions in debate between one character who argues for the importance of the play's explication of the causal linkages and another who expresses frustration with it, mediates between the play and an uncomprehending and impatient audience.[7] The play itself, in all of these respects, seems largely introductory and explanatory, rather than confident, of its causal theme.

Titus Andronicus, however, assumes from the outset a more sophisticated understanding of the causal plot, consistent with its probable appearance, in 1594, at a time in which many in its audiences would have been familiar with the precedent of other plays, including *The Spanish Tragedy.* Plot and causal linkage are given explicit thematic foregrounding in the overt scheming of the malevolent male servant Aaron; and the competition between characters defined by opportunism and causality, such as Aaron, and those defined by feudal honor and obligation, such as Lavinia and Bassianus, is more sharply drawn. In the critical scene of rape and murder, Aaron's ascendancy over Bassianus and Lavinia completes the separation of these two groups. A consequence of this victory is, however, that Lavinia's function is redefined. On one hand, she is located at the end of a causal chain within which her mutilated condition pointedly marks the failure of synchronic and encompassing "natural" relations such as honor and family to provide an effective context for action. On the other, that very process places her at the beginning of a second causal chain in which, by supplying the motive and justification for Titus's reluctant transformation from a loyal feudal retainer to victorious causal plotter, her rape provokes his abandonment of the very values she represents. The structuring of the last half of the play around Titus's revenge, in which Lavinia serves only as an initiating condition, further assures her symbolic obsolescence, graphically confirmed in her death by Titus's hand.

Lavinia's role and the function of gender distinctions in the play as a whole form a two-stage process. In the first, the once inclusive and definitive contexts of "the book of Nature" and "the book of culture," encapsulated within feminized thematics of feudal honor, chastity, and marriage, are marginalized as tragedy's "methodical" privileging of Machiavellian opportunism accedes to center stage.[8] The death of Bassianus and the mutilation of Lavinia are icons of the disintegration of those contexts and their passage into a "history" for which she remains only a dramatic but vestigial trace. That the values which Lavinia and Bassianus represent are still regarded as normative during this first stage is, however, evident in the suspicion with which causal thinking is regarded in the early acts of the play. The demonization of Aaron and Tamora as alien and unscrupulous Machiavellian plotters suggests the extent to which such newly pragmatic values and the views of time, subjectivity, and action they supported were still unassimilated in English society of the early 1590s.

In the second symbolic movement of the play, however, the very qualities of alienation surrounding Aaron and Tamora become the means by which those same values are rehabilitated. In appropriating their methods and learning to plot their defeat under the aegis of Lavinia's revenge, Titus simultaneously domesticates causal thinking and frees it from blame. By defeating the racially marginalized Aaron and disciplining the sexually uncontrolled and foreign Tamora, Titus reconstructs Roman patriarchy with a causal face. And through the transference of causal values from the demonized figures of Machiavellians to the figure of a hero who has acted through a justifiable calculation in the service of personal responsibility, he allows for the recognition of causal thinking as the primary positive value that the tragic narrative has to offer.

In this respect *Titus Andronicus* is typical of the way in which many tragedies process their symbolic contents, assigning and reassigning values to characters and positions as their relative importance changes, while maintaining a consistent and "plotted" movement toward the definition of a new regime. And at least in one respect, it is finally the relationship between the characters Titus and Lavinia that defines that new regime's central features. By overcoming the constraints of his own feudal position, represented at the end of the play by the dissolved claims of family in the battered corpse of Lavinia, Titus argues for a subjectivity ultimately independent of such entanglements, a subjectivity that, though initially highly dependent upon those feminized values, both positive and negative, against which it is initially defined, looks forward to the "universality" of a male subjectivity that is fully causal, objective, and detached—a subjectivity that can operate, in the generalist but highly phallocentric terms of the new science, "beyond gender," that is, beyond any symbolic need for women at all.

That particular victory, for a time achievable within the context of an individualized lyric poetry after Donne, was, for reasons to be considered below, never fully realized in drama, though later developments in tragedies such as *Hamlet* brought it very near completion. Those further developments were significant, both in the movement of this pattern toward completion and in their creation of the circumstances that would, like Lavinia's rape, shift the deployment of gender distinctions toward a substantially different role. At the base of all these changes lie, once again, a question of knowledge and a game of irony in a time of change.

While it is possible to see early tragedies such as *Titus Andronicus* and *The Spanish Tragedy* as having been largely successful in redefining subjectivity in terms of limited causal sequence and a diachronic mapping of time, by 1610, when

Jonson's *The Alchemist* was first performed, it is clear that, whatever their accomplishments, those earlier plays had come to be regarded at least by some as antiquated clichés. Here Jonson's characters construct an elaborate visual parody of Hieronimo, the hero of *The Spanish Tragedy:*

> Fac.: Thou must borrow,
> A *Spanish* suite. Hast thou no credit with the players?
> Drv.: Yes, sir, did you neuer see me play the foole?
> Fac.: I know not Nab: thou shalt, if I can helpe it.
> Hieronymo's old cloake, ruffe, and hat will serue
> Ile tell thee more, when thou bringst'hem.
> (*The Alchemist*, 4.7.67–72)[9]

In the New Comic world of Jonson's middle plays, the kinds of understandings basic to the causal tragic plot were assumptions that only the fools did not share.

The commentary in Jonson's play on the status of *The Spanish Tragedy* is significant not only in showing how much things had changed by 1610 but in pointing to the ways in which the institutions of commercial theater as a representational environment had contributed to that change. As argued earlier, even early plays such as *Titus Andronicus* were ironic in significant ways, commenting on the obsolescence of their predecessors such as *The Spanish Tragedy* as models for the understanding of causality and action. Yet even by the time that *Hamlet* was produced, the pressures for such ironic commentaries and interpretations had drastically increased. Significant proportions of audiences could be presumed to be familiar with such early works and well schooled in the understandings they offered. In a much more aggressive sense, parody and neologism functioned as distancing devices, separating new productions and defining them as new, against the ever widening sea of extant works.[10] The dialectic between audiences and producers, between the conventions of the known and the need for the new, structured a larger chain of causality, linking not just the incidents within a single plot but knowledge and ignorance and play to play in a larger and ever more definitive pattern of mandatory change.

As in Greek and Roman drama, New Comedies such as *The Alchemist*, written fairly late in this process, formed an ironic and retrospective commentary on the conventions of tragedy through the inversion of many of their major features. Less obvious, perhaps, is how fundamental this pattern of ironic inversion was even to the most well known tragedies that preceded it. While even an early play such as *Titus Andronicus* presumed an understanding of the conventions of the revenge plot and its causal construction of time in a more sophisticated way than did *its* predecessors (it was, after all, in its own right a very satiric play), it was far from the elaborate critiques of causal action that were to follow in tragedies such as *Hamlet*. While plays such as *The Spanish Tragedy* and *Titus Andronicus* seem to be based on the assumption of the audience's relative ignorance of causality and sequential time and occupy themselves with their patient demonstration, a play such as *Hamlet* is based on the opposite assumption—that, due to the very popularity and repeated performance of the earlier plays, its audiences would know the conventions of the causal plot and could no longer be entertained with their mere demonstration. That altered circumstance of knowledge and expectation, and the need to escape the collapse into cliché which it threatened, presented substantial challenges for later writers of tragedy while creating the opportunity for greater sophistication.

Unlike the hero of *The Spanish Tragedy,* Hamlet appears to be a sophisticate. Like many Elizabethan playwrights, Hamlet has been to university, and he has studied drama. Like the audiences Jonson frequently berated, Hamlet considers himself more than competent to give advice to professional players, and even to script his own productions. He appears to be intimately acquainted with drama's conventions, and in planning his own play, *The Murder of Gonzago,* demonstrates a confidence not only in the mimetic capabilities of art but also in its potential to affect life. The larger play around him, furthermore, in its metadramatic moments, critical debates, and parodies of older dramas (the "Hecuba" speech perhaps recalling *Dido*), is alive with references to knowledge that the sophisticates among his audiences would share.

Hamlet, like those observing him, is represented as being, in other words, in a position to be acutely self-conscious, not only about his existential position in some represented reality but about his role in the drama that surrounds him and that encases his own (if imaginary) life. Like the sophisticates in the audiences who view him, he is well positioned to understand the deeper metadramatic meaning of his situation, even as the play opens with the appearance of his father's ghost. What Hamlet knows, and what the sophisticates in his audiences must have known having seen *The Spanish Tragedy,* is that, by the conventions of the revenge plot, he is confronted not only with the feudal obligation of his father's death but with his own position as the hero and the "causality" of his fate, in which as hero, he must both kill Claudius and die.[11]

In openly acknowledging on stage the possibilities of such conventionalized knowledge possessed by audiences (audiences who, after all, had come to see a *tragedy*), Shakespeare also acknowledges the emergence of a curious paradox, if not for Hamlet as a character, then at least for Shakespeare as a writer. If the sophisticates in the audience are aware of the conventions of the causal plot, then they know that only two actions are necessary to complete its logic—Hamlet must kill Claudius, and Hamlet must die. But if the logic linking these events to their preconditions has been elaborately and repeatedly mapped by earlier plays, then they can no longer be entertained with its patient demonstration. If these two actions are immediately performed, the play ends in the first act. If, on the other hand, they are properly located in the fifth act, then, by definition, nothing of real "plot" significance can happen in the intervening space. *Hamlet* thus constructs an empty space in which nothing can happen.

The problem, then, was to fill this space with significance, and Shakespeare's response was to devise the character Hamlet, who fills the time with the prevarications, diversions, false starts, and existential commentaries on the condition of being defined as a space, all of which serve both to fill this space and argue for its relevance. Rather than Hamlet creating delay, in other words, it was the unavoidability of the delay that created Hamlet, and the fabled problems of motivation and indecision, as well as the philosophical existentialism of *Hamlet,* were not the products of "character" at all, in the traditional sense, but rather responses to the changed circumstances in which character, and therefore subjectivity, could be constructed in tragedy.

Given these circumstances, several ironies found in *Hamlet* and in its subsequent reception are particularly remarkable. The first, of course, is that Hamlet has persisted for nearly four hundred years as an icon of bourgeois subjectivity, Nietzsche's "man who must choose." James Calderwood ends his sophisticated discussion by reconstructing a humanist analysis, pushing the "real" subjectivity in *Hamlet* back to the author by arguing for Shakespeare's genius in "resistance" to the traditional syntax of plot.[12] Yet Calderwood attributes to the biographical Shakespeare precisely the personal autonomy he has denied Hamlet, who, after all, has always to others seemed to "resist" the role that fate had assigned to him in precisely the same terms. It may be more accurate to say not only that the position of *Hamlet* in the development of Renaissance drama was historically defined by the *inaccessibility* of the "traditional" plot and the necessity of its modification but also that Shakespeare himself was defined, at least as an artist, by these same parameters of change. If it was only by his "delay" that the character Hamlet was able to construct a space within which to exist at all, and only in reflecting on his "fate" that he was able to grant that space significance, then it was only by exploiting the possibilities of this paradox that the historical Shakespeare was able to exist in the public life of the theater by authoring this play. Seen in this light, even *Hamlet*'s philosophy has an arbitrary and sardonic quality: when Hamlet remarks "the readiness is all," he marks not only the final extension of his reasoning but also the arrival of the play at the fifth act within which these very prevarications are no longer necessary to a play that can now move toward closure. The story, in this respect, is not about individuality and free choice but the circumstances of its very formation as an illusion.

If even the most sophisticated humanist approach is to emphasize the continuity of the character Hamlet (or Shakespeare) as an explanation of both dramatic and cultural proportions, other critics have emphasized just the opposite. Catherine Belsey, for example, has argued that Hamlet is "the most discontinuous of Shakespeare's heroes."[13] Yet these apparently opposite positions may finally be two sides of the same coin, both pointing to the larger circumstances in which this particular drama, in both its internal and external aspects, unfolded. The first great theoretician of Greek literacy, Eric Havelock, argued that the heroes of the epics appeared inconsistent and irrational only at the moment in which logical consistency became a social ideal. By such an understanding, Hamlet's inconsistencies, and even his madness, only appear as vestigial features of the old regime defined against the new, the inexorable standard of "literary" logic that the necessities of the play had begun to project.[14]

That very projection, however, points to a second paradox arising from the "causal necessities" of *Hamlet*'s end, but more fully definitive of the plays, such as *Othello*, that would follow. This second paradox is that a Hamlet who *really* understood plot, causality, and linear sequence, and who was *fully* defined in their terms, would not consent to be "tragic" at all. Rather, like the New Comic heroes who replaced him, he would construct a counterplot that subverted the "inevitable" consequences of his fate and turned them to his advantage. At the very least he would abandon his useless and impossible nobility and escape with Ophelia to a life of domestic drama in the Paris suburbs (or perhaps to exercise his wit in a safe Restoration comedy). It was against the full implications of this knowledge and its corresponding abandonment of tragedy and the heroic that Hamlet's discontinuities, misdirections, and madness defended not only this play but also its usefulness to a bourgeois culture too soon to know the restrictions on heroism that its own knowledge would bring. In this sense, *Hamlet* participates par excellence in the game of Renaissance knowledge and duplicity that projects its most solid claims to heroism and the iconic in a diversion from the truth.

The most stunning victory of *Hamlet,* even as viewed through the above analysis, is how fully and completely it extends this figure of the single and isolated hero, however interpreted, to fill center stage. Hamlet and *his* problems: a hero defined not in the first instance by his relation to social institutions or other characters, since their roles have become largely instrumental to his, but by the new institution of his personal fate and his self-absorption within it. In this play, feudal obligation is, finally, only a ghost and a "motive" for a chain of events that would quickly displace it; and the larger, gendered concerns of *Titus Andronicus,* so replete with contextual meanings, become only a backdrop against which this newer drama of individual, masculinized subjectivity can unfold. If Gertrude is the state, then Hamlet is defined by his "personal" alienation from kingship and power.[15] If she is the Oedipal mother, then she is only the causality of the personal past, the childhood that determined not only the trajectory of the present but the future that unfolds as a personal function of the subject. If she is Nature and the Other, against which the speaker, Hamlet, is defined, then she exists to be repressed and to die as a function of *his* death, just as Man in the Baconian world had already begun to repress Nature in the seductive narrative of his own independence.

But perhaps most telling in this drama of the emergence of an independent and "objective," if self-obsessed and masculinized, subjectivity is not the role assigned to Gertrude but rather that assigned to Ophelia, who represents not the past but the faint image of two alternate futurities: one, inaccessible and projected from the past, in which, in her pregnancy with both meaning and progeny, Ophelia would reconstitute with Hamlet the eternity of feudal succession, and the other, barely visible on the horizon of the future, in which she would construct, in the terms already alluded to, the happy world of bourgeois domesticity. In either of these roles Ophelia is defined in this play, finally, not by her power but by the ease of her rejection. Unlike Lavinia in *Titus Andronicus,* Ophelia dies, not by violence but by neglect, a victim not of the necessary obliteration of the values she represents but of the self-absorption of masculine individuality in which she has no place. "I must 'tell' Ophelia's 'story,'" Carol Neely and others have written, but it is indeed a story structured in absence.[16] In considering the fate of later Greek tragedy, Friedrich Nietzsche argued in *The Birth of Tragedy* that "Greek tragedy met an end different from that of her older sister-arts. She died by suicide, in consequence of an irreconcilable conflict; she died tragically, while all the others passed away calmly and beautifully at a ripe old age."[17] It could be argued that the "irreconcilable conflict" for tragedy in the Renaissance emerged with *Hamlet,* defining the plays to follow as stages in the "suicide" or progressive self-destruction of "tragedy" as a viable narrative form.

Ironically, while *Hamlet* may have marked an apotheosis of a kind of successful masculinized subjectivity in tragedy, recent criticism has accurately noted a resurgence of feminine roles in later plays such as *Othello, Lear,* and *The Duchess of Malfi.* There are, of course, many possible explanations for this trend: the rise of a class of relatively independent urban women and the movement within some parts of Protestantism and rationalism to accord women equal status. Within the drama, however, there is another explanation, tied to the further development of plot and subjectivity and the redeployment of gender distinctions along different functional lines. Just as *Titus Andronicus* had shown how the habits of planning and calculation could be shifted from one set of characters to another in the course of their promotion, so later tragedies such as *Othello* would demonstrate the ways in which gender distinctions could be shifted to enforce other categorical differentials just as the functions of the tragic hero in a post-*Hamlet* world were beginning to erode.

The triumph of *Hamlet* is that the character Hamlet can be presented as knowing the conventions and causalities of tragedy adequately enough to anticipate his own fate but not fully enough to conceive of its alternatives. In this particular state of partial awareness, both his frustration and willingness to act remain comprehensible. Just as the successful publication of a neologism precludes its future novelty, however, the articulation of *Hamlet*'s particular state of awareness removes exactly the grounds of his particular claims to ignorance. The bourgeois causal hero who follows knows the futility of such actions. Presented with the motive of revenge he asks, "what's in it for me?" And, as *Hamlet* so amply demonstrates, the answer is self-destruction and death. In the world after *Hamlet*, tragedy is necessarily constructed in very different terms, and the gap between audiences who understand the future and a hero who either cannot or will not accept its terms grows ever wider.

How, then, were audiences to rationalize the existence of a hero whose knowledge was now so much more limited than their own? Shakespeare's solution in *Othello* is to articulate this central structural problem thematically by splitting "the hero" into two competing characters who represent the conflict between what drama had been and what it was to become—between Othello as the waning traditional hero of limited knowledge and fate, in his ignorance pathetic and sacrificial, and Iago as the ascendant hero of plot and causal sophistication, the scheming servant of New Comedy, who, within the confines of tragedy, can once again appear as the mute force of evil.[18] In the victory of Iago, the movement of tragedy toward New Comedy is acted out and given form.[19] Its eventual inheritors are the great causal heroes of the following century—Mirabelle, Robinson Crusoe, and most of all, Milton's Christ—who function by planning, sacrifice, and investment in future rewards, while the fate of the traditional tragic hero, as Jonson demonstrates in *The Alchemist,* is to lie only in parodic subplot encapsulation within a larger game.

While the traditional hero, as *Othello* demonstrates, could for a time survive these changes, he could do so only in a considerably reduced and circumscribed form; the burden then fell on the play to rationalize, if it could not fully justify, the extent of his circumscription. It was Shakespeare's somewhat dubious brilliance to realize just how fully racism in a play such as *Othello* might be used to accomplish these ends: by defining Othello as a black, alien and "inferior" in Venetian society, Shakespeare allowed for the distance that would make Othello's failures and inevitable sacrifice not only acceptable but also satisfying as a form of closure. The audience, like Desdemona, might pity Othello for his suffering, while accepting his downfall as a predictable and "justifiable" consequence of his social transgression. Yet even these "tragic" features point toward comedy. Ironically, in defining Othello as both a black and a mercenary, Shakespeare duplicated those very restrictions that Socrates specified for comedy: convinced that the characters of comedy were inherently demeaning, Socrates argued that they should not be played by citizens but only by slaves and hired aliens.[20]

The close structural identification of *Othello* with New Comedy does not, however, rest simply or even primarily with Othello but with Iago, who, like the "scheming servants" of New Comedies such as Plautus's *Menaechmi* or Jonson's *Volpone*, represents those forces of plot that emerged to dominate the more traditional category of character as even a tragedy such as *Hamlet* had established it. Though a servant in a play still nominally defined by his master, Iago remains at the center of the action, defining its events and charting its causalities, controlling other characters through schemes that become synonymous with the plot itself, and always widening the gap between audience and hero, the audience foreshadowing in their knowledge the certainty of his doom. Iago behaves not like a hero or author who is the source of narrative but like the director or producer who exploits those opportunities that the script provides, positioning characters and coaching them in their roles, timing sequences, and interactions, controlling audiences' perceptions, and subsuming them all to the service of the play and its institutional logic of survival, in which ignorance and sacrifice become his master's only function.

On its most literal level of reifying identity, *Hamlet* had already given some explicit clues as to just how random identity could be in a world defined by action and the causal mechanics of plot. Polonius at the moment of his death is defined, not by his ontological identity as a character but by the arras that defines him as a position in a field of action (whoever is behind the arras must die, a logic extended to grotesque proportions in the later *Revenger's Tragedy*). In *Othello* the extrinsic definition of characters by the syntax of action is further explicated in the theme of substitution that dominates the play's imagery: Cassio is substituted for Iago in promotion, Othello for Roderigo in Desdemona's affections, Iago for Desdemona in Iago's recounting of Cassio's dream, Othello for Iago in Iago's imagined cuckolding. The interchangeability of characters and positions, while perhaps commenting on the emergence of a more fluid bourgeois social structure, internally reveals a system of identity based not on the plenitude and self-sufficiency of characters who define actions but on the displacement of desire in a system of defined action and interchangeable identities, a system detached from any particular human agency or defining vision beyond the aggregate need to survive.

What is "motive" in such an environment? While earlier heroes such as Marlowe's Tamburlaine appear to have created actions, and later heroes such as Hamlet to have had actions thrust upon them, Othello is left to suffer the final indignity of having not only his actions but his motivations visibly constructed for him out of nothing other than the situational necessities of the plot. The creation of motive, in Othello's unfounded jealousy toward Desdemona, is not itself "natural," though it is often explained as such. Hamlet's motive, however ambivalently he may regard it, is clear from the first appearance of the ghost. The creation of Othello's motivation, in contrast, takes nearly the whole play, while its much anticipated "effect," the actual killing of Desdemona, is realized only in its final scenes.

The deferral of "real" motive to Iago, whose nominal jealousy at being passed over in promotion defers it once again toward a generalized system of displacements, is more than just the displacement of motivation from one represented human subject to another: it is rather a diversion basic to the anthropomorphic projection of Iago as a character, through which the entire problem of a more impersonal and institutional motivation can be rationalized within the tragic structure of the play. The motive of *Othello* is not Othello's celebrated jealousy, which, after all, has to be created for him, but neither is it the jealousy of Iago identified as its nominal cause. Rather, it is that silent and unspeakable motive that Iago, in the play's final scene (like Cassio before him in his "drunkenness"), cannot be made to utter—the very necessity that he must act, and act in precisely this manner, for there to be a play at all.

The real motivation in *Othello* is the institutionalization of the theater itself in its circumstance of "literary" and commercial production. In that theater, once fully articulated, authors, texts, and conventions operated only as links in an established productive chain. While the older writers, like older heroes, appeared as the "creators" of a genre, younger writers, like Iago, could establish their own positions only by the apparent manipulations of conventions already well established. In forming New Comedy as the parody of the clichéd conventions of tragedy, they, like Iago, appeared more clearly to be achieving their victories at their "masters'" expense, and at the expense of tragedy itself, which they methodically dismantled and stripped for its parts.[21]

If the increasingly grotesque and exaggerated excesses of the Jacobean stage are any indication, audiences too came to be increasingly located within this system of spectacle and consumption, passivity and detachment, voyeuristically anticipating those horrors they knew were to be their consummation—the punishment of that body that was both "Othello" and themselves—while the world of apparent plenitude and more immediate experience grew ever more remote from their observation. Within this movement, the separation between experience and observation, body and mind, knowledge and action, could only become more absolute. The theater, now the drama of this very expurgation of experience, the body, and the voice before the abstract and analytical world of the text it was helping to produce, moved toward its final obliteration, which was of itself. And it is into this theater, heavy with portents of disaster, that Desdemona, the representation of woman invested once again with a symbolic content not of her own making, had come. But what, beyond victimization, does Desdemona represent?

Othello is produced by the same process that produced *Titus Andronicus* and *Hamlet*, and clearly extends those plays' patterns of violence against women; perhaps less obvious, however, are the ways in which its deployment of gender differentials has shifted in function. In the two earlier plays the displacement of categories of "natural" feudal and familial obligation is reinforced by gendered effects, first in the deliberate brutalization of Lavinia, and later in the more negligent rejection of the solitary Ophelia. The explicit violence directed against these characters seems to lessen as the male subject consolidates his independence within the "causal necessity" of his own fate.

In *Othello*, however, it is precisely this hypermasculinized hero who is most in trouble. While *Hamlet* presents the illusion of a hero coextensive with his fate, *Othello* presumes his fundamental inferiority before it. A hero such as Othello can assert his heroism, in fact, only by extraordinary means—not by his military accomplishments, since the battle with the Turks never actually takes place, nor by his social position, since it is contingent on that same vanishing circumstance, but finally by his murder of Desdemona, who by the end of the play has been revealed to be both the enabling and prohibiting condition of his heroism. Through the persistent theme of substitution, Desdemona comes to operate as a kind of token for heroism and valor. She has been passed from father to husband and matched, in imagination, against many other suitors. She is a match for a "hero," and the standard against which "heroism" is measured. But what is a hero? Desdemona's concern for Othello first gives voice to "his story" and the image of his past heroism, but the pity with which she hears it acknowledges the underlying inequality through which his jealousy, not for what she is but for what he should and can never be, comes to function as a plausible motive for revenge.

In these terms, Othello's jealousy assumes both social and structural dimensions, explicable not only in terms of his social insecurity but also, perhaps more metadramatically, in terms of his deeper jealousy before the *theatrical* conventions of "heroism," the latent order of those "real" tragic heroes whom he can never hope to join but against which this play and this hero must necessarily be judged. The slippage of *Othello*'s conditions of signification toward the "heroic" past of *Hamlet* and other plays is the final link in its system of motives, substitutions, and displacements that define it in an irretrievable cycle of appetency and loss. In this situation, the death of Desdemona becomes inevitable: just as Othello can never escape Desdemona's "pity" as long as she survives him, so also he can never be "equal" to the heroic "story" she represents until that story with its "history" of heroism has been effaced through its final and most complete discreditation—that act so monstrous that it will render the concept of heroism itself obsolete. The final tableau of the play, so definitive in its sexual-political iconography—Othello positioned over the body of the strangled Desdemona—is also symbolic of his metadramatic role, the hero asserting his control over his story by destroying precisely that which had defined it as heroic in the first place, all at the orchestration of the "servant" who, in the metadramatic world, has risen to take his place.

The death of the feminine ideal is linked in *Othello* not with the consolidation of a heroic male subjectivity but with its disintegration, at least in its tragic form, just as the elevation of Desdemona to a kind of heroism in her suffering comes as the tragic conventions that define it move toward exhaustion.[22] *Othello* opens the door to the further and more pathological extensions of this process. In the most "decadent" and parodic of Jacobean tragedies that follow, *The Revenger's Tragedy*, the plot positions occupied by the characters of *Othello* are extended further, as Othello is replaced by the lecherous Duke, now explicitly a villain, Iago by the dubiously heroic and equally conniving Vindice, and Desdemona by the skull of Gloriana, dead nine years before the play's action begins. Gloriana's retrospective ideality, like that of Elizabeth Drury in Donne's *First Anniversary*, functions now only in her absence, for which her death is a necessary precondition. In the climactic scene of the play, arranged by the avenging but pandering Vindice, Gloriana's poisoned skull is presented to the Duke for a kiss, a fitting emblem not only of the necrophilic relationship between this hero and the rotten corpse that tragedy has become, but also of the relationship of drama to its audiences, its pandering presentation of itself to their voyeuristic lusts.[23]

The institutional motive, finally, that places all of these later plays in motion is the motive to continue the symbiotic relationship of authors, theaters, and audiences, through which all of the operations of the theater took place. If plays like *The Spanish Tragedy* and *Hamlet* had established a set of commercially viable conventions, how could they be further exploited? The lessons of *The Spanish Tragedy* and *Hamlet* are that successful implementations of conventions in a competitive commercial environment such as that of Renaissance London both exploit their potential for novelty and make them old; and if the only possibilities left for a play such as *Othello* are to revive those extinct conventions to kill them once again, then even those possibilities would be used. The most melodramatic signature of *Othello*, the revival of Desdemona so that she might die again, a signature echoed more faintly in *Lear*, is an emblem of that process, just as the image of Gloriana's skull puts it further into the past.

The analysis presented here suggests the significant operation of at least some plays in the redefinition of subjectivity in terms of time, causality, and the narrative of personal fate, as well as their operation under the circumstances of a commercial theater as a defined system of sequential change. In these examples, gender distinctions are deployed to enforce the differentiation of other categories in this process, defining emergent categories of privilege while working to discredit those that they replaced. One of the greater ironies of *Othello* is that it shows "identity" in *any* sense to have been tokenized by this process. *Othello* ends as skeptical in its view of causality and the identities it supports as earlier plays had been of the feudal regime they worked to displace; and though it is still convenient to speak of characters and their development in the anthropomorphic and personal terms of their presentation, the actual operation of this or any other political process appears to have a far more impersonal, abstract, and institutional side. All that, of course, is not to obscure its consequences. The functions of the gender distinctions considered here are perhaps most noteworthy in the shifting substructure of symbolic relations that underlies the superficial similarities of their repeated representations of cruelty, but their consequences are likely to have been the same. It is, after all, most often the nature of systems of inequality to produce, through various and subtle means, a very consistent set of results.

Notes

1. All quotations from Shakespeare are from *William Shakespeare: The Complete Works*, ed. Alfred Harbage (Baltimore: Penguin, 1969).

2. For a corresponding argument about Renaissance poetry, see R. L. Kesler, "The Idealization of Women: Morphology and Change in Three Renaissance Texts," *Mosaic* 23 (Spring 1990): 107–26.

3. A more precise definition of "tragedy" lies well beyond the scope of this argument. For a more detailed definition of the revenge subgenre, see R. L. Kesler, "Time and Causality in Renaissance Revenge Tragedy," *University of Toronto Quarterly* 59 (Summer 1990):

474–87. On the notion of closure and its relation to literacy, see esp. Jesse Gellrich, *The Idea of the Book in the Middle Ages: Language Theory, Mythology, and Fiction* (Ithaca: Cornell University Press, 1985); and Peter Bogatyrëv and Roman Jakobson, "Folklore as a Special Form of Creativity," trans. Manfred Jacobson, in *The Prague School: Selected Writings, 1929–1946,* ed. Peter Steiner (Austin: University of Texas Press, 1982), 34–46.

4. Evelyn Fox Keller, *Reflections on Gender and Science* (New Haven: Yale University Press, 1985), esp. 43–65.

5. Carolyn Merchant, *The Death of Nature: Women, Ecology and the Scientific Revolution* (San Francisco: Harper, 1980), 2, 41.

6. For the gradual separation of sixteenth-century drama from its medieval context, see David Bevington, *From "Mankind" to Marlowe: Growth and Structure in the Popular Drama of Tudor England* (Cambridge, Mass.: Harvard University Press, 1962). For parallels in medieval drama to Gellrich's argument, see V. A. Kolve, *The Play Called Corpus Christi* (Stanford: Stanford University Press, 1966), 42. Anthony Gash usefully describes the ways in which such an apparently cohesive system can include significant contestation ("Carnival against Lent: The Ambivalence of Medieval Drama," in *Medieval Literature: Criticism, Ideology, and History,* ed. David Aers [Brighton: Harvester Press, 1986], 74–98).

7. Thomas Kyd, *The Spanish Tragedy,* in *The Works of Thomas Kyd,* ed. Frederick S. Boas, rev. ed. (Oxford: Clarendon Press, 1955).

8. For a discussion of the books of Nature and culture, see Gellrich, *Idea of the Book,* chap. 1.

9. All quotations from Jonson's works are from *Ben Jonson,* ed. C. H. Herford et al., 11 vols. (Oxford: Clarendon Press, 1925–52).

10. Thomas W. Ross reiterates Frederick Boas's assertion that *The Spanish Tragedy* was the most popular play of the period, going through ten editions by 1633 (Ross, introduction to *The Spanish Tragedy,* by Thomas Kyd [Berkeley and Los Angeles: University of California Press, 1968], 1, 11). Philip Edwards speculates that much of its later popularity may have been literary rather than dramatic. This particular play's theatrical history may parallel the more general argument made here about the transitional role of commercial drama in the shift toward a more "literary" environment (Edwards, introduction to *The Spanish Tragedy,* by Thomas Kyd [London: Methuen, 1959], lxvii–lxviii).

11. The "fatalism" of this convention appears to many critics to be its most salient quality. For Charles A. Hallett and Elaine S. Hallett, for example, "It does not matter in the least whether his philosophic point of view is Christian, Humanist, Stoical, or Machiavellian, whether he is a hero or a villain. The fact that he is a revenger determines his fate" (*The Revenger's Madness: A Study of Revenge Tragedy Motifs* [Lincoln: University of Nebraska Press, 1980], 8).

12. James L. Calderwood, *To Be and Not to Be: Negation and Metadrama in "Hamlet"* (New York: Columbia University Press, 1983), 27. See also Kesler, "Time and Causality," 474–87.

13. Catherine Belsey, *The Subject of Tragedy: Identity and Difference in Renaissance Drama* (New York: Methuen, 1985), 41.

14. Eric Havelock, *Preface to Plato* (Cambridge, Mass.: Harvard University Press, Belknap Press, 1963), esp. 197–210.

15. Leonard Tennenhouse argues for this identification for both Gertrude and Lavinia (*Power on Display: The Politics of Shakespeare's Genres* [New York: Methuen, 1986], 106–12).

16. Carol Thomas Neely, "Feminist Modes of Shakespearean Criticism," *Women's Studies* 9 (1981): 11. If the Other becomes "fate" itself, this relationship becomes self-reflexive. See Michel Foucault's comments on the interiorization of sin ("Sexuality and Solitude," in *On Signs,* ed. Marshall Blonsky [Baltimore: Johns Hopkins University Press, 1985], 365–72).

17. Friedrich Nietzsche, *The Birth of Tragedy,* in *The Birth of Tragedy, and The Case of Wagner,* trans. Walter Kaufmann (New York: Vintage, 1967), 76.

18. The parallel between Iago and Aaron is significant, though their functions in their respective plots are different: the early Renaissance imitation of late classical sources would be important to a more detailed investigation (see Kesler, "Time and Causality").

19. The comedic aspects of *Othello* have been acknowledged in various ways by different critics. See, for example, Susan Snyder, "*Othello* and the Conventions of Romantic Comedy," *Renaissance Drama* n.s. 5 (1972): 123–41; Peter Stallybrass, "Patriarchal Territories: The Body Enclosed," in *Rewriting the Renaissance: The Discourse of Sexual Difference in Early Modern Europe,* ed. Margaret W. Ferguson et al. (Chicago: University of Chicago Press, 1986), 136; Carol Thomas Neely, "Women and Men in *Othello:* 'What should such a fool / Do with so good a woman?'" in *The Woman's Part: Feminist Criticism of Shakespeare,* ed. Carolyn Ruth Swift Lenz et al. (Urbana: University of Illinois Press, 1980), 211–39. Stephen Greenblatt compares Iago to Jonson's Mosca (*Renaissance Self-Fashioning: From More to Shakespeare* [Chicago: University Chicago Press, 1980], 233).

20. Plato, *Laws,* in *The Collected Dialogues of Plato,* ed. Edith Hamilton and Huntington Cairns (Princeton: Princeton University Press, 1961), 7 (816e), 1386.

21. Greenblatt's identification of Iago with Mosca points to the enactment of a parallel power struggle internal to drama in this period—namely, between authors and producers, the classic case being that between Jonson and Inigo Jones. See Stephen Orgel, *The Jonsonian Masque* (Cambridge, Mass.: Harvard University Press, 1965).

22. An extension of this thematic, which is beyond the scope of this discussion, is *The Duchess of Malfi,* in which the decline of the male hero in both Ferdinand and Bosola is coupled with the heroism of the Duchess, a heroism defined by its endurance and capability still to claim heroism ("I am Duchess of Malfi still").

23. Stallybrass has noted that Gloriana's skull "is also a negation of genealogy. All mention of Gloriana's family is erased from the play. The reduction of woman to skull, then, is accompanied by the reduction of familial networks." In this respect, as in others which Stallybrass notes, this discursive redefinition is a predictable outcome of the process outlined above, as well as the more general ones of which it is a part ("Reading the Body: *The Revenger's Tragedy* and the Jacobean Theater of Consumption," *Renaissance Drama* n.s. 18 [1987]: 131).

PART 2

6

Theaters, Households, and a "Kind of History" in Elizabeth Cary's *The Tragedy of Mariam*

Rosemary Kegl

> Sly: Is not a comonty a Christmas gambold, or a tumbling-trick?
> Page: No, my good lord, it is more pleasing stuff.
> Sly: What, household stuff?
> Page: It is a kind of history.
> —William Shakespeare, *The Taming of the Shrew* (Ind.2.138–41)

When Sly speculates that the traveling players plan to perform "a Christmas gambold, or a tumbling-trick," the Page corrects his supposed lord: their performance, he says, will be "more pleasing stuff." When Sly associates this more pleasant entertainment with "household stuff," the Page refines Sly's characterization: "It is," he says, "a kind of history." With this refinement, the Page might be stressing that the players' "household stuff" will be "a kind of story"—an extended narrative about Petruchio's attempt to transform Kate "from a wild Kate to a Kate / Conformable as other household Kates" (2.1.276–77)[1] rather than an isolated gambol or a tumbling-trick. And yet it is also worth remembering that the exchange between Sly and the Page is precipitated by the Messenger's announcement that "[y]our honor's players . . . / Are come to play a pleasant comedy"— or, in Sly's words, a "comonty" (Ind.2.129–30). In other words, if the Page's corrections and refinements suggest that this pleasant comedy will take the form of a story about "household stuff," then they also suggest that a pleasant comedy about "household stuff" that is staged by a lord's household players within that lord's household might be termed "a kind of history."

The dialogue between Sly and the Page might seem to be an unlikely point of departure for an analysis of Elizabeth Cary's *The Tragedy of Mariam*.[2] After all, even if we were to assume that Shakespeare's play provides a useful counterpoint to Cary's, there are any number of more promising narrative parallels: both plays are populated by friends, relatives, and servants who are entangled in a series of overlapping marital plots; both meditate on the ingredients necessary for domestic harmony and are notoriously uncomfortable with their outspoken heroines. Yet I find the dialogue compelling not because it provides a narrative parallel to *The Tragedy of Mariam* but because its tendency to function as a lesson in both genre and theatrical practice directs our attention to the household context in which Cary composed—and her audience received—her closet drama.

Categories such as the "domestic" and the "private," when used to describe the theatrical practices with which Cary and her contemporaries would have associated her choice in genre, have made it difficult to sort through the significance of the claim that *The Tragedy of Mariam* is the first extant—and extended—original English drama written by a woman. Or, to formulate the problem in another way, the very categories that have helped us to identify the generic and social contexts for early modern women's dramatic production have made it difficult to sort through the implications of Cary's decision—apparently a decision at which she arrived at least twice—not only to write but, even more precisely, to write a play. The first section of this essay establishes a connection between Cary's closet drama and the dynastic "kind of history" that governed household theatrical practices. The second section analyzes *The Tragedy of Mariam*'s formal imperative—its unusually strict fidelity to one dramatic ideal championed by Philip Sidney, the unity of time. Feminist discussions of Cary's play have tended to emphasize the narrative's social reversal of "all order," including Mariam's verbal authority over her husband and the dissolution of Herod and Mariam's marriage. I argue that *The Tragedy of Mariam*'s formal imperative produces a crisis in genre and consider how this formal reversal of "all order" might help us to analyze the social reversals that structure Cary's narrative. That analysis hinges on the play's uneasy relationship to the excesses of the "popular" stage, on the one hand, and to the dynastic emphasis of the household stage, on the other.[3]

Accounts of late sixteenth- and early seventeenth-century English closet drama generally begin with Mary Sidney's translation of Robert Garnier's *Marc Antoine*, printed in 1592, and address, in addition to *The Tragedie of Antonie*, plays composed over the next fifteen years by Samuel Daniel, Samuel Brandon, Fulke Greville, and William Alexander. Critics who locate *The Tragedy of Mariam* within this dramatic tradition emphasize both its suitability as a form of political critique and its *un*suitability for the stage. The former emphasis derives from what contemporaries regarded as Garnier's tendency to rework Senecan themes in an effort to criticize tyranny and promote political reform—a tendency embraced by many of his English followers and perhaps most notoriously by Daniel, whose *Tragedy of Philotas* brought him to the Privy Council in 1604, charged with sedition for having written sympathetically about the failed Essex rebellion. The latter emphasis derives both from Philip Sidney's remarks about reforming the stage—remarks often thought to have influenced his sister's decision to translate Garnier's play—and from speculation about the conditions under which elite audiences might have received these "reading dramas."[4] For instance, individual audience members might have, in Daniel's words, read a closet drama "in silence," or they might have gathered in households to hear the play read aloud by a single reader or by a number of readers who adopted characters' roles.[5]

It is not terribly surprising that critics have difficulty specifying the practices involved in the reception of these plays. Yet it is somewhat more surprising, particularly given the scarcity of contemporary accounts, that critics are nearly unanimous in categorizing that reception as, at once, "domestic" and "private." I do not mean to suggest that Cary's critics have accepted an absolute distinction between the "public" and the "private" or the association between the "private" and the "domestic" when analyzing *The Tragedy of Mariam*'s narrative of household relations. For example, they note that Cary shapes her narrative around the recognized analogy between order within the family and order within the state, that Cary draws upon closet drama's tradition of advocating political reform, and that her title character's behavior follows from the seventeenth-century claim that religious conviction actually sanctioned both a woman's resistance to her husband and a subject's resistance to her monarch.[6] And yet these categories, the "domestic" and the "private," when used to describe the theatrical practices associated with Cary's play, have tended to obscure the insistence with which English closet dramas defined themselves *as* drama and, more precisely, as drama that existed not in absolute opposition but rather in some uneasy relationship to the stage.

For instance, we might remember that the staging of these plays was apparently not entirely unthinkable. English playwrights, like their French counterparts, modeled their closet dramas on Senecan tragedies. During the last half of the sixteenth and early seventeenth centuries, English authors published or circulated translated and untranslated editions of ancient Greek and Latin drama—many of which, including the tragedies of Seneca in Latin, were performed or declaimed at Whitehall and in England's universities and Inns of Court. In addition, English and French authors often referred to the slight alterations that would be necessary to stage their closet dramas, and, in fact, Daniel was prosecuted by Cecil only after his revised *Philotas* was staged at the Blackfriars.[7] This is not to say that *The Tragedy of Mariam*'s relationship to individual staged plays has been entirely neglected: critics have considered the play's thematic connection to *Antony and Cleo-*

patra, The Merchant of Venice, Othello, and *The Taming of the Shrew;* to household tragedies such as *Arden of Faversham;* and to those plays in the mystery cycles and in the "continental, classicizing" dramatic tradition that featured Herod.[8] These studies have been able to tell us a great deal about the early modern stage conventions that governed outspoken and soft-spoken heroines, racialized "others," murderous wives, and raging tyrants. And yet these studies do not consider *The Tragedy of Mariam*'s uneasy relationship to the stage, and are particularly silent on the play's possible relationship to household theatrical practices.

I find this silence intriguing because, although household theatrical practices are never directly addressed in the criticism, I would argue that their explanatory power is nonetheless registered insistently, if indirectly, in the biographical impulse that has been so pervasive in discussions of Cary's writing—the claim that we might better understand her depiction of the troubled dynastic marriage between Herod and Mariam, Salome's meditations on divorce, and the unjust persecution of Mariam by her husband, her mother, and her husband's relatives if we keep in mind both Cary's arranged marriage to an older and not entirely compatible spouse and the response of that spouse to Cary's conversion to Catholicism, as well as the responses of Cary's parents, Charles I, Queen Henrietta Maria, and the Privy Council. It is also worth keeping in mind—and here I am simply reiterating what critics who are persuaded of the biography's interpretive significance have already noted—that *The Tragedy of Mariam* was first printed in 1613 and that Cary probably composed the play sometime between 1602 and 1608, during the first six years of her marriage to Sir Henry. For most of that time, Cary and her husband were living apart while he was, in turn, serving at court, fighting in the Netherlands, and awaiting ransom in a Spanish prison. In other words, Cary probably wrote *The Tragedy of Mariam*—and it was certainly in print—long before her conversion to Catholicism became public in 1625 and perhaps even some time before the unsuitability of her marriage would have become entirely apparent. And yet, in spite of the fact that neither the date of *The Tragedy of Mariam*'s publication nor the more tentative dates of its composition are terribly new information, many critics have persisted in analyzing the play through the lens of Cary's marriage and conversion. Dympna Callaghan and Marta Straznicky have observed that this emphasis on Cary's biography corresponds to what has been one influential set of scholarly priorities in the study of women's writing.[9] Even taking this observation into account, I would note that Cary's biography has attracted an unusual degree of attention. And I would argue that the persistent scholarly emphasis on Cary's marriage and conversion is a response to the household theatrical tradition that provided one context for *The Tragedy of Mariam*.

A few words about that household tradition. Suzanne Westfall has argued that players attached to great households in the earlier part of the sixteenth century were understood by their contemporaries as quite useful in constructing "a kind of history." According to Westfall, their performances—both those within their lord's household during holidays or celebrations for visiting dignitaries and those in courtyards, inn-yards, town squares, or other households during the players' months of travel—contributed to a fairly explicit attempt, first, to demonstrate the prestige and to assert the political agenda of their lord and, second, to define the evolving relationship between their lord's household and larger regional or national identities. Even those noblemen—like the Lord in the Induction—who did not maintain their own troupes participated in a version of this process when they sponsored household entertainments with the help of traveling players.[10]

By 1572 the right to maintain acting troupes as household servants would have been restricted to persons who possessed at least the status of baronet, and by 1604 would have been even further restricted to members of the royal family. Some powerful households, particularly those concentrated at some distance from the court, apparently succeeded in partially violating these orders—no longer able to serve as patrons to professional acting troupes that performed in the commercial theaters but continuing to serve as patrons to those professional troupes that performed in their lord's household and, as traveling players, in neighboring towns and counties. The remaining households continued to produce entertainments whose players often included some combination of family members, troupes commissioned for short-term engagements, and, particularly during royal progresses, members of the monarch's company. In fact, by focusing her royal progresses on the households of nobility and gentry—rather than religious foundations and royal properties—Queen Elizabeth reinforced the role of household entertainments in creating a dynastic "kind of history" through which the monarch, her hosts, and the Revels Office attempted to define the relationship between large landowners and their local communities, on the one hand, and between those landowners and the central government, on the other. Portions of such entertainments often found audiences beyond those in attendance. For instance, my earlier characterization of *The Tragedy of Mariam* as the "first extant— and extended—original English drama written by a woman" was designed to distinguish Cary's play not only from other closet dramas, including Jane Lumley's translation of *Iphigenia in Aulis* and Mary Sidney's translation of *Marc Antoine,* but also from *Thenot and Piers in Praise of Astraea*—a ten-stanza, sixty-line dramatic dialogue composed by Mary Sidney, performed for the entertainment of the queen in 1592, and printed in 1602. *Thenot and Piers* is not considered an extended dramatic piece because this sort of brief dramatic dialogue generally constituted only one segment of a more extended household entertainment that often included dance, music, tilts, and other forms of pageantry.[11]

Royal progresses provided an occasion for only a small portion of household entertainments, of course. The straightforwardly topical and partisan character of the remaining productions was recognized in Queen Elizabeth's 1559 proclamation which, in keeping with the Act of Uniformity, consolidated and intensified earlier efforts to monitor the religious and political content of dramatic performances, including performances staged within the household. And it was recognized in the Crown's persistent—and apparently well founded—concern that monitoring the content of prologues, interludes, and jigs would prove particularly difficult. Protestant interludes were produced at the households of nobility and upper gentry through the reign of Mary Tudor, and Catholic interludes through the reigns of her sister Elizabeth, James I, and his son Charles. For example, in 1609, only a few years before the publication of *The Tragedy of Mariam,* a group of players led by Christopher and Robert Simpson performed at the home of Sir John Yorke in Nidderdale, West Riding. In addition to staging an extended play, these players performed a brief interlude. During that interlude, a Priest and Minister disputed religious doctrine under the watchful eye of a Fool who, after the Priest emerged victorious, asked the Devil to escort the Minister offstage. At this point, in the words of one witness, "all the people greatlie laughed and rejoiced a longe time together . . . and that some of the said popishe people, who said they had seene the said play acted at the said Sir John Yorkes house in Netherdale, affirmed to some other of their neighbours who had not seene the same, that if they had seene the said play as it was plaid at Gowlthwaite, they would never care for the newe lawe or for goinge to the church more." This interlude seems to have been part of the repertory for which the Simpsons' troupe was well known from at least 1595 through 1616—a repertory in keeping with the performance practices of many of their fellow actors within regions of England that were populated by a large number of recusants.[12]

Although there is no evidence that either Sir Henry's family—the Carys—or his wife's—the Tanfields—sponsored oppositional interludes, there is evidence that members of both families participated in household entertainments. Sir Henry participated in the Twelfth Night masque at Whitehall, written by Thomas Campion to celebrate the 1607 marriage of James Lord Hay, earl of Carlisle; in the masque at Cawsome House, written by Campion to celebrate Queen Anne's progress toward Bath in 1613; and, at Whitehall on New Year's Day of the following year, in Ben Jonson's "Challenge at Tilt," written to celebrate the marriage of the earl of Somerset to Lady Frances Howard. In the same year that Mary Sidney composed *Thenot and Piers,* Queen Elizabeth, at the midpoint of her royal progress, was entertained for two days at Burford, the Tanfield home; the character of any civic or household entertainments that might have celebrated her visit was not recorded. Although Cary would have been a small child during the queen's visit to her family home, her adult years were, according to her earliest biographer, characterized by a love of staged drama, including masques: "[a]fter her lord's death [Elizabeth Cary] never went to masques nor plays, not so much as at the court, though she loved them very much, especially the last extremely; nor to any other such public thing" (224).[13]

I am not suggesting that readers or auditors would have found it difficult to distinguish *The Tragedy of Mariam* from lavish household entertainments such as masques. But I am suggesting that those same readers or auditors would have located Cary's play among a range of household activities, including a dramatic tradition that is overwhelmingly dynastic—that takes as its motivation, and at times as its organizing content, the fate of a single household; that characterizes the household as a network of political and aesthetic preferences; and that views both regional and national identities through the lens of that household. It is *The Tragedy of Mariam*'s association with this household tradition to which critics are responding, however unwittingly, when they note the play's oblique references to Cary's biography and the tentative connections between that biography and the family histories of Herod and Mariam.

In establishing that household productions would have provided one context for *The Tragedy of Mariam,* I temporarily bracketed what I described earlier as closet drama's "uneasy" relationship to the stage. I return to that uneasy relationship as I analyze the play's formal imperative—the Chorus's insistence that the play is faithful to one dramatic ideal championed by Philip Sidney, the unity of time. If, following the Chorus's closing remarks, we are to understand the play's formal imperative as a crisis in genre, then it is worth emphasizing that Cary's depiction of this crisis turns on *The Tragedy of Mariam*'s uneasy relationship to the popular stage, on the one hand, and the household stage, on the other. By focusing on that uneasy relationship, I consider how *The Tragedy of Mariam*'s formal reversal of "all order" might be involved with the more frequently commented upon social reversals that structure its narrative.

Although impressed with the Inner Temple's *Gorboduc,* Sidney notes that the play provides an imperfect "model of all tragedies" because "it is faulty both in place and time.... For where the stage should always represent but one place, and the uttermost time presupposed in it should be, both by Aristotle's precept and common reason, but one day, there is both many days, and many places, inartificially imagined."[14] An adherence to the unities of place and time helped to define closet drama as a genre by providing one index of its distance from the formal errors and immoral excesses that Sidney associated with, in Jean Howard's words, a "popular" stage whose "theatrical representation [was not] in the hands of a properly authorized elite."[15]

In the final stanzas of *The Tragedy of Mariam,* the Chorus implies that, even taking into account the reformist impulses of closet drama, Cary's play demonstrates an unusually strict fidelity to the second of these unities—the unity of time:

> Whoever hath beheld with steadfast eye,
> The strange events of this one only day:
> How many were deceiv'd, how many die,
> That once today did grounds of safety lay!
> It will from them all certainty bereave,
> Since twice six hours so many can deceive.
>
> (5.1.259–64)

As a number of critics have pointed out, this stanza extends to the play's readers its characters' experience of a deceptive temporality. Alexander MacLaren Witherspoon observes that "[Cary] is particularly anxious that the reader shall not forget that the events of the play are supposed to take place within a single day, and she presses the point." Russell Leavenworth adds, "And as for the unity of time, [the reader] is genuinely surprised when the final chorus informs him that this epic panorama of events has occupied but a single day."[16] That surprise could only increase after the subsequent stanzas enumerate the fortunes reversed, the lives and loves unexpectedly lost within "this day alone." And the implausible haste with which "so many changes" occur would only be confirmed if readers were to recall that in the popular treatise that is generally acknowledged to be Cary's primary source for her tale of Herod and Mariam, Thomas Lodge's 1602 translation of Flavius Josephus's *Antiquities of the Jewes,* this dramatic "day's events" unfold over "the space of one whole yeere."[17]

The stanza establishes its bridge between deceived reader and deceived character with a curious reference to vision—"Whoever hath beheld with steadfast eye / The strange events of this one only day"—curious because, although arguably applicable to the reading of closet drama, the reference is perhaps most evocative of a stage audience. I would not want to normalize too quickly Cary's gesture toward the stage. In fact, it is worth recalling that this sort of excessive faithfulness to the unities was a tour de force, fairly typical of contemporary Italian Senecan drama, and generally designed to emphasize the skillful use of stage techniques.[18] Cary's reference to vision, and to the theatrical, is curious, in part because she specifies that her closet drama's tour de force produces a form of temporal disorientation—the sense that the play's events have been compressed into an improbably short amount of represented time—that is remarkably similar to the disorientation that Sidney claims is produced when actors stage the passing of more than a single day: "Now of time they are much more liberal, for ordinary it is that two young princes fall in love. After many traverses, she is got with child, delivered of a fair boy, he is lost, groweth into a man, falls in love, and is ready to get another child, and all this in two hours' space: which how absurd it is in sense, even sense may imagine, and art hath taught, and all ancient examples justified."[19] In other words, *The Tragedy of Mariam*'s strict adherence to the generic expectations of closet drama not only fails to escape but actually manages to approximate the unsettling temporal compression that Sidney associated with the popular stage.

This crisis in genre—the temporal tour de force through which Cary's closet drama tends to replicate rather than reform the excesses of popular productions—finds its most eloquent spokesperson in *The Tragedy of Mariam*'s disoriented stage tyrant. For instance, after being told that the condemned Mariam had predicted that, within three days of her death, he would regret having ordered her execution, Herod more than fulfills his wife's prediction:

> Herod: Three days: three hours, three minutes, not so much,
>   A minute in a thousand parts divided;
>   My penitency for her death is such,
>   As in the first I wish'd she had not died.
>   But forward in thy tale.
> Nuntio: Why, on she went,
>   And after she some silent prayer had said,
>   She did as if to die she were content,
>   And thus to Heav'n her heav'nly soul is fled.
>
>   (5.1.79–86)

Herod's compression of time—his manifestation of regret not three days but one thousandth of a minute after Mariam's execution—is an exaggerated version of the temporal disorientation that Mariam's presence had produced in her husband. Earlier in the day, Herod had described the extension of time that he typically experienced in the absence of his wife and the compression of time that he experienced in her presence:

> Oh, haste thy steps, rare creature, speed thy pace:
> And let thy presence make the day more bright,
> And cheer the heart of Herod with thy face.
> It is an age since I from Mariam went,
> Methinks our parting was in David's days:
> The hours are so increas'd by discontent,
> Deep sorrow, Joshua-like, the season stays:
> But when I am with Mariam, time runs on,
> Her sight can make months minutes, days of weeks:
> An hour is then no sooner come than gone
> When in her face mine eye for wonders seeks.
> (4.1.10–20)

In his exaggerated version of this earlier sense of temporal disorientation, the ranting Herod imagines that time might compress to the point that it would actually reverse itself so that he might alter his wishes from "the first." The impossibility of such a reversal is reinforced by the inexorably chronological character of the Nuntio's account and its consistent movement "forward."

The play immediately restages this confrontation between Herod's desire to "reverse all order" and the Nuntio's insistence upon the irreversibility of events:

> Herod: But art thou sure there doth no life remain?
>   Is't possible my Mariam should be dead?
>   Is there no trick to make her breathe again?
> Nuntio: Her body is divided from her head.
> Herod: Why yet methinks there might be found by art
>   Strange ways of cure; 'tis sure rare things are done
>   By an inventive head, and willing heart.
> Nuntio: Let not, my lord, your fancies idly run.
> (5.1.87–94)

If Cary defines Mariam as the character who "oft . . . with public voice run on" (1.1.1) and Herod as the tyrant who, in keeping with his stage predecessors, "oft . . . with execration sworn" (4.3.118), then in these final passages she also emphasizes that Herod is the character for whom, in the presence of Mariam, "time runs on," and who, after her death, allows his "fancies" to "idly run." In fact, Herod's ranting is perhaps at its most fanciful when the distracted monarch, confronted with the Nuntio's memorably blunt and presumably definitive description of Mariam's death, "Her body is divided from her head," nonetheless insists that his wife might be revived. This ineffective, and apparently irrational, attempt to compress time supports the Chorus's diagnosis that the widowed Herod is left with no position other than that of the stage tyrant who "doth . . . strangely, lunaticly rave" (5.1.287).

How are we to understand the significance of this generic crisis in relation to the social reversal of "all order"—including the dissolution of Herod and Mariam's marriage—that comprises the play's central action? In order to answer this question, it is worth returning once more to the Nuntio's description of Mariam's death—"Her body is divided from her head." The description that is so striking in its anomalously graphic gesture, in report if not in representation, toward the bloody excesses of Senecan productions on the popular stage is equally striking in its conventionalized, almost formulaic, rendition of early modern social disorder. After offering several versions of this common Renaissance bodily image for figuring social hierarchy, Cary makes the severed social body prominent in her play's final act. In this way, she emphasizes that the ranting Herod is unable to accept not only his role in ordering Mariam's execution but also the loss of authority within both family and state that now must follow from his tyrannically indecisive behavior and hasty commands. Mariam is divided from her husband's authority and his subjects from their monarch's authority in part because, unlike Mariam, Herod did not recognize that his authority was located in the royal power to "delay."

Of course, as Herod's earlier temporal disorientation in the presence and absence of Mariam suggests, Herod's authority over his wife and subjects was compromised long before these final scenes. In the play's "Argument" and opening act, we are introduced to Herod's compromised authority through an elaborate network of naming whose diverse constructions of social hierarchy—dynastic, ethnic, national, religious—are brought together by the flexibility of "race" as a category for designating difference in early modern England. The process of assigning and adopting names is also crucial in the biblical narrative of social reversal, the tale of Jacob and Esau, to which these early scenes allude. And that process remains central to *The Tragedy of Mariam* as the play's narrative unfolds through a series of debates about who is entitled to be termed "husband," "wife," "tyrant," "usurper," "friend," or "lord."

Cary's use of the word "style" consistently associates such individual acts of naming with larger issues of form or genre. Salome resents being labeled with "so base a style / As 'foot' to the proud Mariam" (1.4.261–62); Ananell explains that Caesar has crowned Herod with a "larger style than ever" (3.2.45); Constabarus insists that he will fight Silleus "not for Salome . . . but to discharge a coward's style" (2.4.347–48); Herod accuses Mariam of plotting his death "so thy son a monarch might be styl'd" (4.2.208); and Pheroras worries about his inability to "vaunt me in a glorious style, / Nor show my love in far-fetched eloquence" (2.1.75–76). This use of "style"—its double reference to "name" and to "form"—helps to specify Cary's uneasy relationship to both the popular and the household stage, and suggests how *The Tragedy of Mariam*'s crisis in genre might inform the play's social reversals of "all order." For instance, I argued earlier that Herod serves as a spokesperson for the formal imperative through which Cary's closet drama approximates the temporal disorientation that Sidney associated with the errors and excesses of the popular stage. I now would add that Cary's insistence on the formal character of Herod's behavior makes vivid his diminished social authority by emphasizing his tendency to forfeit the "style" of a monarch for the more excessive "style" of a stage tyrant who is, characteristically, unable to "delay."

Throughout this section of the essay, I've defined *The Tragedy of Mariam*'s formal imperative as a crisis in genre precisely because Cary's closet drama tends to replicate rather than reform the excesses of the popular stage. Yet the formal character of Herod's behavior—including his doomed allegiance to the play's temporal logic—points to Cary's uneasy relationship not only to the popular but also to the household stage. If, as I have argued, Cary's readers or auditors might have associated *The Tragedy of Mariam* with a household theatrical tradition, then Cary's use of "style," her double reference to "name" and to "form," would have encouraged her audience to recall the dynastic idiom of that tradition. That idiom characterized the family's household as a network of political and aesthetic preferences and would have viewed both regional and national identities through the lens of that household. Before we turn to the formal imperative that defines Herod's behavior, it is worth remembering that his dynastic authority constitutes a social reversal of "all order." In the first sentence of "The Argument," we are informed that "Herod, the son of Antipater (an Idumean), having crept by the favour of the Romans, into the Jewish monarchy, married Mariam, the [granddaughter] of Hircanus, the rightful king and priest, and for her (besides her high blood, being of singular beauty) he repudiated Doris, his former wife, by whom he had children" (67). By the end of the play's second scene, Mariam's mother, Alexandra, has referred to Herod as "Base Edomite, the damned Esau's heir" (84), "Esau's issue, heir of hell" (100), and an "Idumean" (96) whose status improved only through the generosity of Mariam's grandfather and yet whose fortunate marriage will allow him to "inherit" the crown from "Jacob's child" (85). When Herod usurped the "seat that hath by Judah's race been [fam'd]" (90), he marked himself as an "enemy to royal blood" (91); his true "succession" is "shame" (101),

Alexandra reminds her daughter—"Did not his ancestor his birth-right sell?" (102). In the scene that follows, Mariam taunts Herod's sister, Salome:

> Though I thy brother's face had never seen,
> My birth thy baser birth so far excell'd,
> I had to both of you the princess been.
> Thou parti-Jew, and parti-Edomite,
> Thou mongrel: issu'd from rejected race,
> Thy ancestors against the Heavens did fight,
> And thou like them wilt heavenly birth disgrace.
>
> (1.3.232–38)

Keeping the idiom of the household theatrical tradition in mind, I would argue that Herod's political and aesthetic preferences—including his doomed allegiance to the play's temporal logic—make vivid the absolute limits of a dynastic authority that is, in the play's terms, based on ethnic, national, and religious reversals of "all order."

Yet this account leaves largely unexplained Cary's decision to depict her play's crisis in genre not merely through the formal character of Herod's behavior but, more precisely, through an irreconcilable conflict between Herod's desire that Mariam be revived and the Nuntio's insistence upon her death. As we sort through this conflict, it is worth noting that the Nuntio's position does not function as a simple corrective to Herod's error. In fact, the ineffective ranting of Cary's stage tyrant might be understood as a not entirely fanciful desire that the Nuntio's account remain faithful to the play's narrative logic. As the opening lines of "The Argument" suggest, *The Tragedy of Mariam* is explicitly structured around the repetition of events—"as Sohemus, that had succeeded Josephus' charge, succeeded him likewise in revealing it" (67). Salome will twice rid herself of an unwanted husband. Herod will twice leave Jerusalem and twice return. He will twice order secretly that, in the event of his death, Mariam be executed and, as "The Argument" tells us, his supposedly secret order will twice be revealed to her. Within the logic of such a narrative, it is not entirely fanciful to imagine that Mariam's fate might have repeated that of Herod, whose brother and sister, learning that his death was falsely reported, respond:

> Pheroras: Is Herod then reviv'd from certain death?
> Salome: What? Can your news restore my brother's breath?
>
> (3.2.41–42)

Instead, the unyielding Nuntio insists that Mariam was, quite literally, "out of time" (4.8.557) rather than, as Herod would wish, "timeless" (5.1.229) in her fall.

Given that Herod's tyrannical desire is cast as faithful to the narrative logic of Cary's closet drama, it is somewhat surprising that the Nuntio's account would consistently thwart that desire. Sidney outlines the conventional task of the Nuntio in drama, like closet drama, which attempts to remain faithful to the unities of time and place:

> But they will say, How then shall we set forth a story which containeth both many places and many times? And do they not know that a tragedy is tied to the laws of Poesy, and not of History; not bound to follow the story, but, having liberty, either to feign a quite new matter, or to frame the history to the most tragical convenience? Again, many things may be told which cannot be showed, if they know the difference betwixt reporting and representing. . . . And so was the manner of the ancients took, by some *nuncius* to recount things done in former time or other place.[20]

In *The Tragedy of Mariam,* on the other hand, the conflict between Herod's desire and the Nuntio's account suggests that the latter's report is not only fundamentally incommensurate with the play's strict adherence to the unity of time but also narratively incompatible with the play's represented events. In short, it is the *generic* integrity of Cary's closet drama that the Nuntio's account is designed to subvert.

How are we to interpret this final twist in *The Tragedy of Mariam*'s crisis in genre? I should clarify that I refer to the conflict between the Nuntio and Herod as a crisis in genre because, once again, Cary's closet drama tends to replicate rather than reform the excesses of the popular stage. And I would argue that, once again, this formal crisis points to *The Tragedy of Mariam*'s uneasy relationship not only to the popular stage but also to the domestic stage and the prominence of "name" and "form" in its dynastic "kind of history." However committed Cary might be to her early modern version of ethnic, national, and religious hierarchies, *The Tragedy of Mariam,* like its source story in the Lodge translation of Josephus's *Antiquities,* remains uncomfortable with Mariam's tendency to challenge her husband's authority by offering a competing dynastic narrative. Josephus outlines precisely how Mariam's behavior contributes to her downfall:

> For [Herod] was as inwardly touched with lawfull love of *Mariamme,* as any other of whom the Histories make report: and as touching her, she was both chast and faithfull unto him; yet had she a certaine womanly imperfection and natural frowardnesse, which was the cause that shee presumed too much upon the intire affection wherewith her husband was intangled; so that without regard of his person, who had power and authoritie over others, she entertained him oftentimes very outragiously: All which he endured patiently, without any shew of discontent. But *Mariamme* upbraided and publicly reproached both the kings mother and sister, telling them that they were but abjectly and basely borne. . . . [A]nd from thence also there arose an occasion of greater

accusations and calumniations th[a]n before. . . . [A]nd finally this long contrived and fore-imagined hatred at last brake out violently upon this occasion that ensueth.[21]

The Tragedy of Mariam confirms Josephus's account. After hearing the news of Herod's death, Mariam challenges her husband's dynastic "kind of history"—condemning the murders of her grandfather, Hircanus, and her brother, Aristobulus; questioning the legitimacy of Herod's claim to her family's throne; seconding Alexandra's charge that Herod's biblical "ancestor" sold the family's birthright; comparing the relative ethnic and religious status of her family and of Salome's. "Though I thy brother's face had never seen," Mariam tells her sister-in-law, "My birth thy baser birth so far excell'd / I had to both of you the princess been" (1.3.232–34). When Sohemus informs Mariam that Herod is actually alive, she refuses to conceal her scorn for her husband and his family. That scorn is make visible both by her refusal to rejoin "his bed" (3.3.133) and by her continued attempts to challenge a dynastic history that would legitimate Herod's rule. Sohemus declares that "unbridled speech is Mariam's worst disgrace" (3.3.183). The Chorus concurs:

> Then she usurps upon another's right,
> That seeks to be by public language grac'd:
> And though her thoughts reflect with purest light,
> Her mind if not peculiar is not chaste.
>
> (3.3.239–42)

As a number of critics have noted, Cary defines and redefines what constitutes acceptable "public" speech throughout *The Tragedy of Mariam*. For the purposes of this essay, I would draw attention to the kind of "unbridled speech" that prompts a fairly uniform condemnation from Sohemus, from the Chorus, from Herod, and from Salome: a wife's attempt to offer a dynastic "kind of history" that would challenge her husband's authority precisely by discrediting his family name.

Returning to the final twist in *The Tragedy of Mariam*'s crisis in genre, I would argue that the Nuntio's unyielding account of Mariam's solitary death stages not only the absolute limits of Herod's social authority but, more generally, the absolute substitution of an "ordain'd" (5.1.289) and typological narrative for the play's dynastic "kind of history." That substitution contributes to the play's overtly Christian agenda—including its tendency to offer Mariam as an Old Testament prefiguration of Christ. But that substitution also "solves" what has become a gender problem for the play—subduing Mariam's unseemly challenge to her husband's dynastic authority while managing to retain the ethnic, national, and religious hierarchies on which she had based her objections.

Notes

1. All quotations from Shakespeare are from *The Riverside Shakespeare,* ed. G. Blakemore Evans (Boston: Houghton Mifflin Company, 1974).

2. All quotations from *Mariam* are from Elizabeth Cary, *The Tragedy of Mariam the Fair Queen of Jewry,* ed. Barry Weller and Margaret W. Ferguson (Berkeley and Los Angeles: University of California Press, 1994).

3. In his prefatory letter to *The Muses Sacrifice* (1612), Sir John Davies refers to two of Cary's plays. One of these is apparently the play later published as *The Tragedy of Mariam;* the other, set "in Syracuse," has been lost. For this essay's definition of the "popular" stage, see 136 and 153, n. 15.

4. For work on closet drama and on Senecan influences in the Renaissance theater, I rely on Gordon Braden, *Renaissance Tragedy and the Senecan Tradition: Anger's Privilege* (New Haven: Yale University Press, 1985); E[dmund] K[erchever] Chambers, *The Elizabethan Stage,* 4 vols. (Oxford: Clarendon Press, 1923), 3:cxlv–clxxviii; H[enry] B[uckley] Charlton, *The Senecan Tradition in Renaissance Tragedy: A Re-issue of an Essay Published in 1921* (Manchester: Manchester University Press, 1946), xciv–cc; John W. Cunliffe, *Early English Classical Tragedies* (Oxford: Clarendon Press, 1912), lvi, lxii; Gillian Jondorf, *Robert Garnier and the Themes of Political Tragedy in the Sixteenth Century* (Cambridge: Cambridge University Press, 1969); Russell E. Leavenworth, *Daniel's "Cleopatra": A Critical Study* (Salzburg: Institut für Englische Sprache und Literatur, 1974); Felix E. Schelling, *Elizabethan Drama, 1558–1642,* 2 vols. (New York: Russell and Russell, 1908), 1:40–44 and 2:1–17, and *English Drama* (London: J. M. Dent and Sons, 1914), 141–45; Albert Tricomi, *Anticourt Drama in England, 1603–1642* (Charlottesville: University of Virginia Press, 1989), 53–71; A. W. Ward and A. R. Waller, eds., *The Cambridge History of English Literature,* vols. 5–6, *The Drama to 1642* (1907; reprint, Cambridge: Cambridge University Press, 1949, 1960), pt. 1, 334–35; Alexander MacLaren Witherspoon, *The Influence of Robert Garnier on Elizabethan Drama* (New Haven: Yale University Press; London: Oxford University Press, 1924). "Reading drama" is one of Leavenworth's categories.

5. I take the Daniel phrase from his remarks about the eventual staging of *Philotas.* Those remarks are reproduced in Chambers, *Elizabethan Stage,* 3:275. Coburn Freer is one of the few critics willing to speculate about the reading or performance practices that might have been associated with English Renaissance closet drama ("Mary Sidney: Countess of Pembroke," in *Women Writers of the Renaissance and Reformation,* ed. Katharina M. Wilson [Athens: University of Georgia Press, 1987], 485–86).

6. For discussions of order within the family and within the state, see Frances E. Dolan, *Dangerous Familiars: Representations of Domestic Crime in England, 1550–1700* (Ithaca: Cornell University Press, 1994), 116–19; Barbara Kiefer Lewalski, *Writing Women in Jacobean England* (Cambridge, Mass.: Harvard University Press, 1993), 179–211; Karen L. Raber, "Gender and the Political Subject in *The Tragedy of Mariam,*" *Studies in English Literature 1500–1900* 35 (Spring 1995): 321–43; and Betty S. Travitsky, "Husband-Murder

and Petty Treason in English Renaissance Tragedy," *Renaissance Drama* n.s. 21 (1990): 171–98. Nancy A. Gutierrez, "Valuing *Mariam*: Genre Study and Feminist Analysis," *Tulsa Studies in Women's Literature* 10 (Fall 1991): 233–51; Lewalski, *Writing Women*, 190–201; and Marta Straznicky, "'Profane Stoical Paradoxes': *The Tragedie of Mariam* and Sidnean Closet Drama," *English Literary Renaissance* 24 (Winter 1994): 104–33, locate *The Tragedy of Mariam* within closet drama's tradition of political critique. Elaine V. Beilin, *Redeeming Eve: Women Writers of the English Renaissance* (Princeton: Princeton University Press, 1987), 176; Sandra K. Fischer, "Elizabeth Cary and Tyranny, Domestic and Religious," in *Silent but for the Word: Tudor Women as Patrons, Translators, and Writers of Religious Works*, ed. Margaret Patterson Hannay (Kent, Ohio: Kent State University Press, 1985), 229; and Weller and Ferguson's introduction to *The Tragedy of Mariam*, 11, address religious justifications for a woman's resistance to her husband and a subject's resistance to her monarch.

Margaret W. Ferguson examines the various ways in which the play defines what constitutes an acceptable public voice for a woman ("Running On with Almost Public Voice: The Case of 'E. C.,'" in *Tradition and the Talents of Women*, ed. Florence Howe [Urbana: University of Illinois Press, 1991], 37–67, and "A Room Not Their Own: Renaissance Women as Readers and Writers," in *The Comparative Perspective on Literature: Approaches to Theory and Practice*, ed. Clayton Koelb and Susan Noakes [Ithaca: Cornell University Press, 1988], 93–116). In a longer version of this essay, I consider Ferguson's analyses in terms of the usefulness and limitations of literacy as an analytical category.

7. Braden, *Renaissance Tragedy and the Senecan Tradition*, 104–5; Charlton, *Senecan Tradition in Renaissance Tragedy*, lx–lxi, cxix, cxl–cxli; Cunliffe, *Early English Classical Tragedies*, lvi, lxii; Jondorf, *Robert Garnier and the Themes of Political Tragedy*, 15–16; Schelling, *Elizabethan Drama*, 2:1–17; and Tricomi, *Anticourt Drama in England*, 61–66.

8. Dympna Callaghan discusses the play's relationship to *Antony and Cleopatra* and *The Merchant of Venice* ("Re-Reading Elizabeth Cary's *The Tragedie of Mariam, Faire Queene of Jewry*," in *Women, "Race," and Writing in the Early Modern Period*, ed. Margo Hendricks and Patricia Parker [London: Routledge, 1994], 170–77); Dolan compares the play to *Othello* (*Dangerous Familiars*, 109–20); Maureen Quilligan discusses the relationship between Cary's play and *The Taming of the Shrew* ("Staging Gender: William Shakespeare and Elizabeth Cary," in *Sexuality and Gender in Early Modern Europe: Institutions, Texts, Images*, ed. James Grantham Turner [Cambridge: Cambridge University Press, 1993], 208–32); Weller and Ferguson discuss the play's relationship to *Antony and Cleopatra* and *Othello* (introduction to *The Tragedy of Mariam*, 41–43). Travitsky's "Husband-Murder and Petty Treason" compares *The Tragedy of Mariam* to *Othello* and to *Arden of Faversham*. Weller and Ferguson also emphasize the stage history of "Herod"—primarily as a figure in mystery cycles and in what they refer to as "continental classicizing dramas" (23).

9. For readings of the play that draw on Cary's biography, see Beilin, *Redeeming Eve*, 157–76; Ferguson, "Running On," 37–67; Fischer, "Elizabeth Cary and Tyranny," 225–37; Tina Krontiris, *Oppositional Voices: Women as Writers and Translators of Literature in the English Renaissance* (London: Routledge, 1992), 78–101; Lewalski, *Writing Women*, 179–

213; Betty S. Travitsky, "The *Feme Covert* in Elizabeth Cary's *Mariam*," in *Ambiguous Realities: Women in the Middle Ages and Renaissance,* ed. Carole Levin and Jeanie Watson (Detroit: Wayne State University Press, 1987), 184–96.

For their responses see Callaghan, "Re-Reading Elizabeth Cary's *The Tragedie of Mariam*," 163–77, and Straznicky, "'Profane Stoical Paradoxes,'" 104–33. Laurie J. Shannon also addresses the unusual degree of attention that Cary's biography has received ("*The Tragedie of Mariam:* Cary's Critique of the Terms of Founding Social Discourses," *English Literary Renaissance* 24 [Winter 1994]: 135–53).

For information about Cary's life, I rely on T[homas] Longueville, *Falklands* (London: Longman, Green, and Company, 1897), and Kenneth Murdock, *The Sun at Noon: Three Biographical Sketches* (New York: Macmillan, 1939), 1–39. *The Lady Falkland: Her Life* is reprinted in Weller and Ferguson's edition of *The Tragedy of Mariam*. All citations are from this version of the *Life*. Cary's reference to her disinheritance is recorded in a letter of March 24 to Secretary Conway in *Calendar of State Papers, Domestic Series, Of the Reign of Charles I, 1627–1628* (1858; reprint, Nendeln, Liechtenstein: Kraus Reprint, 1967), 109. For instances of Cary's continued attempts to obtain funding and control over her children's upbringing, see 180, 182, 210, 292, 326, 364.

10. Suzanne R. Westfall, *Patrons and Performance: Early Tudor Household Revels* (Oxford: Clarendon Press, 1990). A number of critics, including David Bevington, *Tudor Drama and Politics: A Critical Approach to Topical Meaning* (Cambridge: Harvard University Press, 1968); Walter Cohen, *Drama of a Nation: Public Theater in Renaissance England and Spain* (Ithaca: Cornell University Press, 1985), 124–29; and Robert Weimann, *Shakespeare and the Popular Tradition in the Theater: Studies in the Social Dimension of Dramatic Form and Function,* ed. Robert Schwartz (Baltimore: The Johns Hopkins University Press, 1978), 100–112, address, like Westfall, the topical nature of early Tudor household productions and yet, unlike Westfall, emphasize the indebtedness of those productions to popular traditions of dramaturgy. In a longer version of this essay, I consider the significance of this debt for an analysis of Cary's closet drama.

11. Glynne Wickham, *Early English Stages, 1300 to 1660,* vol. 1 (London: Routledge and Kegan Paul, 1959), 234–53; vol. 2 (pt. 1 [New York: Columbia University Press, 1963]), 54–149; and Jean Wilson, *Entertainments for Elizabeth I* (Woodbridge: D. S. Brewer, 1980), 38–43. Nancy Cotton discusses Mary Sidney's *Thenot and Piers in Praise of Astraea* (*Women Playwrights in England, c. 1363–1750* [Lewisburg, Pa.: Bucknell University Press; London: Associated University Presses, 1980]).

12. For information about early Protestant interludes, see Paul Whitfield White, *Theatre and Reformation: Protestantism, Patronage, and Playing in Tudor England* (Cambridge: Cambridge University Press, 1993). For information about recusant household performances and the Nidderdale incident, in particular, see Hugh Aveling, *Northern Catholics: The Catholic Recusants of the North Riding of Yorkshire, 1558–1790* (London: Geoffrey Chapman, 1966), 288–91; John Bossy, *The English Catholic Community, 1570–1850* (New York: Oxford University Press, 1976), 83–84; Christopher Howard, *Sir John Yorke of Nidderdale, 1565–1634* (London: Sheed and Ward, 1939), 20–29; M. D. R. Leys, *Catholics in*

England, 1559–1829: A Social History (London: Camelot, 1961), 210–11; North Riding Record Society, *Quarter Sessions Records,* ed. J. C. Atkinson (London: Printed for the Society, 1884), 1:160, the 1609 Six Weeks Sessions. For discussions of Tudor legal responses to the stage, see Wickham, *Early English Stages,* 1:234–53; 2, pt. 1:54–149.

13. Chambers notes Elizabeth's visit to Burford (*Elizabethan Stage,* 4:107) and describes the masques and revels in which Sir Henry participated (3:240–41, 244–45). In turning to Chambers's primary source, John Nichols, *The Progresses, Processions, and Magnificent Festivities, of King James the First, His Royal Consort, Family and Court,* 4 vols. (London: J. B. Nichols, 1828), 2:103–21, 630–40, 725–29, I found a series of discrepancies, which I resolved, in part, by turning to George Edward Cokayne, *The Complete Peerage,* revised and enlarged by Vicary Gibbs (orig. ed., 1910; London: St. Catherine Press, 1959), and *The House of Commons, 1558–1603,* ed. P. W. Hasler, 3 vols. (London: Published for the History of Parliament Trust by H.M.S.O., 1981).

14. Philip Sidney, *An Apology for Poetry,* ed. Geoffrey Shepherd (London: Thomas Nelson and Sons, 1965), 134.

15. Jean E. Howard, *The Stage and Social Struggle in Early Modern England* (London: Routledge, 1994), 42. For the purposes of this essay, I am working with Howard's definition of the "popular" stage.

16. Leavenworth, *Daniel's "Cleopatra,"* 87, and Witherspoon, *Influence of Robert Garnier,* 153. Jonas Barish considers why *The Tragedy of Mariam* seems more suited for the stage than other contemporary closet dramas ("Language for the Study; Language for the Stage," in *The Elizabethan Theatre, XII,* ed. A. L. Magnusson and C. E. McGee [Streetsville, Ont.: P. D. Meany, 1993], 37–43).

17. Weller and Ferguson, *Tragedy of Mariam,* 279.

18. Charlton, *Senecan Tradition,* cxxix–cxxxiii.

19. Sidney, *Apology for Poetry,* 134.

20. Ibid., 134–35.

21. Flavius Josephus, *The Antiquities of the Jewes,* trans. Thomas Lodge, in *The Famous and Memorable Works of Josephus* (London, 1602), 671.

7

Playing the "Scene Self": Jane Cavendish and Elizabeth Brackley's *The Concealed Fancies*

Alison Findlay

The Concealed Fancies was written in 1644 or 1645, when the traditional hierarchies of early modern England were being fundamentally destabilized by the civil war. Care, a servant in the play, comments that "the world's turned upside down since I was young" (5.5.18).[1] The subplot, set in a royalist castle besieged by Parliamentarian forces, self-consciously dramatizes the experience of the sisters Jane Cavendish and Elizabeth Brackley whose home, Welbeck Abbey, was captured by Parliamentarians on 2 August 1644.[2] In a series of domestic scenes attesting to the new sense of social mobility excited by the civil war, servants and aristocrats alike play games which challenge social rank and status. The sisters Luceny and Tattiney, the heroines of the play, test the affections of their suitors, Courtley and Presumption, as a way of educating them about gender roles within marriage. In the most extreme challenge to social hierarchy, Lord Calsindow, the paternal head of the household, declares his intention to marry Toy (a lady's maid) as his "mistress mate" (5.6.54), the word "mistress" implying both an inversion of class structures and the traditional gender order. The intervention of an angel, who condemns Lord Calsindow's politically radical choice as immoral, prevents the highly unconventional match and restores a "proper" sense of order, after which Lord Calsindow betroths his daughters to their suitors.

The Concealed Fancies does not draw a simple parallel between gender and class, between the heroines' quest for autonomy and the political context of the civil war.[3] The questioning of masculine authority in the main, romantic plot does not match with antiroyalist sentiments in the subplot; on the contrary, the protagonists are committed to the royalist cause, as was the authors' family.[4] Cavendish and Brackley, aristocratic authors of a piece of coterie drama, are far removed from the radical behavior of female sectaries or political protesters whose voices shattered conventional images of femininity in the civil war years.⁵ The play does not advocate a sexual revolution; indeed, the overt structure of the main plot is politically conservative. Lord Calsindow returns from exile in act 5 to make a spectacular entrance as a symbol of paternal authority: a father who gives away his daughters in marriage, a king who commands subjects in the little commonwealth of his family. Within this framework, however, Cavendish and Brackley make an extensive and playful use of theater to question the relation of gender and authority within the family.

As a text authored by women, *The Concealed Fancies* self-consciously stages courtship, betrothal, and marriage from a female perspective, appropriating and undermining traditional models of mimesis. When Luceny and Tattiney discuss marriage to their suitors, Luceny tells her younger sister that she will prove a fool in marrying a man who intends to govern her. Tattiney's reply—"do you think, sister, the words saying in the church shall make me mind him more than I do now? He is my servant, for I intend to be his mistress" (2.3.110–14)—alerts us to a contradiction between the socially privileged position of mistress and the subservient role of wife. Instead of intending to "honor and obey" as a wife should, Tattiney vows to remain in command as mistress. The term "mistress" has several potential meanings, on which Tattiney deliberately plays in order to complicate the definition of her role after marriage.⁶ On one hand, "mistress" describes a woman loved and wooed by a man, indicating Tattiney's determination to remain the primary focus of her suitor's affection. Custom will not stale the desire which draws him to her; by maintaining the role of mistress, she will preempt his potential for adultery. The appeal of an illicit liaison will be recontained within the boundaries of marriage because, as a mistress, she will be able to fascinate him with her unpredictable, possibly dangerous behavior. This second sense of "mistress" as one who illicitly occupies the place of a wife (in an unsanctioned relationship with a man) already hints that Tattiney's commitment to the conventional wifely role will be only partial.

To extend the scope of her authority, Tattiney plays on another meaning of the word "mistress," namely a female teacher or ruler of servants. As mistresses, Tattiney and Luceny take up both of these commanding positions: they educate their suitors into the type of husband they want; and they control the household, ruling servants and managing affairs in their father's absence. But the most important significance of the word "mistress" is related to Tattiney's sense of self. Her plan to remain mistress to her husband is made, she says, "as I hope to continue my own" (2.3.108). "Mistress" is thus deployed by Cavendish and Brackley to signify independent identity, a self-fashioned subjectivity. Indeed, the play seems to be original in charging the word with this meaning, as though the authors are deliberately appropriating it, building on its other meanings to create new subject positions for their heroines. Like the multiple meanings of "mistress," gender and subjectivity are intertwined in the play as constructs of performance.

The performance of gender in *The Concealed Fancies* empowers not only the female protagonists but also the authors who stand behind them. The word "mistress," as employed by Tattiney, also refers to a woman who is regarded as an author, patron, or creator. Authorship and authority are clearly connected for Cavendish and Brackley, who in all likelihood wrote *The Concealed Fancies* with a private performance in mind, possibly in their own home, Welbeck Abbey, with themselves as actors.[7] In such a situation, the shifting boundaries between playing and being add another important dimension to the sexual politics of the play. By considering the metatheatrical elements of the text, we can see how *The Concealed Fancies* creates a multisided picture of gender as an unstable, prosthetic production. This has significant consequences for both male and female characters in that it displaces the notion of coherent gendered identity with a model of shifting subject positions.

Luceny and Tattiney both value the status of "mistress," not primarily as a way of exerting erotic power over men (although this is an important trope in the play) but as a mark of autonomy which they are anxious to retain in marriage. Although neither heroine rejects the idea of marriage, each is determined to "continue [her] own" (2.3.108). From their superior position, they put their husbands-to-be through an emotional obstacle course to negotiate equitable partnerships. As Presumption admits, Tattiney "takes the right way to make me tame" (2.2.37).[8] Luceny and Tattiney take advantage of their power as mistresses to mock their suitors and to expose the contradictions which underlie Courtley and Presumption's performances of deference. Through such status games, *The Concealed Fancies* investigates the interplay between social and economic factors and the "proper" codes of masculine and feminine behavior in courtship.

In a period when aristocratic marriages, including those of the authors, were motivated primarily by financial and social exigencies, the preservation of property or inheritance was often more important than the emotional satisfaction to be gained from a match. Marriage was a bargain made between men (the father and the suitor), in which women could be reduced to little more than commodities in a homosocial marketplace. Eve Sedgwick has shown that in "male-dominated" societies, "the large-scale social structures" for maintaining and transmitting patriarchal power are underpinned by male homosocial bonding; "it is crucial," she contends, "to every aspect of social structure within the exchange-of-women framework that heavily freighted bonds between men exist, as the backbone of social form or forms."⁹ Plays performed in the Renaissance commercial theater (with casts composed of men and boy actors) often demonstrate how betrothal was a closed-loop dialogue between men, and the heterosexual marriage market a closed form of homosocial exchange.¹⁰

During the civil war years the need for families of consequence to secure good settlements became even more acute as income from property grew increasingly unpredictable. Rents were often slow in coming in, while higher taxes and payments to the military to prevent pillaging strained resources,¹¹ increasing the pressure to make matches which would ensure a good income. However, mercantile considerations were not solely the province of male suitors. The family of a prospective bride had to be equally certain of her suitor's means since her future position in society would be determined by his financial and social standing. It was the responsibility of the father or elder brother, not of the daughter or mother, to seek the most profitable marriage. A woman who actively promoted her own interests represented a threat because the father's right to dispose of his daughter was the cornerstone of patriarchal power, and her intervention would make the tenure of that power seem uncertain. The ideal was nevertheless complicated in social practice. Drawing on studies in historical sociology and demography, Margaret Ezell has argued that during the seventeenth century a considerable number of women arranged marriages for themselves or for their kin in families where the father was absent, a situation which obviously became more common during the civil war.¹²

The Concealed Fancies considers arranged marriage from the perspective of the usually silenced woman. On one hand, the challenge posed by women who are determined to enter the marketplace themselves is caricatured in the figures of Lady Tranquillity and her maid Toy, both of whom are addicted to self-advancement.¹³ But in the heroines, the authors offer a more sympathetic picture of female intervention, as Luceny and Tattiney's voices break into the normally closed loop of masculine negotiation and expose the injustice of a system which equates them with property. Their father, Lord Calsindow, remains in exile until the end of the play, and although he provides their dowries, the heroines do not resign themselves to the conventional role of passive agents in the matchmaking process. Like Rosalind in *As You Like It* they take advantage of the absence of a controlling father figure to learn more about their suitors, showing a healthy suspicion that Courtley and Presumption's affections are directed less toward them than toward their dowries. Tattiney, for example, accuses Presumption of putting on a romantic performance to deceive her and make her the laughingstock of his true love. Her fear that he is courting only her money reminds us that the role of scornful mistress may also be a form of self-defence against a callous fortune-hunter.

When it comes to their own futures, Luceny and Tattiney balance passion with hardheaded "discretion":

> Tattiney: Pray sister, is he a good fortune?
> Luceny: Yes, and a very good title.
> Tattiney: Then I perceive your discretion likes him.
> Luceny: Aye, and his discretion may very well like me!
> For my father intends to give me a great portion.
> Therefore, I shall not know whether 'tis his wisdom or affection that makes choice of me.
> (1.4.34–40)

Luceny's awareness that she is a valuable commodity on the marriage market makes it difficult for her to accept the servitude befitting a wife. She points out how a good dowry inevitably raises the status of a mistress, so that her eventual subjugation in marriage appears illogical: "I . . . do the more admire why she will contract her family, nobleness and birth, to the servitude of her husband, as if he had bought her his slave, and I'm sure her father bought him for her, for he gave a good portion, and now in sense who should obey?" (Epilogue 43–48). If a woman is furnished with a dowry substantial enough to attract a man's service in courtship, it is only proper that she should continue to command after marriage since her endowment by her father has brought her economic power.

Luceny's argument raises fundamental questions about the organization of the seventeenth-century household. Gender roles in courtship and marriage are exposed as theatrical rather than natural, the changes in status from lover to husband and from mistress to wife making these identities appear unstable. It is ludicrous for the suitors to present themselves as "perpetual servant[s]" (2.2.6) to their mistresses since the seemingly inevitable marriage ceremony will turn the tables and place the women in subservient roles. Luceny and Tattiney recognize that male self-abasement is part of a set of courtship rituals promoting female superiority on a temporary basis. Courtley complains that he "court[s] a wench that doth so truly see" (1.4.111), one who mocks his attempts to pose as a victim, and who knows her own value (1.4.102–8). Once the role of suitor is theatricalized, the role of dominant husband appears equally artificial, a shadow of authority without any natural substance.

The fragility of the patriarchal family is displayed most obviously at the moment of betrothal, when one household fractures and new ones are established. Courtley and Presumption finally win their mistresses by appearing as gods before them in a masque, and by bringing Lord Calsindow home from exile (5.2 and 5.4). The restoration of the father figure apparently transforms the women from domineering mistresses into silent wives. Following Lord Calsindow's return, Luceny and Tattiney say very little in public. Yet the absolute authority of the patriarch does not go unchallenged, as the masque sequence is highly ambiguous. On one level, the authors seem to be imitating the court masque with a nostalgia for the conservative tradition it celebrates: the supremacy of the paternal governor in the home and the kingdom. (Entertainments by Ben Jonson were staged at Welbeck Abbey and Bolsover Castle for the visits of Charles I and Henrietta Maria.)[14] On the other hand, the audience (and the heroines) are aware that the "gods" are merely Courtley and Presumption, dressed up in a last-ditch attempt to win their mistresses' loves. A hint of parody obtains in Luceny and Tattiney's question, "Are you god-cheaters? / Or are we not ourselves?" (5.4.9–10). The hymeneal "gods" are spectacular but very obviously theatrical "cheats" whose power is only a construct of performance, which Luceny and Tattiney, as mistresses of themselves, are able to see. The status of the husband as divinely appointed head of the family is thus simultaneously celebrated and undermined in the play's staging of betrothal.

Luceny and Tattiney's reliance on performance, rather than public speech, to mock matrimonial conventions imitates the method of early modern homilies and conduct books, which present an appearance of marital relations that is belied by the reality underneath. In seventeenth-century England the task of reconciling women to their inferior roles fell largely to preachers and homilists. Valerie Lucas has demonstrated how sermons delivered in church and disseminated in printed form used deft rhetorical stratagems to conceal the true nature of power relations, defining male authority and female subordination as complementary duties to create an illusion of equal partnership.[15] William Whately's discussion of the mutual duties of spouses, in *A Bride-Bush* (1617), is typical of wedding sermons of the period. Whately begins, for example, with the idea that man and wife are "indebted to each other in a reciprocall debt"; yet he goes on to define the husband's two principal duties as "The keeping of his authority, and the using of it," while the wife's are "The first, . . . to acknowledge her inferiority: the next, to carry her self as inferiour."[16]

When alone on stage, Luceny and Tattiney declare war on matrimonial conventions, undoing the hypocrisy of such claims about the equality of spouses:

Tattiney: What, shall not Mr Courtley be your governor when you're married?
Luceny: How often, sister, have your [*sic*] read the Bible over, and have forgotten man and wife should draw equally in a yoke?

Tattiney: I warrant you, sister, I know that text as well as you.
Luceny: How impertinently then dost thou speak?

(2.3.34–41)

Luceny argues that equality means nothing less. She counters Tattiney's words with the implication that preachers like Whately are impertinently misreading the Bible in their examples of so-called equality, and in the Epilogue the heroines criticize the marriage homilies' emphasis on dominance and submission:

Tattiney: I hate those people that will not understand matrimony is to join lovers.
Luceny: But thinks husbands are the rod of authority!

(Epilogue 86–88)

Costume is an important part of the trope of insubordination in marriage. "The Homily on Matrimony," the bedrock of conventional ideas on female subordination, stipulated that a wife should "declare her subjection" through modesty of dress and behavior.[17] But when commanded by her husband, Luceny explains that she "looked soberly, as if I would strictly observe him, yet dressed myself contrary to his instruction" (Epilogue.14–16). The heroines do not crossdress as does Moll Frith, the roaring girl, or Rosalind in *As You Like It*, but their "careless garb" is a synonym for wayward behavior. Tattiney states that Presumption will never see her out of order when she is married "but in a morning, and at night, in my several satin petticoats and waistcoats, and always in my careless garb" (2.3.146–49). Later, she reports that she has strictly followed this policy: "I was myself, and held my petulant garb," writing to him in "as several humours as I will dress myself. His mistress" (Epilogue 78–79, 84–85). She preserves her "self" through costume and triumphantly asserts, "this you may see is an equal marriage" (Epilogue 85).

A more subtle form of subversion is the heroines' mimicry of ideal wifely behavior, a technique which must have had powerful resonance in seventeenth-century society. As Susan Dwyer Amussen has pointed out, people were acutely aware that the reality of marital relations rarely matched the model laid down in conduct books of the time.[18] Scolds and shrews were obvious examples of "unnatural" rebellion, but still more dangerous were those women who appeared to conform but did not genuinely submit themselves to the authority which declared them inferior. Under such circumstances, their obedience was merely a performance of subjection. Whately's *A Bride-Bush* cautions husbands that in the case of some wives "the heart goes against that which the hand performes; and thou art disliked inwardly, though perhaps obeyed in shew: and if obedience come not from the heart, can it last long?"[19] *The Concealed Fancies* plays on this gap between genuine and counterfeit submission. A key moment occurs during Luceny's song before her wedding: looking in a mirror at the image of herself as bride-to-be, she vows:

> Why then, a wife in show appear,
> Though monkey I should dare;
> And so upon the marriage day
> I'll look as if obey.
>
> (5.6.3–6)

Luceny's brother Stellow, who has overheard her, responds with a song which characterizes her refusal to submit as indicative of an unstable gender hierarchy:

> Now do I hear the ladies, what wagers they will lay,
> Saying, surely you'll disallow obey;
> Truly I know not what you mean, cry you and look away,
> What act you mean to be the scene, lost wagers each must pay.
>
> (5.6.7–12)

Luceny elaborates on her scheme to subvert the principle of wifely subjection while appearing to conform:

> Now do I view myself by all so looked upon,
> And thus men whispering say, faith she's already gone,
> For wit or mirth I plainly see,
> That she a wife will be.
> No sir, say I, a wit above
> Is Hymen's monkey love.
>
> (5.6.12–17)

In the manuscript, the lack of punctuation makes the meaning of the final lines difficult to decipher, but if we read the word "monkey" as an adjective qualifying love, then Luceny's reply claims that her wit, that is, her ability to mimic wifely obedience in marriage, places her above the so-called wise men.

The mirror scene brings into relief the psychological underpinning of performance. The incident highlights how Cavendish and Brackley manipulate patriarchal models of mimesis for their own purposes in ways which look forward to Luce Irigaray's *Speculum of the Other Woman* where Irigaray politicizes the mirror as a feminist tool. Instead of a reflective surface designed to confirm the primacy of the male subject (and the woman's lack), the mirror and the process of imitation become the means of destabilizing the relationship between truth and illusion, so that the subject is plunged into a world of imitations without origins—"a mimetic system [which] is not referable to one model, one paradigm . . .

dominated by Truth."[20] Irigaray shows that in Freudian theory the woman provides a mirror image of the man by substituting her lack of a penis with penis envy, the desire to be like him. He is the ideal form of which she can become only a copy through admiration. Because her penis envy is necessary to reinforce his sense of self, woman is constructed as a negative (castrated) projection of man, reflecting his desire for a mirror image of himself.[21] If, however, like Luceny, the woman does not perceive herself purely in terms of lack, then the reflection becomes a hollow representation, lacking the fullness (of female envy) required to substantiate the male position as primary subject or "truth." When a woman has fashioned a positive sense of self, as has Luceny, the image she offers is only a mimicry of otherness. Irigaray's reconfiguration of female mimesis is especially significant for our understanding of the role of mimicry in *The Concealed Fancies*. In *This Sex Which Is Not One* Irigaray further contends that by playing with mimesis and mimicking models of femininity, woman can "convert a form of subordination into an affirmation, and thus begin to thwart it."[22] In *The Concealed Fancies* Luceny does not construct herself opposite the masculine "true" form of her prospective husband. Luceny-as-bride in the mirror stands opposite the Luceny whose independent will has been firmly established in the play. In this female mimetic pattern she projects an insincere, two-dimensional type of wifely conformity, one which refuses to believe in the ideology which declares her inferior. By means of mimicry she outmaneuvers the men who assert that "she a wife will be" and who believe that "she's already gone," that is, disappeared into marriage. Luceny plays out "Hymen's monkey love," a subversive performance which places her "a wit above" the men's attempts to silence her into nothing.

In seventeenth-century England insincere performance of the wifely role was perceived by the writers of conduct books as a dangerous problem. Thomas Gataker's marriage sermon *A Wife In Deed*[23] cautions that a woman who is a wife only in show is not a true part of the marital body (151). Gataker describes her, in a striking list of similes, as *"an eye of glasse,* or *a silver nose,* or *an ivorie tooth,* or *an iron hand,* or *a wooden leg"* (151). Without full mental and spiritual subjection, she can only be prosthetic, a *"Shadow without Substance"* (149). Gataker's text admits the possibility that the submissive wife is a fiction created by the rhetoric of domestic conduct books. Although women, he writes, may have been married in public, with witnesses, exchange of rings, and ceremonies performed by bishops or even archbishops, they may still not be wives. In a rigidly patriarchal model of mimesis, he counsels them to examine themselves by using the gospel as a "Looking-glasse . . . to shew thee what thou art," and to measure themselves against the models of wifely subjection put forth by St Peter and St Paul. If they do not like what they find, "it is not the fault of the Glasse, but their owne" (154). Significantly, Gataker identifies those women who illicitly occupy the place of wives as mistresses: "A wife then, say those *Apostles,* is one, that is *subject and obedient to her Husband as her head.* But many by this *Rule,* will hardly prove *wives;* being *Mistresses* . . . rather than *wives,* to those *that have them,* or rather *whom they have*" (154). Mistresses are women who take the name of wife but who overrule their partners, offering to guide and govern those who should be their guides, command those who should be their masters. According to Gataker's classification of wives, Luceny and Tattiney's behavior in *The Concealed Fancies* marks them out as shadows without substance. Vowing to remain mistresses in spirit, they will only mimic the wifely role.

Female mimicry thus represents a significant threat to patriarchy because it deconstructs the traditional mimetic pattern and the ideology inscribed within it. For Irigaray, mimicry creates a world of mimesis without referent or origin, making (male) "truth" itself illusory. In *Speculum of the Other Woman* she rewrites Plato's theory of imitation, showing how all objects and representations are equally false because "reality," such as it is, is constructed from shadows, reflections, mirror play. Elin Diamond observes that Irigaray's model is particularly relevant to the theatrical arena, in that it simultaneously exploits and undermines patriarchal mimesis through a process which Diamond calls "mimesis-mimicry, in which the production of objects, shadows and voices is excessive to the truth/illusion structure of mimesis, spilling into mimicry, multiple 'fake offspring.'"[24] *The Concealed Fancies* employs mimesis-mimicry to fracture the gendered human subject. The heroines enact numerous contradictory parts of themselves through imagined and actual scenarios with their husbands and suitors. Their performances as mistresses, nuns, and dutiful (silent) daughters reproduce the discourse of male-authored texts in ways which destabilize the authority of the originals. In a parodic rehearsal of wifely obedience, Luceny tells Tattiney: "My destruction is that when I marry Courtley I shall be condemned to look upon my nose whenever I walk; and when I sit at meat, confined by his grave wink, to look upon the salt; and if it be but the paring of his nails, to admire him" (2.3.47–52). Luceny caricatures the conventional poses of female subjection: keeping the eyes lowered, raising them only to admire the husband's actions, however insignificant these may be. Perhaps in performance she accompanies the words with physical gestures to make the parody three-dimensional. Luceny anticipates another performance of deference, in front of her mother-in-law, assuring Tattiney: "though I look obedient and civil to her, I will let her discretion understand in silence, that I know myself, and that I deserve thanks for coming into her family" (2.3.124–27). Mistress Courtley will immediately see through Luceny's mimicry of wifely subservience and perceive that Luceny too is mistress of herself. Luceny knows her own value, as someone who has brought a rich dowry into the house and has not internalized the inferior role assigned to her.

The servant Pert recognizes how liberating the technique of mimesis-mimicry is for the heroines, saying, "this lady that I mean will have her several scenes, now wife, then mistress, then my sweet Platonic soul, and then write in the like several changes of mistress, not only to confirm love, but provoke love" (4.5.55–59). Luceny and Tattiney repeatedly rewrite themselves through performance, the kaleidoscope of shifting images of woman which they present indicating that all identity is imitation. Their strategic mimicry enables them to convert their final subordination into affirmation while confusing the men who wish to exert husbandly authority over them. When asked about his relationship with Tattiney, Presumption laments, "my misfortune is, she knows her scene self too well" (1.1.3–4), her plurality undermining Presumption's own sense of self. By the end of the play he has become "a compound of he-knows-not-what," a mixture of contradictory roles in which "he appears himself" (Epilogue 69, 73). Each character "knows [the] scene self too well," as no more than a prosthetic construct.

Since playing the "scene self" exposes the unitary subject as an illusion, it might seem a dangerous course of action for female protagonists whose goal is to "continue [their] own." If both male and female identity is equally performative, however, the need to assert a fixed sense of self becomes irrelevant. Once male primacy as "truth" or "origin" is destabilized by mimesis-mimicry, the context for self-determination becomes theatrical. In this way, *The Concealed Fancies* explores the consequences of the shift to an enactment of gender. Luceny and Tattiney nowhere attempt to transcend the level of performance to establish a stable sense of self. Each woman's wish to "continue her own" is not a desire to remain the same, but to remain mistress of the roles she plays. The heroines embrace the possibilities offered by performance (including the potential for mimicry), engendering a multiplicity of often contradictory identities.

More remarkable is the fact that the female duplicity involved in mimicry meets with approval from Courtley, who in scene 1 declares, "My mistress truly I would have / A pretty monkey, yet seem grave" (1.1.58–59). His wish for a partner with a split subjectivity (modest wife/playful mistress) seems motivated partly by desire; nevertheless, as the speech continues, it becomes clear that he actively encourages behavior which exposes the fragility of the patriarchal order that privileges him. The roles of wife and mistress, and the subject positions they offer, exist in dangerous proximity. The first, played out in public, has the appearance of deference but is always closely shadowed by the presence of the "mistress," the self-determining intelligence which endows women with the wit to mimic subjection. Courtley explains:

> Her stature I would have each see
> A wife or mistress she may well then be,
> In private know no matrimony law
> In public all should think I did her awe,
> Her petulance I'd only have with me
> With others stately for to be,
> I would not have her think of wife
> Nor me as husband to make strife,
> But justly have her fraught with wit,
> So by me, pretty man, may sit.
>
> (1.1.62–71)

Although in public Luceny must play the dignified wife, in awe of her husband, neither she nor Courtley must internalize the conventional gender roles dictated by the terms "husband" and "wife." He would not have her *think* of herself as a wife, nor should he think of himself as a husband "to make strife." Instead, he envisages a private utopia in which the "law" of matrimony and the gendered status relationship which it produces are unknown. Once the roles of husband and wife are removed, gender no longer determines conduct. In the final line, there is even a hint of the blurring of sexual identities. As an autonomous subject fraught (or endowed) with her own "wit," Luceny becomes a "pretty man" who sits as an equal beside Courtley. Whenever the word "pretty" has been used in the play, it has referred to a female character; here, too, its combination with "man" demonstrates the disturbance of male and female as fixed concepts, as well as the gender attributes linked to each sex.

In suggesting that even biological categories are molded by the discursive fields in which they are played out, *The Concealed Fancies* complicates the relationship between sex, gender, and performance. Judith Butler has shown that "the presumption of a binary gender system implicitly retains belief in a mimetic relation of gender to sex whereby gender mirrors sex," and that this pattern of mimesis is mistaken since there is no original or natural identity on which gender can be fashioned.[25] The configuration of bodies into sexes which exist in binary relation to one another is itself a cultural phenomenon, another imitation rather than an origin. The contingency of sexual identity in early modern England is hinted at in *The Concealed Fancies,* not through parodic repetitions such as crossdressing but through moments of discontinuity such as the one Courtley imagines. Courtley's speech gives a rare glimpse into the possibility of gender disturbance whereby "*man* and *masculine* might just as easily signify a female body as a male one," and even biological categories take on a performative aspect.[26] As categories lacking differentiation, gender and sex are part of the world of performance, their validity depending upon reenactment in public to reaffirm collective "truths" about identity and agency.[27] In Courtley's speech the boundaries between public and private realms blur just as the binary opposition between genders dissolves. He separates Luceny's public and private behavior but then invites the audience into that utopian space where she sits beside him in wit. He would "have each see" her potential to be both wife and mistress. The insight we are allowed into the private realm shows that the opposition of sexual identities within a relationship of dominance and subordination is not a natural given—it is generated by means of a series of regulatory practices and constituted by performance. In light of this exposé, Courtley's authority as husband is reduced to the same parodic status as Luceny's subjection.

Why should Courtley undermine the very ideology which places him in a dominant subject position? I believe the best way to explain his unusual behavior is to turn to the text's authorship. Cavendish and Brackley use their own power as mistresses, as governors over the world of the play, to bring a utopian vision of marital relations into a semipublic arena. The acknowledgement of gender instability by a man is integral to their project of exploiting performance to break down suppositions of male primacy. Courtley's admission that his power over Luceny is theatrical, that his gendered identity is just as much a cultural construct as hers, opens the possibility of a relationship of reciprocity and equality between men and women.

Luceny and Tattiney's success in outwitting their husbands depends to a large extent upon their own facility with language. Luceny's observation, "we have been brought up in the creation of good languages, which will make us ever ourselves" (2.3.142–44), alerts us to the close connection between characters and authors, a feature which extends the effect of "enacting gender" beyond the stage. Like Luceny and Tattiney, Jane Cavendish and Elizabeth Brackley re-create themselves through their own discourse. Like the heroines, they have been "brought up in the creation of good languages, which will make us ever our selves." The Cavendish household provided an atmosphere of creativity, both literary and theatrical. William Cavendish was the author of several plays as well as prose texts on horsemanship and government. He encouraged all of his children, sons and daughters, to write, telling Jane: "Sweet Jane, I know you are a rare inditer / And hath the pen of a most ready writer," and Elizabeth: "Bess, you must write too; write but what you think. / Now you're a girl, dissemble when you link."[28] The first part of the directive to Elizabeth shows the value of writing in asserting subjectivity, while in the second part the word "dissemble" suggests mimicry of "proper" feminine behavior. Betrothal marks a transition from one role to the other in that "link" here means "to couple" or, more specifically, to "get married."[29] As an unmarried "girl" Elizabeth can write what she thinks, but marriage will bring with it the need to dissemble.

As Margaret Ezell notes, Jane Cavendish and Elizabeth Brackley offer no excuse for their writings in the manuscript presentation volume which includes *The Concealed Fancies*.[30] They make no effort to "dissemble" or hide their literary achievements to comply with orthodox ideas of women's silence. On the contrary, by styling themselves as part of a royalist literary coterie, they perform a type of literary sex-change. Writing within a homosocial tradition (which reaffirmed bonds between threatened male royalists), Jane and Elizabeth cross gender boundaries to sit beside the Cavalier poets like "pretty men."[31] The Cavendish family circle provided a specialized arena in which gender and status could be debated, and *The Concealed Fancies* depends vitally on that context. Its dramatization of the prosthetic nature of gender draws on an intersection of the dominant ideologies governing marital relations (and women's behavior) in seventeenth-century England, and the coterie in which these conventions were already being questioned: a coterie in which women were encouraged to write, talk, and debate alongside men. The Cavendish household, with its shared consciousness of gender as performance, is a significant factor in the play's interrogation of gender.

In spite of the absence of external evidence about a private production of the play involving Jane and Elizabeth, there are many textual clues which suggest parallels between characters and authors. Throughout *The Concealed Fancies* references to acting, scene-shifting, and costume make the play inescapably metatheatrical. Courtley and Presumption introduce the heroines as self-assured actors and vow to "see how they will act their scenes" (1.1.52–53), referring both to the characters who outwit them in the performance of courtship and to the actors behind those roles who have composed the scenes. The fact that Courtley and Presumption agree to observe each other's wooing implies that they have offstage presences, watching from the audience as both actors and characters when they are not performing. Luceny and Tattiney's first appearance emphasizes *their* dual identities. Luceny asks her sister "Prithee, tell me how you acted your scene?" (1.4.2–3) and she goes on to describe her own performance with Courtley. References to scenes already played, or played offstage, imply a connection between the scripted performance and other forms of self-presentation in the household and beyond,[32] performances guided by a set of socially accepted practices.

The term "posture" is used in both main plot and subplot to refer to a self-conscious role which advertises an attitude. Luceny and Tattiney adopt "posture[s] of coyness" (1.1.55) which their suitors find impossible to fathom. In the Ballamo plot, the cousins use "postures" to strike a defiant riposte to the Parliamentarian forces. Sh. (whose name is never given in a fuller form in the text), takes the theatrical metaphor further by comparing herself, captured by the enemy, to the tragic figure of Cleopatra: "could they have thought me worthy to have adorned their triumphs. I would have performed his gallant tragedy and so have made myself glorious for time to come" (3.4.15–18). Again the dividing line between types of performance is unclear. The words "his gallant tragedy" may refer to a dramatization of the story, possibly Shakespeare's play. However, to be led in triumph by the Parliamentary commander would have been theatrical in itself, a "royal" spectacle. Such lines must have had a striking effect when spoken within the walls of the besieged Welbeck Abbey. The characters' translation of what was the Cavendish sisters' own situation into dramatic terms comments on what the authors have done in this very scene. Like the cousins in the Ballamo plot, Jane and Elizabeth were actors in a piece over which they had little control beyond the presentation of their own roles in response to circumstances. Their optimistic belief that "the scene would change again" (3.4.8) and the Parliamentarian siege would be lifted is counterpointed by the image of defeat in the reference to Cleopatra. Only their position as writers of the play gives them the authority to compose an optimistic future.

Other speeches in the play reinforce the strong possibility that Luceny and Tattiney were performed by the authors. Presumption's praise of Tattiney's picture (4.4.21–28) reproduces Jane's poem, "On My Sister Brackley's Picture," identifying Tattiney with Elizabeth.[33] The epilogues highlight the speakers' multifaceted identities as protagonists, as authors of their own scenes, and as the "scene selves" which they create there. Luceny's line—"That puts me in mind of my epilogue" (Epilogue 90)—translates her from character to actor and writer, leading into the verse epilogue where she becomes spokeswoman for the whole production company.

When we take into account the probable performance conditions of *The Concealed Fancies* the full effect of mimesis-mimicry becomes apparent. If Cavendish and Brackley did produce the play as a private theatrical at Welbeck Abbey, their identities as actors add another level to the multilayered representations of self, differentiating the play from texts like *As You Like It* and *Epicoene*. Martin Esslin employs the term "cubed semiosis" to describe the complex relationship between actor, role, and audience in dramatic representation. The actor stands for a character who, in turn, can be seen as representative of a type or class of person (the actor playing Rosalind in *As You Like It*, for example, stands for aristocratic heiresses). Behind these two layers of semiosis (the particular and the abstract) the audience remains aware of the performer whose identity exerts its own erotic, magnetic energy. Like the character and the type, the actor's personality is a powerful generator of meaning.[34] In plays written for public stages the presence of boy actors behind female roles reveals the impossibility of fixing absolute gender demarcations. The absorption of male into female and female into male is constantly foregrounded in these texts, reminding the audience of the "other" which disrupts the illusion of unified, self-contained subjectivity. In *The Concealed Fancies* the presence of female performers creates a different effect. The reference to Cleopatra in the subplot effects a contrast between the player's ability to re-create herself on stage and the tradition of boy actors playing female roles. Alluding indirectly to Shakespeare's *Antony and Cleopatra* (5.2.215), the cousin Sh. celebrates how she "practised Cleopatra" herself in her captivity (3.4.13–14), unlike the male performer who can only "boy" Cleopatra's greatness, creating a split between performer and role. In *The Concealed Fancies* the slippage between author, actress, and character evokes gender sameness rather than difference. Instead of seeing immediate gender discontinuity (the male body and the female role), the audience of *The Concealed Fancies* was confronted with actors who demonstrated the performative nature of gender within the "appropriate" male or female bodies for their characters, bodies which were revealed as performative, gendered entities produced by the various stylized acts which constructed their reality.

The coexistence of female actors, authors, and characters on stage would have blurred the boundaries between performance and subjectivity, particularly in a performance space like the Cavendish home where acting on stage and off occurred within the same space. Behind the characters of Luceny and Tattiney stand the Cavendish sisters. Rather than functioning as continuations of their offstage personae, the fictional roles may have given the sisters an opportunity to present selves or "fancies" (that is, aspects of themselves which they wished to develop) which would usually have been concealed. An audience at Welbeck Abbey might have been surprised by the differences between the sisters' ordinary behavior and their performances in role. They make explicit reference to their own voices in the prologues, the first asking the ladies not to blush and craving the gentlemen's indulgence for a female performer, before bidding them be silent (a witty reversal of the usual dictates on women's silence contained within a conventional appeal to the audience on behalf of the performers). The second prologue, who behaves much more coyly, declares that there is no offensive plot behind the play, and, not wishing to be censured for speaking "too long," retires, only to go on to perform, of course.

The blending of character, type, and actress in *The Concealed Fancies* allows the female authors to use the play for their own purposes. Since the games played by Luceny and Tattiney are also "played" by the performers, the roles can perhaps be read as part of Cavendish and Brackley's endeavors to negotiate their own identities in relation to their husbands and suitors. Other poems in the manuscript volume suggest attitudes toward performance that are similar to those held by Luceny and Tattiney. In "The Pert One, or otherwise, My Sister Brackley," Jane commends Elizabeth's ability to balance discretion and independence as a model for wives: "For you can tell how to bee free & wise / Therefore for wives you are the onely syse."[35] When the play was written, Elizabeth was already married to John Egerton, Viscount Brackley. It had been an arranged marriage for which she had been given a dowry of £12,000, a sum which apparently was not sufficient to cover the debts on the Egerton estate. However, when civil war broke out she was still living with her family at the Cavendish home for the reason that she was "too young to be bedded."[36] For Elizabeth, then, the play's treatment of the transition between the roles of mistress and wife would have been especially pertinent.[37]

Jane's attitude to marriage, as evidenced in her writings, seems to promote the model advocated by the heroines in *The Concealed Fancies*. She echoes Luceny closely in one of her letters where she writes that she and her husband are still like lover and mistress.[38] In "A Songe" she offers a pattern of behavior to preserve the affections of a husband and wife once they marry:

> Now if a wife doe knowe hir scene
> What neede shee care what hee doth meane
> Soe n'er his foole hee should hir winn
> For that's a matrimoniall sinn
>
> Now let them conclude in love to each
> And not that language by awe to teach
> For that will then appeare to bee
> Ther's noe free quarter for a shee
>
> Now see I them each other to face
> Upon good grounds to keepe their place
> Soe if one get the Victory
> The other should a conquest see.[39]

The reference to "knowing a scene" immediately draws attention to the importance of performance in maintaining a proper balance of autonomy and cooperation. Jane's belief that it is wrong to make a wife a fool is shared by Courtley (3.3.92–93). In the poem she argues that if the partners love one another, the dominance and submission model of marriage will appear unjust since it offers no space for female self-expression. Instead she recommends a pattern whereby both wife and husband can "keepe their place" and achieve "Victory" or concede "conquest" as appropriate.

In *The Concealed Fancies* Luceny and Tattiney's behavior is directed toward this same goal of companionship in marriage. They want to be able to speak their minds freely as mistresses, and to appear as "modest" wives. The combination of these apparently irreconcilable roles is achieved through the mask of conformity in public and the private assertion of independent will, via witty mimicry. The sisters' technique of limited, covert subversion matches that of the authors themselves. In performance, the effect of mimesis-mimicry protects Cavendish and Brackley from direct association with the characters' more controversial views, yet alerts the audience to the idea that there is no difference between playing on or off stage. All apparent conformity may be mimicry, all expressions of duty mere performances of subjection. With the Cavendish sisters as actors, *The Concealed Fancies* was not simply a piece of entertainment. The multiple images of woman as actor and author of herself, together with the special coterie for which the play was written, allowed Jane Cavendish and Elizabeth Brackley to transcend the limits placed on them by theatrical and social convention.

Notes

1. The manuscript of the play, together with several occasional poems and a masque, "A Pastorall," are located in the Bodleian Library (Bod. Rawl. MS Poet. 16). Nathan Comfort Starr has published a transcript, "*The Concealed Fansyes:* A Play by Lady Jane Cavendish and Lady Elizabeth Brackley," in *PMLA* 46 (1931): 802–38. A modernized spelling edition of the play is included in S. P. Cerasano and Marion Wynne-Davies, eds., *Renaissance Drama by Women: Texts and Documents* (London: Routledge, 1996). All quotations are taken from this edition.

2. Jane Cavendish (1621–69) and Elizabeth Brackley (1626–63) were the daughters of William Cavendish, duke of Newcastle, by his first wife Elizabeth Bassett. They wrote "The Concealed Fansyes" before Newcastle's marriage in 1645 to Margaret Cavendish. Welbeck Abbey was recaptured briefly for the king in July 1645 but the Parliamentarians regained control and on 13 Nov. 1645 it was disgarrisoned. The earl of Manchester reported that "Newcastle's daughters, and the rest of his children and family" were in Welbeck when it was captured. A letter sent to Lord Fairfax on 17 Apr. 1645 is signed by Jane and Frances Cavendish but Elizabeth Brackley is also mentioned in a postscript. See Starr, "The Concealed Fancies: A Play," 803–4; and A. S. Turberville, *A History of Welbeck Abbey and Its Owners,* vol. 1: *1539–1755* (London: Faber and Faber, 1938), 112–13.

3. It is tempting to align class and gender in the play as common elements in a pattern of inversion, whereby familial disorder, with the "woman on top," forms part of a wider discourse designed to identify threats to patriarchal rule in the kingdom (see, for example, Natalie Zemon Davis, *Society and Culture in Early Modern France* [London: Duck-

worth, 1975], 124–51, and Martin Ingram, "Ridings, Rough Music and Mocking Rhymes in Early Modern England," in *Popular Culture in Seventeenth-Century England*, ed. Barry Reay [London: Routledge, 1988], 166–97). William Gouge's *Of Domesticall Duties* (London, 1622) was typical in defining the family as "a little common-wealth" (18), but in spite of the close relationship between the family and the state in the early modern imagination, we must appreciate that these are different spheres of life.

4. William Cavendish, for example, had been tutor to Prince Charles and had led forces to fight for the king in the north until the defeat at Marston Moor; his daughters' manuscript containing *The Concealed Fancies* also includes laudatory poems addressed to the king and queen and His Highness the Prince of Wales. For details of William Cavendish's activities, see Margaret Cavendish's biography *The Life of William Cavendish, First Duke of Newcastle* (London, 1667), in *The Lives of William Cavendish, Duke of Newcastle, and of His Wife, Margaret Duchess of Newcastle*, ed. Mark Antony Lower (London: John Russell Smith, 1872). Margaret's evaluation of her husband's success as a military commander omits some important details and exaggerates others (see Henry Ten Eyck Perry, *The First Duchess of Newcastle and Her Husband as Figures in Literary History*, Harvard Studies in English 4 [Boston: Ginn and Co., 1918]). The poems to members of the royal family are found in the sisters' paginated manuscript volume (Bod. Rawl. MS Poet. 16), 9, 12.

5. See Keith Thomas, "Women and the Civil War Sects," *Past and Present* 13 (1958): 42–62.

6. *Oxford English Dictionary*, 2d ed., *s.v.* "mistress."

7. No records exist of an actual performance of the play, but for suggestions that it may have been performed in the Cavendish household see Marion Wynne-Davies's introduction to the text in *Renaissance Drama by Women*, and Susan Wiseman, "Gender and Status in Dramatic Discourse: The Duchess of Newcastle," in *Women, Writing, History, 1640–1740*, ed. Isobel Grundy and Susan Wiseman (London: Batsford, 1992), 161–63. The roles of the three cousins at Ballamo would probably have been envisaged for (and perhaps performed by) Jane, Elizabeth, and their younger sister Frances. Elizabeth and Jane could have doubled these small roles with the parts of Luceny and Tattiney, until the final scene where the cousins do not speak. Presumption could possibly have been played by John Egerton. A performance of *The Concealed Fancies*, directed by Alison Findlay and Jane Milling, was staged at Bretton Hall, 14 Dec. 1994. For details of the play's performability see Alison Findlay, Stephanie Hodgson-Wright, and Gweno Williams, "'The Play Is Ready to Be Acted': Women and Dramatic Production 1570–1670," *Women's Writing* (special issue: *Early Modern Women Dramatists*, ed. Marion Wynne-Davies [forthcoming 1998]). Lisa Hopkins discusses teaching the play, in "Judith Shakespeare's Reading: Teaching *The Concealed Fancies*," *Shakespeare Quarterly* 47 (Winter 1996): 396–406. On Cavendish and Brackley's place in an emerging female dramatic tradition see Ros Ballaster, "The First Female Dramatists," in *Women and Literature in Britain, 1500–1700*, ed. Helen Wilcox (Cambridge: Cambridge University Press, 1996), 267–90.

8. The role of courted mistress in the play may be modeled on Queen Henrietta Maria.

The entertainments which she shaped and in which she acted at court were in part a means to assert herself (see Erica Veevers, *Images of Love and Religion: Queen Henrietta Maria and Court Entertainments* [Cambridge: Cambridge University Press, 1989]). Lines from one of the manuscript poems to the queen (Bod. Rawl. MS Poet. 16:9) are reworked into Courtley's and Presumption's speeches in praise of their mistresses in *The Concealed Fancies* (4.4.22–36), suggesting that Jane and Elizabeth regarded the queen as a model of strength.

9. Eve Kosofsky Sedgwick, *Between Men: English Literature and Male Homosocial Desire* (New York: Columbia University Press, 1985), 25, 86. See also Miriam Slater, *Family Life in the Seventeenth Century: The Verneys of Claydon House* (London: Routledge and Kegan Paul, 1984), 61–63.

10. In Shakespeare's *The Taming of the Shrew*, for example, neither daughter is privy to the negotiations which will determine her future. In the Induction to the play, the page Bartholemew's disguise points up the "absence" of women (Ind. 1.103–30, and 2.99–110). The female prizes are literally "presented" by men since the roles are performed by boy actors. (All quotations from Shakespeare are from *The Complete Works*, ed. Stanley Wells and Gary Taylor [Oxford: Clarendon Press, 1988].) In Jonson's *Epicoene* (1609) the betrothal similarly revolves around a financial relationship between men: Morose, Dauphine, and the boy whom he hires to play the part of Epicoene, the "Silent Woman" of the play's title. Dauphine needs the boy actor not because the silent woman takes an active part in the negotiations, but because Morose will not believe that such a creature exists (*Epicoene*, ed. R. V. Holdsworth [London: Benn, 1979]). Richard Brome's later play *The Damoiselle* (1638) satirizes the commodification of women even further in a plot in which a supposed innkeeper plans to raffle his daughter's virginity. Marriage and prostitution appear disturbingly similar in a commercialized culture in which men determine the dowries or "prices" of all the female characters. The title character (or "Damoiselle") is in fact a young man disguised in a plot to recover his inheritance (*The Damoiselle or The New Ordinary*, in *The Dramatic Works of Richard Brome Containing Fifteen Comedies*, 3 vols. [London: J. Pearson, 1873], 1:375–468).

11. Slater, *Family Life in the Seventeenth Century*, 80.

12. Margaret J. M. Ezell, *The Patriarch's Wife: Literary Evidence and the History of the Family* (Chapel Hill: University of North Carolina Press, 1987), 17–34.

13. Marion Wynne-Davies suggests that the character of Lady Tranquillity may be based on Margaret Lucas, whom William Cavendish married in December 1645. Reports of his "inappropriate" courtship, with a woman over thirty years younger than himself, may have been passed on to Jane and Elizabeth by the two Cavendish brothers Henry and Charles (*Renaissance Drama by Women*, 129).

14. See *The King's Entertainment at Welbeck* (1633) and *Love's Welcome at Bolsover* (1634) in *Ben Jonson*, ed. C. H. Herford, Percy Simpson, and Evelyn Simpson (Oxford: Clarendon Press, 1925–52), 7:787–814. The entertainments are discussed with reference to Welbeck Abbey and Bolsover Castle by Cedric C. Brown, "Courtesies of Place and Arts of Diplomacy in Ben Jonson's Last Two Entertainments for Royalty," *Seventeenth Century* 9 (Autumn 1994): 147–71.

15. R. Valerie Lucas, "Puritan Preaching and the Politics of the Family," in *The Renaissance Englishwoman in Print: Counterbalancing the Canon,* ed. Anne M. Haselkorn and Betty S. Travitsky (Amherst: University of Massachusetts Press, 1990), 228–29. See also Mary Beth Rose, *The Expense of Spirit: Love and Sexuality in English Renaissance Drama* (Ithaca: Cornell University Press, 1988), 124–31.

16. William Whately, *A Bride-Bush or A Wedding Sermon* (London, 1617), 1, 18, 36. On early modern marriage sermons see also Kathleen M. Davies, "The Sacred Condition of Equality: How Original Were Puritan Doctrines of Marriage?" *Social History* 5 (1977): 563–80; and William Haller and Melville Haller, "The Puritan Art of Love," *Huntington Library Quarterly* 5 (Feb. 1941–42): 235–72.

17. "Homily on Matrimony" (1547), in *Certain Sermons or Homilies Appointed to be read in churches in the time of Queen Elizabeth of famous memory and now thought fit to be reprinted by Authority from the Kings Most Excellent Majesty* (Oxford, 1683), 322. Thirty-nine editions of the First Book of Homilies were in print between 1547 and 1650.

18. Susan Dwyer Amussen, *An Ordered Society: Gender and Class in Early Modern England* (Oxford: Basil Blackwell, 1988), passim.

19. Whately, *Bride-Bush,* 29.

20. Luce Irigaray, *Speculum of the Other Woman,* trans. Gillian C. Gill (Ithaca: Cornell University Press, 1985), 292. For a discussion of Irigaray's rewriting of Platonic mimesis, see Elin Diamond, "Mimesis, Mimicry, and the 'True-Real,'" *Modern Drama* 32 (Mar. 1989): 58–72.

21. Irigaray, *Speculum of the Other Woman,* 51–54. On Irigaray's critique of Freudian mimesis see Toril Moi, *Sexual/Textual Politics: Feminist Literary Theory* (London: Routledge, 1985), 127–35.

22. Luce Irigaray, *This Sex Which Is Not One,* trans. Catherine Porter and Carolyn Burke (Ithaca: Cornell University Press, 1985), 76.

23. Gataker's *A Wife In Deed* was originally written for the marriage of Sir Robert and Lady Brilliana Harley and first published in 1623. In 1637 it was reprinted in Thomas Gataker, *Certain Sermons First Preached and After Published, at severall times* (London, 1637). All quotations are taken from the 1637 edition.

24. Irigaray, *Speculum of the Other Woman;* Diamond, "Mimesis, Mimicry, and the 'True-Real,'" 65.

25. Judith Butler, *Gender Trouble: Feminism and the Subversion of Identity* (New York: Routledge, 1990), 6.

26. Ibid., 6.

27. Ibid., 140.

28. See Turberville, *History of Welbeck Abbey and Its Owners,* 1:45–46. Dale B. J. Randall recognizes the extensive literary activities of the family, though his dismissal of *The Concealed Fancies* as "not a bad game for a couple of beleaguered young women to play" diminishes its significance ("The Cavendish Phenomenon," in *Winter Fruit: English Drama, 1642–1660* [Lexington: University Press of Kentucky, 1995], 313–36, quotation on 326).

29. *Oxford English Dictionary,* 2d ed., s.v. "link."

30. Margaret M. J. Ezell, "'To Be Your Daughter in Your Pen': The Social Functions of Literature in the Writings of Lady Elizabeth Brackley and Lady Jane Cavendish," *Huntington Library Quarterly* 51 (Autumn 1988): 281–96.

31. On the homosocial character of Cavalier writing see Earl Miner, *The Cavalier Modes from Jonson to Cotton* (Princeton: Princeton University Press, 1971), 275; and Ezell, "'To Be Your Daughter in Your Pen,'" 287.

32. On the importance of the household context see Alison Findlay, "'She Gave You the Civility of the House': Household Performance in *The Concealed Fancies*," in *Readings in Renaissance Women's Drama,* ed. Susan P. Cerasano and Marion Wynne-Davies (forthcoming, London: Routledge).

33. Bod. Rawl. MS Poet. 16:22.

34. Martin Esslin, *The Field of Drama* (London: Methuen, 1987), 59–60.

35. Bod. Rawl. MS Poet. 16:11.

36. Mark Anthony Lower, ed., *The Lives of William Cavendish, Duke of Newcastle and of His Wife Margaret, Duchess of Newcastle* (London: John Russell Smith, 1872), 123–24.

37. Many of the ideas expressed by the heroines find echoes in Elizabeth Brackley's private meditation, "Considerations concerning marriage," from the manuscript in the British Library "True Copies of certaine Loose Papers left by ye Right honorable Elizabeth, Countesse of Bridgewater, Collected and Transcribed together here since her Death Anno dom. 1663," BL Egerton 607, 150–61. (All subsequent references are to this paginated manuscript.) Elizabeth begins by directly confronting the issue of female submission, pointing out that "Some account of marriage as an unhappy life, by reason there is an obedience must belong from the wife to the Husband" (150). Although this statement appears to be radical, in fact it follows the "Homily on Matrimony" which acknowledges that women "must specially feel the grief and pains of their Matrimony, in that they relinquish the Liberty of their own Rule." Elizabeth does not claim that women should rule their husbands as mistresses as do the heroines of *The Concealed Fancies,* but neither does she regard women's subjection as the natural consequence of male superiority. Given the duty of obedience, she proposes that women should debate with themselves "whether or no they could esteeme of such a person so as to value his Judgement, and in matters of consequence to yeild to his councell" before entering into marriage (151–52). The character Tattiney uses playacting to test Presumption's attitudes throughout the wooing process, and she succeeds in transforming him from a potentially tyrannical governor to a "discreet husband" (Epilogue 80). If the romantic plot of *The Concealed Fancies* is intimately related to the Cavendish sisters' own marital relationships, then it may be that Elizabeth took the opportunity offered by the performance to discover whether she could esteem John Egerton and respect his judgment.

In "Considerations Concerning Marriage" Elizabeth, like the homilists, presents marriage as a partnership, but she is careful to stress the importance of equality of affection and of free speech. She outlines a model of feminine behavior like that promoted by the heroines of *The Concealed Fancies,* arguing that a wife should not be "over awed by her owne Fancyes" (156) or strong will. If she is "hye, and lofty, and willfull" this will drive away her husband (154–55). On the other hand, a wife should not be "so meeke, and lowe in spirit," in "Subjection," as to drive away her husband simply because he believes she would rather be alone (153–54). Neither should she be "in such awe of him, as a servant of his Master, as not to speake, to contradict the least word he saith, but to have an affection and love to him, as a friend, and so to speake their mind and opinion freely to him" (152–53). The extant records suggest that Elizabeth's own marriage matched this model of love, affection, and free exchange of ideas. John Egerton's epitaph notes that he had enjoyed twenty-two years of companionship in "the sweet society of the Best of Wives"; and Jane Cavendish praises Egerton in one of her poems as the pattern for husbands, combining love, faithfulness, and wisdom (see Betty Travitsky, "'His Wife's Prayers and Meditations': MS Egerton 607," in *The Renaissance Englishwoman in Print: Counterbalancing the Canon,* ed. Haselkorn and Travitsky, 241–60, esp. 241); and Betty S. Travitsky, "Reconstructing the Still, Small Voice: The Occasional Journal of Elizabeth Egerton," *Women's Studies* 19.2 (1991): 193–200. Jane's poem in praise of Brackley is located in Bod. Rawl. MS Poet. 16: 19.

38. Portland MS PW1.88, University of Nottingham Library, quoted in *Kissing the Rod: An Anthology of Seventeenth-Century Women's Verse,* ed. Germaine Greer et al. (London: Virago, 1988), 108.

39. Bod. Rawl. MS Poet. 16:26.

8

The Introduction of Actresses in England: Delay or Defensiveness?

Michael Shapiro

In the past several decades, English-speaking audiences on both sides of the Atlantic have seen all-male productions of *As You Like It.* Clifford Williams directed one for the National Theatre in 1967, which he revived in 1974 with a different cast for a North American tour. Cheek by Jowl, a British company, which had taken its production on world tour, performed at the Brooklyn Academy of Music in October and December of 1994. Neither company attempted to replicate the particular pattern of all-male casting used in the original production of c. 1600. On Shakespeare's stage, female roles were customarily taken by "play-boys," that is, youths in late adolescence, who were younger and probably slighter in build than adult male performers. As apprentices and hirelings rather than fully fledged actors or sharers in the company, "play-boys" probably occupied a lower social status than the adult male actors playing adult male characters. In the two recent all-male productions, however, Rosalind was played by very experienced adult performers—Ronald Pickup and Gregory Floy for the National, Ronnie Lester for Cheek by Jowl.[1] Even with play-boys, the effects of such cross-gender casting for modern audiences would be different from what they were for Elizabethan spectators. For us it is a novelty; for them it was the norm.

For centuries, in fact, the use of male actors in female roles had been normative not only in England but throughout the West. Stephen Orgel has recently characterized the retention of cross-gender casting in England as "a uniquely English solution to the universal European disapproval of actresses."[2] Orgel makes the additional point that retention per se of tradition is not an adequate explanation for a continuing cultural practice, especially one being abandoned in neighboring countries. Whereas Orgel sees the English commercial stage as unique in its use of female impersonators, I would describe it as late in introducing actresses.

In this essay I want to explore some of the possible reasons for that lateness. I have not found explanations based on English sexual attitudes to be fully convincing, especially when those attitudes occur in other European societies which find different ways to come to terms with the employment of actresses during the same period. The first task then is to question the uniqueness of the English solution and to interrogate explanations based on the assumptions of that uniqueness. The second task is to seek alternative hypotheses for the late introduction of actresses on the English stage. I want to direct the inquiry away from cultural attitudes toward gender and toward the economics of the English commercial theater, specifically toward the training of actors and demands of touring, in the hope that such a shift in the way we define the problem might lead to the discovery of new documentary evidence.

English Acting Troupes and the All-Male Tradition of European Theater

Acting had been an all-male activity in ancient Greece as well as in the official theaters of Rome, although the popular Roman festival of Floralia featured a farcical and bawdy style of mime which included female performers.[3] In medieval Europe, most officially sanctioned theatrical activity took place under the auspices of all-male ecclesiastical institutions, despite some evidence of performances in nunneries and of limited participation by girls or young women in French and English biblical plays or cycles put on by craft guilds.[4] There are also traces of women appearing all over Europe as itinerant entertainers, probably as singers, dancers, and acrobats, under such names as *joculatores* or *jongleurs*.

Nowhere in Europe did women act in plays performed by professional theater troupes until Italian popular touring companies, the commedia dell'arte, employed actresses in the 1560s: "the first record . . . is the appearance in a troupe list of 1564 of a certain Lucrezia Senese."[5] In the three centuries since the introduction of actresses, audiences have come to accept the use of women in female roles as natural, when in fact it is merely conventional and at one time was considered innovative. Perhaps the appropriate question is not why the English theater resisted the use of actresses until 1660, but rather why real women replaced female impersonators.

Glynne Wickham answers this question in terms of decorum: a growing demand for verisimilitude in the theaters of Italy, first largely in regard to scenic design, led to an equivalent demand for verisimilitude in the casting of female roles.[6] However, the productions which first used scenic design to suggest domestic interiors or realistic street facades were those mounted by private academies, in which men continued to play female roles long after actresses appeared in plays performed by the popular troupes. The popular troupes themselves were slower to adopt verisimilitude in scenic design, for as itinerant companies they used trestle-and-board stages easily set up in marketplaces or halls.

The kind of aesthetic inconsistency Wickham describes was evidently not perceived as a problem. As Michael Anderson remarks about a drawing of the celebrated actress Isabella Andreini performing on a crude stage, "It may seem strange that the foremost actress of her day should appear on a stage which, in scenic terms, is no better equipped than that of the Zanni performing in the *piazza* or the most modest of *stanze*."[7] Casting practices also undermined verisimilitude: while the Isabellas and other chaste upper-class romantic heroines were played by the earliest actresses, who were often relatives of the male members of the company, the low comic roles of female servants, who often engaged in raucous and bawdy farce, were played by men. In two cast lists, that of I Comici Uniti from Padua in 1584 and that of Uniti from Genoa in 1614, the character of Franceschina is assigned to a man. One suspects that the families involved, no less than the civic authorities, had no wish to see their female relatives engage in coarsely eroticized slapstick, such as the scene from the *Recueil Fossard* collection in which Pantalon is spying on Harlequin through the curtains as the latter reaches his right hand under the skirt and between the thighs of Francesquina.[8]

A more obvious explanation than Wickham's for the introduction of actresses is commercial: popular troupes exploited the appeal of actresses when and where civic and ecclesiastical authorities did not stop them from doing so. The innovation was not welcomed everywhere, for public performances by women were seen as too provocative by those in power, who sometimes feared that actresses were engaging in prostitution. Despite such resistance, the use of actresses spread throughout Europe, although not in any simple linear fashion, as a rapid overview will indicate.

Even in Italy, women were forbidden to act in public in certain localities. In Rome in 1588, a troupe known as the Desiosi (also known as Company of Diana because of its association with an actress named Diana Ponti) was ordered by Pope Sixtus V to replace their actresses with boys. He subsequently banned women from performing publicly throughout the Papal States, a decree which held (with some exceptions) until late in the eighteenth century. This papal ban included singers as well as actresses, so that in Rome, as elsewhere in Italy, voices in the upper registers were supplied by castrati.[9]

In Spain, actresses, as opposed to dancers and singers, probably did not appear until an Italian troupe petitioned the authorities for permission to use its women in 1587. The practice was subsequently adopted by competing Spanish companies, not without clerical opposition, although some of that opposition was bought off by the promise to donate a portion of playhouse profits to orphanages, hospitals, and poorhouses maintained by the religious confraternities which controlled the Madrid theaters.[10] Even after actresses were permitted on the Spanish stage in 1587, they were outlawed between 1596 and 1600 and carefully regulated thereafter: they had to be married women, accompanied by their husbands, not visited more than twice backstage by male spectators, and they were forbidden to wear costumes considered too revealing. Ursula Heise notes that Spanish authorities were troubled by female characters adopting male disguise and tried to curtail if not forbid it in a series of edicts, fearful that male attire revealed women's bodies and thus accentuated rather than veiled female sexuality. Spanish clerics were apparently divided over whether the danger of using men in female roles was more acute than that of using women. Heise links objections to female impersonation to an intense and violent wave of persecution of homosexuals which swept over Spain in the sixteenth century, although the reissuing of edicts outlawing such cross-gender casting suggests that companies continued the practice, perhaps using both men and women in female roles.[11]

In France, there is evidence of actresses even before the arrival of Italian popular troupes. An actress named Marie Fairet and her manager signed a contract at Bourges in 1545, but the use of actresses on a regular basis followed the arrival of the Italian popular companies, which played at court and publicly in Paris in the early 1570s. A French troupe introduced actresses in Bordeaux in 1598 and shortly thereafter in Paris.[12]

What emerges from this admittedly rough and schematic survey of the introduction of actresses in Italy, France, and Spain is a steady, if nonlinear, increase in their use on the commercial stage, but with important countercurrents. (Throughout Europe, noncommercial productions such as those under the auspices of all-male institutions like academies, schools, and universities, of course remained all-male.) In the Protestant countries of northern Europe, theatrical representation of women is no less complicated than in the Catholic countries to the south. In Geneva in 1546, for example, a local troupe applied to the town council for permission to perform a dramatization of the Acts of the Apostles. E. K. Chambers summarizes the case:

> The council ordered the book of the piece to be submitted to Calvin, and agreed that it should be performed, should his report be favourable. Calvin and the other ministers did not much like the proposal, more particularly as the players declined to give alms to the poor out of the profits of the enterprise. It so happened, however, that one of the ministers, Abel Poupin, was himself the author of the play and partly because of this, and partly because he was not sure that an attempt to prevent the performance would be successful, Calvin seems to have persuaded his colleagues to offer no objec-

tion. . . . A preacher of fiery temper, Michel Cop, got into the pulpit and denounced the play, accusing the women performers of a shameless desire to display themselves in public and thereby ensnare the eyes of men.[13]

Although Calvin agreed with Cop's objection, invoking Tertullian's antitheatrical authority, he justified his earlier decision to permit the play on grounds of expediency. The following year, the council refused to permit a performance by a troupe evidently consisting of Richard Chaultemps and his wife and children, although other plays on classical and religious subjects were permitted. In 1572, the Synod of Nimes outlawed the performance of all but strictly educational plays within the French reformed church.[14]

If women playing female characters caused a problem for Calvin and his followers, so did the casting of young men or boys in such roles. In a sermon in 1556, Calvin cited the prohibition of crossdressing in Deuteronomy 22.5 as an absolute rule. By contrast, his successor at Geneva, Theodore Beza, author of Christian humanist plays such as *Abraham's Sacrifice,* fully supported cross-gender casting. According to Richard Braithwait, Beza "constantly affirmed, that it was not only lawfull for them to set forth and act those *Playes,* but for Boyes to put on womens apparell for the time."[15] Puritan opinion, at least in Geneva, could waver in regard to the representation of women by actresses or male performers, for either women or the images of women could, from their point of view, stir the erotic imagination; some English antitheatrical writings also grant such evocative power to male performers themselves.

In Holland, the picture is also mixed. Touring troupes in the sixteenth century may have used actresses, but productions by the Chambers of Rhetoric were all-male affairs. Female roles were taken not only by boys but according to some accounts by older men as well. The first actresses did not appear in Dutch commercial theaters until 1655, and even then they often shared female roles with male performers.[16]

The retention of cross-gender casting by the English commercial companies must be judged against this variegated history of female representation by both men and women in early modern Europe. Whether Catholic or Protestant, religious and some civic officials feared that any display of women could be disruptive to social order, whether the display was by real women exhibiting their own bodies or by female impersonators creating theatrical representations of women. In England, productions at the universities often evoked considerable anxiety over the issue of female impersonation.[17] On the Continent, the Jesuits, who were as strongly influenced by Deuteronomy 22.5 as the English antitheatricalists, initially prohibited female characters or female costumes in their school productions ("nec persona ulla muliebris vel habitus introducatur"), but eventually relaxed this rule in order to produce plays based on heroines such as Judith.[18] English antitheatrical tracts, some written by and for Puritans, denounce cross-gender casting as a violation of the biblical injunction against crossdressing. They would probably have objected to women onstage with equal vigor, as Nashe slyly suggests in his defense of the English system of cross-gender casting: "Our Players are not as the players beyond sea, a sort of squirting baudie Comedians, that have whores and common Curtizens to playe womens partes, and forbeare no immodest speech or unchast action that may procure laughter."[19] In fact, although instances of social crossdressing such as the *Hic Mulier* movement evoked considerable anxiety in the period, especially when women wore male attire, I tend to agree with Alan Nelson's conclusion that for most of the English antitheatricalists the real target was drama per se, and the biblical injunction against crossdressing was simply a handy weapon in that campaign.[20]

There was throughout early modern Europe a pervasive impulse to control women's freedom of movement and association in order to restrict their sexual activity. Ironically, English women enjoyed relatively greater freedom of movement in their daily lives than did most women on the Continent, especially in Spain. All over Europe, theatrical displays of female sexuality aroused intense fears and invited rigid forms of regulation if not outright prohibition. Such fears were expressed by antitheatricalist writers in both Catholic and Protestant countries, and they seem as agitated when women performers displayed their own bodies, faces, and voices as when skilled male performers created theatrical illusions of women. Some societies preferred male performers as the lesser of two evils, although this solution raised two other fears. One was that the erotic allure of the crossdressed male actor might be sexually arousing to male spectators.[21] A second fear was the effeminization of male spectators through their enthrallment either by the crossdressed male performer per se or by the character he portrayed. Thus Heise concludes her comparison of English and Spanish antitheatrical writings by noting that both movements construct the theater, regardless of whether women or men play female roles, as an essentially "female" spectacle which threatens to sap the virility of male spectators, the dominant and most significant faction of the audience, rendering them unfit for positions of military or civic leadership and robbing the nation of economic vitality. Despite her indebtedness to Orgel's work, Heise finally expresses doubt that English "cultural anxieties about the nature of male identity" were "due to the convention of *male* crossdressing in particular" (my emphasis) and concludes that "the same dynamic would have asserted itself had women been admitted to the stage."[22]

The reasons why English troupes preserved the practice of cross-gender casting might more readily be linked to such factors as protection of male employment, the maintenance of recruitment and training systems already in place, the lack of a pool of potential actresses, and the relative advantages or disadvantages of touring with women.

The Training of Actors in Early Modern England

As throughout western Europe, one strand of English theatrical activity grew out of all-male institutions—grammar schools, universities, and chapel choirs. Another strand grew out of the work of small traveling troupes which toured throughout England and whose activities are now being chronicled in *Records of Early English Drama* (REED) volumes. Extant casting lists from the latter half of the sixteenth century indicate that most companies comprised six or eight men and two boys who usually doubled in any number of female and juvenile roles.[23] The larger London companies, like Shakespeare's, typically comprised twelve full-time adult members, or sharers, and three or four younger male performers to take female and juvenile roles. At about nineteen, as in the case of Ezekiel Fenn, the play-boys were ready to assume adult male roles, and, one presumes, to relinquish female roles to younger boys. There is no evidence that any female roles were played by grown men in the London commercial theaters before 1642.[24]

Play-boys entered the adult acting companies either as apprentices or as "covenant servants." Those described as apprentices were bound to an individual adult actor rather than to a company. In return for fees paid by a parent or guardian, the actor housed the boy and undertook to teach him the profession of acting. Starting ages for apprentice actors could vary from about ten to sixteen, and the length of service from three to ten years. By contrast, most apprenticeships in the craft guilds started around twenty and lasted about seven years, only occasionally ending before the age of twenty-four. Acting apprenticeships probably began earlier so that, once trained, the play-boys could perform for several years in female roles before the onset of puberty, which occurred later than it does now, made them better suited to adult male roles.[25]

Two pieces of literary evidence suggest that young male actors were leased by the week. Captain Tucca, a character in Ben Jonson's *Poetaster* (1601) considers offering his two "pyrgi," or boy servants, to the actor, Histrio: "What wilt thou give mee a weeke, for my brace of beagles, here, my little point-trussers?" Tucca has the boys demonstrate their skill in a variety of roles, until Histrio seems ready to make a deal—"what will you ask for 'hem a weeke, Captaine?"—only to have Tucca refuse on the grounds that the player would peddle them as catamites ("sell 'em for enghles"). Venus, the deaf Tire-woman in Jonson's *Christmas, His Masque* (1616), brags about the acting abilities of her son, a "Prentise in Love-lane with a

Bugle-maker," who will play Cupid in the masque: "I forsooth, he'le say his part, I warrant him, as well as ere a Play boy of 'em all: I could ha' had money enough for him, an I would ha' beene tempted, and ha' let him out by the weeke, to the Kings Players: Master *Burbadge* has beene about and about with me; and so has old Mr. *Hemings* too, they ha' need of him."[26] The passage is rich in self-reflexive irony because in all likelihood Venus herself was represented by a "play-boy."

Fragments of documentary evidence suggest that boy actors were sometimes leased and sometimes apprenticed, but to individuals rather than companies. On December 19, 1597, Henslowe recorded the purchase of a boy named James Bristowe for eight pounds from the actor William Augusten and subsequently records payments of three shillings per week he received from the company for the use of Bristowe's services. Decades later, in 1633, John Shank testified that he paid forty pounds for a boy named John Thompson. Susan Baskervil received seven shillings per week from a troupe playing at the Red Bull for the services of a boy who had previously been apprenticed to her late son, William Browne, an actor, who died in 1634.[27]

The apprenticeship system continued into the Caroline periods, even as it blended into another system, that of the training or nursery company. Earlier in the seventeenth century, members of grammar school and chorister troupes such as Nathan Field eventually found employment in adult companies. In 1629, efforts were made to create a juvenile or nursery company, when Richard Gunnell and William Blagrave established the Children of the Revels at the Salisbury Court Theater "to train and bring up certain boys in the quality of playing with intent to be a supply of able actors to your Majesty's Servants of the Blackfriars," that is, the King's Men.[28] But Blagrave acquired at least one member of that troupe, Stephen Hammerton, by buying the remaining nine years of his apprenticeship from a merchant tailor. Similarly, in 1636–37, Christopher Beeston founded another juvenile company, "Beeston's Boys," or the King's and Queen's Young Company, to play at the Cockpit, perhaps on the model of the Salisbury Court Company of a few years earlier. After Beeston's death in 1637, his son William managed the troupe until it was dissolved in 1642. Even during the interregnum, when the London theaters were officially closed, William Beeston tried to establish a clandestine troupe of youthful actors at the Cockpit. As Beeston testified in a lawsuit a year or so later, he laid out a substantial sum in 1650 to repair the theater after acquiring it "and after that took prentices and covenant servants to instruct them in the quality of acting and fitting for the stage."[29]

The phrase "covenant servants" suggests an alternative to apprenticeships as a method of recruiting; evidently the boys were regarded as personal property, to be sold or rented for theatrical performers. The price of boys, as of everything else, had risen since Henslowe had bought and leased James Bristowe, perhaps through general inflation and perhaps because talented or trained young male actors had become an increasingly valued commodity as the London theatrical industry expanded. In a legal document dated 1635, the Burbage family recalled that the King's Men acquired some of the actors from the Children of the Queen's Revels when they took over Henry Evans's lease of the Blackfriars theater in 1608, evidently to replenish their own supply of young male actors, "the boys daily wearing out."[30] In the Caroline period, training companies were started, as we have seen, presumably to augment the supply of youthful male performers, but some adult troupes might still have recruited their own play-boys to take juvenile and female roles.

However the play-boys were recruited, there is testimony to their skill in acting. Writing about a performance of *Othello* by the King's Men at Oxford in 1610, Henry Jackson commented in his Latin diary on the power of the young male playing Desdemona: "she always acted the matter very well, in her death moved us still more greatly; when lying in bed she implored the pity of those watching with her countenance alone."[31] Some post-Restoration accounts of the earlier female impersonators strike a different note: Colley Cibber disparaged these "Boys, or young Men of the most effeminate Aspect" as "ungain Hoydens,"[32] but one suspects that he is denigrating the theater of the previous age to praise that of his own.

Perhaps the strongest reason for the continued exclusion of women from the stage was a desire on the part of male actors to preserve the profession of acting as a site for male employment. The apprenticeship system itself need not have prevented English troupes from bringing young women into their ranks, for some crafts did take female apprentices. In any case, there was no actors' guild in England and although many actors maintained active membership in craft guilds, only three recorded cases of theatrical apprenticeship were channeled through those institutions.[33]

Even if women were theoretically eligible for theatrical apprenticeships, the economic climate for female employment outside of the home or family business was deteriorating. For most of the sixteenth century, women were being pushed out of economic niches they had occupied earlier. Modifying a time-honored practice of female impersonation in order to include women in acting troupes would probably have seemed threatening to male performers accustomed to all-male companies (one composed of sharers in the case of the King's Men) in which many had learned the craft by starting with juvenile female roles, the very roles women would usurp should they enter the profession.

Shortly after the Restoration, one group of actors had to be compelled by economic and legal pressure to act alongside women. This was a troupe of veteran performers, all of them professionally active before 1642, whom Michael Mohun led at the Red Bull in defiance of the monopolies granted to companies led by Killigrew and Davenant, as well as of the efforts of Sir Henry Herbert, Master of the Revels, to assert his authority over the renewed commercial theatrical life of London by taxing the companies. Mohun's group evidently revived theatrical practices from the Caroline period. In a petition to the king dated October 13, 1660, the troupe complained that it owed Herbert no fees as he was unable to protect them from Killigrew, who pressured them to join his company and forced them to accept a set of new theatrical practices: "Mr. Killegrew having your Majesties former Grante suppress us, untill wee had by convenant obleiged our selves to Act with Woemen a new Theatre and Habitts according to our Scaenes."[34] Mohun, incidentally, was remembered by James Wright in *Historia Histrionica* as having performed the female role of Bellmente in Shirley's *Love's Cruelty* (1631) both before and after the Restoration.[35] Although actresses were already a great attraction, Mohun and his group apparently revived the theater as they had known it, and were reluctant to admit women to the fraternal order of stage players and perhaps even to share roles with them. The bias continued even after women became established on the London stage, for no actress ever became a full sharer of a company until 1695.[36] Until that point, production costs had been kept low by the suppression of actresses' compensation, but costs had been lower still when female roles were played by male apprentices and male "covenant servants."

The First English Actresses

In 1660, when the theaters reopened, the few available trained female impersonators were eighteen years older than they had been when the theaters closed in 1642. Evidently some, such as Michael Mohun, resumed earlier female roles, and it is possible that Thomas Jordan was alluding to just such superannuated "boy actresses" in his barb at "men act that are between / Forty and Fifty, wenches of fifteen."[37] Other, younger performers, such as Edward Kynaston (born in 1643), William Betterton (born in 1644), and James Nokes (birthdate unknown), were initially great successes in female roles, and for a brief time, female roles were taken by both men and women, but very quickly the use of actresses became standard. Pepys mentions "the first time that ever I saw women come upon the stage" in his entry for January 3, 1661, but Andrew Newport had already written two weeks earlier to Sir Richard Leveson on December 15, 1660, that "Upon our stages we have women actors, as beyond seas."[38] When Charles II authorized the resumption of playing by chartering two companies, he issued patents in May and August 1660, but the clause specifically permitting actresses first appeared in a revised patent dated January 15, 1662. The inserted passage notes that in "many plays, formerly acted . . . the womens parts therein have been acted by men in the habits of women, at which some have taken offence." The revised patent then proposes to remedy that situation, although by 1662 actresses had already been performing on the London stage for over two years: "And we do likewise permit and give leave that all the womens parts to be acted in either of the two said companies for the time to come, may be performed by women, so long as these recreations, which, by reason of the aforesaid, were scandalous and offensive, may by such reformation be esteemed not only harmless delights, but useful and instructive representations of humane life, to such of our good subjects as shall resort to see the same."[39] Despite the king's high moral tone, the display of women's bodies, accentuated by theatrical costume—especially the display of legs made possible by the donning of doublet and hose in the disguised heroine plays—was a powerful playhouse attraction.[40]

Why, we must ask again, did England's commercial theaters wait until 1660 to adopt a practice which had for some decades been commonplace in many areas on the continent? There was never, so far as I know, any legal statute prohibiting the appearance of women onstage, and indeed aristocratic women, like their male counterparts, often appeared as nonspeaking dancers in masques performed in the Jacobean court, an elite setting where any moral objections to the display of female bodies were overpowered by the desire of the queen and her ladies to perform. Italian companies, presumably with female performers, occasionally visited England, playing largely but not entirely at court. There is evidence of widespread familiarity with their work, although not always with their use of female performers.[41] French troupes employing actresses played in London in 1629 and 1635.[42] The former attracted significant audiences, for Prynne refers to "French women Actors in a play not long since personated in Black friars Playhouse to which there was great resort," adding a note which gives the date as Michaelmas 1629.[43]

The place to see women onstage was abroad, and Englishmen traveling on the Continent often reported on this novelty. Thomas Coryate, who visited Venice in 1610, is typical: "Here I observed certaine things that I never saw before. For I saw women acte, a thing that I never saw before, though I have heard that it hath beene sometimes used in London, and they performed it with as good a grace, action, gesture, and whatsoever convenient for a Player as ever I saw any masculine Actor."[44] Coryate sought out all manner of exotica during his travels—

for example, Jewish circumcisions and Venetian courtesans, so that one would think that he of all people would have taken advantage of any available opportunity to see women perform in London playhouses. Perhaps he is referring to touring Italian troupes, possibly to the appearance of Queen Anne and several aristocratic women in Jacobean court masques. Scholars are puzzled.

In the Caroline court, Aurelian Townshend's masque, *Tempe Restor'd,* featured two female singers, a Mme. Coniacke and a Mrs. Shepherd, while other women appeared in masquelike pastorelles.[45] By the 1630s, playhouse audiences seemed receptive to the idea of female performers. A character in James Shirley's *The Ball* (1639) comments that women actors are "a thing much desir'd in England," while a character in Richard Brome's *The Court Beggar* (1640) refers both to the current practice of female impersonation and the current interest in actresses: "If you have a short speech or two, the boy's a pretty actor, and his mother can play her part—women actors now grow in request."[46] Nevertheless, up to the time the theaters closed in 1642, we know of no actresses who appeared in the commercial theaters of London nor in productions by itinerant troupes outside of London. For the average English theatergoer (and many women went to plays too) all-male casting was, and was accepted as, standard practice. Still, one wonders why some shrewd English theatrical entrepreneur like Philip Henslowe did not attempt to gain a commercial advantage over his competitors by adapting the new continental fashion of employing actresses.

Perhaps the delay in introducing actresses on the English stage may have been caused by the difficulty of finding women with the kind of education and training who would be willing to enter a field traditionally seen as one remove from prostitution. Moll Frith, the model for Moll Cutpurse in Dekker and Middleton's *The Roaring Girl,* once made a kind of guest appearance on the stage of the Fortune in 1611. She did so not as an actress but as an eccentric celebrity of marginal social status and ambiguous gender who represented a version of herself. She was not someone amenable to the rigorous training needed to gain steady employment as an actress. In the years before the closing of the theaters, it is not clear that there was a class of women who might have entered the acting profession were it possible to do so. It is hard to imagine many literate girls or young women whose families would have allowed them to become apprentices (which would have meant leaving home and moving into the master's house) at an age probably even earlier than the usual one for other crafts or for entering domestic service.

Although biographical information is scanty and of dubious accuracy, most early Restoration actresses came from the ranks of "dowerless daughters of the genteel poor," that is, from impoverished middle-class families and in some cases from royalist families ruined by the civil war.[47] When actresses did finally appear on the English stage, only one—Susannah Mountfort—was the daughter of an actor, and one or two others were said to have been raised in theatrical families. By 1660 the commercial stage had made some gain in social stature: the two London companies were chartered by the king and relied heavily on an elite clientele. Whether the primary task of the actress was to represent the behavior of upper-class heroines or to advertise her own beauty and charm before male playgoers, the theater, having no young men trained to play female roles, came to rely on a class of young women who by virtue of their family's social backgrounds would require a minimum of training in order to represent dramatic heroines on the Restoration stage. Such a class of women may not have been as readily available or desperate for livelihood before 1642, nor was there a class of literate courtesans with expertise in, say, music and dance, who might also have furnished acting troupes with a supply of female performers.

Restoration actresses, while not recruited from the ranks of courtesans, often became involved in sexual liaisons of varying degrees of permanence with male spectators, and in a few cases became prostitutes after leaving the stage. While some actresses signaled their availability, others, like Anne Bracegirdle, were praised for keeping admirers at bay. There was considerable discussion over the family backgrounds of Restoration actresses, largely a coded discourse about whether particular female performers were of a class and descent that made them sexually available to male playgoers or whether their social origins might somehow help them deflect unwanted sexual advances.

In Italy, most of the earliest actresses were wives and sisters of actors, and presumably entered family businesses under the protection of male relatives. One of the most famous, Isabella Andreini, was held in respectful adulation during her lifetime: "her admirers [went] to great length to stress her virtue and high moral tone."[48] Although suspected of prostitution, actresses on the Continent seem to have been related by marriage or blood to male performers, and thus worked in what amounted to family businesses. In England, the obvious economic advantages to such an arrangement may have been thwarted by the resistance of male actors, as has been suggested, or may have been outweighed by economic liabilities.

Actresses as Liabilities for Itinerant Acting Troupes

The REED archives and forthcoming volumes may contain evidence about the presence of women in provincial touring companies, but thus far none has come to my attention. To judge from Edward Alleyn's letters to his wife back home,

English actors of the seventeenth century did not take their wives and families with them when they went on provincial tours. Italian touring companies, which were as we have seen essentially family businesses, did include female relatives, but it is not clear why English troupes were not organized around family units. The economic advantages of such a modus operandi are obvious, to say nothing of the possible drawing power of female performers. What factors might then have rendered so obvious an innovation ineffective from the economic point of view?

Scholars are only now realizing the importance of touring to the theatrical industry of early modern England, in part because of the extensive documentation in the REED volumes of theatrical activity outside of London. Andrew Gurr puts it succinctly: "Travelling dictated all the early playing practices. The habits that went with it lasted through much of the early Stuart period when London playing became secure."[49]

To gain an audience, a traveling company had to secure permission from a lord mayor or magistrate or some other local authority. Companies with women might have found it hard to secure such permission, not only because of the association of actresses with prostitution or promiscuity, a common assumption throughout western Europe in the late medieval and early modern periods, but because of a series of laws beginning in the 1570s making parishes responsible for any illegitimate children born there. There was great pressure to force the fathers of such children to marry the women they had impregnated but when it was not possible to identify, locate, or coerce such fathers, responsibility fell upon local communities.[50]

At the same time, there was great social upheaval and displacement in rural England, owing to the enclosure of common grazing lands and other changes in the agrarian economy, as well as to overpopulation and inflation. These displacements produced large numbers of homeless, most of them gravitating toward London in search of employment but some wandering without so clear a purpose. The Vagabond Acts of Tudor England attempted to curtail the movement of impoverished vagrants, while another series of laws, known as the Poor Laws, endeavored to set forth the charitable responsibilities of local communities and to give them power to prevent "sturdy beggars" from elsewhere from draining communal resources designated for their own deserving poor. In earlier forms of Vagabond Laws, common players of interludes were grouped with other categories of undesirable vagrants, but after 1572 exception was made for actors who could show that they were in the employ of someone of the rank of baron or above. To distinguish themselves from "masterless men" and other indigent wanderers, itinerant acting troupes were required to show local authorities patents or licenses identifying themselves as servants of some master before they were given permission to perform in a given community.[51] The local constables who enforced such laws, constituting a rotating volunteer police force such as the one caricatured in *Much Ado about Nothing*, might have kept an eye out for women late in pregnancy and so prevented any actress with child from entering the town, delivering her baby, and abandoning it to the charge of the local citizens.[52] In practice, companies with women might have aroused the suspicion of local officials that the actresses were either prostitutes when not onstage or might leave bastard children behind when the troupe left town to resume its travels.

Recently discovered diary entries belonging to Sir Henry Herbert, Master of the Revels, indicate that wives in some branches of the entertainment industry accompanied their husbands, or were licensed to do so in the early Stuart period. On August 20, 1622, Herbert thus records the payment of ten shillings for the granting of "a license to Thommas Barrell with one man his wife & children to toss a pike for a year." Exactly one year to the day later, he granted "a license to Marke Bradley with his wife to make shewe of a Ramme with 4 horns for a year." On August 25, 1624, he granted "A license to William Smith & Jane his wife with two assistants to shewe *a birde called a Starr* for 6 months."[53] Wives like those referred to in these entries were not actresses but there does seem to have been a niche for family businesses, at least at the lower end of the itinerant entertainment industry.

In a few recorded cases such women, or the family troupe they toured with, received a less than cordial welcome, evoking the kind of suspicion which theater companies employing actresses might well have elicited. Thomas Wyatt and his wife Joan, who had been licensed by Herbert's predecessor as Master of the Revels, Sir George Buc, "for the shewynge of one Peter Williams a man monstrously deformed," were thus brought before a magistrate in Norwich on June 16, 1618, and told "to shew him this present day & no longer." On September 27, 1614, Ciprian de Roson with "his wife & two assistantes," who had been licensed by Buc "to shewe feates of activity together with A Beast Called an Elke [were] nowe enjoyned to depart the Cytty [of Norwich] this present day upon payne of whippynge."[54]

It is not clear that these troupes were sent packing because of the presence of women, or suspicions or accusations attending on their presence, although one is tempted to draw such an inference after reading the following extract from the Constables' Accounts of Manchester for 1624–25 involving a blind fiddler and his wife, where the distinction between itinerant entertainer and beggar might have easily become blurred in the eyes of the arresting constable(s), perhaps because the wife was pregnant: "Robert Cowbornne beeinge a blind man A ffiddler and his wiffe beeinge Taken beggine shee beinge verye great with Child and beeinge putt in the Dungeon whilest the passe was makeinge beeinge not past halffe ane howere was delivered of a Child which was christned and they were both kept o the townes chardges till shee was churched whiche was xiiii^teen dayes."[55]

Given the large numbers of wayfaring homeless, the ancient and prejudicial ambiguities between actors and vagabonds and between actresses and prostitutes, plus a fear of being burdened with some other parish's bastards, provincial theatrical troupes may have anticipated that traveling with women would jeopardize their ability to secure the permission they needed from local authorities in order to perform. If so, even the London troupes may have felt it would be uneconomical to train women to play female roles for their own playhouses and then substitute male actors in the same roles during provincial tours. Such a system of dual casting was, however, precisely what Italian popular troupes did in order to play both in the Papal States, where actresses were forbidden, and elsewhere in Italy where they were allowed. English troupes could have used their play-boys in the provinces and their actresses in London, unless, as was suggested earlier, male actors clung to the time-tested system of casting which had nourished many of their own careers.

If these hypotheses have any merit, then the economics of theater may help explain why casting men as women remained the standard practice of the English theater until 1642, and only changed after theater was revived in 1660 under a vastly altered set of conditions. Framing the issue in such terms suggests an answer based on specific conditions affecting the theater before and after the Restoration: for example, gendered rivalries, concern over employment opportunities, methods of recruitment, managerial assessment of practicality, availability of potential actresses, and other factors which seem no less distinctively English than the cultural attitudes Orgel invoked. Formulating the issue as Orgel did in the late 1980s—"Why were women more upsetting than boys to the English?"[56]— invites an answer based on male fears of female sexuality. The manifestations of that fear, at least those aspects of rigidly patriarchal culture cited by Orgel, seem fairly widespread throughout Europe and thus lack power to explain what is said to be "a distinctively English solution to the nearly universal disapproval of actresses." In some parts of the Continent, as I have suggested, such fears were assuaged by a willingness to entrust the control of actresses' sexuality to their male relatives. In general, Orgel argues in *Impersonations* for a more fluid and flexible sense of gender and sexuality than many feminist and queer-theory scholars have allowed. One of the culture-specific factors which might have enabled the English companies' practice of cross-gender casting was the lack, in England, despite Puritan rhetoric, of the kind of "morbid fear of homoeroticism as such"[57] observable in, say, Spain and Venice. Other such factors are the presence of a significant number of assertive women in early modern England, some of whom were sexually attracted to younger males, and a greater freedom of social movement permitted women in England than elsewhere in Europe. The result of this unique social mix was an atmosphere in which, as Orgel suggests, the construction of sexuality and gender was more fluid than in other parts of Europe: "The transvestite actor was indispensable to Renaissance England; but (or, perhaps, therefore) the figure was never fully naturalized. He was essential precisely as a construct, always available to interrogate, unsettle, reinterpret the norms, which were always conceived to be unstable—the interrogation, indeed, was as essential a part of the never-ending attempt at stabilization."[58] But even if one grants a greater flexibility in England than elsewhere in Europe regarding the norms of sexual behavior and gender identity, it is not clear to me whether Orgel is arguing that the practice of cross-gender casting was the cause or the effect of what he takes to be English efforts both to interrogate and to stabilize those norms.

In short, this circularity suggests that as Orgel moved from the earlier article to the recent book, he seems to have lost interest in causal explanations of the English delay in admitting actresses to their commercial acting companies and to have chosen instead to pursue broader questions of cultural history. Some theater historians, however, may seek specific explanations for the timing of the introduction of actresses on the English stage, and for that reason I offer a set of hypotheses derived largely from what we know of the organization and economic conditions of early modern theater both in England and on the Continent.

Notes

1. Reviews of the National Theatre productions are cited in Michael Shapiro, *Gender in Play on the Shakespearean Stage* (Ann Arbor: University of Michigan Press, 1994), 259, n. 2. For reviews of the Cheek by Jowl production, see Ben Brantley, "How to Call a Play into Being by Smearing a Man with Mud," *New York Times,* Oct. 6, 1994, C:17; Vincent Canby, "As You Like It," *New York Times,* Oct. 16, 1994, 2:5; and Richard Corliss, "Something to Sing About: A Very Traditional British Cast Finds Rapture in *As You Like It,*" *Time* 144 (Dec. 12, 1994): 84.

2. Stephen Orgel, "Nobody's Perfect," *South Atlantic Quarterly* 88 (1989): 7–8. In his recent book, *Impersonations: The Performance of Gender in Shakespeare's England* (Cambridge: Cambridge University Press, 1996), Orgel expands this earlier inquiry into the use of male actors to play female roles in pre-Restoration English commercial theater and seems less interested in possible explanations or causes of cross-gender casting than he is in broader explorations of the construction of gender and sexuality in early modern England and in our own culture.

3. Lesley Ferris, *Acting Women: Images of Women in the Theatre* (New York: New York University Press, 1989), 32–33.

4. Elissa Weaver, "Spiritual Fun: A Study of Sixteenth-Century Tuscan Convent Theater," in *Women in the Middle Ages and the Renaissance: Literary and Historical Perspectives,* ed. Mary Beth Rose (Syracuse, N.Y.: Syracuse University Press, 1986), 173–205; Meg Twycross, "'Transvestism' in the Mystery Plays," *Medieval English Theatre* 5 (1983): 133; and James Stokes, "The Wells Cordwainers Show: New Evidence Concerning Guild Entertainments in Somerset," *Comparative Drama* 19 (Winter 1985–86): 336.

5. Kenneth Richards and Laura Richards, *The Commedia dell'Arte: A Documentary History* (London: Basil Blackwell for the Shakespeare Head Press, 1990), 39. See also Paul C. Castagno, *The Early "Commedia dell'Arte" 1550–1621,* American University Studies series 26, Theatre Arts 13 (New York: Peter Lang, 1994), 53; Richard Andrews, *Scripts and Scenarios: The Performance of Comedy in Renaissance Italy* (Cambridge: Cambridge University Press, 1992), 224, 258, n. 65; Kathleen M. Lea, *Italian Popular Comedy,* 2 vols. (Oxford: Clarendon Press, 1934), 1:113–14; and Kathleen McGill, "Women and Performance: The Development of Improvisation by the Sixteenth-Century Commedia dell'Arte," *Theatre Journal* 43 (Mar. 1991): 61.

6. Glynne Wickham describes this change as the substitution of image for emblem (*Early English Stages, 1300 to 1660,* vol. 2 [pt. 1 (London: Routledge and Kegan Paul, 1963)], 10).

7. Michael Anderson, "Making Room: Commedia and the Privatisation of the Theatre," in *The Commedia dell'Arte from the Renaissance to Dario Fo,* ed. Christopher Cairns, in The Italian Origins of European Theatre 6, Papers of the Conference of the Society for Italian Studies, Nov. 1988 (Lewiston, N.Y.: Edwin Mellen Press, 1989), 85; see also Kenneth Richards and Laura Richards, *Commedia dell'Arte,* 88–90.

8. Pierre Louis Duchartre, *The Italian Comedy,* trans. Randolph T. Weaver (New York: Dover, 1966), 90, 93, 320; Kenneth Richards and Laura Richards, *Commedia dell'Arte,* 268; Frances Barasch, "Francesquina, the Transvestite Clown and Shakespeare's Maidservants," paper presented at the World Shakespeare Congress, Tokyo, 1991.

9. According to Ireneo Sanesi, the cardinals granted a license to the Desiosi so long as they agreed to perform "without women" (*"senza donne"*) (*La Commedia,* 2d ed. [Milan: Villardi, 1954], 1:508). I wish to thank Janet Smarr for translating this passage. Carlo Goldoni (b. 1707), records first seeing actresses during a visit to Rimini, "where women are admitted on the boards, and we do not see there, as at Rome, men without beards." See *Memoires of Carlo Goldoni,* ed. William A. Drake, trans. John Black (New York: Knopf, 1926), 15. See also Kenneth Richards and Laura Richards, *Commedia dell'Arte,* 67; Rosamond Gilder, *Enter the Actress: The First Women in the Theatre* (Boston: Houghton Mifflin, 1931), 64; John Roselli, "The Castrati as a Professional Group and a Social Phenomenon," *Acta Musicologica* 60 (1988): fasc. 2 (May-Aug.), 143–79. Roselli sees the castration of vocally talented boys in a time of economic depression and Christian asceticism as a more extreme economic gamble than entering religious orders, where celibacy was enforced by vow rather than by the surgeon's knife.

10. Melveena McKendrick, *Theatre in Spain, 1490–1700* (Cambridge: Cambridge University Press, 1989), 48–49; and N. D. Shergold, *A History of the Spanish Stage* (Oxford: Clarendon Press, 1967), 143ff. Ms. Luz Vega-Vega informs me that medieval and Renaissance Spanish records sometimes refer to female instrumentalists, singers, and dancers under such terms as *juglaresa,* but it is not clear whether they can be considered actresses. Ursula K. Heise argues that a *Pragmatica* of 1534, regulating performers' dress, refers to female as well as male *comediantes,* so that the Italian troupe was petitioning for a return to a previous practice ("Transvestism and the Stage Controversy in Spain and England, 1580–1680," *Theatre Journal* 44 [Oct. 1992]: 357–74). Such a request, however, would have been unnecessary had actresses still been employed in Spanish companies.

11. Heise, "Transvestism," 359–60, 366–68.

12. W. L. Wiley, *The Early Public Theatre in France* (Cambridge, Mass.: Harvard University Press, 1960), 20–25, 87–91; and Gilder, *Enter the Actress,* 82–99.

13. E. K. Chambers, *The Elizabethan Stage,* 4 vols. (Oxford: Clarendon Press, 1923), 1:246–47.

14. Ibid., 1:247–49.

15. Richard Braithwait, *The English Gentleman* (London, 1630), quoted in Paul Whitfield White, *Theatre and Reformation: Protestantism, Patronage, and Playing in Tudor England* (Cambridge: Cambridge University Press, 1992), 234, n. 29.

16. Henk Gras, "All Is Semblative a Woman's Part?" (Ph.D. diss., University of Utrecht, 1991), 431. Leslie Hotson reports that an English actor-manager, George Jolly, who led a traveling troupe on the Continent, was the first to bring actresses onstage in Frankfurt-am-Main in the 1650s (*The Commonwealth and Restoration Stage* [Cambridge, Mass.: Harvard University Press, 1928], 171).

17. See J. W. Binns, "Women or Transvestites on the Elizabethan Stage? An Oxford Controversy," *Sixteenth Century Journal* 5 (Summer 1974): 95–120; Shapiro, *Gender in Play,* 38–39, 146–47.

18. Edna Purdie, "Jesuit Drama," in *Oxford Companion to the Theatre,* ed. Phyllis Hartnoll, 3d ed. (Oxford: Oxford University Press, 1967), 508. In 1591, an official revision of the rules permitted only those female roles which were absolutely necessary, while a dispensation of 1602 required such characters to be modest and serious and only rarely introduced (509).

19. Thomas Nashe, *Pierce Pennilesse His Supplication to the Divill,* in *The Works of Thomas Nashe,* ed. Ronald B. McKerrow, 5 vols. (London: Sidgwick and Jackson, 1910), 1:215.

20. Shapiro, *Gender in Play,* 15–28; Alan Nelson, "Cross-dressing in English Renaissance Theatre: Business as Usual," paper presented at the Sixteenth Century Studies Conference, St. Louis, Mo., 1993. As Nelson points out, their failure to encourage or at least allow plays with only male characters gives the game away. Orgel makes a similar point about antitheatricalists' attacks on theater for fostering homoerotic behavior: "the Puritan charge that theatre promotes homosexuality appears because to the Puritan mind theatre is felt to be dangerous, not the other way round" (*Impersonations,* 41).

21. John Rainolds compares young male actors playing women to Sporus, Nero's ho-

mosexual favorite, while Prynne, citing Stubbes, refers to cases of men "who have beene despaerately enamored with Players Boyes thus clad in womans apparell, so farre as to solicite them by words, by Letters, even actually to abuse them" (quoted in Shapiro, *Gender in Play*, 38; see 37–41, 143ff.). I am aware of current controversies in our attempts to understand homoeroticism in early modern England, but for purposes of my argument rely on Alan Bray's ground-breaking book, *Homosexuality in Renaissance England* (London: Gay Men's Press, 1982). As Bray has noted, except for antitheatrical tracts and a few satirical poems, it is rare in early modern England to find male homosexuality linked to crossdressing. Indeed, outside of the theater and folkloric rites (mostly rural rather than urban), it is rare to find any evidence at all of male crossdressing in England. See also Shapiro, *Gender in Play*, 37–41.

22. Heise, "Transvestism," 371. English antitheatricalist tracts are discussed by Orgel, *Impersonations*, 27–30, and by Laura Levine, *Men in Women's Clothing: Anti-Theatricality and Effeminization, 1579–1642* (Cambridge: Cambridge University Press, 1994).

23. Doubling schemes are printed in David Bevington, *From "Mankind" to Marlowe* (Cambridge: Harvard University Press, 1962), 265–73. See also Shapiro, *Gender in Play*, 32–34.

24. J. B. Streett, "The Durability of Boy Actors," *Notes and Queries* 218 (1973): 461–65. My information about acting apprenticeship comes from Gerald Eades Bentley, *The Profession of Player in Shakespeare's Time, 1590–1642* (Princeton: Princeton University Press, 1984), 113–46; and *The Jacobean and Caroline Stage*, 7 vols. (Oxford: Clarendon Press, 1941–68), 2:433–34; T. J. King, *Casting Shakespeare's Plays: London Actors and Their Roles*, (Cambridge: Cambridge University Press, 1992), 48–49, 77.

25. Steve Rappaport, *Worlds within Worlds: Structures of Life in Sixteenth-Century London* (Cambridge: Cambridge University Press, 1989), 295ff.; and Richard Rastall, "Female Bodies in All-Male Casts," *Medieval English Theatre* 7 (1985): 28–35.

26. *Ben Jonson*, ed. C. H. Herford and Percy Simpson (Oxford: Clarendon Press, 1925–52); *Poetaster* (vol. 4), 3.4.205–7, 3.4.273–76; and *Christmas, His Masque* (vol. 7), ll. 119, 132–37.

27. Bentley, *Profession of Player*, 126–28.

28. G. E. Bentley, "The Salisbury Court Theater and Its Boy Players," *Huntington Library Quarterly* 40 (Feb. 1977), 137. Although masters of children's troupes held the power to impress or take up children, Henry Clifton's Star Chamber suit of 1601 identifies one of the Blackfriars actors, Alvery Trussel, as having been "an apprentice to one Thomas Gyles," choirmaster of Paul's (quoted in Harold N. Hillebrand, *The Child Actors* [New York: Russell and Russell, 1964], 161). Hillebrand also reprints a contractual agreement dated November 14, 1606, in which Alice Cooke agrees, in effect, to apprentice her son Abel for three years to Thomas Kendall, one of the managers of the Blackfriars troupe, "to be practiced and exercised in the . . . qualitye of playinge" (198).

29. Bentley, *Profession of Player*, 144.

30. Sharers Papers of Cuthbert and Richard Burbage, as quoted in Bentley, *Profession of Player*, 140.

31. Translated by Andrew Gurr, in *The Shakespearean Stage, 1574–1642*, 2d ed. (Cambridge: Cambridge University Press, 1980), 209, following Geoffrey Tillotson, "*Othello* and *The Alchemist* at Oxford in 1610," *Times Literary Supplement*, July 20, 1933, 494.

32. Colley Cibber, *An Apology for the Life of Mr. Colley Cibber*, 2 vols. (London: John C. Nimmo, 1889), 2:90.

33. Stephen Orgel, citing K. D. M. Snell's *Annals of the Labouring Poor: Social Change and Agrarian England, 1660–1900* (New York: Cambridge University Press, 1985), finds a surprising number of women admitted to the artisanal guilds in the sixteenth century, but notes a significant decline by the early seventeenth century (*Impersonations*, 72–73). Comparison of theater apprenticeships with those of craft guilds may be less relevant than Orgel believes: (1) As Rappaport argues, as part of a general decline in the economic status of women, they were gradually being squeezed out of craft guilds, but it is incorrect to infer that they were also squeezed out of the acting profession in that they were never a part of it (*Worlds within Worlds*, 36–42); (2) Bentley finds that only three of the theatrical apprentices served actors who belonged to craft guilds, and although he suggests that Apprentice Books might yield more, I know of no examples which have come to light (*Profession of Player*, 125–26). The relative paucity of theatrical apprenticeships taking the form of craft-guild apprenticeships seems to refute the suggestion made by Orgel "that the initial impulse of acting troupes toward the guild system came from . . . its promise of respectability within the city structure, rather than from its utility as an enabling mechanism for theatrical apprentices" (*Impersonations*, 64–68, quotation on 68). The whole issue of theatrical apprenticeships is very cloudy as we do not know what percentage of apprentices did or did not go on to become adult actors nor what percentage of adult actors entered the profession through some route other than apprenticeship.

34. [Sir Henry Herbert], *The Control and Censorship of Caroline Drama: The Records of Sir Henry Herbert, Master of the Revels, 1623–73*, ed. N. W. Bawcutt (Oxford: Clarendon Press, 1996), 235. I am not sure what is meant by "Habitts according to our Scaenes."

35. James Wright, *Historia Histrionica* (London, 1699), quoted in Bentley, *Profession of Player*, 123.

36. Sandra Richards, *The Rise of the English Actress* (New York: St. Martin's Press, 1993), 8.

37. Thomas Jordan, *A Royal Arbour of Loyal Poesie*, quoted in John Harold Wilson, *All the King's Ladies: Actresses of the Restoration* (Chicago: University of Chicago Press, 1958), 6.

38. For information on Kynaston, Betterton, and Nokes, see Philip H. Highfill, Kalman A. Burnim, and Edward A. Langhans, *A Biographical Dictionary of Actors, Actresses, Musicians, Dancers, Managers, and Other Stage Personnel in London, 1660–1800*, 17 vols. (Carbondale: Southern Illinois University Press, 1984), 9:79, 2:101–2, and 11:40–41. Even after the introduction of actresses, and contrary to Charles's revised patent, Nokes continued to play female roles, especially older women, such as the Nurse in *Romeo and Juliet* and in Henry Nevil Payne's *The Fatal Jealousy* (1672), for which he won the nickname of "Nurse." See also the entries for other known female impersonators in the years im-

mediately following the Restoration: Edward Angel (1:83), Mr. Floyd (5:314), and John Mosely (10:329). Pepys's entry and Newport's letter are quoted in *The London Stage, 1660–1800,* ed. William Van Lennep, 3 vols. (Carbondale: Southern Illinois University Press, 1965), 1:12 and xxiv.

39. Quoted in Henry Wysham Lanier, *The First English Actresses* (New York: Players, 1930), 42–43. To replace the systems of apprenticeship and covenant servants, under which training girls would have been difficult, one or two nursery companies developed in the years after the reopening of the theaters. See Hotson, *Commonwealth and Restoration Stage,* 176–96.

40. Katharine Eisaman Maus, "'Playhouse Flesh and Blood': Sexual Ideology and the Restoration Actress," *ELH* 46 (Winter 1979): 595–617. While Samuel Pepys's diary reflects his great delight with performances by Kynaston and by a number of actresses, John Evelyn's journal records his sense of the moral decline of the stage and his reluctance to attend plays, citing, among other reasons, the erotic power of actresses to arouse male spectators: "Women now (& never 'til now) permitted to appear & act, which inflaming severall young noble-men & gallants, became their whores, & to some their Wives." See *London Stage,* 1:12, 96, 119.

41. Lea, *Italian Popular Comedy,* 2:352–58.

42. For evidence of French troupes in London, see Herbert's *Control and Censorship,* 169, 191, 193.

43. William Prynne, *Histrio-Mastix* (1633), quoted in Gras, "All Is Semblative," 528. Gras casts doubt on the evidence that French actresses were unpopular with London spectators. J. P. Collier, *History of English Dramatic Poetry and Annals of the Stage* (1832), as quoted by Gras, cites a letter from Thomas Brande to Archbishop Laud to the effect that a female troupe of "vagrant French players . . . were hissed, hooted, and pippin-pelted from the stage." Gras declares that this letter can no longer be found where Collier claimed to have seen it, suggesting that it is Collier's invention. Perhaps the French company, probably comprising men and women, was unsuccessful. Gras cites a letter (unknown to Collier) from John Mead to Martin Stuteville, dated October 31, 1629, which reports that "certain French comedians, presuming to play before an English auditory in a playhouse, whereto belonged far better actors, were hissed off the stage," but there is no evidence of the French actresses being singled out for disapprobation. Sir Henry Herbert returned part of their licensing fees "in respect of their ill fortune," which suggests no lack of favor in the eyes of this court official (*Control and Censorship,* 169).

44. Thomas Coryate, *Coryate's Crudities* (London, 1611), 247. For commentary on this passage and other English travelers' accounts of actresses on the continent, see Shapiro, *Gender in Play,* 42. Orgel cites evidence of occasional performances by women in mystery plays, Tudor pageants, early Stuart masques, and court pastorelles, and notes the novel cameo appearance of Moll Frith on the Fortune stage in 1611, but there is no evidence of women acting in plays performed by an English commercial company before 1660 (*Impersonations,* 4–7).

45. Aurelian Townshend, *The Poems and Masques,* ed. Cedric C. Brown (Reading: Whiteknights Press, 1983), 96, 98; Chambers, *Elizabethan Stage,* 1:371, n. 4; Bentley, *Jacobean and Caroline Stage,* 4:549–50, 917; and Suzanne Gossett, "'Man-maid, Begone!': Women in Masques," *English Literary Renaissance* 18 (Winter 1988): 96–113. Sophie Tomlinson notes the controversy over the idea of women as actresses, and describes how this discourse blurred the difference between women's participation in theatrical performance and in national politics ("She That Plays the King: Henrietta Maria and the Threat of the Actress in Caroline Culture," in *The Politics of Tragicomedy: Shakespeare and After,* ed. Gordon McMullan and Jonathan Hope [London: Routledge, 1992], 189–207).

46. Quoted in Sandra Richards, *Rise of the English Actress,* 1, 261, n. 4.

47. Wilson, *All the King's Ladies,* 10; for brief biographies of actresses, see appendix A. See also Sandra Richards, *Rise of the English Actress,* 3–7; Kristina Straub, *Sexual Suspects: Eighteenth-Century Players and Sexual Ideology* (Princeton: Princeton University Press, 1992), 90–91; and Elizabeth Howe, *The First English Actresses: Women and Drama, 1660–1700* (Cambridge: Cambridge University Press, 1993).

48. Andrews, *Scripts and Scenarios,* 190; Gilder, *Enter the Actress,* 67–81. Spanish authorities, as we have seen, tried to ensure that actresses did not practice prostitution. William O. Beeman describes how, in the rare instances when women enacted female roles in Iranian theatrical presentations, they took great pains to show that they were performers and not prostitutes: "One was married and always had her husband close at hand. Another brought her aged mother and always sat with her when not onstage. A third had a baby that she would nurse conspicuously. All these devices were designed to prevent the men in the audience from approaching the women" ("Mimesis and Travesty in Iranian Traditional Theatre," in *Gender in Performance: The Presentation of Difference in the Performing Arts,* ed. Laurence Senelick [Hanover: University Press of New England, 1992], 22).

49. Andrew Gurr, *The Shakespearian Playing Companies* (Oxford: Clarendon Press, 1996), 36; Bentley, *Profession of Player,* 177–205; Sally-Beth MacLean, "Tour Routes: 'Provincial Wanderings' or Traditional Circuits?" *Medieval and Renaissance Drama in England* 6 (1993), 1–14; Leeds Barroll, *Politics, Plague, and Shakespeare's Theater* (Ithaca: Cornell University Press, 1991), 106–11, 227–32; Virginia Gildersleeve, *Government Regulation of the Elizabethan Drama* (New York: Columbia University Press, 1908), 21–43.

50. See G. R. Quaife, *Wanton Wenches and Wayward Wives* (London: Croom Helm, 1979), 202–24; and Martin Ingram, *Church Courts, Sex, and Marriage in England, 1570–1640* (Cambridge: Cambridge University Press, 1987), 150ff.

51. Paul Slack, *Poverty and Policy in Tudor and Stuart England* (London: Longman, 1988); A. L. Beier, *Masterless Men: The Vagrancy Problem in England, 1560–1640* (London: Methuen, 1985), 43. In a statement of rules and procedures from William Lambarde's *The Duties of Constables [,] Borsholders, Tithing Men* (London, 1583), which was often reprinted during the period, I can find no suggestion of this anxiety over the fear of women vagrants burdening local communities with newborn offspring. There are hints to be found in A. V. Judges, *Elizabethan Underworld* (London: George Routledge, 1930), xlvii; and Beier, *Mas-*

terless Men, 53–54. I have found no explicit mention of what seems like the obvious fear that itinerant male actors, like all "masterless men," might seduce local women and so leave behind them illegitimate offspring who would have to be supported by the parish.

52. For discussion and examples of local concern with illegitimacy, see Susan Dwyer Amussen, *An Ordered Society: Gender and Class in Early Modern England* (New York: Columbia University Press, 1988), 111–17; see F. G. Emmison, *Elizabethan Life,* 5 vols. (Chelmsford: Essex County Council, 1970–80), vol. 2, *Morals and the Church Courts* (1973), on the same issue as well as on the related offense of "harbouring unmarried mothers" (25–31).

53. [Herbert], *Control and Censorship,* 154.

54. *Records of Early English Drama: Norwich,* ed. David Galloway (Toronto: University of Toronto Press, 1991), 142, 156–57.

55. *Records of Early English Drama: Lancashire,* ed. David George (Toronto: University of Toronto Press, 1991), 68.

56. Orgel, "Nobody's Perfect," 8.

57. Orgel, *Impersonations,* 35–36ff.

58. Ibid., 108.

9

Staging the Female Playgoer: Gender in Shakespeare's Onstage Audiences

Laurie E. Osborne

In his address "To Gentlewomen Citizens of London" at the end of *The Schoole of Abuse* (1579) Stephen Gosson singles out the female playgoer as particularly vulnerable. By speaking to the female citizens separately and in different terms from those he has used to outline the threats to the male audience, Gosson positions the female audience as different. Greater than his fear of the inevitable corruption engendered by watching the theatrical spectacle is his anxiety lest these women become spectacles themselves, available to the uncontrolled desires and attentions of the men at the theater. Gosson describes the woman playgoer's vulnerability specifically in terms of the gaze: "Thought is free: you can forbidde no man, that vieweth you, to noate you and that noateth you, to iudge you, for entring to places of suspition. Wilde Colts, when they see their kinde, begin to bray; & lusty bloods, at the showe of faire women, give a wanton sigh or a wicked wish."[1] Thus singled out as, involuntarily, most likely to cross the boundary between spectator and spectacle, the female playgoer differs from the male playgoer who will, according to Gosson, be aroused by the play's presentation of lust as well as by the women in the audience. While the men may consciously adopt sexual display, the women in the audience appear dangerously vulnerable to the gaze.

However suggestive Gosson's remarks might be, critics who want to explore the Renaissance female playgoer face considerable obstacles. There are two possible strategies: first, gathering the limited evidence of actual women in the audience, through sources such as prologues, epilogues, antitheatrical pamphlets, letters, diaries, and court records; second, examining how Renaissance playwrights represent the female audience. In the first category, both Andrew Gurr and, in a more limited form, Richard Levin, have catalogued references to the female playgoer, all the while lamenting the paucity of the available documentary evidence.[2]

S. P. Cerasano and Marion Wynne-Davies include such materials in their recent collection, *Renaissance Drama by Women,* but the resources available, particularly before 1600, are quite scarce.[3] In a sophisticated elaboration of the second approach, Jean E. Howard argues persuasively in her reading of *The Wise Woman of Hogsdon* that female playgoers learn to enter transgressively into theatrical circulation; in effect, the theater allows them, as well as the male playgoer, possession of the desiring gaze.[4] Although Howard's argument is useful, mine differs in significant ways. Whereas her approach invokes theatrical strategies outside of official playgoing, I focus on representations of staged productions within plays rather than on the portrayal of women in audiences of the period. Moreover, I assume that an individual playwright's ongoing representation of the playgoing public is a significant context for considering the female audience. Shakespeare's representations of his audience are conservative and therefore cannot yield a complete picture of the Renaissance female playgoer. However, his very conservatism serves to mark out quite clearly the potential of gender differences among playgoers. In Shakespeare's plays in particular, onstage female playgoers are more constrained in their responses and actions, more limited by status, and more vulnerable to the male playgoer's attentions than are the female spectators in other plays of the period who use theatrical behaviors outside overtly theatrical contexts.

Shakespeare's female playgoers differ drastically from their male counterparts. Whereas the men in the onstage audience—like the wild colts braying—often seek to take over and even become the show, the women always risk and resist slipping from spectator to spectacle. Such slippage potentially moves the female playgoer from a position of power to one of vulnerability. As spectators, women prove crucial to Shakespeare's onstage productions; they offer the occasion for theater, and sometimes their very presence creates theater. When they slip into the dangerous position of spectacle, however, they become vulnerable to the sexual "noating" and appropriation by men. This position also, paradoxically, carries potential power—after all, the staged male playgoers frequently compete to control or even become the spectacle themselves, often in order to attract the women.

Before examining *Love's Labor's Lost* and *Hamlet* specifically, a few general observations. First, in the representations of plays and their audiences, Shakespeare uniformly adopts the conventions of the public theater: all the players are male and mostly adult, rather than the child actors associated with the companies which played in the private theaters. Yet all of Shakespeare's playlets are private performances in households or courts. As a result, none of his internal productions encounters a citizen audience like Nell and George in Francis Beaumont's *The Knight of the Burning Pestle* or the Gossips in Ben Jonson's *The Staple of News.*[5]

Instead, the players he stages are normally of a lower class than their noble audiences, and those staged audiences are themselves more uniformly upperclass than the blend of classes that frequented the public theater.[6] Just as important, the authorities who commission these productions are inevitably male and usually of rank: the Lord in *The Taming of the Shrew,* the King of Navarre in *Love's Labor's Lost,* Duke Theseus in *A Midsummer Night's Dream,* Hamlet in *Hamlet,* and Prospero in *The Tempest.* Thus in Shakespeare's self-conscious representations, "formal" theatrical experiences—where both the audiences and the players on stage are aware of their relative positions—are thoroughly male-dominated as well as rigidly hierarchical.

Some critics read this predominance of private and courtly plays within Shakespeare's dramas as both reflecting and controlling the playwright's ideal audience, that is, the educated nobility.[7] However, just as important, these productions, though private and therefore presumably able to accommodate women on stage as did the court masques, also present the male dominance of theatrical enterprise.[8] To this extent, Shakespeare's deliberate metadramas fully enact the patriarchal system of the Renaissance theater which Kathleen McLuskie details in "The Patriarchal Bard."[9] However, as in both public and private theaters, the theatrical productions staged within Shakespeare's plays are invariably presented to an audience of both male and female characters.

By characterizing these performances as private, Shakespeare removes them from the theaters, the "places of suspition" that Gosson claims will lead the men in the audience both to judge and to desire the female playgoer. Within Shakespeare's plays, the public theater, which both empowers the female playgoer and leaves her open to "noating," gives way to private performances only, complete with basically homogeneous audiences. The resulting secure hierarchies of class inevitably privilege the noble audiences over the common players, creating an unusually stable theatrical situation.

Yet, even within these private performances, Shakespeare's female playgoers prove to be both vulnerable sexual spectacles and figures empowered by their involvement in theater. If anything, the differences between male and female playgoers are more striking than those represented in other metadramatic plays like Beaumont's *Knight of the Burning Pestle:* the male playgoers actively seek to become the spectacle rather than just spectators, but the female playgoers try to maintain their "safe" positions as audience members although constantly at risk of becoming the show. In Shakespeare's "courtly" internal performances, variations and movement in class or social status determine the degree to which a particular female playgoer can negotiate her double position as spectator and spectacle.

A cursory examination suggests that Shakespeare's onstage female playgoers are most notable for their silence, quite unlike the male playgoers in their sometimes unexpected lack of response. The production of *The most lamentable comedy and most cruel death of Pyramus and Thisby* (1.2.11–12) in *A Midsummer Night's Dream* reproduces this familiar audience dynamic.[10] All the male playgoers mock and disrupt the play whereas all the new brides except Hippolyta are noticeably silent. Only the woman of the highest status responds verbally to the production, setting her at the same level of interaction with performance as the Duke and the lesser gentlemen, Demetrius and Lysander. Here, as in *Hamlet* and *Love's Labor's Lost*, the men make spectacles out of themselves in response to performance; the women are always already both spectacle and spectator and, like Hippolyta, frequently insist on their roles as spectators. Even though antitheatrical pamphleteers like Gosson, Northbrooke and Rainolds often characterize the female audience as a group, Shakespeare's internal productions suggest that variations in class can influence the female playgoer's relationship to the spectacle she surveys.[11]

In the case of *Love's Labor's Lost*, the rigidly masculine world which the King of Navarre tries to establish in his court reflects the insistent patriarchy of the theater. Navarre so carefully guards against the excesses that Gosson associates with the theater that his academy starts out as an inversion of Gosson's *Schoole of Abuse*.[12] The King's masculine society requires mortification of the senses rather than the arousal of appetites which purportedly occurs in the theater. The King eliminates the very abuses that taint England's former virtues, according to Gosson: "banquetting, playing, pyping, and dauncing, and all suche delightes as may winne us to pleasure or rocke us in sleepe" (*Schoole of Abuse*, C1). The King of Navarre also forbids women to come within a mile of his school on pain of losing their tongues, and "If any man be seen to talk with a woman within the term of three years, he shall endure such public shame as the rest of the court can possible devise" (1.1.129–32). Thus the King's most stringent requirements undo the feature of the public theater audience which most concerns Gosson. Predictably, the other rigors imposed upon the courtiers pale beside the final requirement that they not talk with women.

As long as the King stands firm, he banishes the abuses that Gosson so thoroughly associates with the theater and creates a school that will restore masculine fame and heroism. However, when Shakespeare places on stage Navarre's academy, constructed along the same educational models as Gosson's "Schoole," he also displays the academy as revealingly vulnerable both to the female gaze and to theatricality. The arrival of the Princess of France and her ladies undoes the King's academy almost before it starts and simultaneously transforms it into a place of theatrical display and a school of abuses—with a difference. In *Love's Labor's Lost,* women are literally the occasion for theater, and their eyes produce a crescendo of informal theatrical "productions," culminating in the formal theater of the Pageant of the Nine Worthies. This fact makes literal the concerns expressed in Gosson's tract that women in effect cause theatricality and spectacle by their attendance. Gosson warns that the men in the theater indulge in "Such ticking, such toying, Such smiling, such winking, and such manning them [the women] home, when the sportes are ended, that it is a right Comedie to mark their behaviour, to watch their conceates" (*Schoole of Abuse,* C2). The men in the theater willfully become the spectacle through their treatment of the women.

The initial foray into performance in *Love's Labor's Lost* illustrates this "Comedie," as Navarre and the lords reveal how the eyes of the newly arrived ladies produce such playing. As first Berowne, then the King, then Longaville, and finally Dumaine declare their love and hide to overhear the next lover's vows, Shakespeare creates a layered eavesdropping scene in which the revelations sound a common theme: the ladies have conquered with their eyes. Berowne, the first oathbreaker, struggles against his love, but fails: "I will not love; . . . I will not. O but her eye—by this light, but for her eye, I would not love her; yes, for her two eyes" (4.3.8–10). The King then enters and begins his sonnet by describing the Princess's "eyebeams" as sweeter than the golden sun kissing the dew, only to hide and observe Longaville, whose sonnet opens, "Did not the heavenly rhetoric of thine eye, / 'Gainst whom the world cannot hold argument, / Persuade my heart to this false perjury?" (4.3.58–60). Finally Dumaine enters, and all three who are now hidden overhear his exclamation about "divine Kate": "By heaven, the wonder in a mortal eye!" (4.3.83). One by one they claim their beloved's eyes as the reason for their oathbreaking and abandonment of the academy. The easy Petrarchanism of these compliments insists on the originating power of the female gaze, the importance of which is underscored later in this scene as well as in the court's appearance as Muscovites before the women.

In the second half of this scene, each man successively emerges and challenges the ones arriving after him. Berowne appears last and exposes the oathbreaking in the series of declarations and the hypocrisy of each man as he mocks his successor on the scene. However, Berowne's ascendancy is only temporary, eclipsed by the appearance of a woman, Jaquenetta. By bringing Berowne's letter and thus revealing his hypocrisy, Jaquenetta, accompanied by Costard, becomes—temporarily—a very powerful audience. Although she cannot even read Berowne's sonnet, she disrupts his self-presentation. When Berowne responds by exclaiming, "O, dismiss this audience, and I shall tell you more" (4.3.206), his direction signals the end of Jaquenetta's function as a flawed but crucial audience to the men's entrance into theatricality. Both she and Costard can be readily turned aside as audience figures because of their lower status and because of their marginal involvement in the relations between Navarre's court and the Princess's entourage.

In the courtiers' next, more self-conscious theatrical enterprise, they cannot so easily dismiss the female audience. The men disguise themselves as Muscovites and plan to perform before an unknowing audience, the ladies. However, forewarned by Boyet, the ladies mask themselves and exchange the love tokens they have received so that the disguised suitors will each woo the wrong lady. The Princess and her ladies possess both rank and wit enough to maintain their critical, deflating stance. As the court of Navarre moves still closer to engaging in overt theater, the courtiers now willingly embrace the playing and dancing which Gosson so deplores, but the women resist.

The Princess and her court take full advantage of the fact that they are to be unknowing audience to the lords' performances as well as objects of the desiring male gaze. The Princess's fair demeanor can be taken for Rosaline's dark complexion behind the mask so that the King does not realize that he is wooing the lady he has just roundly criticized as "black as ebony" (4.3.243). Moreover, when the lords unmask and return, the Princess and her court follow Rosaline's suggestion and

> complain to them what fools were here,
> Disguis'd like Muscovites, in shapeless gear;
> And wonder what they were, and to what end
> Their shallow shows and prologue vildly penn'd
> . . . .
> Should be presented at our tent to us.
> (5.2.302–5, 307)

In effect, the men have empowered their female audience by presenting themselves as the spectacle. As a response, the women's strategy effectively establishes them as the superior noble audience to a poor show. The comedy thus validates female spectatorship, but only in the noblewomen and only in informal theatrical situations.

Throughout this series of situations which approach theater, the women prove a powerful audience, but, in the one *formal* play, the Pageant of the Nine Worthies, the female spectators undergo a striking transformation in influence and function. Throughout the "official" pageant, the ladies, except for the Princess herself, are silent, as in *Dream*. The court of Navarre, in contrast, is vocally abusive to the heroic figures of the pageant. Perhaps in an effort to prove the "show worse than the King's and his company" (5.2.513), Berowne, Dumaine, and Longaville interrupt the players and taunt them throughout their speeches.[13] In fact they so completely drown out Judas Machabeus's speech, putting him "out of countenance," that Holofernes finally complains, "This is not generous, not gentle, not humble" (5.2.629). Only the Princess sympathizes, "Alas, poor Machabeus, how hath he been baited!" (5.2.631). The men continue to embrace their roles as spectacles for the ladies during the formal pageant; however, the women's responses to theatricality change, inflected along class lines.

Because of her status, the Princess can not only insist upon the pageant over the King's initial objections but can also oppose the men who interrupt the players. Moreover, the Princess often comments favorably, as when she gives "great thanks [to] Pompey" in response to his appeal after the men mock him. After Boyet and Berowne interrupt Nathaniel, she even encourages him: "The conqueror is dismay'd. Proceed, good Alexander" (5.2.567). The Princess becomes the only playgoer who is actively heeding and encouraging the performance. Armado turns to her specifically when the men prevent him from speaking his role as Hector: "But I will forward with my device. Sweet royalty, bestow on me the sense of hearing" (5.2.662–64). The Princess's answer makes it perfectly clear that she accepts her part as his auditor: "Speak, brave Hector, we are much delighted" (5.2.665). With this appeal to the princess and her ratification, Armado seeks to change the response to the pageant.

However, the transformation that ensues revises both the pageant and its audience. At the very moment when Armado abandons the male audience in favor of the more receptive female one, Dumaine reinterprets Hector's gallant adoration of her slipper into a bawdy pun suggesting that he cannot love her by the yard (penis), and Berowne provokes Costard to reveal Jaquenetta's pregnancy. The empowerment of the Princess as an audience results in sexual joking and the revelation of Jaquenetta's condition. In the formal theatrical situation, despite the weakness of the players, the powers demonstrated earlier by the Princess and her court wane noticeably. Suddenly they are silenced and vulnerable before the kind of sexual joking that they casually dismissed during the informal playing.

The disruptions of the pageant underscore the female audience's unusual blend of vulnerability and influence, both tied to the status of the female playgoer in question. Although some critics insist that Marcade's entrance undoes the pageant as well as the courtship plot of the comedy, in fact, the production of the Nine Worthies is doubly interrupted, first by Berowne's apparent intervention just as Armado appeals to the Princess and second by Marcade's news of her father's death.[14] When Costard's announcement of Jaquenetta's pregnancy successfully derails the pageant, his news could easily signify an intrusion of reality.[15] However, since Berowne motivates this revelation as Armado acknowledges the Princess as a powerful audience, the particular "reality" which intrudes is significant.[16]

After all, Jaquenetta is both the first female spectacle and the first female spectator of the all-male production of love sonnets. Costard first mentions her after Armado has observed him conversing with her in the park at the very beginning of the play; she becomes the spectacle of female sexuality and the first violation of the King's rules. When she enters in act 4, scene 3, her possession of Berowne's letter to Rosaline not only undoes his mocking commentary about the other lovers but temporarily places her as one of the Princess's ladies. Jaquenetta's fleeting identification as a powerful yet vulnerable audience resonates with the later invocation of her pregnancy. This display of female sexuality, though only present in description, insists on the vulnerability of women exposed to the gaze—especially since Armado's desires for Jaquenetta have been provoked by his watching her in the park with Costard. Her sexual presence as an object of the male gaze underscores the way Armado's theatrical attentions to the Princess subject her to bawdy innuendo.

In addition to temporarily silencing the Princess, the female spectacle also transforms the production. Whether the assertion of paternity is accurate or, as Dorothea Kehler persuasively argues, a false accusation staining Armado's honor, this challenge turns the pageant's stilted announcements of male heroism into vivid action.[17] The play develops a dramatic tension and momentum it previously lacked, in part because the male playgoers stop interrupting the pageant with criticism and start promoting the action; their cooperation and participation occurs only after the female spectacle has replaced the female spectator as the focus of attention. This transformation of the absent Jaquenetta into spectacle silences the Princess, the most powerful and most vocal female playgoer.

However, with Marcade's news, the death of male patriarchal authority signals the elevation of the Princess to Queen and restores her authority and influence. Although Berowne actually dismisses the Worthies and their battle, at this point the Queen and her ladies hold sway over both the men and the interpretation of *all* the theatrics offered so far. They dismiss the Lords' courtship as merely a jest to pass the time, so that Berowne laments that their "wooing doth not end like an old play: / Jack hath not Gill. These ladies' courtesy / Might well have made our sport a comedy" (5.2.874–76). Now both the Queen and her ladies speak and impose tasks on their would-be lovers. Berowne's insistent complaints that the ladies' requirements undo the dictates of comedy and the time allotted for a play are significant indications that the Princess and her court intend to accept courtship only when they are no longer placed in the female playgoer's paradoxical position of power and vulnerability.[18] However, despite the ladies' seemingly effective moves to escape their place as an official female audience, the comedy closes with the epilogue of the Nine Worthies, encouraged now by the King's more generous response to Armado's request. The song, which is hardly a learned dialogue, also once more raises the issue of female frailty in the Spring section's insistence on "'Cuckoo, cuckoo'—O word of fear, / Unpleasing to a married ear!" (5.2.910–11).

The oscillation in influence between the female audience and the male audience during the official theater which closes *Love's Labor's Lost* registers the very different investment of the male and female playgoer in the theatrical production: the female playgoer is always vulnerable to being "noated," as Gosson puts it, to being judged as sexually available and desirable, whereas the male playgoer always seeks control over the theatrical display, sometimes becoming the spectacle himself. The vulnerability of the female playgoer is thus doubly dangerous: it endangers the female playgoer who could slip against her will from spectator to spectacle, and it endangers the male playgoer's investment in re-creating himself for her because she herself could become the more powerful spectacle. Given that all the players and playwrights are men, the seemingly exclusive male authority over performance, vested in players and playwrights, can slip most dangerously in response to the status and influence of a particularly powerful female playgoer, like the Princess of France or Queen Elizabeth.

Hamlet's theatrical productions establish even more emphatically the patriarchal control over theater—and the paradoxical position of the female audience. In Hamlet's first encounter with the players, he demands that the actor recite a speech to him. The resulting impromptu performance offers the most thoroughly masculine theater since *Taming,* where even the female playgoer, Bartholomew as Sly's wife, is male. For Hamlet's speech, the actors, the director, and the audience, made up of Polonius, Rosencrantz, Guildenstern, and Hamlet himself, are entirely male. In fact Hamlet ironically draws attention to this situation by addressing the boy-actress and suggesting that he has grown too close to manhood to pretend to be a woman any longer: "What, my young lady and mistress! by' lady, your ladyship is nearer to heaven than when I saw you last, by the altitude of a chopine. Pray God your voice, like a piece of uncurrent gold, be not crack'd within the ring" (2.2.426–30). Women are present in this scene only in the loss of "womanhood" imagined for the boy-actress. Hamlet's theater here is more than masculine: he chooses it, he starts to perform it, and he watches it. From his own enjoyment in controlling and hearing this speech, Hamlet imagines that he can aim another drama, *The Murder of Gonzago,* at a single man, Claudius. This scene carries the rigidly patriarchal mechanism of Renaissance theater to its extreme.

However, the speech also emphasizes the significance of class in relationship to theatrical display and its pleasures. In *Hamlet,* drama is always vulnerable to appropriation and multiple interpretations. His use of an all-male theatrical company to affect an elite male audience never fully succeeds, because the audiences of these performances always include multiple classes and, during the official performance, both sexes. In the first scene, Polonius interrupts the player's speech twice: to complain about its length and to relieve the player's apparent distress. He also seconds Hamlet's own interruption to praise the description of the mobled queen. Polonius's vocal presence denies Hamlet full control over his production and demonstrates that, even with its singular appeal, the speech can be challenged by multiple listeners and not-so-elite audiences.[19]

The more subtle undermining of this scene as a patriarchal exemplum occurs within the speech itself: powerful female spectators haunt even this all-male performance. In fact, Hamlet's initial request insists on the importance of the female audience; he calls for "One speech . . . I chiefly lov'd, 'twas Aeneas' [tale] to Dido" (2.2.445–46). The context of this tale, Aeneas narrating the story to the queen he loves and betrays, positions even this all-male performance specifically in terms of performing for a woman. Dido is the formal audience to Aeneas's tale, aware that she listens just as he displays the spectacle of the Trojan war for her.

However, this brief invocation of formal theater is not the only example of female spectatorship. Hamlet demands that the player continue beyond Pyrrhus's regicide with the description of Queen Hecuba. As a result, the scene of Pyrrhus's hesitation and violence opens with one queen listening to Aeneas's tale and closes with another responding to the scene of her husband's murder:

> When she saw Pyrrhus make malicious sport
> In mincing with his sword her [husband's] limbs,
> The instant burst of clamor that she made,
> Unless things mortal move them not at all,
> Would have made milch the burning eyes of heaven,
> And passion in the gods.
>
> (2.2.513–18)

Pyrrhus's hesitation is just a pause before the act of bloody vengeance, allowing Hamlet to reunderstand his own wavering in his revenge on Claudius as the prelude to bloody vengeance. However, when Hamlet insists on hearing about Hecuba, he demands the presentation of a witness who resists the violence of the scene and requires sympathy for the victim.

If Hecuba's reactions potentially influence the gods who hear her grieve, she certainly affects the actor who weeps, Polonius and Hamlet who note those tears, and the audience of Shakespeare's play. However, Hecuba's grief-stricken response does more than merely guide the audience's reaction, the function of the female audience first explored by Marianne Novy.[20] Within the overtly male, apparently self-involved version of theater which Hamlet invokes, this demand for Hecuba reinforces the inescapable importance of a female audience first signaled in Aeneas's tale to Dido. Moreover, the description of Hecuba imagines her as a spectator. Aeneas's speech accords Hecuba a certain power in her curious double presence as both spectator and spectacle. First invoked by sight in "Who, ah woe, had seen the mobled queen," Hecuba almost immediately becomes a spectacle of excessive sexuality, the reputed mother of fifty children who "for a robe, / About her lank and all o'er-teemed loins, / A blanket, in the alarm of fear caught up" (2.2.507–9). The linked sexuality and maternity of the figure move the larger audience; as a spectator to the slaughter of Priam, her response "unless things mortal move them not at all— / Would have made milch the burning eyes of heaven" (2.2.518–19). Hecuba's presence crystallizes the multiple possibilities of the speech which Hamlet has requested for his own pleasure and reveals the inevitably multiple positions offered to the theatrical audience: identification with Pyrrhus's vengeance, reactions to the half-clad display of Hecuba's fecund and sexual body, and sympathy for her wild grief as spectator to her husband's slaughter.

Although Hecuba is not a formal audience viewing a theatrical display, the narrative of her informal spectatorship is offered in a performance for another queen, Dido. In that situation, Aeneas's speech before his female audience represents and rewrites female spectatorship as both sexual display and evocative emotional power. In the excerpted speech as demanded by Hamlet, Hecuba, as the mourning queen, inevitably invokes Queen Gertrude who then becomes part of the formal audience to Hamlet's *Mousetrap*. Whereas the queenly figures of Hecuba and Dido are embedded in the context and text of this speech, *The Murder of Gonzago* plays before an audience that includes women.

Hamlet intends the play to "catch the conscience of the King" (2.2.605); however, Claudius is not the only one watching. Once again, Hamlet himself insists on invoking the involvement of the female spectators. Rejecting a seat at his mother's side, presumably so that he can better watch the King and Queen, Hamlet chooses Ophelia as "metal more attractive" (3.2.110). As the play progresses, his attentions to Ophelia deliberately transform her from an audience member to an object of gaze and sexual appropriation. His jesting insists on her sexual identity as he turns her modest avowal that she "think[s] nothing" into "a fair thought to lie between maids' legs" (3.2.117–18). His sexual bantering develops from general comments about female sexuality to specific complaints about his mother's hasty marriage and finally to the suggestion of sexual union between himself and Ophelia—"It would cost you a groaning to take off mine edge," he says (3.2.249–50).

Hamlet's behavior, which enacts Gosson's predictions of "eyes to their lappes . . . marking in their eares . . . Such ticking, such toying" (*Schoole of Abuse*, C2), meets with Ophelia's resistance. Hamlet begins with sexual puns which Ophelia tries not to acknowledge. She rejects his suggestion that she has misinterpreted his offer to lie in her lap as she rejects his assessment of his mother's brief mourning. When he hyperbolically claims that Gertrude has mourned but two hours, she replies factually that it has been twice two months. His wordplay founders on her literal responses. Despite his attempts to make her into the spectacle, Ophelia turns her attention to the dumbshow. In effect she displaces her confusion about Hamlet's suggestive comments into watching the play, much as, in *Taming*, Bartholomew as the Lady protects "herself" from the sexual attentions of "her" husband by directing "her" attention to the play. Ophelia directs Hamlet's attention to the dumbshow by asking, "What means this, my lord?" When Hamlet replies cryptically, she offers her own interpretation: "Belike this show imports the argument of the play" (3.2.139–40). In response to her further interest in what the play means, Hamlet suggests that Ophelia herself is the show:

> Ophelia: Will 'a tell us what this show meant?
> Hamlet: Ay, or any show that you will show him. Be not you asham'd to show, he'll not shame to tell you what it means.
>
> (3.2.143–46)

He places Ophelia, and by implication women, as the spectacle to be interpreted as much as the dumbshow is. And Ophelia again rejects his view and directs her attention to the play, "You are naught, you are naught. I'll mark the play" (3.2.147).

This progression is doubly significant. Ophelia's openly knowing responses to his sexual jokes have been interpreted both as sure evidence that their relationship is well established and as proof that she, like Gertrude, partakes of tainted female sexuality. More important, however, her responses develop through her viewing of the play and through Hamlet's insistent sexual teasing as the play progresses. The broader significance of their interaction during the play-within-the-play lies in the link Hamlet forges between sexuality and theater—but only with the female playgoer of lower status, a character warned about her social inferiority by her brother and thoroughly subjected to her father's will.

Gertrude proves less vulnerable than Ophelia because of her rank and her maternal authority over her son. Hamlet comments twice on the Player-Queen's promises, first to note the wormwood of her comments and second to comment

"If she should break it now!" (3.2.224) after the Player-Queen concludes her speech. Unlike Ophelia, who responds to him even when she does not follow his meaning, Gertrude ignores both of his pointed comments. Finally he addresses his mother directly: "Madam, how like you this play?" (3.2.229). Her response, "The lady doth protest too much" (3.2.230), critiques the play's art and resists Hamlet's efforts to establish *her* as the display for critical attention.[21] In part because Claudius, king to her queen, intervenes to question Hamlet, Gertrude more easily resists Hamlet's efforts to place her as the sexual spectacle than Ophelia does. Gertrude's refusal to identify with the Player-Queen, which becomes more evident during the closet scene, suggests that female resistance to becoming the show is enabled by the status of the woman as well as by her adoption of the authority implicit in judging the performance. Gertrude is both more vulnerable—her actions are being staged—and more in control than Ophelia.

In consequence, both Gertrude and Ophelia occupy an uneasy place between spectator and spectacle during this scene. This focus on female playgoers is all the more surprising since what Hamlet ostensibly expects is that Claudius will become the spectacle:

> . . . I have heard
> That guilty creatures sitting at a play
> Have by the very cunning of the scene
> Been strook so to the soul that presently
> They have proclaim'd their malefactions.
> (2.2.588–92)

While the female audience's apparent status as spectacle associates the women with Claudius (and more importantly with Claudius's guilt), both Ophelia and Gertrude resist Hamlet's attempts to identify them as the sexual spectacle in the play and refuse to acknowledge guilt even as much as Claudius does when he halts the play and draws all eyes by calling for light. Ultimately, the women occupy a different position from the male playgoers—distinct from Horatio who observes both the play and the audience, and separate from Claudius who stops the play upon discovering that his crime is on display.

In fact, Claudius's disruption of the performance transforms both him and Hamlet into the spectacles on display. Whether the players' performance or Hamlet's summary of the forthcoming action provokes the king's violent reaction, Claudius becomes the object of the gaze. Hamlet, on the other hand, deliberately positions himself as part of the show from the start; as Ophelia suggests: "You are as good as a chorus, my lord" (3.2.245). Even more striking, Hamlet takes over performing once the players' production has been interrupted. After

Claudius has departed, Hamlet starts to recite poetry, implying that his performance would "with [two] Provincial roses on my raz'd shoes, get me a fellowship in a cry of players" (3.2.276–78). As male playgoers, both Hamlet and Claudius interrupt the production and *actively* usurp the spectacle of performance; the female playgoers, threatened with becoming the objects on display, resist with greater or lesser success.

In Shakespeare's plays, both male and female playgoers interact with and affect performance, but they do so quite differently. Male interaction takes the form of self-display, active intervention, and, in several cases, the complete derailment of performance leading to unexpected new conclusions. This model persists in the most controlling of male playgoers, Prospero, who disrupts the wedding masque, his only formal production, and becomes the object of Ferdinand's and Miranda's wondering gaze. Female audiences, including the silenced Miranda, intrude far less actively, often encouraging the performance and acknowledging that they are paying attention and even approving.

Nevertheless, several of these plays suggest that the female playgoer is the necessary condition of performance as well as a potentially distracting spectacle herself. The occasion for the production in *The Tempest,* like that of *A Midsummer Night's Dream,* is a wedding; the King of Navarre authorizes the Pageant of the Nine Worthies to entertain the Princess. Moreover, Hamlet's inspiration for his *Mousetrap* arises from the player's speech, itself framed through Dido and Hecuba as a production offered for a female audience and incomplete without its internal audience to Priam's slaughter.

Although Shakespeare's female playgoers do not directly or willfully intervene to alter performance, the mere presence of the female playgoer raises the potential that *she* will become the spectacle, overwhelming the carefully planned production or even the performance as rescripted by male intervention. The female playgoer's ability to resist becoming spectacle or at least to control the kind of spectacle which she becomes depends on her social status. Female rulers, like the Princess of Navarre and Gertrude, resist heavy-handed attempts to treat them as spectacles rather than spectators. Less highly placed women, like Ophelia or the Princess's ladies, either try to insist on the performance as the spectacle rather than themselves or remain silent. The complex doubled spectatorship of Dido and Hecuba during the player's speech suggests just how complicated the interaction between spectatorship and becoming the spectacle can be, even for powerful women.

These representations of deliberate theater within the plays are very much at odds with the theatrical powers which Shakespearean women from Portia to Paulina exhibit during informal playing. In *The Merchant of Venice,* after playing the judicious audience to Shylock's complaints, Portia restages the trial of Antonio, punishes Shylock, and for good measure wheedles her own ring and control over her body from her unwitting husband. In *The Winter's Tale,* the former queen's waiting woman controls both the jealous King Leontes and the silenced, immobilized Queen Hermione. Paulina's lower status is irrelevant to her staging of Hermione as statue, and, despite claims that she fears to be taken as a witch, she seems unconcerned about becoming the spectacle herself. Yet in Shakespearean plays where the theater is explicitly staged—with mutually aware players, audiences, and directors—Shakespeare stages the female spectator in a complex, uncomfortable position of having to negotiate between being and watching the show.

In Shakespeare's plays, female characters may exercise dramatic powers outside the theater without regard to status or personal exposure, but within official theatrical situations, even those same female characters—like the Princess and her court—suddenly change and become vulnerable. These interactions of class and gender in Shakespeare's onstage audiences reveal the particular pressures on the female audience. The female playgoers' status, sexual experience or inexperience, and resulting vulnerability to male playgoers' "noating" of them, all contribute to their relationships with the spectacles they observe and the spectacles they are constantly in danger of becoming. Often charged with more sympathy, generosity, and fair judgment of performance, Shakespeare's female playgoers are also overcharged with the burden of being both the bearer of the gaze which creates theater and the object of the gaze which "noats her and judges her."

Notes

1. Stephen Gosson, *The Schoole of Abuse* (1579; reprint, New York: Da Capo Press, 1972), F2.

2. Andrew Gurr, *Playgoing in Shakespeare's London* (Cambridge: Cambridge University Press, 1987), 56–65 (in appendix 2 Gurr extracts contemporary records documenting playgoing); Richard Levin, "Women in the Renaissance Theatre Audience," *Shakespeare Quarterly* 40 (Summer 1989): 165–74. See also Ann Jennalie Cook, *The Privileged Playgoers of Shakespeare's London* (Princeton: Princeton University Press, 1981).

3. S. P. Cerasano and Marion Wynne-Davies, *Renaissance Drama by Women: Texts and Documents* (London: Routledge, 1996).

4. Jean E. Howard, "Scripts and/versus Playhouses: Ideological Production and the Renaissance Public Stage," in *The Matter of Difference: Materialist Feminist Criticism of Shakespeare,* ed. Valerie Wayne (Ithaca: Cornell University Press, 1991), 221–36. See also Howard's *The Stage and Social Struggle in Early Modern England* (New York: Routledge, 1994). Several critics are involved in further meditations on female spectatorship; Dympna

Callaghan presented a paper at the 1997 Shakespeare Association of America Conference entitled "The Equine Phallus and the Fantasy of Female Spectatorship," and Valerie Traub is currently working on the theater and female pleasure in the early modern period. Shakespeare's very conservatism in representing the female spectator serves as counterpoint to these investigations which often center around either nontheatrical accounts of female spectatorship or around medical discourses about female pleasure.

5. See my "Female Audience and Female Authority in *The Knight of the Burning Pestle*," *Exemplaria* 3 (Fall 1991): 491–518.

6. Andrew Gurr notes that social class was peculiarly mixed in the public theater, where theatrical professionals might indeed be playing to both their betters and their inferiors (*Playgoing*, 54–62).

7. Alvin B. Kernan, "Shakespearian Comedy and Its Courtly Audience," in *Comedy from Shakespeare to Sheridan: Change and Continuity in the English and European Dramatic Tradition: Essays in Honor of Eugene M. Waith*, ed. A. R. Braunmuller and J. C. Bulman (Newark: University of Delaware Press, 1986), 91–93.

8. See also Alan Nelson, "Women in the Audience of the Cambridge Plays," *Shakespeare Quarterly* 41 (Fall 1990): 333–36.

9. Kathleen McLuskie, "The Patriarchal Bard: Feminist Criticism and Shakespeare," in *Political Shakespeare: New Essays in Cultural Materialism*, ed. Jonathan Dollimore and Alan Sinfield (Ithaca: Cornell University Press, 1985), 88–108.

10. All quotations from Shakespeare are from *The Riverside Shakespeare*, ed. G. Blakemore Evans (Boston: Houghton Mifflin, 1974).

11. See Cerasano and Wynne-Davies, *Renaissance Drama by Women*, 161–64.

12. By taking this perspective on Navarre's academy, I am not necessarily contradicting Maurice Hunt's argument that Renaissance audiences would have linked the academy with the King of Navarre and his dealing (and double dealing) with Queen Elizabeth ("The Double Figure of Elizabeth in *Love's Labor's Lost*," *Essays in Literature* 19 [Fall 1992]: 173–92).

13. Katharine Eisaman Maus sees this abuse as the court's response to the tainting of noble names and fame ("Transfer of Title in *Love's Labour's Lost*: Language, Individualism, Gender," in *Shakespeare Left and Right*, ed. Ivo Kamps [New York: Routledge, 1991], 213–14).

14. Joseph Chaney argues that all the festivities in the play are interrupted: "Nathaniel falters, Holofernes stumbles, Armado trembles. Each is cut short by mockery, and finally the show itself is interrupted when Marcade brings word that the King of France is dead" ("Promises, Promises: *Love's Labor's Lost* and the End of Shakespearean Comedy," *Criticism* 35 [Winter 1993]: 41–65, quotation on 51).

15. For Caroline Asp, Jaquenetta's pregnancy introduces reality ("*Love's Labour's Lost*: Language and the Deferral of Desire," *Literature and Psychoanalysis* 35, no. 3 [1989]: 1–21), and, for Maus, in "Transfer of Title in *Love's Labour's Lost*," it functions as part of the conceptual differences in the ladies' approach to language (219–20).

16. The stage direction in the Quarto text says only that Berowne steps forward after

Armado, but most editors supply an interaction with Costard which apparently provokes the ensuing events.

17. Dorothea Kehler, "Jaquenetta's Baby's Father: Recovering Paternity in *Love's Labor's Lost*," *Renaissance Papers* (1990): 45–54.

18. Hunt usefully summarizes the arguments associating the Princess of France with Elizabeth and argues for Elizabeth's doubled presence as both glorious queen and threatening female ruler with whom courtship was nonproductive or futile. In fact he so identifies the Princess of France with Elizabeth that there is no place to consider the ebb and flow of her influence in the final scene ("Double Figure of Elizabeth").

19. Annabel Patterson also starts from Hamlet's injunctions to the players in considering Shakespeare's relationship with his audience (*Shakespeare and the Popular Voice* [Oxford: Basil Blackwell, 1989], 13–31).

20. Marianne Novy, "Shakespeare's Female Characters as Actors and Audience," in *The Woman's Part: Feminist Criticism of Shakespeare,* ed. Carolyn Ruth Swift Lenz, Gayle Greene, and Carol Thomas Neely (Urbana: University of Illinois Press, 1980), 256–70.

21. Carolyn Heilbrun was one of the first to point out that Gertrude's character in the play demonstrates judgment and depth, rather than merely lust ("The Character of Hamlet's Mother," *Shakespeare Quarterly* 8 [Autumn 1957]: 201–6).

10

Gender, Rhetoric, and Performance in John Webster's *The White Devil*

Christina Luckyj

John Webster's *The White Devil* has long provoked anxiety among its critics. The arraignment scene, in which Vittoria defends herself magnificently against charges of murder and adultery, has been widely celebrated as "one of the great moments of the English stage."[1] Yet unlike Desdemona in *Othello* or Hermione in *The Winter's Tale*, Vittoria is clearly implicated in the crimes of which she is accused. Her response to Bracciano's importunities has not in fact been "frosty" (3.2.202), as she claims it has; indeed, she has eschewed the "loathed cruelty" (1.2.209) of the Petrarchan mistress by embracing her lover openly in the first act (213).[2] And, while her agency is never entirely clear, she goes on to recount a dream in which (at least according to Flamineo) she instructs Bracciano to "make away his Duchess and her husband" (1.2.256). Male villain-heroes may not be uncommon in Jacobean tragedy (viz. Vindice in *The Revenger's Tragedy*), but female figures such as Vittoria who arouse admiration and reprehension are rare indeed. In most early modern drama, as Bracciano puts it, "Woman to man / Is either a god or a wolf" (4.2.89–90). Critics therefore continue to dispute the meaning of Vittoria's performance in the trial scene. Some simply label her a hypocrite and Webster a moralist: D. C. Gunby, for example, asserts that "we should acknowledge the truth of his [Monticelso's] asseveration that 'If the devil / Did ever take good shape, behold his picture.'"[3] Others find hypocrisy not in Vittoria but in Webster himself, who thus commits "an artistic insincerity—a lie in the poet's heart,"[4] and indulges his penchant for "vivid sympathetic insights at the expense of ethical coherence."[5] More recently, Catherine Belsey has deflected blame from the dramatist to his culture, associating Vittoria's "discursive mobility" with the unstable and discontinuous place of women in early modern England, when "in the family as in the state women had no single, unified, fixed position from which to speak."[6] From different perspectives, then, critics have identified the trial scene with disjuncture and dissembling (Vittoria's, Webster's or the culture's), despite its powerful impact on the stage. I shall argue that such anxieties about performance, especially as it constitutes gender identity, are in fact self-consciously articulated and managed by *The White Devil* itself.

Like many early modern texts, *The White Devil* invests its anxieties about performance in women. "O ye dissembling men!" cries Vittoria, who is promptly corrected by Flamineo: "We suck'd that, sister / From women's breasts, in our first infancy" (4.2.179–80). Women are "politic" (1.2.21) performers whose pretense to virtue masks a voracious sexual appetite and whose apparent tears are "but moonish shades of griefs or fears" (5.3.187). Despite the proliferation of male disguises, in the rhetoric of *The White Devil* performance is frequently gendered female. To Isabella's plea that he exhibit some marital affection, Bracciano cries, "O dissemblance" (2.1.171); seeing Vittoria's tears at his ill-treatment, he remarks scornfully, "Procure but ten of thy dissembling trade, / Ye'd furnish all the Irish funerals / With howling" (4.2.93–95). Female theatricality is of course a common misogynist trope in early modern texts; in *Much Ado about Nothing,* Claudio mouths an antifeminist cliché in his indictment of Hero's "performance": "O, what authority and show of truth / Can cunning sin cover itself withal!" (4.1.35–36).[7] If theatricality in men could be a powerful means of "self-fashioning," Weidemann points out that "theatricality in a woman suggests that her identity has somehow become inauthentic or alienated, akin to that of a professional actor."[8] Joseph Swetnam's notorious *Araignment of lewde, idle, froward and unconstant women* (1615) recycles commonplaces in declaring that "a woman which is faire in showe is foule in condition, she is like unto a glow-worme which is bright in the hedge and black in the hand."[9] Such a construction relies on a stable and privileged masculine capacity to "see through" feminine dissimulation, and make clear distinctions between outside and inside.[10] *The White Devil,* however, problematizes this masculine privilege. In this play, as I shall argue, men are as implicated as women in the theatrical practices they abhor; women appropriate theater as a form of power; and performance is revealed as constitutive, as the "true" and the "adulterate" become indistinguishable (1.1.49–50).

"I account this world a tedious theatre," cries the Duchess of Malfi, "For I do play a part in't 'gainst my will" (4.1.83–84). Like the Duchess, Vittoria in her trial and Isabella in her rejection of Bracciano "play a part." Unlike the Duchess, however, whose participation in her brother's sadistic "spectacle" (4.1.57) is involuntary, the women of *The White Devil* embrace theatricality, offering extraordinarily self-conscious performances. In the trial scene, Vittoria constructs herself as an actor both in the courtroom and on the stage. When she rejects the lawyer's use of Latin, for example, on the grounds that "amongst this auditory /

Which come to hear my cause, the half or more / May be ignorant in't" (3.2.15–17), her remark applies to the Red Bull audience rather than to the learned ambassadors. When Isabella almost slavishly repeats Bracciano's ceremony of divorce, she at first appears to be masochistically increasing the anguish of her "piteous and rent heart" by acting out her "sad ensuing part" (2.1.223–24) in a script that has been written by her husband. But Bracciano's declaration that "this divorce shall be as truly kept / As if the judge had doomed it" (2.1.196–97) becomes in Isabella's version "And this divorce shall be as truly kept, / As if in thronged court a thousand ears / Had heard it" (255–57)—a remark that glances at the Red Bull audience itself. Why do both women, victims in the fictional world, display this kind of metadramatic awareness? And why, at the height of their performances, do both women threaten to violate established gender boundaries? "O that I were a man, or that I had power / To execute my apprehended wishes" (2.1.242–43), cries Isabella. Similarly, at a central moment of self-assertion, Vittoria declares that her "defense, of force, like Perseus / Must personate masculine virtue to the point" (3.2.135–36). "Personate" had by the early seventeenth century become a new and specifically theatrical term:[11] Webster himself uses it in his character of "An Excellent Actor" to assert that "what we see him personate, we thinke truely done before us."[12] While it could mean "represent, embody," it was also commonly used to mean "imitate, feign, counterfeit."[13] The verb again foregrounds Vittoria's theatricality: in the theater one cannot represent without counterfeiting. But why, for both Isabella and Vittoria, is metatheater so closely associated with crossing gender lines? In part, it is clear that to become tragic subjects (authors and agents of their own choices), women must *act* in both senses of the word—take action and play a (male) role. Yet even as they appropriate masculine power, they also exceed mere role-playing to reveal a heightened awareness of the theater itself, and this has important implications for the play.

Despite Flamineo's proposal that Vittoria be attired "in a page's suit" (4.2.209) to facilitate her escape from the house of convertites, literal crossdressing—with its potential for playful masquerade and the destabilizing of gender[14]—never occurs in *The White Devil*. By this time, as Michael Shapiro points out, such transvestism had become a distinctly old-fashioned device.[15] And when Isabella and Vittoria crossdress rhetorically, they appear at first to mirror the many other women in early modern plays whose expressed longing to turn into men emphasizes by contrast their immutable and essential "feminine" natures. In *The Duchess of Malfi*, the Duchess may defy Bosola with "Were I a man / I'd beat that counterfeit face into thy other" (3.5.117–18), but her fantasy of masculine violence must give way to her gently controlling, indirect tale of the feminized salmon/victim. In Middleton and Rowley's *The Changeling*, Beatrice-Joanna may sigh, "Would creation

... Had form'd me man," but her attempt to realize the "freedom" of a man (2.2.107–8, 109)[16] actually delivers her into the power of DeFlores, who fetishizes and essentializes her virginal female body. Similarly, in Shakespeare's *Much Ado about Nothing,* Beatrice may cry repeatedly, "O that I were a man!" (4.1.303, 306, 317), but she must finally acknowledge that she "cannot be a man with wishing" (322–23), and she defers to Claudio's agency. Such fantasies of crossing gender lines are destined to remain merely fantasies partly because these women endorse a gender system from which they are necessarily excluded. Like the anonymous author of the crossdressing pamphlet *Haec Vir,* who finally defends female transvestism as a reification of traditional masculine value,[17] Beatrice laments a world in which "manhood is melted into curtsies, valour into compliment, and men are only turned into tongue, and trim ones, too" (4.1.319–21). Women seek to turn into men only because men are not doing their job; the value of that job is never in question. Similarly, in *The White Devil,* Isabella's cry, "O that I were a man" (2.1.242), draws attention not only to what she lacks but also to her brother's ineffectual defense on her behalf. The jealous tirade that follows appears to confirm her irrational feminine nature: while Francisco associates her with the (typically female) "fury" (244), Bracciano implies that her "humour" (and perhaps her forced abstinence from marital intercourse) has led to the rising of her "stomach" (271–72), akin to the rising womb, a common symptom of hysteria. In the trial scene, Vittoria tenders her "modesty / And womanhood" (3.2.132–33) before she reluctantly, "of force" (135), adopts a masculine pose in her own defense. At first glance, rhetorical "crossdressing" appears to be a conventional means of heightening the illusion of femininity that is crucial to an all-male theatrical company.

In *The White Devil,* however, the simple dichotomy between essential feminine identity and masculine disguise is problematized by metatheatrical presentation. For one thing, Isabella is deliberately constructing and playing out a female stereotype; the feminine is clearly a matter of performance here. For another, the violent fantasies of a "foolish, mad, / And jealous woman" (2.1.263–64) are also constructed as the "apprehended wishes" of a "man" (242–43):

> To dig the strumpet's eyes out, let her lie
> Some twenty months a-dying, to cut off
> Her nose and lips, pull out her rotten teeth,
> Preserve her flesh like mummia, for trophies
> Of my just anger!
>
> (2.1.245–49)

Here is a fantasy of dismemberment which parodies the Petrarchan *blazon* (already parodied by Flamineo at 1.2.114–18) and anticipates Bracciano's own later rage against Vittoria, his threat to "cut her into atomies" (4.2.40). As the scene builds in tension, Isabella's breathless rage gives way to an increasingly firm control of the stage, as she directs the movements of the male characters (250–52) and repeats, even as she parodies, Bracciano's vow of divorce. Isabella's performance, despite its apparently "feminine" irrationality, actually gets her the "power" (242) of a man: whereas earlier she attempts to placate Bracciano gently when he commands her to "take [her] chamber" (154), here she defies her brother's issue of the same command (269) and refuses to "stay a minute" (270). The fetishized kiss that Isabella earlier desires (156–57) and Bracciano refuses and then transfers to her hand to mark perversely the "latest ceremony of... love" (193) is finally bestowed at Isabella's command (252). After making him kiss her, she reinscribes his discourse: whereas he refers to her "love" (200) for him, she recasts it sardonically as her "former dotage" (259). Francisco identifies Isabella as both a madwoman and a male cuckold who merits "horns" (266). The final impact of the scene is to illuminate a double standard at work: while the male characters construct Isabella's divorce ceremony as quixotic feminine ravings to be easily dismissed (273–74), Bracciano's vow—cast in the same words—is "fixed" (205) and immutable. In her "part" (224), however, Isabella plays out both the hysterical impotence of the jealous woman and the tyrannical potency of the autonomous male. The contrived theatricality of the scene exposes both as culturally authorized modes of self-display.

In *The White Devil*, perspective is frequently shifting and unreliable, and subjectivity frequently foregrounded—this is a world in which, as Flamineo says, "men at sea think land and trees and ships go that way they go" (1.2.154–56), and "they that have the yellow jaundice, think all objects they look upon to be yellow" (108–9). That Isabella can play masculine and feminine parts at once, blurring gender boundaries, exposes gender as a matter of perception as well as self-construction. Similarly, in the trial scene Vittoria represents herself simultaneously as a railing shrew taking a "woman's poor revenge / Which dwells but in the tongue" (3.2.283–84) and as a commanding rhetorician, usurping "masculine virtue" (136). Both Isabella's and Vittoria's performances deconstruct traditional gendered antitheses and expose them as contingent on subjective construction.[18]

It is worthwhile here to recall briefly some of the cultural debate surrounding real crossdressed women: it was common, for example, to assume, as does Richard Brathwait's *English Gentlewoman* (1631), that crossdressed women "labour to purchase them opinion of *esteeme*, by their unwomanly expressions of valour."[19] Female transvestism was clearly constructed as a desire to imitate masculine modes. Imitation, however, also opens a space for masquerade, parody, and caricature. Judith Butler points out that "in imitating gender, drag implicitly reveals the imitative structure of gender itself."[20] In *As You Like It,* for example, Rosalind imagines herself with "a swashing and a martial outside / As many other mannish cowards have / That do outface it with their semblances" (1.3.120–22). Her imitation of masculinity promises to expose its artificial construction through parody. Indeed, masculine extravagance (the sartorial equivalent of the braggadocio) was frequently displaced onto women in a burgeoning consumer economy; Karen Newman suggests that "the furor over cross-dressing may owe more to an objection to women's sharing in the male privilege of *excess* in dress than to specifically masculine attire."[21] Thus female transvestites are horrifying partly because they figure *masculine* theatricality, read here not as power but as degeneration. In *Hic Mulier* (1620), the author finds in female transvestism a critique of masculine behaviour when s/he denounces women who desire to be "man in body by attire, man in behavior by rude complement, man in nature by aptness to anger, man in action by pursuing revenge, man in wearing weapons, man in using weapons," and rails against crossdressed women for imitating the worst aspects of men: "The long hair of a woman is the ornament of her sex . . . the long hair of a man, the vizard for a thievish or murderous disposition. And will you cut off that beauty to wear the other's villainy?"[22] Along with this pamphlet's clear anxiety about women's access to male privilege is a hint that such behavior functions as a critique of men. If, as Valerie Lucas points out, this pamphlet "betrays how men fashion the female transvestite as a mirror image of masculine violence,"[23] the female transvestite may in turn appropriate that mirror image and reflect it back at men. Crossdressed women, like the effeminized men discussed by Laura Levine, threaten to reveal "that there is no masculinity in itself but only masculinity insofar as it is staged and performed."[24]

Similarly, the women of *The White Devil* who usurp masculine rhetoric are positioned not only to gain access to male privilege but also to offer a savage critique of that privilege. Isabella's repetition of Bracciano's vow, for example, apparently intended to salvage his reputation, actually exaggerates and caricatures his pose: she parodies his autocratic appropriation of the authority of a "judge" (2.1.197) by upping the ante to "a thousand ears" and "a thousand lawyers" (256–57).[25] Her performance of Bracciano's machismo foregrounds its inherent theatricality. At the center of her trial, Vittoria claims that her "defense, of force, like Perseus / Must personate masculine virtue" (3.2.135–36). Heightening the artifice of her performance, she self-consciously alludes to Ben Jonson's 1609 *Masque of Queens* in which Perseus, "expressing *heroicall* and *masculine Vertue,*"[26] arrives to rout the antimasque of witches and usher in twelve famous queens dressed as warriors for battle. As Perseus, Vittoria by implication represents her opponents as witches (demonized masculine women) from whose "cursed accusation"—

maleficia—she is justified in defending herself; at the same time she identifies herself not with the idealized and disempowered Queen Anne but with the King, the controlling extratheatrical presence in the masque embodied by Perseus.[27] Furthermore, Vittoria "crossdresses" to emulate masculinity—like real seventeenth-century women modeling themselves on heroic hermaphrodites—while she constructs it as a theatrical performance of the most distant and artificial kind. (The Red Bull, of course, catered to an audience at the other end of the social spectrum than the court masque.) Since the line is unpunctuated in the quarto, her offer to "personate masculine virtue to the point" suggests a perfectly detailed ("to the point") portrait of masculinity—a theatrical sketch, perhaps even a "character" to vie with Monticelso's character of a whore presented earlier.[28]

While it is difficult to attribute a parodic impulse to Vittoria herself, it is possible to trace in Vittoria's masculine theatricality Webster's profound ambivalence toward his male hero. It is surely important that, even as Vittoria invokes "masculine virtue," this commodity is in short supply in the play. When, for example, Bracciano intervenes as Vittoria's "champion" (3.2.180) during the trial, his rhetoric is grossly fraudulent and self-aggrandizing. His claim to have been motivated by "charity . . . which should flow / From every generous and noble spirit, / To orphans and to widows" (161–63) is a cowardly attempt at inventing an alibi. He then resorts to violent threats and lordly Latin tags, finally exiting on the line, "Nemo me impune lacessit" (179) and abandoning his lover so that (as Vittoria herself points out) "[t]he wolf may prey the better" (3.2.180). However, perhaps the play's most obvious exposure of masculinity as a precarious and risible construction comes earlier, when Bracciano's son, the young prince Giovanni, dons a suit of armour and tosses his "pike" (2.1.110)—a common euphemism for penis—while declaring his plan to "press the women to the war / And then the men will follow" (135–36). Though Francisco announces that "a good habit makes a child a man" (137), Giovanni makes the swaggering Bracciano of the second act by analogy look like a child.[29] Similarly, Vittoria's accomplished performance of masculinity exposes those cultural paradigms that underlie the rhetorical posturing of the men in this play.

Indeed, the main thrust of Vittoria's trial scene is that no one is exempt from performance, and that all performance is contingent on interpretation. Monticelso, for example, offers to read Vittoria's flushed cheeks as a sign of her inauthenticity: "I shall be plainer with you, and paint out / Your follies in more natural red and white / Than that upon your cheek" (3.2.51–53). Vittoria's deceptive show is like the whore's use of cosmetics; the Cardinal invokes a misogynist commonplace which metonymically figures a gilded exterior masking a corrupt interior. However, since the boy actor used paint to play a woman,[30] the Cardinal's charge (however true) loses its misogynist force and becomes simply antitheatrical. Moreover, he participates in the performance he condemns when he adopts the metaphor of applying cosmetics to describe his own rhetorical strategies. Vittoria then contests his reading: "O you mistake," she corrects him. "You raise a blood as noble in this cheek / As ever was your mother's" (53–55). "The shameful blush," writes Bevington, "may represent one of two opposite responses: dismay and confusion at an undeserved accusation or admission of guilt."[31] By foregrounding this sign, Vittoria exposes its contingency on perception and on theatrical representation: it is as likely to manifest the confused dismay of a noblewoman as the cheap artifice of a whore. Later, the Cardinal draws attention to her sumptuous attire by charging: "She comes not like a widow: she comes armed / With scorn and impudence. Is this a mourning habit?" (121–22). In reply, Vittoria points out: "Had I foreknown his death as you suggest, / I would have bespoke my mourning" (123–24)—in her case, mourning attire would signify not grief but guilt. Far from simply exposing Vittoria as a hypocrite or avoiding the problem altogether (as critics suggest), the trial scene of *The White Devil* openly contests the intelligibility of performance.

Despite her metatheatrical awareness, then, Vittoria is consistently antitheatrical. She begins the scene by pointedly invoking an "auditory" (3.2.15), thus taking the part of playwrights such as Webster who sought "full and understanding" ("To the Reader," ll. 6–7) listeners rather than the gaping spectators of the common stages.[32] By contrast, the Cardinal insistently foregrounds the visual in a protracted display of misogynistic scopophilia, alternately inviting and rejecting "ocular proof" of Vittoria's corruption. "Observe this creature" (57), "look upon this creature" (120), "See my lords" (63, 129), he instructs the ambassadors (and the theater audience). On the one hand, the Cardinal continually draws attention to Vittoria's appearance. On the other hand, he insists that her appearance is no guide to her inner reality:

> You see my lords what goodly fruit she seems,
> Yet like those apples travellers report
> To grow where Sodom and Gomorrah stood:
> I will but touch her and you straight shall see
> She'll fall to soot and ashes.
>
> (3.2.63–67)

This kind of standard antifeminist fare is reiterated in the Cardinal's description of a whore as "Sweet meats which rot the eater: in man's nostril / Poisoned perfumes" (81–82). What is significant here is the paradox underlying his rhetoric: what he seeks to prove by *sight* can never be *seen,* and must always therefore be subject to doubt. The final absurdity comes when he both invokes and dismisses his audience's visual sense: "If the devil / Did ever take good shape behold his picture" (216–17). The Cardinal depends not only on the stability of outward signs but also on their utter deceptiveness; Vittoria consistently foregrounds the latter. At the same time, she challenges the misogynist notion that men can penetrate women scopically by splitting herself into subject and object: as, in act 1, she is both controlling narrator and terrified victim of her own dream (1.2.230–48), in the trial scene she is both the detached observer who offers to "give aim" to guide her enemies' shots and the object of those shots, "at the[ir] mark" (3.2.24). This puts Vittoria, rather than the Cardinal, in control of the object of representation, herself.

Continually focused on the crudely visual spectacle, the Cardinal himself is as deeply implicated in performance as the woman he condemns. Vittoria points out, "It doth not suit a reverend cardinal / To *play* the lawyer thus" (3.2.60–61; emphasis added). In his construction, Vittoria is a "counterfeit" jewel (141) whose adulterous affair "would be played o'th'stage, / But that vice many times finds such loud friends / That preachers are charmed silent" (249–51). The line repays closer examination: from his predictable opening equation of illicit sexuality with promiscuous theater, the Cardinal moves surprisingly to ally himself *with* the theater, an instrument used by "preachers" to expose "vice." His antitheatricality doubles back on itself, as he fashions himself as supporter, rather than opponent, of the stage.

In response, Vittoria foregrounds her own theatricality—theatricality which signals not her hypocrisy but the conditions of performance itself. For the theater can stage only outward signs of inner truths; as Katharine Maus points out, "spectacle depends upon, sometimes betrays, but never fully manifests a truth that remains shrouded, indiscernible, or ambiguous."[33] After insisting on the ambiguity of visible signs, Vittoria significantly lays claim to an interiority that is simply impregnable: "For know that all your strict combined heads, / Which strike against this mine of diamonds, / Shall prove but glassen hammers, they shall break" (3.2.143–45). Vittoria's only real defense against the Cardinal's two-pronged attack is to withdraw into unknowable inwardness, to lay claim to "thoughts" (230) to which outward signs can bear no witness. This interiority is, however, quite different from Hamlet's "that within which passes show" (*Hamlet* 1.2.85), which intimates an "authentic inner reality"[34] or private subjective space. "This mine of diamonds" is defined not by what is within but by what is without—dense and impenetrable, it dazzles the eye of the beholder without giving him a point of access. In other words, Vittoria foregrounds not only the indeterminacy of those signs used to define and incriminate her but also the inaccessibility of subjectivity itself. She thus reappropriates misogynist notions of feminine indeterminacy for her own ends.[35] By fashioning herself as a performer, Vittoria can distance herself from her own self-representation and open a space for her subjectivity, a subjectivity defined by negation and absence, by what cannot be represented. It is hardly surprising that she later withdraws into a silence which defies exegesis (4.2.188). By foregrounding Vittoria's unintelligibility, the play challenges its own production of theatrical spectacle.

Anxiety about theatrical spectacle—its constitutive power, its possible duplicity—haunts *The White Devil* far beyond its representations of gender. The conjurer, for example, before revealing the double murder in dumb show to Bracciano, unexpectedly agonizes about the distinction between his own "strong-commanding art" (2.2.22) and mere "juggling tricks" (14), inauthentic performances. His overanxious insistence on the authenticity of his conjuring betrays an anxiety not only about the tenuous distinction between black and white magic but also about the art of theater itself. After the dumb shows, in which the two murders are played out before his eyes, Bracciano inexplicably remarks: "'Twas quaintly done, but yet each circumstance / I taste not fully" (2.2.38–39). Does his commendation of acts "quaintly done" apply to the murders, or the means of their discovery, and are these separable? Is it nagging uncertainty about the gap between representation and reality that underlies his need for further confirmation? This moment is followed by the conjurer's assurance that the real will immediately impinge on them as guards "come with purpose to apprehend / Your mistress" (48–49), but his words are never confirmed; instead, the stage is cleared and reality elided by theatrical convention. The conjurer's initial distinction between legitimate theater—making the real visible—and illegitimate theater—manufacturing illusion—is made only to be confounded. A similar moment recurs in act 4, when Isabella's ghost is "conjured" by Francisco. Is the ghost in fact an objectively "real" ghost of revenge tragedy erroneously dismissed by a new Machiavellian revenger? Or is the ghost a figment of Francisco's "melancholy" (4.1.108), of "Thought, [which] as a subtle juggler, makes us deem / Things supernatural which have cause / Common as sickness" (4.1.106–8)? The issue is never resolved for the audience. Underlying all this is of course a theatrical joke: such uncertainty imitates theater itself, which is both as real as actors on a stage (the ghost exists) and as illusory as their playing of roles (the ghost never exists). With Flamineo's mock suicide in the final act, Webster daringly forces his audience to confront the constitutive power of illusion when it is finally revealed as mere theater—theater in which pistols never hold bullets and death never occurs, yet in which audience desire and expectation are transformative. Antonelli recognizes this when he advises Lodovico at the opening of the play:

> Perfumes the more they are chafed, the more they render
> Their pleasing scents, and so affliction
> Expresseth virtue fully, whether true,
> Or else adulterate.
>
> (1.1.47–50)

His casual remark hints at the play's underlying trope: that "expression" (literally, the action of pressing out; figuratively, the manifestation or performance) finally effaces distinctions between the "true" and the "adulterate." Outward signs and performances are not only unreliable guides to inner essences, they also transform them, rendering any distinction between enactment and pretense meaningless.

That life itself is theater, theater thus an image of theater, was of course a commonplace of the age. The *theatrum mundi* conceit is pithily expressed by that "laboured and understanding" playwright admired by Webster ("To the Reader," ll. 40–41), Ben Jonson: "I have considered our whole life is like a play, wherein every man, forgetful of himself, is in travail with expression of another. Nay we so insist in imitating others, as we cannot, when it is necessary, return to ourselves."[36] The power inherent in theatrical modes of "self-fashioning" has been frequently emphasized by new historicist critics; recently, however, some critics have exposed the anxieties hinted at by Jonson that inevitably accompany such a contingent construction of identity. Maus argues that "in a culture in which truth is imagined to be inward and invisible . . . theatrical representation becomes subject to profound and fascinating crises of authenticity."[37] Laura Levine attends to the "profound sense of powerlessness" generated by the notion that "things lack or are believed to lack an independent existence apart from their own theatricalizations"; her study identifies such contingency with masculine identity in particular.[38] Theater may actually have dangerous constitutive power, as Jonson suggests. Virtue is "fully" expressed by affliction; whether it is "true" or "adulterate" virtue may be irrelevant. Such fears and fantasies about performance are crucial to *The White Devil* and especially to its representations of gender.

I have argued that *The White Devil* is as theatrically self-aware as its female characters; like them, it pushes anxieties about gender and performance to the surface by exposing all its characters—male and female—as implicated in performance. Furthermore, it challenges the notion that such performances can be easily decoded; rather, they are exposed as contingent on fallible, subjective interpretation. The deepest fear haunting the play is, of course, the fear that there is nothing behind or beneath the performance, no fixed self or gender.[39] *The White Devil* provisionally manages this fear by illuminating performance as a necessary and useful component in the construction of identity. If, in this play, perspectives are shifting and no single reading is definitive, then identity is as fluid and malleable as the performance which "expresseth" it. In Isabella's case, for example, the "piteous and rent heart" (2.1.223) supposed to underlie her "part," is effectively expressed in her decision to "rail and weep" (230); self and performance are effortlessly elided. What we see is a study in the actor's "personation" of his part; while we are always aware of his artifice, if the performance is good we are simultaneously convinced by his "real" passion. However she attempts to close off her performance and reintroduce distinctions between self and part, between silent "killing griefs" (2.1.277) and loquacious tirade, Isabella succeeds only in revealing the constitutive power of theater. Similarly, that Vittoria is invariably remembered in the theater for her heroic posture—for "something fine, proud and wonderfully defiant"[40]—is not accidental: it is proof of the same constitutive power. Her performance actually shapes her identity, if only because we as spectators participate in the shaping.[41] Paradoxically, Vittoria's antitheatricality helps her stage herself successfully. And, though *The White Devil* exposes the theatricality of gender, Bracciano dies like the "princes" (5.3.35) of *de casibus* tragedy and Vittoria can claim she is "too true a woman" (5.6.221) to feel fear at the prospect of death. However, *The White Devil*'s self-consciousness about crossdressing and theater, so often articulated explicitly by Vittoria, should make us aware of the provisional and contingent nature of identity, gender, and performance for all the characters in this play.

Notes

1. Jack Landau, "Elizabethan Art in a Mickey Spillane Setting." *Theatre Arts* 39 (1955); reprinted in *Webster: The White Devil and the Duchess of Malfi: A Casebook*, ed. R. V. Holdsworth (London: Macmillan, 1975), 234.

2. All references to the play are to John Webster, *The White Devil*, ed. Christina Luckyj, The New Mermaids (London: A and C Black, 1996).

3. D. C. Gunby, "Critical Introduction" to *The White Devil*, in *The Works of John Webster*, vol. 1, ed. D. C. Gunby, David Carnegie, Antony Hammond, and Doreen Delvecchio (Cambridge: Cambridge University Press, 1995), 76.

4. Ian Jack, "The Case of John Webster," *Scrutiny* 16 (1949); reprinted in *John Webster: A Critical Anthology*, ed. G. K. Hunter and S. K. Hunter (Harmondsworth: Penguin, 1969), 162.

5. Madeleine Doran, *Endeavors of Art: A Study of Form in Elizabethan Drama* (Madison: University of Wisconsin Press, 1954), 355.

6. Catherine Belsey, *The Subject of Tragedy: Identity and Difference in Renaissance Drama* (London: Methuen, 1985), 160.

7. All references to Shakespeare are from *The Riverside Shakespeare*, ed. G. Blakemore Evans (Boston: Houghton Mifflin, 1974).

8. Heather L. Weidemann, "Theatricality and Female Identity in Mary Wroth's *Urania*," in *Reading Mary Wroth: Representing Alternatives in Early Modern England*, ed. Naomi J. Miller and Gary Waller (Knoxville: University of Tennessee Press, 1991), 194.

9. Joseph Swetnam, *Araignment of lewde, idle, froward, and unconstant women* (London, 1615), 12–13. Webster was fond of the image of the glowworm for the deceptiveness of appearances, and used it twice: in *The White Devil*, Flamineo ironically uses the phrase to praise Mulinassar (the disguised Francisco) for his ability to distinguish reality from illusion (5.1.41–42); in *The Duchess of Malfi*, Bosola repeats it in an attempt to strip the Duchess of her illusions of greatness (4.2.144–45) (John Webster, *The Duchess of Malfi*, ed. Elizabeth M. Brennan, The New Mermaids [London: Ernest Benn, 1964]). In both cases the speaker's own claim to penetrate theatrical appearance to uncover a plainer truth is problematized.

10. Carol Cook makes a similar observation about Shakespeare's *Much Ado about Nothing*: "Masculine privilege is contingent on the legibility of women, and the ambiguous signifying power of women's 'seeming' is the greatest threat to the men of Messina" ("'The Sign and Semblance of Her Honor': Reading Gender Difference in *Much Ado about Nothing*," in *Shakespeare and Gender: A History*, ed. Deborah Barker and Ivo Kamps [London: Verso, 1995], 76).

11. Andrew Gurr, *The Shakespearean Stage, 1574–1642*, 3d ed. (Cambridge: Cambridge University Press, 1992), 99.

12. John Webster, "An Excellent Actor," in *The Complete Works of John Webster*, ed. F. L. Lucas, 4 vols. (London: Chatto and Windus, 1927), 4:43.

13. Gunby, Carnegie, Hammond, and Delvecchio point out that "*personate* was used in widely divergent senses at this time," though they find in its metatheatrical usage an antifeminist agenda: Vittoria is passing herself off fraudulently as a man (*Works of John Webster*, 1:298–99).

14. Much has been written about the potential for subversion when boy actors play women crossdressing as men, particularly in Shakespeare's comedies: see, for example, Jean E. Howard's "Crossdressing, the Theatre and Gender Struggle in Early Modern England" (*Shakespeare Quarterly* 39 [Winter 1988]: 418–40) and Catherine Belsey's "Disrupting Sexual Difference: Meaning and Gender in the Comedies," in *Alternative Shakespeares*, ed. John Drakakis (London: Methuen, 1985), 166–90.

15. Shapiro comments that Flamineo's "suggestion might even be a shared joke among the three characters, along with the spectators, for by 1612 the female page had become a cliché on the English stage" (*Gender in Play on the Shakespearean Stage: Boy Heroines and Female Pages* [Ann Arbor: University of Michigan Press, 1994], 25).

16. Thomas Middleton and William Rowley, *The Changeling*, ed. N. W. Bawcutt (London: Methuen, 1958).

17. *Haec Vir*, while offering a spirited defense of women's right to crossdress, nonetheless ends with a reassertion of the gender hierarchy: "Cast then from you our ornaments and put on your own armor; be men in shape, men in show, men in words, men in actions, men in counsel, men in example" (in *Half Humankind: Contexts and Texts of the*

Controversy about Women in England, 1540–1640, ed. Katherine Usher Henderson and Barbara F. McManus [Urbana: University of Illinois Press, 1985], 288).

18. Sheryl A. Stevenson also notes the moments of female impersonation in *The White Devil,* and suggests that these contribute to a blurring of gender distinctions ("'As Differing as Two Adamants': Sexual Difference in *The White Devil,*" in *Sexuality and Politics in Renaissance Drama,* ed. Carole Levin and Karen Robertson [Lewiston, N.Y.: Edwin Mellen, 1991], 164). Her conclusion, however, differs from mine; she claims that "In Isabella and Vittoria, masculinity becomes a mask which seems at the same time a hidden aspect of self" (166). I am suggesting that, far from turning into men, Isabella and Vittoria problematize both masculinity and notions of a hidden self.

19. Richard Brathwait, *The English Gentlewoman* (London, 1631), 24.

20. Judith Butler, *Gender Trouble: Feminism and the Subversion of Identity* (London: Routledge, 1990), 137.

21. Karen Newman, *Fashioning Femininity and English Renaissance Drama* (Chicago: University of Chicago Press, 1991), 21.

22. *Hic Mulier,* in *Half Humankind,* ed. Usher and McManus, 270.

23. Valerie Lucas, "*Hic Mulier:* The Female Transvestite in Early Modern England," *Renaissance and Reformation* n.s. 12 (1988): 73.

24. Laura Levine, *Men in Women's Clothing: Anti-theatricality and Effeminization, 1579–1642* (Cambridge: Cambridge University Press, 1994), 56.

25. Stevenson points out that "Isabella's duplication of Bracciano's mocking, ceremonial divorce offers evidence that the play's women deliberately mirror men" ("'As Differing as Two Adamants,'" 164).

26. *The Masque of Queenes* in *Ben Jonson,* ed. C. H. Herford et al., 11 vols. (Oxford: Clarendon, 1941), 7:302, l. 365.

27. Suzanne Gossett suggests that in the *Masque of Queenes,* "Perseus represents King James" ("'Man-maid, Begone!': Women in Masques," in *Women in the Renaissance: Selections from "English Literary Renaissance,"* ed. Kirby Farrell, Elizabeth H. Hagemann, and Arthur Kinney [Amherst: University of Massachusetts Press, 1990], 123). If so, there may be some complex ironies at work here: Vittoria crossdresses as King James, who was virulently opposed to real crossdressed women and in 1620 instructed the clergy to inveigh against the practice.

28. The line has often been repunctuated by editors. Both the new Cambridge edition (*Works of John Webster,* vol. 1, ed. Gunby, Carnegie, Hammond, and Delvecchio) and John Russell Brown's Revels edition of *The Duchess of Malfi* (London: Methuen, 1964), following Lucas, add a break in the line so that it reads "Must personate masculine virtue—to the point!" (3.2.136). The unbroken line in the quarto, however, heightens its theatrical self-consciousness.

29. Giovanni is still a child, and so his dependence on women is childishly and charmingly overt, even as he dons the apparel and attitudes of early modern men (just illustrated in the swaggering confrontation between Francisco and Bracciano). Coppélia Kahn comments on the "disparity between men's social dominance and their peculiar emotional

vulnerability to women" in the construction of early modern manhood (*Man's Estate: Masculine Identity in Shakespeare* [Berkeley and Los Angeles: University of California Press, 1981], 12).

30. I thank Brian Gibbons for bringing this to my attention.

31. David Bevington, *Action Is Eloquence: Shakespeare's Language of Gesture* (Cambridge, Mass.: Harvard University Press, 1984), 96.

32. Gurr points out that Renaissance playwrights "valued their poetry much more than the 'shows' of the common stage, and consequently rated hearing far above seeing as the vital sense for the playgoer" (*Playgoing in Shakespeare's London* [Cambridge: Cambridge University Press, 1987], 85).

33. Katharine Eisaman Maus, *Inwardness and Theater in the English Renaissance* (Chicago: University of Chicago Press, 1995), 210.

34. Catherine Belsey, *The Subject of Tragedy: Identity and Difference in Renaissance Drama* (London: Methuen, 1985), 41.

35. Elizabeth Harvey points out that "there is a difference between being consigned to a marginalized position by the patriarchal order and voluntarily (and self-consciously) occupying that position as a strategy for subverting the dominant discourse" (*Ventriloquized Voices: Feminist Theory and English Renaissance Texts* [London: Routledge, 1992], 57).

36. Jonson, "Timber, or Discoveries," in *Ben Jonson,* ed. Ian Donaldson (Oxford: Oxford University Press, 1985), 551.

37. Maus, *Inwardness and Theater,* 32.

38. Levine, *Men in Women's Clothing,* 7, 70–71.

39. This fear is one of the central concerns discussed by Levine.

40. Benedict Nightingale, "Snared by a Sinister World," *The Times,* 19 June 1991, 18. Nightingale is praising Josette Simon's Vittoria in the 1991 National Theatre production directed by Philip Prowse.

41. The claim I am making here for Webster's demand that his audience recognize both the constitutive power of theater and its deceptive instability is similar to Dena Goldberg's argument: "And just as the play warns us not to believe everything we hear or see, it demands, nonetheless, that we make a judgment of some kind. To demand that an audience be both active and skeptical in relation to one's own play is remarkable in itself and is asking a great deal, even of a Jacobean audience" ("'By Report': The Spectator as Voyeur in Webster's *The White Devil,*" *English Literary Renaissance* 17 [Winter 1987]: 84).

Bibliography

Primary Sources

Aristotle. *The Works of Aristotle.* Trans. E. S. Forster. Vol. 7. Oxford: Clarendon Press, 1927.

Banister, John. *The Historie of Man.* London, 1578. STC 1359.

Batman uppon Bartholome. London, 1582.

Bawcutt, N. W. "New Revels Documents of Sir George Buc and Sir Henry Herbert." *Review of English Studies* n.s. 35 (1984): 316–31.

Beaumont, Francis, and John Fletcher. *The Dramatic Works in the Beaumont and Fletcher Canon.* Gen. ed. Fredson Bowers. 7 vols. Cambridge: Cambridge University Press, 1966–89.

Bodin, Jean. *Method for the Easy Comprehension of History.* Trans. Beatrice Reynolds. New York: Columbia University Press, 1945.

———. *The Six Bookes of a Commonweale* (1606). Ed. Kenneth Douglas McRae. Trans. Richard Knolles. Cambridge, Mass.: Harvard University Press, 1962.

Borde, Andrew. *The Fyrst Boke of the Introduction of Knowledge* (1548). London: Early English Text Society, 1870.

Brackley, Elizabeth. "True Coppies of certaine Loose Papers left by ye Right honourable Elizabeth, Countesse of Bridgewater, Collected and Transcribed together here since her Death Anno Dom. 1663." BL Egerton 607.

Brathwait, Richard. *The English Gentlewoman.* London, 1631.

Brome, Richard. *A Critical Edition of Brome's "The Northern Lasse".* Ed. Harvey Freid. New York: Garland, 1980.

———. *The Dramatic Works of Richard Brome Containing Fifteen Comedies.* 3 vols. London: Pearson, 1873.

Browne, Thomas. *The Works of Sir Thomas Browne.* Ed. Geoffrey Keynes. Vol. 2. Chicago: University of Chicago Press, 1963.

Bulwer, John. *Anthropometamorphosis: Man Transform'd; Or, The Artificial Changeling.* London, 1650.

Burton, Robert. *The Anatomy of Melancholy.* Oxford, 1621.

Calendar of State Papers, Domestic Series, Of the Reign of Charles I, 1627–1628 (1858). Reprint. Nendeln, Liechtenstein: Kraus, 1967.

Cary, Elizabeth. *The Tragedy of Mariam the Fair Queen of Jewry.* Ed. Barry Weller and Margaret W. Ferguson. Berkeley and Los Angeles: University of California Press, 1994.

Cavendish, Jane, and Elizabeth Brackley. "Poems, Songs, a Pastorall and a Play by the Right Honourable Lady Jane Cavendish and Lady Elizabeth Brackley." Bod. Rawl. MS Poet, 16.

Cavendish, Margaret. *The Life of William Cavendish, First Duke of Newcastle* (1667). In *The Lives of William Cavendish, Duke of Newcastle, and of his Wife, Margaret Duchess of Newcastle,* ed. Mark Anthony Lower. London: John Russell Smith, 1872.

Cerasano, S. P., and Marion Wynne-Davies, eds. *Renaissance Drama by Women: Texts and Documents.* London: Routledge, 1996.

Certain Sermons or Homilies Appointed to be Read in Churches in the Time of Queen Elizabeth. Oxford, 1683.

Charron, Pierre. *Of Wisdome.* Trans. Samson Lennard. Amsterdam: Scholars' Facsimiles, 1971.

Chauliac, Guy de. *The Cyrurgie of Guy de Chauliac.* Ed. Margaret S. Ogden. Early English Text Society. [Oxford: Oxford University Press, 1971.]

Cibber, Colley. *An Apology for the Life of Mr. Colley Cibber.* 2 vols. London: John C. Nimmo, 1889.

Cokayne, George Edward. *The Complete Peerage.* 1910. Rev. Vicary Gibbs. London: St. Catherine Press, 1959.

Coryate, Thomas. *Coryate's Crudities.* London, 1611.

Crooke, Helkiah. *Microcosmographia. A Description of the Body of Man.* London, 1618.

Cupid's Banishment: A Masque Presented to her Majesty by the Young Gentlewomen of the Ladies Hall, Deptford, May 4, 1617. Ed. C. E. McGee. *Renaissance Drama* n.s. 19 (1988): 227–64.

Davies, Sir John. Prefatory Letter. *The Muses Sacrifice.* London, 1612.

Dekker, Thomas. *The Non-Dramatic Works of Thomas Dekker.* Ed. Alexander B. Grosart. 5 vols. 1884–86. Reprint. New York: Russell and Russell, 1963.

Du Laurens, Andre. *A Discourse of the Preservation of the Sight: of Melancholike Diseases; of Rhuemes, and of Old Age.* Trans. Richard Surphlet. Oxford, 1599.

Ferrand, Jacques. *Treatise on Lovesickness* (1623). Ed. and trans. Donald A. Beecher and Massimo Ciavolella. Syracuse, N.Y.: Syracuse University Press, 1990.

Ford, John. *The Lover's Melancholy.* Ed. R. F. Hill. Manchester: Manchester University Press, 1985.

Freud, Sigmund. *Collected Papers.* Trans. Joan Riviere. 5 vols. New York: Basic Books, 1959.

———. *The Standard Edition of the Complete Psychological Works of Sigmund Freud.* Ed. and trans. James Strachey. 24 vols. London: Hogarth Press, 1953–73.

Galen, Claudius. *Opera Omnia.* Ed. C. G. Kühn. Vols. 1 and 2. Leipzig, 1821.

Garzoni, Tomasso. *The Hospitall of Incurable Fooles.* Trans. E. Blount. London, 1600.

Gataker, Thomas. *Certain Sermons First Preached and After Published, at severall Times.* London, 1637.

[Goldoni, Carlo.] *Memoires of Carlo Goldoni*. Ed. William A. Drake. Trans. John Black. New York: Knopf, 1926.

Gosson, Stephen. *The Schoole of Abuse*. New York: Da Capo Press, 1972 [facsimile reprint of 1579 edition].

Gouge, William. *Of Domesticall Duties: Eight Treatises*. London, 1622.

Goulart, Simon. *Admirable and Memorable Histories Containing the Wonders of Our Time*. Trans. Edward Grimeston. London, 1607.

Greer, Germaine, et al., eds. *Kissing the Rod: An Anthology of Seventeenth-Century Women's Verse*. London: Virago, 1988.

Guillemeau, Jacques. *Child-birth, or The Happy Deliverie of Women*. London: Hatfield, 1612.

Haec-Vir: or The Womanish-Man: Being An Answere to a late Booke intituled Hic-Mulier. In *Half Humankind: Contexts and Texts of the Controversy about Women in England, 1540–1640*, ed. Katherine Usher Henderson and Barbara F. McManus, 277–89. Urbana: University of Illinois Press, 1985.

Harrison, William. *The Description of England* (1587). In vol. 1 of *Holinshed's Chronicles of England, Scotland, and Ireland*. 6 vols. London, 1807–8.

[Herbert, Sir Henry.] *The Control and Censorship of Caroline Drama: The Records of Sir Henry Herbert, Master of the Revels, 1623–73*. Ed. N. W. Bawcutt. Oxford: Clarendon Press, 1996.

Hic Mulier; or, the Man-Woman: Being a Medicine to cure the Coltish Disease of the Staggers in the Masculine-Feminines of our Times, Expressed in a brief Declamation. In *Half Humankind: Contexts and Texts of the Controversy about Women in England, 1540–1640*, ed. Katherine Usher Henderson and Barbara F. McManus, 264–76. Urbana: University of Illinois Press, 1985.

Highfill, Philip H., Kalman A. Burnim, and Edward A. Langhans. *A Biographical Dictionary of Actors, Actresses, Musicians, Dancers, Managers, and Other Stage Personnel in London, 1660–1800*. 17 vols. Carbondale: Southern Illinois University Press, 1984.

Hippocratic Writings. Ed. G. E. R. Lloyd. Trans. J. Chadwick and W. N. Mann. London: Penguin, 1978.

Howard, Christopher. *Sir John Yorke of Nidderdale, 1565–1634*. London: Sheed and Ward, 1939.

Huarte, Juan. *Examen de ingenios, The Examination of mens Wits*. Englished by R. Carew. Printed by A. Islip for R. Watkins, 1594. STC 13890.

———. *The Examination of Men's Wits* (1594). Trans. Richard Carew. Gainesville, Fla.: Scholars' Facsimiles and Reprints, 1959.

Jonson, Ben. *Ben Jonson*. Ed. C. H. Herford et al. 11 vols. Oxford: Clarendon Press, 1925–52.

———. *Ben Jonson*. Ed. Ian Donaldson. Oxford: Oxford University Press, 1985.

———. *Ben Jonson's Plays and Masques*. Ed. Robert Adams. New York: Norton, 1979.

———. *Ben Jonson: The Complete Masques*. Ed. Stephen Orgel. New Haven: Yale University Press, 1969.

———. *Epicoene*. Ed. R. V. Holdsworth. London: Benn, 1979.

Jorden, Edward. *A Briefe Discourse of a Disease called the Suffocation of the Mother*. London, 1603. STC reel 757.

Josephus, Flavius. *The Antiquities of the Jews.* Trans. Thomas Lodge. London, 1602.
Judges, A. V. *The Elizabethan Underworld: A Collection of Tudor and Early Stuart Tracts and Ballads.* London: George Routledge, 1930.
Klein, Joan Larsen. *Daughters, Wives, and Widows: Writings by Men about Women and Marriage in England, 1500–1640.* Urbana: University of Illinois Press, 1992.
Kyd, Thomas. *The Works of Thomas Kyd.* Ed. Frederick S. Boas. Rev. ed. Oxford: Clarendon Press, 1955.
Lacan, Jacques. "Desire and the Interpretation of Desire in *Hamlet.*" Trans. James Hulbert. In *Literature and Psychoanalysis: The Question of Reading: Otherwise,* ed. Shoshana Felman. *Yale French Studies* 55/56 (1977): 11–52.
———. *Écrits: A Selection.* Trans. Alan Sheridan. New York: Norton, 1977.
———. *Feminine Sexuality: Jacques Lacan and the École Freudienne.* Ed. Juliet Mitchell and Jacqueline Rose. Trans. Jacqueline Rose. New York: Norton, 1982.
———. *The Four Fundamental Concepts of Psycho-Analysis.* Ed. Jacques-Alain Miller. Trans. Alan Sheridan. New York: Norton, 1981.
———. "Introduction to the Names-of-the-Father Seminar." Trans. Jeffrey Mehlman. *October* 40 (1987): 81–95.
———. *The Seminar of Jacques Lacan: Book II: The Ego in Freud's Theory and in the Technique of Psychoanalysis 1954–1955.* Ed. Jacques-Alain Miller. Trans. Sylvana Tomaselli. New York: Norton, 1988.
The Lady Falkland: Her Life. In *The Tragedy of Mariam the Fair Queen of Jewry,* ed. Barry Weller and Margaret W. Ferguson, 183–275. Berkeley and Los Angeles: University of California Press, 1994.
Lally, Steven, ed. *The Aeneid of Thomas Phaer and Thomas Twyne* (1584). Reprint. New York: Garland, 1987.
Lambarde, William. *The Duties of Constables [,] Borsholders, Tithing Men.* London, 1583.
Lemnius, Levinus. *The Touchstone of Complexions.* Trans. Thomas Newton. London, 1581.
Longueville, T[homas]. *Falklands.* London: Longman, Green, and Co., 1897.
Mandeville's Travels. Ed. and trans. Malcolm Letts. Vol. 1. London: Hakluyt Society, 1953.
Marlowe, Christopher. *The Tragedie of Dido Queene of Carthage.* In vol. 1 of *The Complete Works of Christopher Marlowe,* ed. Roma Gill. Oxford: Clarendon Press; New York: Oxford University Press, 1987.
Middleton, Thomas, and William Rowley. *The Changeling.* Ed. N. W. Bawcutt. London: Methuen, 1958.
Milles, Thomas. *The Treasurie of Auncient and Moderne Times.* London, 1613.
Montaigne, Michel de. *The Complete Essays of Montaigne.* Trans. Donald M. Frame. Stanford: Stanford University Press, 1965.
Moryson, Fynes. *Shakespeare's Europe: Unpublished Chapters of Fynes Moryson's Itinerary.* Ed. Charles Hughes. London: Sherratt and Hughes, 1903.
Nashe, Thomas. *Pierce Pennilesse His Supplication to the Divill.* In *The Works of Thomas Nashe,* ed. Ronald B. McKerrow. 5 vols. London: Sidgwick and Jackson, 1910.
Nichols, John. *The Progresses, Processions, and Magnificent Festivities, of King James the First,*

His Royal Consort, Family and Court. 4 vols. London: Printed by and for J. B. Nichols, 1828.

Nietzsche, Friedrich. *The Birth of Tragedy, and The Case of Wagner*. Trans. Walter Kaufmann. New York: Vintage, 1967.

North Riding Record Society. *Quarter Sessions Records*. Ed. J. C. Atkinson. Vol. 1. London, 1884.

Ovid. *Publius Ovidius Naso: The XV Bookes Entytuled Metamorphosis*. Trans. Arthur Golding. London, 1567. STC 18956. Reprint. Amsterdam: Walter J. Johnson and Theatrum Orbis, 1977.

Peacham, Henry. *The Complete Gentleman [1622], The Truth of Our Times [1638], and The Art of Living in London [1642]*. Ed. Virgil B. Heltzel. Ithaca: Cornell University Press, 1962.

Plato. *The Collected Dialogues of Plato*. Ed. Edith Hamilton and Huntington Cairns. Princeton: Princeton University Press, 1961.

Plutarch. "Of the Naturall Love or Kindnes of Parents to their Children." In *The Philosophie, Commonlie Called The Morals*, trans. Philemon Holland. London, 1603.

The "Problemes" of Aristotle. London: Arnold Hatfied, 1597. STC 764.

Prynne, William. *Histrio-Mastix: The Player's Scourge or Actor's Tragedy* (1633). New York: Garland, 1974.

Raynold, Thomas. *The Byrth of Mankynde, Otherwise Named The Womans Booke*. London, 1545.

Records of Early English Drama: Lancashire. Ed. David George. Toronto: University of Toronto Press, 1991.

Records of Early English Drama: Norwich. Ed. David Galloway. Toronto: University of Toronto Press, 1991.

Richards, Kenneth, and Laura Richards. *The Commedia dell'Arte: A Documentary History*. London: Basil Blackwell for the Shakespeare Head Press, 1990.

Sandys, George. *Ovid's Metamorphoses English'd*. Oxford, 1632.

Sanesi, Ireneo. *La Commedia*. 2d ed. Milan: Villardi, 1954.

Scot, Reginald. *The Discoverie of Witchcraft*. London, 1584.

Shakespeare, William. *The Complete Works*. Ed. Stanley Wells and Gary Taylor. Oxford: Clarendon Press, 1988.

———. *Much Ado about Nothing*. Ed. Sheldon P. Zitner. Oxford: Oxford University Press, 1994.

———. *The Pelican Shakespeare*. Ed. Alfred Harbage. New York: Viking Press, 1977.

———. *The Riverside Shakespeare*. Ed. G. Blakemore Evans. Boston: Houghton Mifflin, 1974. 2d ed. 1997.

———. *William Shakespeare: The Complete Works*. Ed. Alfred Harbage. Baltimore: Penguin, 1969.

Sidney, Philip. *An Apology for Poetry*. Ed. Geoffrey Shepherd. London: Nelson, 1965.

Spevack, Marvin, ed. *A New Variorum Edition of Shakespeare: Antony and Cleopatra*. New York: Modern Language Association of America, 1990.

Statius, Publius Papinius. *Statius.* Trans. J. H. Mozley. 2 vols. London: Heinemann; New York: Putnam's, 1928.

Swetnam, Joseph. *The Araignment of Lewde, Idle, Froward and Unconstant Women or the Vanity of Them, Choose you Whether.* London, 1615.

Tacitus. *The Agricola and the Germania.* Trans. H. Mattingly and S. A. Handford. Middlesex: Penguin, 1970.

Townshend, Aurelian. *The Poems and Masques.* Ed. Cedric C. Brown. Reading, Eng.: Whiteknights Press, 1983.

Vaughan, William. *Approved Directions for Health, both Naturall and Artificiall.* London, 1612.

Vicary, Thomas. *The Anatomie of the Bodie of Man.* Ed. Frederick J. Furnivall and Percy Furnivall. Early English Text Society, e.s. 53. 1888. Reprint. Millwood, N.Y.: Kraus, 1975.

Virgil. *Aeneis.* In *The Aeneid of Thomas Phaer and Thomas Twyne [1584]: A Critical Edition,* ed. Steven Lally. New York: Garland, 1987.

Walkington, Thomas. *The Opticke Glasse of Humors. Wherein the Foure Complections are Succinctly Painted Forth.* London, 1607.

———. *The Opticke Glasse of Humors* (1631). New York: Scholars' Facsimiles, 1981.

Webster, John. *The Complete Works of John Webster.* Ed. F. L. Lucas. 4 vols. 1927. Reprint. London: Chatto and Windus, 1966.

———. *The Duchess of Malfi.* Ed. John Russell Brown. London: Methuen, 1964.

———. *The White Devil.* Ed. Christina Luckyj. New Mermaids. London: A and C Black, 1996.

———. *The Works of John Webster.* Ed. D. C. Gunby et al. Vol. 1. Cambridge: Cambridge University Press, 1995.

Whately, William. *A Bride-Bush or A Wedding Sermon.* London, 1617. STC 25296.

Wilson, Jean. *Entertainments for Elizabeth I.* Woodbridge: D. S. Brewer, 1980.

Wright, Thomas. *The Passions of the Mind in General* (1604). Ed. William Webster Newbold. New York: Garland, 1986.

Secondary Sources

Adams, Parveen. "A Note on the Distinction between Sexual Division and Sexual Differences." In *The Woman in Question,* ed. Parveen Adams and Elizabeth Cowie, 102–9. London: Verso; Cambridge, Mass.: MIT Press, 1990.

Adelman, Janet. *The Common Liar: An Essay on "Antony and Cleopatra."* New Haven: Yale University Press, 1973.

———. *Suffocating Mothers: Fantasies of Maternal Origin in Shakespeare, "Hamlet" to "The Tempest."* London: Routledge, 1992.

Aers, David. *Community, Gender, and Individual Identity: English Writing 1360–1430.* New York: Routledge, 1988.

Amussen, Susan Dwyer. *An Ordered Society: Gender and Class in Early Modern England.* Oxford: Basil Blackwell, 1988.

Anderson, Michael. "Making Room: Commedia and the Privatisation of the Theatre." In *The Commedia Dell'Arte from the Renaissance to Dario Fo,* ed. Christopher Cairns, 74–97. Italian Origins of European Theatre 6. Papers of the Conference of the Society for Italian Studies, Nov. 1988. Lewiston, N.Y.: Edwin Mellen Press, 1989.

Anderson, Ruth Leila. *Elizabethan Psychology and Shakespeare's Plays.* New York: Russell and Russell, 1966.

Andrews, Jonathan. "Bedlam Revisited: A History of Bethlem Hospital 1634–1770." Ph.D. diss., Queen Mary and Westfield College, London University, 1991.

Andrews, Richard. *Scripts and Scenarios: The Performance of Comedy in Renaissance Italy.* Cambridge: Cambridge University Press, 1992.

Asp, Caroline. "*Love's Labour's Lost:* Language and the Deferral of Desire." *Literature and Psychoanalysis* 35, no. 3 (1989): 1–21.

Aveling, Hugh. *Northern Catholics: The Catholic Recusants of the North Riding of Yorkshire, 1558–1790.* London: Geoffrey Chapman, 1966.

Babb, Lawrence. *The Elizabethan Malady: A Study of Melancholia in English Literature from 1580 to 1642.* East Lansing: Michigan State College Press, 1951.

Bakhtin, Mikhail. *Rabelais and His World.* Trans. Hélène Iswolsky. 1965. Reprint. Bloomington: Indiana University Press, 1984.

Ballaster, Ros. "The First Female Dramatists." In *Women and Literature in Britain, 1500–1700,* ed. Helen Wilcox, 267–90. Cambridge: Cambridge University Press, 1996.

Barasch, Frances. "Francesquina, the Transvestite Clown and Shakespeare's Maidservants." Paper presented at the World Shakespeare Congress, Tokyo, 1991.

Barish, Jonas. "Language for the Study; Language for the Stage." In *The Elizabethan Theatre, XII,* ed. A. L. Magnusson and C. E. McGee, 37–43. Streetsville, Ont.: P. D. Meany, 1993.

Barkan, Leonard. *Transuming Passion: Ganymede and the Erotics of Humanism.* Stanford: Stanford University Press, 1991.

Barker, Deborah, and Ivo Kamps, eds. *Shakespeare and Gender: A History.* London: Verso, 1995.

Barroll, Leeds. *Politics, Plague, and Shakespeare's Theater.* Ithaca: Cornell University Press, 1991.

Bartels, Emily. *Spectacles of Strangeness: Imperialism, Alienation, and Marlowe.* Philadelphia: University of Pennsylvania Press, 1993.

Baswell, Christopher. *Virgil in Medieval England: Figuring the "Aeneid" from the Twelfth Century to Chaucer.* Cambridge: Cambridge University Press, 1995.

Beecher, Donald A. "Antiochus and Stratonice: The Heritage of a Medico-Literary Motif in the Theatre of the English Renaissance." *Seventeenth Century* 5, no. 2 (1990): 113–32.

Beeman, William O. "Mimesis and Travesty in Iranian Traditional Theatre." In *Gender in Performance: The Presentation of Difference in the Performing Arts,* ed. Laurence Senelick, 14–25. Hanover, N.H.: University Press of New England, 1992.

Beier, A. L. *Masterless Men: The Vagrancy Problem in England, 1560–1640.* London: Methuen, 1985.

Beilin, Elaine V. *Redeeming Eve: Women Writers of the English Renaissance.* Princeton: Princeton University Press, 1987.

Belsey, Catherine. "Disrupting Sexual Difference: Meaning and Gender in the Comedies." In *Alternative Shakespeares,* ed. John Drakakis, 166–90. London: Methuen, 1985.

———. *The Subject of Tragedy: Identity and Difference in Renaissance Drama.* London: Methuen, 1985.

Bentley, Gerald Eades. *The Jacobean and Caroline Stage.* 7 vols. Oxford: Clarendon Press, 1941–68.

———. *The Profession of Player in Shakespeare's Time, 1590–1642.* Princeton: Princeton University Press, 1984.

———. "The Salisbury Court Theater and Its Boy Players." *Huntington Library Quarterly* 40 (Feb. 1977): 129–49.

Bernal, Martin. *Black Athena: The Afroasiatic Roots of Classical Civilization.* Vol. 1: *The Fabrication of Ancient Greece, 1785–1985.* New Brunswick, N.J.: Rutgers University Press, 1987.

Bevington, David. *Action Is Eloquence: Shakespeare's Language of Gesture.* Cambridge, Mass.: Harvard University Press, 1984.

———. *From "Mankind" to Marlowe: Growth and Structure in the Popular Drama of Tudor England.* Cambridge, Mass.: Harvard University Press, 1962.

———. *Tudor Drama and Politics: A Critical Approach to Topical Meaning.* Cambridge, Mass.: Harvard University Press, 1968.

Binns, J. W. "Women or Transvestites on the Elizabethan Stage? An Oxford Controversy." *Sixteenth Century Journal* 5 (Summer 1974): 95–120.

Bliss, Lee. *The World's Perspective: John Webster and the Jacobean Drama.* Sussex: Harvester, 1983.

Boas, F. S. *Christopher Marlowe: A Biographical and Critical Study.* Oxford: Clarendon Press, 1940.

Bogatyrëv, Peter, and Roman Jakobson. "Folklore as a Special Form of Creativity." Trans. Manfred Jacobson. In *The Prague School: Selected Writings, 1929–1946,* ed. Peter Steiner, 34–46. Austin: University of Texas Press, 1982.

Bossy, John. *The English Catholic Community, 1570–1850.* New York: Oxford University Press, 1976.

Braden, Gordon. *Renaissance Tragedy and the Senecan Tradition: Anger's Privilege.* New Haven: Yale University Press, 1985.

Brantley, Ben. "How to Call a Play into Being by Smearing a Man with Mud." *New York Times,* 6 Oct. 1994, sec. C, 17.

Bray, Alan. "Homosexuality and the Signs of Male Friendship in Elizabethan England." *History Workshop Journal* 29 (Spring 1990): 1–19.

———. *Homosexuality in Renaissance England.* London: Gay Men's Press, 1982.

Bredbeck, Gregory W. "B/O—Barthes's Text/O'Hara's Trick." *Publications of the Modern Language Association of America* 108 (Mar. 1993): 268–82.

———. *Sodomy and Interpretation: Marlowe to Milton.* Ithaca: Cornell University Press, 1991.

Brooke, C. F. Tucker. *The Life of Marlowe and "The Tragedy of Dido Queen of Carthage."* Vol. 1 of *The Works and Life of Christopher Marlowe.* Ed. R. H. Case. London: Methuen, 1930–33.

Brown, Cedric C. "Courtesies of Place and Arts of Diplomacy in Ben Jonson's Last Two Entertainments for Royalty." *Seventeenth Century* 9 (Autumn 1994): 147–71.

Bullough, Vern L. *Sex, Society, and History.* New York: Science History Publications, 1976.

Butler, Judith. "Against Proper Objects." *Differences: More Gender Trouble: Feminism Meets Queer Theory* 6 (Summer/Fall 1994): 1–26.

———. *Bodies That Matter: On the Discursive Limits of "Sex."* New York: Routledge, 1993.

———. *Gender Trouble: Feminism and the Subversion of Identity.* New York: Routledge, 1990.

———. "Performative Acts and Gender Constitution: An Essay in Phenomenology and Feminist Theory." 1988. Reprinted in *Performing Feminisms: Feminist Critical Theory and Theatre,* ed. Sue-Ellen Case, 270–82. Baltimore: Johns Hopkins University Press, 1990.

Cady, Joseph. "'Masculine Love,' Renaissance Writing, and the 'New' Invention of Homosexuality." *Journal of Homosexuality* 23, nos. 1 and 2 (1992): 9–40.

Calderwood, James L. *To Be and Not to Be: Negation and Metadrama in "Hamlet."* New York: Columbia University Press, 1983.

Callaghan, Dympna. "The Equine Phallus and the Fantasy of Female Spectatorship." Paper presented at the Shakespeare Association of America Conference, Washington, D.C., 1997.

———. "Re-Reading Elizabeth Cary's *The Tragedie of Mariam, Faire Queene of Jewry.*" In *Women, "Race," and Writing in the Early Modern Period,* ed. Margo Hendricks and Patricia Parker, 163–77. London: Routledge, 1994.

Canby, Vincent. "As You Like It." *New York Times,* 16 Oct. 1994, sec. 2, 5.

Cantor, Paul A. *Shakespeare's Rome: Republic and Empire.* Ithaca: Cornell University Press, 1976.

Cartelli, Thomas. *Marlowe, Shakespeare, and the Economy of Theatrical Experience.* Philadelphia: University of Pennsylvania Press, 1991.

Case, Sue-Ellen, ed. *Performing Feminisms: Feminist Critical Theory and Theatre.* Baltimore: Johns Hopkins University Press, 1990.

Castagno, Paul C. *The Early "Commedia dell'Arte" (1550–1621).* American University Studies series 26, Theatre Arts 13. New York: Peter Lang, 1994.

Cawley, Robert Ralston. *The Voyagers and Elizabethan Drama.* London: Oxford University Press, 1938.

Chambers, E[dmund] K[erchever]. *The Elizabethan Stage.* 4 vols. Oxford: Clarendon Press, 1923.

Chaney, Joseph. "Promises, Promises: *Love's Labor's Lost* and the End of Shakespearean Comedy." *Criticism* 35 (Winter 1993): 41–65.

Chaplin, Joyce. "Natural Philosophy and an Early Racial Idiom in North America: Comparing English and Indian Bodies." *William and Mary Quarterly* 54 (1997): 229–52.

Charlton, H[enry] B[uckley]. *The Senecan Tradition in Renaissance Tragedy: A Re-issue of an Essay Published in 1921.* Manchester: Manchester University Press, 1946.

Chase, Cynthia. "'Transference' as Trope and Persuasion." In *Discourse in Psychoanalysis and Literature,* ed. Shlomith Rimmon-Kenan, 211–32. London: Methuen, 1987.

Cixous, Hélène. "Castration or Decapitation." Trans. Annette Kuhn. *Signs* 7, no. 1 (1981): 41–55.

Clément, Catherine. *The Lives and Legends of Jacques Lacan.* Trans. Arthur Goldhammer. New York: Columbia University Press, 1983.

Cohen, Walter. *Drama of a Nation: Public Theater in Renaissance England and Spain.* Ithaca: Cornell University Press, 1985.

———. "Political Criticism of Shakespeare." In *Shakespeare Reproduced: The Text in History and Ideology,* ed. Jean E. Howard and Marion F. O'Connor, 18–46. New York: Methuen, 1987.

Collier, J. P. *History of English Dramatic Poetry and Annals of the Stage.* London, 1831.

Cook, Ann Jennalie. *The Privileged Playgoers of Shakespeare's England.* Princeton: Princeton University Press, 1981.

Cook, Carol. "'The Sign and Semblance of Her Honor': Reading Gender Difference in *Much Ado about Nothing.*" In *Shakespeare and Gender: A History,* ed. Deborah Barker and Ivo Kamps, 75–103. London: Verso, 1995.

Copjec, Joan, ed. *Supposing the Subject.* London: Verso, 1994.

Corliss, Richard. "Something to Sing About: A Very Traditional British Cast Finds Rapture in *As You Like It.*" *Time* 144 (12 Dec. 1994): 84.

Crewe, Jonathan. "In the Field of Dreams: Transvestitism in *Twelfth Night* and *The Crying Game.*" *Representations* 50 (Spring 1995): 101–21.

Cunliffe, John W. *Early English Classical Tragedies.* Oxford: Clarendon Press, 1912.

Curtius, Ernst Robert. *European Literature in the Latin Middle Ages.* New York: Bollingen, 1953.

D'Amico, Jack. *The Moor in English Renaissance Drama.* Tampa, Fla.: University of South Florida Press, 1991.

Danby, John. "*Antony and Cleopatra:* A Shakespearean Adjustment." In *New Casebooks: Antony and Cleopatra,* ed. John Drakakis, 33–55. New York: St. Martin's Press, 1994.

Dannenfeldt, Karl H. "Egypt and Egyptian Antiquities in the Renaissance." *Studies in the Renaissance* 6 (1959): 7–27.

Davies, H. Neville. "Jacobean *Antony and Cleopatra.*" In *New Casebooks: Antony and Cleopatra,* ed. John Drakakis, 126–65. New York: St. Martin's Press, 1994.

Davies, Kathleen M. "The Sacred Condition of Equality: How Original Were Puritan Doctrines of Marriage?" *Social History* 5 (1977): 563–80.

Davies, Natalie Zemon. *Society and Culture in Early Modern France.* London: Duckworth, 1975.

Diamond, Elin. "Mimesis, Mimicry, and the 'True-Real.'" *Modern Drama* 32 (Mar. 1989): 58–72.

Dixon, Suzanne. *The Roman Mother.* Norman: University of Oklahoma Press, 1988.

Dolan, Frances E. *Dangerous Familiars: Representations of Domestic Crime in England, 1550–1700.* Ithaca: Cornell University Press, 1994.

———. "Taking the Pencil out of God's Hand: Art, Nature, and the Face-Painting Debate in Early Modern England." *Publications of the Modern Language Association of America* 108 (Mar. 1993): 224–39.
Doran, Madeleine. *Endeavors of Art: A Study of Form in Elizabethan Drama.* Madison: University of Wisconsin Press, 1954.
Dover, Kenneth. "Greek Homosexuality and Initiation." In *Homosexuality in the Ancient World,* ed. Wayne R. Dynes and Stephen Donaldson, 127–46. Studies in Homosexuality 1. New York: Garland, 1992.
Drakakis, John. "'Fashion It Thus': *Julius Caesar* and the Politics of Theatrical Representation." In *Materialist Shakespeare,* ed. Ivo Kamps, 280–91. London: Verso, 1995.
———, ed. *New Casebooks: Antony and Cleopatra.* New York: St. Martin's Press, 1994.
Dubrow, Heather. "Friction and Faction: New Directions for New Historicism." *Monatshefte* 84 (Summer 1992): 212–19.
———. "Navel Battles: Interpreting Renaissance Gynecological Manuals." *American Notes and Queries* n.s. 5 (1992): 67–71.
Duchartre, Pierre Louis. *The Italian Comedy.* Trans. Randolph T. Weaver. New York: Dover, 1966.
Dusinberre, Juliet. *Shakespeare and the Nature of Women.* New York: Macmillan, 1975.
Eccles, Audrey. *Obstetrics and Gynaecology in Tudor and Stuart England.* Kent, Ohio: Kent State University Press, 1982.
Edwards, Philip. Introduction to *The Spanish Tragedy,* by Thomas Kyd, i–lxx. The Revels Plays. London: Methuen, 1959.
Ellis, Havelock. "Christopher Marlowe." In *Christopher Marlowe,* ed. Havelock Ellis, xxix–xlviii. London: Unwin; New York: Scribner's [1903].
Emmison, F. G. *Elizabethan Life.* 5 vols. Chelmsford: Essex County Council, 1970–80.
Epstein, Julia. "Either/Or—Neither/Both: Sexual Ambiguity and the Ideology of Gender." *Genders* 7 (Spring 1990): 99–142.
Erickson, Peter. *Patriarchal Structures in Shakespeare's Drama.* Berkeley and Los Angeles: University of California Press, 1985.
Esslin, Martin. *The Field of Drama.* London: Methuen, 1987.
Ezell, Margaret J. M. *The Patriarch's Wife: Literary Evidence and the History of the Family.* Chapel Hill: University of North Carolina Press, 1987.
———. "'To Be Your Daughter in Your Pen': The Social Functions of Literature in the Writings of Lady Elizabeth Brackley and Lady Jane Cavendish." *Huntington Library Quarterly* 51 (Autumn 1988): 281–96.
Ferguson, Margaret W. "A Room Not Their Own: Renaissance Women as Readers and Writers." In *The Comparative Perspective on Literature: Approaches to Theory and Practice,* ed. Clayton Koelb and Susan Noake, 93–116. Ithaca: Cornell University Press, 1988.
———. "Running On with Almost Public Voice: The Case of 'E. C.'" In *Tradition and the Talents of Women,* ed. Florence Howe, 37–67. Urbana: University of Illinois Press, 1991.
Ferris, Lesley. *Acting Women: Images of Women in the Theatre.* New York: New York University Press, 1989.

Findlay, Alison. "'She Gave You the Civility of the House': Household Performance in *The Concealed Fancies.*" In *Readings in Renaissance Women's Drama,* ed. Susan P. Cerasano and Marion Wynne-Davies. Forthcoming, London: Routledge.

Findlay, Alison, Stephanie Hodgson-Wright, and Gweno Williams. "'The Play Is Ready to Be Acted': Women and Dramatic Production 1570–1670." *Early Modern Women Dramatists.* Special issue of *Women's Writing,* ed. Marion Wynne-Davies (forthcoming 1998).

Fink, Z. S. "Milton and the Theory of Climatic Influence." *Modern Language Quarterly* 2 (1941): 67–80.

Finke, Laurie A. "Painting Women: Images of Femininity in Jacobean Tragedy." In *Performing Feminisms: Feminist Critical Theory and Theatre,* ed. Sue-Ellen Case, 223–36. Baltimore: Johns Hopkins University Press, 1990.

Fischer, Sandra K. "Elizabeth Cary and Tyranny, Domestic and Religious." In *Silent but for the Word: Tudor Women as Patrons, Translators, and Writers of Religious Works,* ed. Margaret Patterson Hannay, 225–37. Kent, Ohio: Kent State University Press, 1985.

Ford, John. *The Lover's Melancholy.* Ed. R. F. Hill. Manchester: Manchester University Press, 1985.

Foucault, Michel. *The History of Sexuality.* Trans. Robert Hurley. 3 vols. 1978. Reprint. New York: Vintage, 1978–87.

———. *Madness and Civilization: A History of Insanity in the Age of Reason.* Trans. Richard Howard. New York: Vintage, 1988.

Freer, Coburn. "Mary Sidney: Countess of Pembroke." In *Women Writers of the Renaissance and Reformation,* ed. Katharina M. Wilson, 481–90. Athens: University of Georgia Press, 1987.

Gagnier, Regenia. "Feminist Postmodernism: The End of Feminism or the Ends of Theory?" In *Theoretical Perspectives on Sexual Difference,* ed. Deborah L. Rhode, 21–30. New Haven: Yale University Press, 1990.

Gallop, Jane. *Reading Lacan.* Ithaca: Cornell University Press, 1985.

Garber, Marjorie. *Vested Interests: Cross-Dressing and Cultural Anxiety.* New York: Routledge, 1992.

Gash, Anthony. "Carnival against Lent: The Ambivalence of Medieval Drama." In *Medieval Literature: Criticism, Ideology, and History,* ed. David Aers, 74–98. Brighton: Harvester Press, 1986.

Gellrich, Jesse. *The Idea of the Book in the Middle Ages: Language Theory, Mythology, and Fiction.* Ithaca: Cornell University Press, 1985.

Gilder, Rosamund. *Enter the Actress: The First Women in the Theatre.* Boston: Houghton Mifflin, 1931.

Gildersleeve, Virginia. *Government Regulation of the Elizabethan Drama.* New York: Columbia University Press, 1908.

Gillies, John. *Shakespeare and the Geography of Difference.* Cambridge: Cambridge University Press, 1994.

Glacken, Clarence J. *Traces on the Rhodian Shore: Nature and Culture in Western Thought from Ancient Times to the End of the Eighteenth Century.* Berkeley and Los Angeles: University of California Press, 1967.

Gohlke, Madelon. "'I Wooed Thee with My Sword': Shakespeare's Tragic Paradigms." In *Representing Shakespeare: New Psychoanalytic Essays,* ed. Murray M. Schwartz and Coppélia Kahn, 170–87. Baltimore: Johns Hopkins University Press, 1980.
Goldberg, Dena. "'By Report': The Spectator as Voyeur in Webster's *The White Devil.*" *English Literary Renaissance* 17 (Winter 1987): 67–84.
Goldberg, Jonathan. *Sodometries: Renaissance Texts, Modern Sexualities.* Stanford: Stanford University Press, 1992.
Gossett, Suzanne. "'Man-maid, Begone!': Women in Masques." *English Literary Renaissance* 18 (Winter 1988): 96–113. Reprinted in *Women in the Renaissance: Selections from English Literary Renaissance,* ed. Kirby Farrell, Elizabeth H. Hagemann, and Arthur Kinney, 118–35. Amherst: University of Massachusetts Press, 1990.
Gras, Henk. "All Is Semblative a Woman's Part?" Ph.D. diss., University of Utrecht, 1991.
Grazia, Margreta de. "The Motive for Interiority: Shakespeare's *Sonnets* and *Hamlet.*" *Style: Texts and Pretexts in the English Renaissance* 23 (Fall 1989): 430–44.
Greenblatt, Stephen. *Renaissance Self-Fashioning: From More to Shakespeare.* Chicago: University of Chicago Press, 1980.
———. *Shakespearean Negotiations: The Circulation of Social Energy in Renaissance England.* Berkeley and Los Angeles: University of California Press, 1988.
Grosz, Elizabeth. *Jacques Lacan: A Feminist Introduction.* London: Routledge, 1990.
Gueguen, Pierre-Gilles. "Transference as Deception." In *Reading Seminar XI: Lacan's Four Fundamental Concepts of Psychoanalysis,* ed. Richard Feldstein, Bruce Fink, and Maire Jaanus, 77–90. Albany: State University of New York Press, 1995.
Gurr, Andrew. *Playgoing in Shakespeare's London.* Cambridge: Cambridge University Press, 1987.
———. *The Shakespearean Playing Companies.* Oxford: Clarendon Press, 1996.
———. *The Shakespearean Stage, 1574–1642.* 2d ed. Cambridge: Cambridge University Press, 1980. 3d ed., 1992.
Gutierrez, Nancy A. "Valuing *Mariam:* Genre Study and Feminist Analysis." *Tulsa Studies in Women's Literature* 10 (Fall 1991): 233–51.
Hall, Kim F. *Things of Darkness: Economies of Race and Gender in Early Modern England.* Ithaca: Cornell University Press, 1995.
Haller, William, and Melville Haller. "The Puritan Art of Love." *Huntington Library Quarterly* 5 (Jan. 1941–42): 235–72.
Hallett, Charles A., and Elaine S. Hallett. *The Revenger's Madness: A Study of Revenge Tragedy Motifs.* Lincoln: University of Nebraska Press, 1980.
Halperin, David M. *One Hundred Years of Homosexuality and Other Essays on Greek Love.* New York: Routledge, 1990.
Harbage, Alfred. *Shakespeare and the Rival Traditions.* New York: Macmillan, 1952.
———. *Shakespeare's Audience.* 1941. Reprint. New York: Columbia University Press, 1958.
Harris, Jonathan Gil. "'Narcissus in Thy Face': Roman Desire and the Difference It Fakes in *Antony and Cleopatra.*" *Shakespeare Quarterly* 45 (Winter 1994): 408–25.
Harvey, Elizabeth D. *Ventriloquized Voices: Feminist Theory and English Renaissance Texts.* London: Routledge, 1992.

Hasler, P. W., ed. *The House of Commons, 1558–1603*. 3 vols. London: Published for the History of Parliament Trust by H.M.S.O., 1981.

Havelock, Eric. *Preface to Plato*. Cambridge, Mass.: Harvard University Press, Belknap Press, 1963.

Heilbrun, Carolyn. "The Character of Hamlet's Mother." *Shakespeare Quarterly* 8 (Autumn 1957): 201–6.

Heise, Ursula K. "Transvestism and the Stage Controversy in Spain and England, 1580–1680." *Theatre Journal* 44 (Oct. 1992): 357–74.

Heller, Thomas C., et al., eds. *Reconstructing Individualism: Autonomy, Individuality, and the Self in Western Thought*. Stanford: Stanford University Press, 1986.

Herrup, Cynthia. "Law and Morality in Seventeenth Century England." *Past and Present* 106 (Feb. 1985): 102–23.

Hexter, Ralph. "Sidonian Dido." In *Innovations of Antiquity*, ed. Ralph Hexter and Daniel Selden, 332–84. New York: Routledge, 1992.

Hillebrand, Harold N. *The Child Actors*. 1926. Reprint. New York: Russell and Russell, 1964.

Holderness, Graham, Nick Potter, and John Turner. *Shakespeare out of Court: Dramatizations of Court Society*. New York: St. Martin's Press, 1990.

Hopkins, Lisa. "Judith Shakespeare's Reading: Teaching *The Concealed Fancies*." *Shakespeare Quarterly* 47 (Winter 1996): 396–406.

Hotson, Leslie. *The Commonwealth and Restoration Stage*. Cambridge, Mass.: Harvard University Press, 1928.

Howard, Jean E. "Crossdressing, the Theatre, and Gender Struggle in Early Modern England." *Shakespeare Quarterly* 39 (Winter 1988): 418–40.

———. "Scripts and Playhouses: Ideological Production and the Renaissance Public Stage." In *The Matter of Difference: Materialist Feminist Criticism of Shakespeare,* ed. Valerie Wayne, 221–36. Ithaca: Cornell University Press, 1991.

———. *The Stage and Social Struggle in Early Modern England*. New York: Routledge, 1994.

Howe, Elizabeth. *The First English Actresses: Women and Drama, 1660–1770*. Cambridge: Cambridge University Press, 1992.

Hunt, Maurice. "The Double Figure of Elizabeth in *Love's Labor's Lost*." *Essays in Literature* 19 (Fall 1992): 173–92.

Ingram, Martin. *Church Courts, Sex, and Marriage in England, 1570–1640*. Cambridge: Cambridge University Press, 1987.

———. "Ridings, Rough Music and Mocking Rhymes in Early Modern England." In *Popular Culture in Seventeenth-Century England,* ed. Barry Reay, 129–63. London: Routledge, 1988.

Irigaray, Luce. "The Female Gender." In *Sexes and Genealogies,* trans. Gillian C. Gill, 105–23. 1987. Reprint. New York: Columbia University Press, 1993.

———. *Speculum of the Other Woman*. Trans. Gillian C. Gill. Ithaca: Cornell University Press, 1985.

———. *This Sex Which Is Not One*. Trans. Catherine Porter and Carolyn Burke. Ithaca: Cornell University Press, 1985.

Jaanus, Maire. "The *Démontage* of the Drive." In *Reading Seminar XI: Lacan's Four Fundamental Concepts of Psychoanalysis,* ed. Richard Feldstein, Bruce Fink, and Maire Jaanus, 119–36. Albany: State University of New York Press, 1995.

Jack, Ian. "The Case of John Webster." *Scrutiny* 16 (1949). Reprinted in *John Webster: A Critical Anthology,* ed. G. K. Hunter and S. K. Hunter, 157–64. Harmondsworth: Penguin, 1969.

Jameson, Fredric. *Marxism and Form.* Princeton: Princeton University Press, 1971.

———. *The Political Unconscious: Narrative as a Socially Symbolic Act.* Ithaca: Cornell University Press, 1981.

Jardine, Alice. *Gynesis: Configurations of Woman and Modernity.* Ithaca: Cornell University Press, 1985.

Jardine, Lisa. *Still Harping on Daughters: Women and Drama in the Age of Shakespeare.* Sussex: Harvester Press, 1983. Reprint. New York: Columbia University Press, 1989.

———. "Twins and Travesties: Gender, Dependency and Sexual Availability in *Twelfth Night.*" In *Erotic Politics: Desire on the Renaissance Stage,* ed. Susan Zimmerman, 27–38. New York: Routledge, 1992.

Jed, Stephanie H. *Chaste Thinking: The Rape of Lucretia and the Birth of Humanism.* Bloomington: Indiana University Press, 1989.

Jondorf, Gillian. *Robert Garnier and the Themes of Political Tragedy in the Sixteenth Century.* Cambridge: Cambridge University Press, 1969.

Jones, Ann, and Peter Stallybrass. "Fetishizing Gender: Constructing the Hermaphrodite in Renaissance Europe." In *Body Guards: The Cultural Politics of Gender Ambiguity,* ed. Julia Epstein and Kristina Straub, 80–111. New York: Routledge, 1991.

Jordan, Winthrop. *White over Black: American Attitudes toward the Negro, 1550–1812.* Chapel Hill: University of North Carolina Press, 1968.

Kahn, Coppélia. *Man's Estate: Masculine Identity in Shakespeare.* Berkeley and Los Angeles: University of California Press, 1981.

Kamps, Ivo. "Materialist Shakespeare: An Introduction." In *Materialist Shakespeare: A History,* ed. Ivo Kamps, 1–19. London: Verso, 1995.

Kastan, David Scott. *Shakespeare and the Shapes of Time.* Hanover, N.H.: University Press of New England, 1982.

Kehler, Dorothea. "Jaquenetta's Baby's Father: Recovering Paternity in *Love's Labor's Lost.*" *Renaissance Papers* (1990): 45–54.

Keller, Evelyn Fox. *Reflections on Gender and Science.* New Haven: Yale University Press, 1985.

Kernan, Alvin B. "Shakespearian Comedy and Its Courtly Audience." In *Comedy from Shakespeare to Sheridan: Change and Continuity in the English and European Dramatic Tradition,* ed. A. R. Braunmuller and J. C. Bulman, 91–101. Newark: University of Delaware Press, 1986.

Kesler, R. L. "The Idealization of Women: Morphology and Change in Three Renaissance Texts." *Mosaic* 23 (Spring 1990): 107–26.

———. "Time and Causality in Renaissance Revenge Tragedy." *University of Toronto Quarterly* 59 (Summer 1990): 474–87.

King, T. J. *Casting Shakespeare's Plays: London Actors and Their Roles.* Cambridge: Cambridge University Press, 1992.

Kofman, Sarah. *The Enigma of Woman: Woman in Freud's Writings.* Trans. Catherine Porter. Ithaca: Cornell University Press, 1985.

Kolve, V. A. *The Play Called "Corpus Christi."* Stanford: Stanford University Press, 1966.

Konstan, David, and Martha Nussbaum, eds. *Sexuality in Greek and Roman Society.* Special issue of *Differences* 2, no. 1 (1990).

Kristeva, Julia. *Desire in Language: A Semiotic Approach to Literature and Art.* Ed. Leon S. Roudiez. Trans. Thomas Gora, Alice Jardine, and Leon S. Roudiez. New York: Columbia University Press, 1980.

———. *Tales of Love.* Trans. Leon S. Roudiez. New York: Columbia University Press, 1987.

Krontiris, Tina. *Oppositional Voices: Women as Writers and Translators of Literature in the English Renaissance.* London: Routledge, 1992.

Landau, Jack. "Elizabethan Art in a Mickey Spillane Setting." *Theatre Arts* 39 (1955). Reprinted in *Webster: The White Devil and the Duchess of Malfi: A Casebook,* ed. R. V. Holdsworth, 233–35. London: Macmillan, 1975.

Lanier, Henry Wysham. *The First English Actresses.* New York: Players, 1930.

Laplanche, Jean. *Life and Death in Psychoanalysis.* Trans. Jeffrey Mehlman. Baltimore: Johns Hopkins University Press, 1976.

Laqueur, Thomas. *Making Sex: Body and Gender from the Greeks to Freud.* Cambridge, Mass.: Harvard University Press, 1990.

———. "Orgasm, Generation, and the Politics of Reproductive Biology." *Representations* 14 (Spring 1986): 1–41.

Lea, Kathleen M. *Italian Popular Comedy.* 2 vols. Oxford: Clarendon Press, 1934.

Leavenworth, Russell E. *Daniel's "Cleopatra": A Critical Study.* Salzburg: Institut für Englische Sprache und Literatur, 1974.

Lee, Jonathan Scott. *Jacques Lacan.* Amherst: University of Massachusetts Press, 1991.

Levin, Richard. "Women in the Renaissance Theatre Audience." *Shakespeare Quarterly* 40 (Summer 1989): 165–74.

Levine, Laura. *Men in Women's Clothing: Anti-Theatricality and Effeminization, 1579–1642.* Cambridge: Cambridge University Press, 1994.

———. "Men in Women's Clothing: Anti-Theatricality and Effeminization from 1579 to 1642." *Criticism* 28 (Spring 1986): 121–43.

Lewalski, Barbara Kiefer. *Writing Women in Jacobean England.* Cambridge, Mass.: Harvard University Press, 1993.

Leys, M. D. R. *Catholics in England, 1559–1829: A Social History.* London: Camelot Press, 1961.

Loomba, Ania. "The Color of Patriarchy." In *Women, "Race," and Writing in the Early Modern Period,* ed. Margo Hendricks and Patricia Parker, 17–34. London: Routledge, 1994.

———. *Gender, Race, Renaissance Drama.* Manchester: Manchester University Press, 1989.

Lorde, Audre. *Sister Outsider: Essays and Speeches.* New York: Crossing Press, 1984.

Lucas, Valerie R. "*Hic Mulier:* The Female Transvestite in Early Modern England." *Renaissance and Reformation* n.s. 12 (1988): 65–84.

———. "Puritan Preaching and the Politics of the Family." In *The Renaissance Englishwoman in Print: Counterbalancing the Canon,* ed. Anne M. Haselkorn and Betty S. Travitsky, 224–40. Amherst: University of Massachussetts Press, 1990.

MacCallum, M. W. *Shakespeare's Roman Plays and Their Background.* London: Macmillan, 1910.

MacCannell, Juliet Flower. *Figuring Lacan: Criticism and the Cultural Unconscious.* London: Croom Helm, 1986.

MacDonald, Joyce Green. "Sex, Race, and Empire in Shakespeare's *Antony and Cleopatra.*" *Literature and History* 5, no. 1 (1996): 60–77.

MacDougall, Hugh A. *Racial Myth in English History: Trojans, Teutons, and Anglo-Saxons.* Hanover, N.H.: University Press of New England, 1982.

MacInnes, Ian. "Decoding Cold Blood: Climate Theory and Military Science in *Henry V.*" Paper presented at annual meeting, Shakespeare Association of America, Chicago, Mar. 1995.

Maclean, Ian. *The Renaissance Notion of Woman: A Study in the Fortunes of Scholasticism and Medical Science in European Intellectual Life.* Cambridge: Cambridge University Press, 1980.

MacLean, Sally-Beth. "Tour Routes: 'Provincial Wanderings' or Traditional Circuits?" *Medieval and Renaissance Drama in England* 6 (1993): 1–14.

MacLure, Millar, ed. *Christopher Marlowe: The Critical Heritage, 1588–1896.* London: Routledge, 1979.

Marshall, Cynthia. "Man of Steel Done Got the Blues: Melancholic Subversion of Presence in *Antony and Cleopatra.*" *Shakespeare Quarterly* 44 (Winter 1993): 385–408.

Martindale, Charles, and Michelle Martindale. *Shakespeare and the Uses of Antiquity: An Introductory Essay.* London: Routledge, 1990.

Maus, Katharine Eisaman. *Inwardness and Theater in the English Renaissance.* Chicago: University of Chicago Press, 1995.

———. "'Playhouse Flesh and Blood': Sexual Ideology and the Restoration Actress." *ELH* 46 (Winter 1979): 595–617.

———. "Transfer of Title in *Love's Labour's Lost:* Language, Individualism, Gender." In *Shakespeare Left and Right,* ed. Ivo Kamps, 205–23. New York: Routledge, 1991.

———. "A Womb of His Own: Male Renaissance Poets in the Female Body." In *Sexuality and Gender in Early Modern Europe: Institutions, Texts, Images,* ed. James Grantham Turner, 266–88. Cambridge: Cambridge University Press, 1993.

McGee, C. E., and John C. Meagher. "Preliminary Checklist of Tudor and Stuart Entertainments: 1485–1558." *Research Opportunities in Renaissance Drama* 25 (1982): 31–114.

———. "Preliminary Checklist of Tudor and Stuart Entertainments: 1588–1603." *Research Opportunities in Renaissance Drama* 24 (1981): 51–155.

———. "Preliminary Checklist of Tudor and Stuart Entertainments: 1603–1613." *Research Opportunities in Renaissance Drama* 27 (1984): 47–126.

———. "Preliminary Checklist of Tudor and Stuart Entertainments: 1614–1625." *Research Opportunities in Renaissance Drama* 30 (1988): 17–128.

McGill, Kathleen. "Women and Performance: The Development of Improvisation by the Sixteenth-Century Commedia dell'Arte." *Theatre Journal* 43 (Mar. 1991): 59–69.

McKendrick, Melveena. *Theatre in Spain, 1490–1700*. Cambridge: Cambridge University Press, 1989.

McLuskie, Kathleen. "The Act, the Role, and the Actor: Boy Actresses on the Elizabethan Stage." *New Theatre Quarterly* 3 (May 1987): 120–30.

———. "The Patriarchal Bard: Feminist Criticism and Shakespeare." In *Political Shakespeare: New Essays in Cultural Materialism*, ed. Jonathan Dollimore and Alan Sinfield, 88–108. Ithaca: Cornell University Press, 1985.

Merchant, Carolyn. *The Death of Nature: Women, Ecology and the Scientific Revolution*. San Francisco: Harper, 1980.

Miner, Earl. *The Cavalier Modes from Jonson to Cotton*. Princeton: Princeton University Press, 1971.

Miola, Robert S. *Shakespeare's Rome*. Cambridge: Cambridge University Press, 1983.

Moi, Toril. *Sexual/Textual Politics*. London: Routledge, 1985.

Mullaney, Steven. *The Place of the Stage: License, Play, and Power in the Drama of Shakespeare and His Contemporaries*. Chicago: University of Chicago Press, 1988.

Murdock, Kenneth. *The Sun at Noon: Three Biographical Sketches*. New York: Macmillan, 1939.

Neely, Carol Thomas. "Constructing Female Sexuality in the Renaissance: Stratford, London, Windsor, Vienna." In *Feminism and Psychoanalysis*, ed. Richard Feldstein and Judith Roof, 209–29. Ithaca: Cornell University Press, 1989.

———. "The Cultural Re-gendering of Madness in Early Modern England: The History of Case Histories and the Jailor's Daughter's Cure." Paper presented at the seminar on Shakespeare and the Arts of Healing. Annual Meeting of the Shakespeare Association of America, Atlanta, 1993.

———. "Feminist Modes of Shakespearean Criticism: Compensatory, Justificatory, Transformational." *Women's Studies* 9, no. 1 (1981): 3–15.

———. "Women and Men in *Othello*: 'What should such a fool / Do with so good a woman?'" In *The Woman's Part: Feminist Criticism of Shakespeare*, ed. Carolyn Ruth Swift Lenz, Gayle Greene, and Carol Thomas Neely, 211–39. Urbana: University of Illinois Press, 1980.

Nelson, Alan. "Cross-dressing in English Renaissance Theatre: Business as Usual." Paper presented at the Sixteenth Century Studies Conference, St. Louis, Mo., 1993.

———. "Women in the Audience of the Cambridge Plays." *Shakespeare Quarterly* 41 (Fall 1990): 333–36.

Newman, Karen. *Fashioning Femininity and English Renaissance Drama*. Chicago: University of Chicago Press, 1991.

Nightingale, Benedict. "Snared by a Sinister World." *The Times*, 19 June 1991: 18.

Novy, Marianne. "Shakespeare's Female Characters as Actors and Audience." In *The*

Woman's Part: Feminist Criticism of Shakespeare, ed. Carolyn Ruth Swift Lenz, Gayle Greene, and Carol Thomas Neely, 256–70. Urbana: University of Illinois Press, 1980.

Nyquist, Mary. "'Profuse, Proud Cleopatra': 'Barbarism' and Female Rule in Early Modern English Republicanism." *Women's Studies: An Interdisciplinary Journal* 24, nos. 1–2 (1994): 85–130.

Oliver, H. J. Introduction to Christopher Marlowe, *Dido, Queen of Carthage* and *The Massacre at Paris,* ed. H. J. Oliver, xix–xxvi. The Revels Plays. Cambridge, Mass.: Harvard University Press, 1968.

Orgel, Stephen. *Impersonations: The Performance of Gender in Shakespeare's England.* Cambridge: Cambridge University Press, 1996.

———. *The Jonsonian Masque.* Cambridge, Mass.: Harvard University Press, 1965.

———. "Nobody's Perfect: Or Why Did the English Stage Take Boys for Women?" *South Atlantic Quarterly* 88 (Winter 1989): 7–29.

———. "The Subtexts of *The Roaring Girl.*" In *Erotic Politics: Desire on the Renaissance Stage,* ed. Susan Zimmerman, 12–26. New York: Routledge, 1992.

Osborne, Laurie. "Female Audience and Female Authority in *The Knight of the Burning Pestle.*" *Exemplaria* 3 (Fall 1991): 491–518.

Ovid. *Publius Ovidius Naso: The XV Bookes Entytuled Metamorphosis.* Trans. Arthur Golding. London, 1567. STC 18956. Reprint. Amsterdam: Walter J. Johnson and Theatrum Orbis Terrarum, 1977.

Panofsky, Erwin. *Studies in Iconology: Humanistic Themes in the Art of the Renaissance.* New York: Harper and Row, 1962.

Park, Katharine, and Robert A. Nye. "Destiny Is Anatomy." *New Republic,* 18 Feb. 1991: 53–57.

Parker, Andrew, and Eve Kosofsky Sedgwick. "Introduction: Performativity and Performance." In *Performativity and Performance,* ed. Parker and Sedgwick, 1–18. New York: Routledge, 1995.

Parker, Patricia. "Gender Ideology, Gender Change: The Case of Marie Germain." *Critical Inquiry* 19 (Winter 1993): 337–64.

———. "Romance and Empire: Anachronistic *Cymbeline.*" In *Unfolded Tales: Essays on Renaissance Romance,* ed. George M. Logan and Gordon Teskey, 189–207. Ithaca: Cornell University Press, 1989.

Paster, Gail Kern. *The Body Embarrassed: Drama and the Disciplines of Shame in Early Modern England.* Ithaca: Cornell University Press, 1993.

———. "The Unbearable Coldness of Women: Women's Imperfection in the Humoral Economy." *English Literary Renaissance* (forthcoming in December 1998).

Patterson, Annabel. *Shakespeare and the Popular Voice.* Oxford: Basil Blackwell, 1989.

Payne, Deborah C. "Reified Object or Emergent Professional? Retheorizing the Restoration Actress." In *Cultural Reading of Restoration and Eighteenth-Century English Theater,* ed. J. Douglas Canfield and Deborah C. Payne, 13–38. Athens: University of Georgia Press, 1992.

Perry, Henry Ten Eyck. *The First Duchess of Newcastle and Her Husband as Figures in Literary History.* Boston: Ginn, 1918.

Purdie, Edna. "Jesuit Drama." In *Oxford Companion to the Theatre,* ed. Phyllis Hartnoll. 3d ed. Oxford: Oxford University Press, 1967.
Quaife, G. R. *Wanton Wenches and Wayward Wives.* London: Helm, 1979.
Quilligan, Maureen. "Staging Gender: William Shakespeare and Elizabeth Cary." In *Sexuality and Gender in Early Modern Europe: Institutions, Texts, Images,* ed. James Grantham Turner, 208–32. Cambridge: Cambridge University Press, 1993.
Quint, David. *Epic and Empire: Politics and Generic Form from Virgil to Milton.* Princeton: Princeton University Press, 1993.
Raber, Karen L. "Gender and the Political Subject in *The Tragedy of Mariam.*" *Studies in English Literature 1500–1600* 35 (Spring 1995): 321–43.
Rackin, Phyllis. "Androgyny, Mimesis, and the Marriage of the Boy Heroine on the English Renaissance Stage." *Publications of the Modern Language Association of America* 102 (Jan. 1987): 29–41.
———. "Historical Difference/Sexual Difference." In *Privileging Gender in Early Modern England,* ed. Jean R. Brink, 37–63. Sixteenth Century Essays and Studies 23. Kirksville, Mo.: Sixteenth Century Journal Publishers, 1993.
———. "Shakespeare's Boy Cleopatra, the Decorum of Nature, and the Golden World of Poetry." *Publications of the Modern Language Association of America* 87 (Mar. 1972): 201–12.
Ragland-Sullivan, Ellie. *Jacques Lacan and the Philosophy of Psychoanalysis.* Urbana: University of Illinois Press, 1986.
Randall, Dale B. J. *Winter Fruit: English Drama, 1642–1660.* Lexington: University Press of Kentucky, 1995.
———. *Jonson's Gypsies Unmasked: Background and Theme of "The Gypsies Metamorphos'd."* Durham, N.C.: Duke University Press, 1975.
Rappaport, Steve. *Worlds within Worlds: Structures of Life in Sixteenth-Century London.* Cambridge: Cambridge University Press, 1989.
Rastall, Richard. "Female Bodies in All-Male Casts." *Medieval English Theatre* 7 (1985): 28–35.
Richards, Sandra. *The Rise of the English Actress.* New York: St. Martin's Press, 1993.
Richlin, Amy. *The Garden of Priapus: Sexuality and Aggression in Roman Humor.* Rev. ed. New York: Oxford University Press, 1992.
Rose, Mary Beth. *The Expense of Spirit: Love and Sexuality in English Renaissance Drama.* Ithaca: Cornell University Press, 1988.
———. "Where Are the Mothers in Shakespeare? Options for Gender Representation in the English Renaissance." *Shakespeare Quarterly* 42 (Fall 1991): 291–314.
———. "Women in Men's Clothing: Apparel and Social Stability in *The Roaring Girl.*" *English Literary Renaissance* 14 (Autumn 1984): 367–91.
Roselli, John. "The Castrati as a Professional Group and a Social Phenomenon." *Acta Musicologica* 60 (1988); fasc. 2 (May-August): 143–79.
Ross, Thomas W. Introduction to *The Spanish Tragedy,* by Thomas Kyd, ed. Thomas W. Ross, 1–10. Fountainwell Drama Texts. Berkeley and Los Angeles: University of California Press, 1968.

Saslow, James. *Ganymede in the Renaissance: Homosexuality in Art and Society.* New Haven: Yale University Press, 1986.
Schelling, Felix E. *Elizabethan Drama, 1558–1642.* Vols. 1 and 2. New York: Russell and Russell, 1908.
———. *English Drama.* London: Dent, 1914.
Schiesari, Juliana. *The Gendering of Melancholia: Feminism, Psychoanalysis, and the Symbolics of Loss in Renaissance Literature.* Ithaca: Cornell University Press, 1992.
Schleiner, Winfried. *Melancholy, Genius, and Utopia in the Renaissance.* Wiesbaden: Harrassowitz, 1991.
———. "Prospero as a Renaissance Therapist." *Literature and Medicine* 6 (1987): 54–60.
Scott, Joan W. "Gender: A Useful Category of Historical Analysis." *American Historical Review* 91 (Dec. 1986): 1053–75.
Sedgwick, Eve Kosofsky. *Between Men: English Literature and Male Homosocial Desire.* New York: Columbia University Press, 1985.
Senelick, Laurence, ed. *Gender in Performance: The Presentation of Difference in the Performing Arts.* Hanover, N.H.: University Press of New England, 1992.
Sergent, Bernard. *Homosexuality in Greek Myth.* Trans. Arthur Goldhammer. Boston: Beacon Press, 1986.
Shannon, Laurie J. "*The Tragedie of Mariam:* Cary's Critique of the Terms of Founding Social Discourses." *English Literary Renaissance* 24 (Winter 1994): 135–53.
Shapiro, Michael. *Children of the Revels: The Boy Companies of Shakespeare's Time and Their Plays.* New York: Columbia University Press, 1977.
———. *Gender in Play on the Shakespearean Stage: Boy Heroines and Female Pages.* Ann Arbor: University of Michigan Press, 1994.
Shepherd, Simon. *Marlowe and the Politics of Elizabethan Theatre.* New York: St. Martin's Press, 1986.
Shepherdson, Charles. "The *Role* of Gender and the *Imperative* of Sex." In *Supposing the Subject,* ed. Joan Copjec, 158–84. London: Verso, 1994.
Shergold, N. D. *A History of the Spanish Stage.* Oxford: Clarendon Press, 1967.
Shumaker, Wayne. *The Occult Sciences in the Renaissance: A Study in Intellectual Patterns.* Berkeley and Los Angeles: University of California Press, 1972.
Sinfield, Alan. *Faultlines: Cultural Materialism and the Politics of Dissident Reading.* Berkeley and Los Angeles: University of California Press, 1992.
Singh, Jyotsna. "Renaissance Antitheatricality, Antifeminism, and Shakespeare's *Antony and Cleopatra.*" *Renaissance Drama* n.s. 20 (1989): 99–121.
Siraisi, Nancy G. *Medieval and Early Renaissance Medicine.* Chicago: University of Chicago Press, 1990.
Skinner, Marilyn. *Reading Dido: Gender, Textuality, and the Medieval Aeneid.* Minneapolis: University of Minnesota Press, 1994.
Slack, Paul. *Poverty and Policy in Tudor and Stuart England.* London: Longman, 1988.
Slater, Miriam. *Family Life in the Seventeenth Century: The Verneys of Claydon House.* London: Routledge and Kegan Paul, 1984.

Smith, Bruce R. *Homosexual Desire in Shakespeare's England: A Cultural Poetics.* Chicago: University of Chicago Press, 1991.

Snell, K. D. M. *Annals of the Labouring Poor.* Cambridge: Cambridge University Press, 1988.

Snowden, Frank M., Jr. *Before Color Prejudice: The Ancient View of Blacks.* Cambridge, Mass.: Harvard University Press, 1983.

Snyder, Susan. "*Othello* and the Conventions of Romantic Comedy." *Renaissance Drama* n.s. 5 (1972): 123–41.

Sprengnether, Madelon. "The Boy Actor and Femininity in *Antony and Cleopatra.*" In *Shakespeare's Personality,* ed. Norman N. Holland et al., 191–205. Berkeley and Los Angeles: University of California Press, 1989.

Stallybrass, Peter. "Patriarchal Territories: The Body Enclosed." In *Rewriting the Renaissance: The Discourses of Sexual Difference in Early Modern Europe,* ed. Margaret W. Ferguson et al., 123–42. Chicago: University of Chicago Press, 1986.

———. "Reading the Body: *The Revenger's Tragedy* and the Jacobean Theater of Consumption." *Renaissance Drama* n.s. 18 (1987): 121–48.

———. "Transvestism and the 'Body Beneath': Speculating on the Boy Actor." In *Erotic Politics: Desire on the Renaissance Stage,* ed. Susan Zimmerman, 64–83. New York: Routledge, 1992.

Stallybrass, Peter, and Allon White. *The Politics and Poetics of Transgression.* London: Methuen, 1986.

Starr, Nathan Comfort. "*The Concealed Fansyes:* A Play by Lady Jane Cavendish and Lady Elizabeth Brackley." *Publications of the Modern Language Association of America* 46 (1931): 802–38.

Stevenson, Sheryl A. "'As Differing as Two Adamants': Sexual Difference in *The White Devil.*" In *Sexuality and Politics in Renaissance Drama,* ed. Carole Levin and Karen Robertson, 159–74. Lewiston, N.Y.: Mellen, 1991.

Stokes, James. "The Wells Cordwainers Show: New Evidence Concerning Guild Entertainments in Somerset." *Comparative Drama* 19 (Winter 1985–86): 332–46.

Straznicky, Marta. "'Profane Stoical Paradoxes': *The Tragedie of Mariam* and Sidnean Closet Drama." *English Literary Renaissance* 24 (Winter 1994): 104–33.

Straub, Kristina. *Sexual Suspects: Eighteenth-Century Players and Sexual Ideology.* Princeton: Princeton University Press, 1992.

Streett, J. B. "The Durability of Boy Actors." *Notes and Queries* 218 (1973): 461–65.

Tennenhouse, Leonard. *Power on Display: The Politics of Shakespeare's Genres.* New York: Methuen, 1986.

Thomas, Edward. Introduction to *The Plays of Christopher Marlowe,* vii–xv. London: Dent, 1909.

Thomas, Keith. "Women and the Civil War Sects." *Past and Present* 13 (1958): 42–62.

Thomas, Vivian. *Shakespeare's Roman Worlds.* London: Routledge, 1989.

Thompson, Ann. "Women/'Women' and the Stage." In *Women and Literature in Britain 1500–1700,* ed. Helen Wilcox, 100–116. Cambridge: Cambridge University Press, 1996.

Tomlinson, Sophie. "She That Plays the King: Henrietta Maria and the Threat of the Actress in Caroline Culture." In *The Politics of Tragicomedy: Shakespeare and After,* ed. Gordon McMullan and Jonathan Hope, 189–207. London: Routledge, 1992.

Traub, Valerie. *Desire and Anxiety: Circulations of Sexuality in Shakespearean Drama.* London: Routledge, 1992.

———. "The (In)significance of 'Lesbian' Desire in Early Modern England." In *Erotic Politics: Desire on the Renaissance Stage,* ed. Susan Zimmerman, 150–69. New York: Routledge, 1992.

Travitsky, Betty S. "The *Feme Covert* in Elizabeth Cary's *Mariam.*" In *Ambiguous Realities: Women in the Middle Ages and Renaissance,* ed. Carole Levin and Jeanie Watson, 184–96. Detroit: Wayne State University Press, 1987.

———. "'His Wife's Prayers and Meditations': MS Egerton 607." In *The Renaissance Englishwoman in Print: Counterbalancing the Canon,* ed. Anne M. Haselkorn and Betty S. Travitsky, 241–60. Amherst: University of Massachusetts Press, 1990.

———. "Husband-Murder and Petty Treason in English Renaissance Tragedy." *Renaissance Drama* n.s. 21 (1990): 171–98.

———. "Reconstructing the Still, Small Voice: The Occasional Journal of Elizabeth Egerton." *Women's Studies* 19, no. 2 (1991): 193–200.

Tricomi, Albert. *Anticourt Drama in England, 1603–1642.* Charlottesville: University of Virginia Press, 1989.

Turberville, A. S. *A History of Welbeck Abbey and Its Owners.* Vol. 1: *1539–1755.* London: Faber and Faber, 1938.

Twycross, Meg. "'Transvestism' in the Mystery Plays." *Medieval English Theatre* 5 (1983): 123–80.

Van Lennep, William, ed. *The London Stage, 1660–1800.* 3 vols. Carbondale: Southern Illinois University Press, 1965.

Veevers, Erica. *Images of Love and Religion: Queen Henrietta Maria and Court Entertainments.* Cambridge: Cambridge University Press, 1989.

Vickers, Nancy J. "The Body Re-membered: Petrarchan Lyric and the Strategies of Description." In *Mimesis from Mirror to Method, Augustine to Descartes,* ed. John D. Lyons and Stephen G. Nichols, Jr., 100–109. Hanover, N.H.: University Press of New England, 1982.

———. "Diana Described: Scattered Woman and Scattered Rhyme." *Critical Inquiry* 8 (Winter 1981): 265–79.

Wack, Mary Frances. *Lovesickness in the Middle Ages: The "Viaticum" and Its Commentaries.* Philadelphia: University of Pennsylvania Press, 1990.

Ward, A. W., and A. R. Waller, eds. *The Cambridge History of English Literature.* Vols. 5–6, *The Drama to 1642.* 1907. Reprint. Cambridge: Cambridge University Press, 1949, 1960.

Watkins, John J. *The Specter of Dido: Spenser and Virgilian Epic.* New Haven: Yale University Press, 1995.

Wayne, Valerie, ed. *The Matter of Difference: Materialist Feminist Criticism of Shakespeare.* Ithaca: Cornell University Press, 1991.

Weaver, Elissa. "Spiritual Fun: A Study of Sixteenth-Century Tuscan Convent Theater." In *Women in the Middle Ages and the Renaissance: Literary and Historical Perspectives,* ed. Mary Beth Rose, 173–205. Syracuse: Syracuse University Press, 1986.

Weeks, Jeffrey. *Sexuality.* London: Routledge, 1986.

Weidemann, Heather L. "Theatricality and Female Identity in Mary Wroth's *Urania.*" In *Reading Mary Wroth: Representing Alternatives in Early Modern England,* ed. Naomi J. Miller and Gary Waller, 191–209. Knoxville: University of Tennessee Press, 1991.

Weimann, Robert. *Shakespeare and the Popular Tradition in the Theater: Studies in the Social Dimension of Dramatic Form and Function,* ed. Robert Schwartz. Baltimore: Johns Hopkins University Press, 1978.

Weller, Barry, and Margaret W. Ferguson. Introduction to *The Tragedy of Mariam the Fair Queen of Jewry,* by Elizabeth Cary ed. Barry Weller and Margaret Ferguson, 1–59. Berkeley and Los Angeles: University of California Press, 1994.

Westfall, Suzanne R. *Patrons and Performance: Early Tudor Household Revels.* Oxford: Clarendon Press, 1990.

Whigham, Frank. "Reading Social Conflict in the Alimentary Tract: More on the Body in Renaissance Drama." *ELH* 55 (Summer 1988): 333–50.

White, Paul Whitfield. *Theatre and Reformation: Protestantism, Patronage, and Playing in Tudor England.* Cambridge: Cambridge University Press, 1993.

Wickham, Glynne. *Early English Stages, 1300 to 1660.* 3 vols. in 4. London: Routledge and Kegan Paul; New York: Columbia University Press, 1959–81.

Wiley, W. L. *The Early Public Theatre in France.* Cambridge, Mass.: Harvard University Press, 1960.

Wilson, John Harold. *All the King's Ladies: Actresses of the Restoration.* Chicago: University of Chicago Press, 1958.

Winkler, John J. *Constraints of Desire: The Anthropology of Sex and Gender in Ancient Greece.* New York: Routledge, 1992.

Wiseman, Susan. "Gender and Status in Dramatic Discourse: The Duchess of Newcastle." In *Women, Writing, History, 1640–1740,* ed. Isobel Grundy and Susan Wiseman, 159–77. London: Batsford, 1992.

Witherspoon, Alexander MacLaren. *The Influence of Robert Garnier on Elizabethan Drama.* New Haven: Yale University Press; London: Oxford University Press, 1924.

Woodbridge, Linda. *Women and the English Renaissance: Literature and the Nature of Womankind, 1540–1620.* Urbana: University of Illinois Press, 1984.

Woods, Gregory. "Body, Costume, and Desire in Christopher Marlowe." *Journal of Homosexuality* 23, nos. 1 and 2 (1992): 69–84.

Wynne-Davies, Marion. "The Queen's Masque: Renaissance Women and the Seventeenth-Century Court Masque." In *Gloriana's Face: Women, Public and Private, in the English Renaissance,* ed. S. P. Cerasano and Marion Wynne-Davies, 79–104. Detroit: Wayne State University Press, 1992.

Zimmerman, Bonnie. "What Has Never Been: An Overview of Lesbian Feminist Criticism." In *Making a Difference: Feminist Literary Criticism,* ed. Gayle Greene and Coppélia Kahn, 177–210. 1985. Reprint. London: Routledge, 1990.

Zimmerman, Susan. "Disruptive Desire: Artifice and Indeterminacy in Jacobean Comedy." In *Erotic Politics: Desire on the Renaissance Stage,* ed. Zimmerman, 39–63. New York: Routledge, 1992.

Žižek, Slavoj. *The Sublime Object of Ideology.* London: Verso, 1989.

Contributors

JANET ADELMAN is professor of English at the University of California, Berkeley. Her most recent book on Shakespeare is *Suffocating Mothers: Fantasies of Maternal Origin, "Hamlet" to "The Tempest"* (Routledge, 1992).

VIVIANA COMENSOLI is professor of English at Wilfrid Laurier University in Waterloo, Ontario. She has published essays on Renaissance drama and culture, and is the author of *"Household Business": Domestic Plays of Early Modern England* (University of Toronto Press, 1996) and co-editor of *Discontinuities: New Essays on Renaissance Literature and Criticism* (University of Toronto Press, 1998).

ALISON FINDLAY lectures on Renaissance literature at the University of Lancaster. Her publications include "Hamlet: A Document in Madness," in *New Essays on "Hamlet,"* ed. Mark Thornton Burnett and John Manning (AMS Press, 1994) and *Illegitimate Power: Bastards in Renaissance Drama* (Manchester University Press, 1994).

MARY FLOYD-WILSON is assistant professor of English at Yale University. She has published essays in *Women's Studies* and the *South Atlantic Review,* and is the author of "Temperature, Temperance, and Racial Difference in Ben Jonson's *The Masque of Blackness,*" forthcoming in *English Literary Renaissance.*

ROSEMARY KEGL is associate professor of English at the University of Rochester and director of the Susan B. Anthony Institute for Gender and Women's Studies. She has published essays on Margaret Cavendish, Andrew Marvell, George Puttenham, William Shakespeare, and two seventeenth-century Quaker women, Katherine Evans and Sarah Chevers. She is the author of *The Rhetoric of Concealment: Figuring Gender and Class in Renaissance Literature* (Cornell University Press,

1994) and is currently at work on a study of theatrical practices and the gendering of intellectual activity in sixteenth- and seventeenth-century England.

R. L. KESLER is associate professor of English at Oregon State University, where he teaches sixteenth- and seventeenth-century British literature, American Indian literature, linguistics, and the history of literacy. During the past four years he has been primarily involved in the creation of a new ethnic studies department.

CHRISTINA LUCKYJ is associate professor of English at Dalhousie University in Nova Scotia. Her publications include "Acting *The Duchess of Malfi:* An Optimist's View" in *The Elizabethan Theatre* 13 (1994); "'A Moving Rhetoricke': Women's Silences and Renaissance Texts" in *Renaissance Drama* n.s. 24 (1993); and the New Mermaids edition of John Webster's *The White Devil* (A and C Black, 1996). She has recently completed a full-length study of gender and silence in early modern texts.

JOYCE GREEN MACDONALD is associate professor of English at the University of Kentucky. She is the editor of *Race, Ethnicity, and Power in Renaissance Drama* (Fairleigh Dickinson University Press, 1996) and has published articles on gender and race in Shakespearean performance and in eighteenth-century drama.

LAURIE E. OSBORNE is associate professor of English at Colby College in Waterville, Maine. She has published articles on *Much Ado about Nothing, Twelfth Night,* and *The Knight of the Burning Pestle.* Her book, *The Trick of Singularity: "Twelfth Night" and the Performance Editions,* has recently been published by the University of Iowa Press.

ANNE RUSSELL is associate professor of English at Wilfrid Laurier University, where she teaches courses in early modern drama and literature. Her publications include articles on the critical and performance history of Shakespeare as well as a critical edition of Aphra Behn's *The Rover* (Broadview Press, 1994).

MICHAEL SHAPIRO is professor of English at the University of Illinois at Urbana-Champaign. He has also taught at the City College of New York, Cornell University, and Reading University (England). He is the author of *Children of the Revels: The Boy Companies of Shakespeare's Time and Their Plays* (Columbia University Press, 1977) and *Gender in Play on the Shakespearean Stage* (University of Michigan Press, 1994), as well as of numerous essays, notes, and reviews on English Renaissance drama. He is the cofounder and artistic director of the Revels Players.

ALAN WALWORTH is assistant professor of English and theater at the College of Wooster in Wooster, Ohio. He recently completed his Ph.D. dissertation, "Displacing Desires in Early Modern Drama," at the University of Illinois at Urbana-Champaign.

Index

Adams, Parveen, 3, 16n11
Adelman, Janet, 5, 6, 7, 8, 23, 73, 86, 88, 96n79; *Suffocating Mothers,* 42n4, 51n38, 52n44, 92–93n23, 93n25, 95n58
Aetius of Amida, 55
Alexander of Tralles, 55
Alexander, William, 136
Alleyn, Edward, 189
Amussen, Susan Dwyer, 160, 200n52
Anderson, Michael, 179
Anderson, Ruth Leila, 95n67
Andreini, Isabella, 179, 189
Andrews, Richard, 199n48
Angel, Edward, 198n38
Anne, Queen (England), 140, 188
Arden of Faversham, 138, 151n8
Aristotle, 17n14, 21, 23, 38, 44n7, 52n40, 78, 142
Aristotle's Masterpiece, 45n16
Asp, Caroline, 216n15
Augusten, William, 184
Aveling, Hugh, 152n12

Babb, Lawrence, 53, 93n30
Bakhtin, Mikhail, 6, 8, 17n15, 54, 56, 57, 58, 60, 63, 68n12, 69nn26–27, 73
Ballaster, Ros, 172n7
Banister, John, 28, 29, 30, 45n13; *The Historie of Man,* 27
Barish, Jonas, 153n16
Barkan, Leonard, 110n21, 110n24

Barrell, Thommas, 191
Bartels, Emily, 108n7, 109n11
Bartholomaeus Anglicus, 95n65
Baskervil, Susan, 184
Bassett, Elizabeth, 171n2
Baswell, Christopher, 109n12
Batman uppon Bartholome, 91n11, 95n65
Beaumont, Francis, *The Knight of the Burning Pestle,* 14, 202, 203
Beecher, Donald, 53, 54, 67–68n5
Beeman, William O., 199n48
Beeston, Christopher, 184
Beier, A. L., 199–200n51
Beilin, Elaine V., 151n6, 151n9
Belsey, Catherine, 16n10, 123, 218, 230n14
Bentley, G. E., 196n24, 196n28, 196n30, 197n33
Berkeley, William, *The Lost Lady,* 89, 96n84
Bernal, Martin, 93n30
Betterton, William, 186, 197n38
Bevington, David, 131n6, 152n10, 196n23, 225
Beza, Theodore, *Abraham's Sacrifice,* 181
Blagrave, William, 184
Boas, F. S., 97–98, 109n10, 131n10
Bodin, Jean, 76, 81, 91n10, 93n24
Bogatyrëv, Peter, 131n3
Borde, Andrew, 88
Bossy, John, 152n12
Bracegirdle, Anne, 189
Brackley, Elizabeth, 12, 154–56, 166–71, 171n2, 172n7, 173n13, 175n37; "Considerations con-

cerning marriage," 175n37. *See also* Cavendish, Jane
Braden, Gordon, 150n4, 151n7
Bradley, Marke, 191
Brathwait, Richard, 181; *English Gentlewoman,* 222
Brande, Thomas, 198n43
Brandon, Samuel, 136
Brantley, Ben, 193n1
Bray, Alan, 108n8, 112n34, 196n21
Bredbeck, Gregory W., 108n8, 111n26
Bristowe, James, 184, 185
Brome, Richard, 6; *The Court Beggar,* 188; *The Damoiselle,* 173n10; *The English Moor,* 96n84; *The Northern Lasse,* 61, 64
Brooke, C. F. Tucker, 97
Brown, Cedric C., 173n14
Brown, John Russell, 231n28
Browne, Thomas, 88; *Pseudodoxia Epidemica,* 79, 80
Browne, William, 184
Buc, Sir George, 191
Bullough, Vern L., 45n16, 46n17
Bulwer, John, 88; *Anthropometamorphosis,* 80
Burnim, Kalman A., 197n38
Burton, Robert, *Anatomy of Melancholy,* 55, 65, 68–69n14, 69n15, 69n17, 69nn23–24
Butler, Judith, 2, 3, 17n18, 57, 165, 222

Cady, Joseph, 112n34
Calderwood, James L., 122
Callaghan, Dympna, 138, 151n8, 152n9, 215–16n4
Calvin, John, 180–81
Campion, Thomas, 140
Canby, Vincent, 193n1
Carew, R., 45n12
Cartelli, Thomas, 108n7
Cary, Elizabeth, 11; *The Tragedy of Mariam,* 11, 135–49, 150n3, 150–51n6, 151n8, 152n9, 153n16
Cary, Sir Henry, 138, 140, 153n13
Case, Sue-Ellen, 17n18
Cavendish, Charles, 173n13
Cavendish, Henry, 173n13

Cavendish, Jane, 12, 154–56, 166–71, 171n2, 173n13; *The Concealed Fancies,* 12, 154–71, 172n7; *A Pastorall,* 171n1
Cavendish, Margaret, 172n4, 173n13
Cavendish, William, 166, 171n2, 172n4, 173n13
Cawley, Robert Ralston, 95n63, 95n65
Cecil, Lord, 137
Cerasano, S. P., 18n20, 202
Chambers, E. K., 150nn4–5, 153n13, 180
Chaney, Joseph, 216n14
Chaplin, Joyce, 91n7
Charles I (England), 138, 140, 159
Charles II (England), 187
Charles IX (France), 60
Charles, Prince of Wales, 172n4
Charlton, H. B., 150n4, 151n7
Charron, Pierre, 92n15
Chase, Cynthia, 62, 70n28
Chauliac, Guy de, *The Cyrurgie of Guy de Chauliac,* 27, 45n11
Chaultemps, Richard, 181
Cibber, Colley, 185
Cixous, Hélène, 58, 60
Clément, Catherine, 57
Clifton, Henry, 196n28
Cohen, Walter, 16n9, 152n10
Cokayne, George Edward, 153n13
Collier, J. P., 198n43
Coniacke, Mme., 188
Cook, Ann Jennalie, 18n24
Cook, Carol, 230n10
Cooke, Alice, 196n28
Cop, Michel, 181
Corliss, Richard, 193n1
Coryate, Thomas, 187; *Coryate's Crudities,* 198n44
Cotton, Nancy, 152n11
Cowborne, Robert, 191
Crewe, Jonathan, 43n7
Crooke, Helkiah, 28, 37, 38, 40, 42, 52n45; *Microcosmographia,* 36, 39, 41, 49–50n29, 50n30, 50n32, 51nn34–35
Cunliffe, John W., 150n4, 151n7
Cupid's Banishment, 18n20
Curtius, Ernst, 110n24

D'Amico, Jack, 92n18
Danby, John, 96n75, 96n77
Daniel, Samuel, 136; *Tragedy of Philotas*, 137, 150n5
Dannenfeldt, Karl, 77
Davenant, William, 186
Davies, H. Neville, 92n20
Davies, Sir John, *The Muses Sacrifice*, 150n3
Davies, Kathleen M., 174n16
Davis, Natalie Zemon, 171n3
Dekker, Thomas: *Lanthorne and Candle-Light*, 88; *The Roaring Girl*, 188
Diamond, Elin, 12, 163, 174n20
Dixon, Suzanne, 110n17
Dolan, Frances E., 113n36, 150n6, 151n8
Donne, John, 119; *First Anniversary*, 129
Dover, Kenneth J., 110n18
Drakakis, John, 15n2, 90n2
Du Laurens, Andre, *Preservation of the Sight*, 55, 68n14, 69n17, 69nn23–24
Dubrow, Heather, 44n7, 45n12, 48n27
Dusinberre, Juliet, 111n29
Duval, Jacques, 45n14; *Des Hermaphrodites*, 48n28

Eccles, Audrey, 46n19, 48n27
Edwards, Philip, 131n10
Egerton, John, Viscount Brackley, 170, 172n7, 175–76n37
Elizabeth I (England), 139, 140
Ellis, Havelock, 97
Emmison, F. G., 200n52
Epstein, Julia, 17n14
Erickson, Peter, 82, 93n23
Esslin, Martin, 168
Evans, Henry, 185
Evelyn, John, 198n40
Ezell, Margaret J. M., 16n10, 157, 167, 175n31

Fairet, Marie, 180
Fenn, Ezekiel, 183
Ferguson, Margaret W., 15n6, 15n9
Ferrand, Jacques, *A Treatise on Lovesickness*, 68n5, 93n38
Ficino, Marsilio, 77

Field, Nathan, 184
Findlay, Alison, 11, 12, 172n7, 175n32
Finke, Laurie A., 9, 17n17
Fischer, Sandra K., 151n6, 151n9
Flavius Josephus. *See* Josephus, Flavius
Fletcher, John, 6; *The Mad Lover*, 66; *The Noble Gentleman*, 62, 65; *Two Noble Kinsmen*, 53, 61, 62, 63
Floy, Gregory, 177
Floyd, Mr., 198n38
Floyd-Wilson, Mary, 7
Ford, John, 6; *The Lover's Melancholy*, 62, 65
Foucault, Michel, 3, 4, 17n12, 53, 54, 98, 108n8, 109n17, 132n16
Freer, Coburn, 150n5
Freud, Sigmund: on castration, 56; on melancholia, 55, 56, 58, 63; on transference, 54, 59–60, 62, 68n9, 69–70n28, 71n54
Frith, Moll, 198n44
Furnivall, Frederick J., 44–45n10
Furnivall, Percy, 44–45n10

Gagnier, Regenia, 15n3
Galen, 55; "one-sex" model, 4–6, 17n14, 25–28, 30, 31, 32, 36–42, 44n7, 45n12, 45n16, 49nn28–29, 52n40
Gallop, Jane, 71n68
Garber, Marjorie, 17n11
Garnier, Marie, 49n28
Garnier, Robert, *Marc Antoine*, 136, 137
Garzoni, Tomasso, *Hospitall of Incurable Fooles*, 55, 68n14, 69n17
Gash, Anthony, 131n6
Gataker, Thomas, *A Wife in Deed*, 162–63, 174n23
Gilder, Rosamund, 199n48
Gillies, John, 93n26, 94n57, 95n64
Glacken, Clarence J., 90–91n7
Gohlke, Madelon. *See* Sprengnether, Madelon
Goldberg, Dena, 232n41
Goldberg, Jonathan, 98, 108n8
Goldoni, Carlo, 194n9
Gossett, Suzanne, 18n20, 231n27
Gosson, Stephen, 14, 203, 206, 209; *The Schoole of Abuse*, 19n25, 201, 204, 205, 212

Gouge, William, 172n3
Goulart, Simon, 60; *Admirable and Memorable Histories,* 55, 59, 68n14, 69n17, 69nn23–24
Gras, Henk, 198n43
Grazia, Margreta de, 43, 49n29
Greenblatt, Stephen, 4, 17nn11–12, 25, 40, 41, 43nn5–6, 44n9, 45n14, 48n26, 49n28, 103, 108n7, 112n30, 132n19, 132n21
Greville, Fulke, 136
Guillemeau, Jacques, *Child-birth,* 36, 48n27
Gunby, D. C., 218, 230n13, 231n28
Gunnell, Richard, 184
Gurr, Andrew, 19n24, 190, 201, 215n2, 216n6, 232n32
Gutierrez, Nancy A., 151n6

Haec Vir, 221, 230n17
Hall, Kim F., 92n22, 94n53
Haller, Melville, 174n16
Haller, William, 174n16
Hallett, Charles A., 131n11
Hallett, Elaine S., 131n11
Halperin, David, 112n34
Hammerton, Stephen, 184
Harbage, Alfred, 18n24
Harris, Jonathan Gil, 85, 90n1, 95n68
Harrison, William, 91nn10–11
Harvey, Elizabeth D., 43n7, 232n35
Havelock, Eric, 123
Hay, James, Earl of Carlisle, 140
Heilbrun, Carolyn, 217n21
Heise, Ursula, 180, 182, 195n10
Henrietta Maria, Queen, 138, 159, 172n8
Henry IV (France), 55
Henslowe, Philip, 184, 185, 188
Herbert, Sir Henry, 186, 191, 197n34, 198n43
Heywood, Thomas, *Wise Woman of Hogsdon,* 202
Hexter, Ralph, 109n12
Hic Mulier, 182, 223
Highfill, Philip, 197n38
Hippocrates, 17n14, 78, 91n11
Hodgson-Wright, Stephanie, 172n7
"Homily on Matrimony," 160, 174n17, 175n37
Hopkins, Lisa, 172n7

Hotson, Leslie, 195n16, 198n39
Howard, Christopher, 152n12
Howard, Lady Frances, 141
Howard, Jean E., 13, 15n2, 19nn24–25, 44n7, 142, 153n15, 202, 230n14
Howe, Elizabeth, 199n47
Huarte, Juan, 91n10; *Examen de ingenios, Examination of mens Wits,* 45n12, 51–52n40, 77, 78
Hunt, Maurice, 216n12, 217n18

Ingram, Martin, 172n3
Irigary, Luce, 3, 12, 161–62, 163, 174n20, 174n21

Jackson, Henry, 185
Jakobson, Roman, 131n3
James I (England), 140
Jameson, Fredric, 8, 17n15
Jardine, Alice, 3
Jardine, Lisa, 14, 19n26, 104, 112n31
Jed, Stephanie H., 109n14
Jolly, George, 195n16
Jonas, Richard, *De partu hominis,* 46n19, 46n21
Jondorf, Gillian, 150n4, 151n7
Jones, Ann Rosalind, 44n7
Jonson, Ben, 121, 159, 228; *The Alchemist,* 120, 125; "Challenge at Tilt," 140; *Christmas, His Masque,* 183; *Epicoene,* 168, 173n10; *Gypsies Metamorphosed,* 89; *King's Entertainment at Welbeck,* 159, 173n14; *Love's Welcome at Bolsover,* 159, 173n14; *Masque of Blackness,* 86, 95–96n71; *Masque of Queens,* 223; *Poetaster,* 183; *The Staple of News,* 202; *Volpone,* 126
Jordan, Thomas, 186
Jordan, Winthrop D., 91n7
Jorden, Edward, *A Briefe Discourse of a Disease,* 48n27, 68n14
Josephus, Flavius, *Antiquities of the Jewes,* 142, 148, 149
Judges, A. V., 199n51

Kahn, Coppélia, 52n44, 231–32n29
Kamps, Ivo, 1, 15n2
Kegl, Rosemary, 11

Kehler, Dorothea, 208
Keller, Evelyn Fox, 116
Kendall, Thomas, 196n28
Kesler, R. L., 8, 9, 130nn2–3, 132n18
Killigrew, Thomas, 186
Kofman, Sarah, 59, 60
Kolve, V. A., 131n6
Kristeva, Julia, 67
Krontiris, Tina, 151n9
Kyd, Thomas, *The Spanish Tragedy*, 117, 118, 119, 120, 129, 130
Kynaston, Edward, 186, 197n38, 198n40

Lacan, Jacques, 54, 56, 57, 60, 62, 63, 64, 65, 66, 68n12, 69n25
Lambarde, William, *The Duties of Constables*, 199n51
Langhans, Edward E., 197n38
Lanier, Henry Wysham, 198n39
Laplanche, Jean, 67
Laqueur, Thomas, 4, 5, 25, 41, 44n9, 45n15, 51n34, 103; *Making Sex*, 4, 17nn12–14, 27, 32, 40, 43n6, 45n16, 47n23, 49nn28–29, 50n33, 51n40
Laud, William, archbishop of Canterbury, 198n43
Leavenworth, Russell E., 142, 150n4, 153n16
Lemnius, Levinus, *Touchstone of Complexions*, 55, 68n14, 69n17, 69n24
Leo Africanus, 95n65
Lester, Ronnie, 177
Leveson, Sir Richard, 186
Levin, Richard, 19n24, 201
Levine, Laura, 14, 19n26, 44n7, 104, 196n22, 223, 228
Lewalski, Barbara Kiefer, 16n10, 18n20, 150–51n6, 151–52n9
Leys, M. D. R., 152–53n12
Lodge, Thomas, translations of Flavius Joesphus by, 142, 148
Longueville, T., 152n9
Loomba, Ania, 16n6, 90n2
Lorde, Audre, 16n8
Lucan, *Pharsalia*, 98
Lucas, Margaret, 173n13
Lucas, Valerie, 159, 223

Luckyj, Christina, 12, 14, 15
Lumley, Jane, translation of *Iphigenia in Aulis* by, 139

MacCallum, M. W., 92n19
MacCannell, Juliet Flower, 63, 67
MacDonald, Joyce Green, 8, 9, 92n19, 92n22
MacInnes, Ian, 94n56
Maclean, Ian, 47–48n24
Mandeville's Travels, 95n65
Marin le Marcis, 45n14, 48n28
Marlowe, Christopher, 8; *Dido Queene of Carthage*, 8, 9, 97–108; *Hero and Leander*, 98
Marshall, Cynthia, 94n55, 96n78
Martindale, Charles, 92n19
Martindale, Michelle, 92n19
Mary Tudor, Queen, 140
Maus, Katherine Eisaman, 58, 198n40, 216n13, 216n15, 226, 228
McGee, C. E., 18n19
McLuskie, Kathleen, 103, 112n30, 203
Mead, John, 198n43
Meagher, John C., 18n19
Merchant, Carolyn, 116–17
Middleton, Thomas, 6; *The Changeling*, 220; *More Dissemblers Besides Women*, 89; *The Nice Valour*, 61; *The Roaring Girl*, 188; *The Spanish Gipsy*, 89
Milles, Thomas, 60; *The Treasurie of Auncient and Moderne Times*, 68n14, 69n23
Milling, Jane, 172n7
Milton, John, 79, 125; *Paradise Lost*, 23
Miner, Earl, 175n31
Miola, Robert S., 92n19
Mohun, Michael, 186
Montaigne, Michel de, 28, 29, 49n28
Moryson, Fynes, 78
Mosely, John, 198n38
Moulton, Ian Frederick, 109n10
Mountfort, Susannah, 189
Mullaney, Steven, 1, 15n1
Murdock, Kenneth, 152n9

Nashe, Thomas, 182
Neely, Carol Thomas, 3, 16n9, 51n35, 51n39, 124, 132n19

Nelson, Alan, 182, 195n20
Newman, Karen, 3, 16n10, 59, 223
Newport, Andrew, 186
Nichols, John, 153n13
Nietzche, Friederich, 124
Nightingale, Benedict, 232n40
Nokes, James, 186, 197n38
Northbrooke, John, 204
Novy, Marianne, 211
Nye, Robert A., 44n7
Nyquist, Mary, 92n22

Ogden, Margaret S., 45n11
Oliver, H. J., 97, 109n10
Orgel, Stephen, 41, 43–44n7, 49–50n29, 50n32, 51n36, 51n39, 52n41, 112n31, 112n33, 177, 182, 192–93, 193n2, 195n20, 196n22, 197n33, 198n44
Osborne, Laurie E., 12, 14
Ovid, *Metamorphoses*, 8, 98, 100, 102, 105, 106

Panofsky, Erwin, 110n21
Paré, Ambroise, 28, 29, 48n27, 49n28
Park, Katherine, 44n7
Parker, Andrew, 18n18
Parker, Patricia, 17n14, 44n7, 49n28, 51n39, 92n20
Paster, Gail Kern, 44n7, 45n15, 48n25, 68n12, 71n50, 73, 96n76, 96n78
Patterson, Annabel, 219n19
Payne, Henry Nevil, *The Fatal Jealousy*, 197n38
Peacham, Henry, *The Complete Gentleman*, 95n60
Pepys, Samuel, 186, 198n38, 198n40
Perry, Henry Ten Eyck, 172n4
Pickup, Ronald, 177
Plautus, *Menaechmi*, 126
Plutarch, *The Philosophie*, 52n45
Pollard, A. W., 46n20
Potter, Nick, 1, 15n1
Poupin, Abel, 180
Problemes of Aristotle, The, 30, 31, 32, 35, 42, 45n16, 46n18, 48n26
Prowse, Philip, 232n40
Prynne, William, 196n21; *Histrio-Mastix*, 18n20, 198n43

Pseudo-Aristotle, 91n11
Purdie, Edna, 195n18

Quilligan, Maureen, 151n8
Quint, David, 109n13, 110n23

Raber, Karen L., 150n6
Rackin, Phyllis, 91n13, 111n29
Ragland-Sullivan, Ellie, 64
Rainolds, John, 195n21, 204
Randall, Dale B. J., 96n81, 174n28
Rappaport, Steve, 197n33
Raynold, Thomas, 34, 42, 52n45; *The Byrth of Mankynde*, 32, 33, 36, 46nn19–22, 47nn23–24, 48nn24–27
Redgrave, G. R., 46n20
REED (*Records of Early English Drama*), 183, 189, 190
Revenger's Tragedy, The. See Tourneur, Cyril
Richards, Sandra, 199n47
Richlin, Amy, 110n17
Rose, Mary Beth, 8, 16n9, 17n15
Roselli, John, 194n9
Roson, Ciprian de, 191
Ross, Thomas W., 131n10
Rowley, William, *The Changeling*, 220; *The Spanish Gipsy*, 89

Saintsbury, George, 97
Sandys, George, 113n38
Sanesi, Ireneo, 194n9
Saslow, James, 110n21
Scaliger, Julius Caesar, 48n24
Schelling, Felix E., 150n4, 151n7
Schiesari, Juliana, 58
Schleiner, Winfried, 53, 54, 67n4, 69n14
Scot, Reginald, *The Discoverie of Witchcraft*, 68n14
Scott, Joan W., 15, 19n27
Sedgwick, Eve Kosofsky, 19n18, 156, 173n9
Selenick, Laurence, 19n27
Seneca, 137, 143, 145, 150n4
Sergent, Bernard, 110n18
Shakespeare, William, 5, 14, 52n45, 202; *Antony and Cleopatra*, 5, 7, 8, 23, 24, 25, 42, 42n3, 43n4, 73–90, 137–38, 151n8, 169; *As

You Like It, 23, 62, 157, 160, 168, 177, 223; comedies, one-sex model and, 39, 40, 41; *Hamlet,* 9, 10, 14, 24, 114, 116, 119–26, 128–30, 168, 202, 203, 204, 209, 210–14, 226; *Henry VI,* 42; *Julius Caesar,* 93n24; *King Lear,* 124; *Love's Labor's Lost,* 14, 202, 203, 204, 205, 209; *Measure for Measure,* 95n68; *Merchant of Venice,* 23, 66, 138, 151n8, 214–15; *Midsummer Night's Dream,* 14, 203, 204, 214; *Much Ado about Nothing,* 191, 219, 221; *Othello,* 9, 10, 114, 116, 123–30, 138, 151n8, 185, 218; *Romeo and Juliet,* 197n38; *Taming of the Shrew,* 135, 138, 151n8, 173n10, 203, 209, 212; *Tempest,* 203, 214; *Titus Andronicus,* 9, 74, 91n9, 114, 116, 118–21, 124–25, 128; *Twelfth Night,* 23; *Two Noble Kinsmen,* 53, 61, 62, 63; *Winter's Tale,* 215, 218
Shannon, Laurie J., 152n9
Shapiro, Michael, 12, 13, 111n28, 193n1, 196n21, 198n44, 220, 230n15
Shepherd, Mrs., 188
Shepherd, Simon, 108n8, 113n37
Shepherdson, Charles, 17n11
Shirley, James, 6; *The Ball,* 188; *Love Tricks,* 62, 66; *Love's Cruelty,* 186
Sidney, Mary, 136; *Thenot and Piers,* 139, 141, 152n11; translation of Garnier's *Marc Antoine* by, 139
Sidney, Philip, 11, 137, 141; on unities, 141–42, 143, 146, 148
Simon, Josette, 232n40
Simpson, Christopher, 140
Simpson, Robert, 140
Sinfield, Alan, 43n7, 51n39
Singh, Jyotsna, 43n4
Siraisi, Nancy G., 91n8
Sixtus V, Pope, 179
Slater, Miriam, 173n9
Smith, Bruce R., 108n8, 110n19
Snell, K. D. M., 197n33
Snowden, Frank, 93n27
Snyder, Susan, 132n19
Socrates, 126
Somerset, Earl of, 141
Spevack, Marvin, 95n62
Sprengnether, Madelon, 42n3, 52n44

Stallybrass, Peter, 42n3, 43–44n7, 58, 59, 68n12, 69n27, 71n50, 132n19, 132n23
Starr, Nathan Comfort, 171n2
Statius, *Thebaid,* 102, 106
Stevenson, Sheryl A., 231n18, 231n25
Straub, Kristina, 199n47
Straznicky, Marta, 138, 151n6
Stubbes, Philip, 196n21; *Anatomie of Abuses,* 104
Stuteville, Martin, 198n43
Swetnam, Joseph, 219

Tacitus, 78, 79
Tennenhouse, Leonard, 75
Tertullian, 181
Thomas, Edward, 97
Thomas, Vivian, 92n19
Thompson, Ann, 11
Thompson, John, 184
Tomlinson, Sophie, 11, 18n20, 199n45
Tourneur, Cyril, *The Revenger's Tragedy,* 126, 129, 218
Townshend, Aurelian, 199n45; *Tempe Restor'd,* 188
Traub, Valerie, 51n39, 52n43, 68n12, 72n72, 111n29, 216n4
Travitsky, Betty S., 150–51n6, 151n8, 152n9, 176n37
Tricomi, Albert, 150n4, 151n7
Trussel, Alvery, 196n28
Turberville, A. S., 171n2

Vaughan, William, *Approved Directions for Health,* 55, 59, 68n14
Veevers, Erica, 18n20, 173n8
Vega-Vega, Luz, 195n10
Vesalius, *Fabrica,* 47n23
Vicary, Thomas, 26, 27; *The Anatomie of the Bodie of Man,* 44n10
Virgil, *Aeneid,* 8, 98–102, 105, 106, 107, 109n12, 110n23

Wack, Mary Frances, 71n60
Walkington, Thomas, 91n10; *Opticke Glasse of Humors,* 55, 68n14, 69n17, 69nn23–24
Walworth, Alan, 6, 7, 8

Watkins, John, 109n12
Webster, John, *The Devil's Law-Case*, 96n84; *The Duchess of Malfi*, 124, 132n22, 220, 230n9; *The White Devil*, 14, 15, 218–29, 230n9
Weeks, Jeffrey, 5, 17n14
Weidemann, Heather L., 219
Weimann, Robert, 152n10
Weller, Barry, 151n6
Westfall, Suzanne R., 11, 139, 152n10
Whately, William, *A Bride-Bush*, 50n31, 159–60, 174n16
Whigham, Frank, 67, 72n71
White, Allon, 68n12
White, Paul Whitfield, 152n12
Wickham, Glynne, 152n11, 178, 179, 194n6
Williams, Clifford, 177
Williams, Gweno, 172n7
Williams, Peter, 191
Wilson, Jean, 152n11

Wilson, John Harold, 199n47
Wise Woman of Hogsdon, 202
Wiseman, Susan, 172n7
Witherspoon, Alexander MacLaren, 142, 150n4
Woodbridge, Linda, 16n10
Woods, Gregory, 113n37
Wright, James, 186
Wright, Thomas, 91n10; *The Passions of the Mind in General*, 79, 94nn49–50
Wyatt, Joan, 191
Wyatt, Thomas, 191
Wynne-Davies, Marion, 18n20, 172n7, 173n13, 202

Yorke, Sir John, 140

Zimmerman, Bonnie, 9, 17n16
Zimmerman, Susan, 51n39
Žižek, Slavoj, 54